POWER FOR SANITY

William Cullen Bryant by Samuel F. B. Morse, 1829. National Academy of Design.

POWER FOR SANITY
Selected Editorials of
WILLIAM CULLEN BRYANT, 1829–1861

Compiled and Annotated
by
WILLIAM CULLEN BRYANT II

The lucidity of his comment and the keenness of his criticism set the editor apart from shriller contemporaries, and made him a power for sanity in a scurrilous generation.

—Vernon Louis Parrington, 1927

Fordham University Press
New York
1994

Copyright © 1994 by FORDHAM UNIVERSITY PRESS
All rights reserved.
LC 93-44266
ISBN 0-8232-1543-1 *(clothbound)*
ISBN 0-8232-1544-x *(paperback)*

Library of Congress Cataloging-in-Publication Data

Bryant, William Cullen, 1794-1878.
   Power for sanity : selected editorials of William Cullen Bryant, 1829-1861 / by William Cullen Bryant II.
     p.   cm.
   Selection of editorials from the New York evening post, 1829-1861.
   Includes bibliographical references and index.
   ISBN 0-8232-1543-1 : $30.00. — ISBN 0-8232-1544-X (pbk.) : $20.00
   1. United States—Politics and government—1815-1861—Sources.
I. Title.
E415.7.B79   1994
320.973—dc20   93-44266
                                                                        CIP

Printed in the United States of America

In Memory of Donald Cross Bryant
Teacher, Scholar, and Caring Brother

CONTENTS

Acknowledgments	xv
Foreword	xvii
Introduction	xix
Editorial Note	xxvii

EDITORIALS:

1829

John Quincy Adams Gives Way to Jackson. March 5	1

1832

Effect of Climate on Age. March 1	1
A Leaf from Mrs. Trollope's Memorandum Book. July 9	4
Jackson's Veto of the Bank Recharter. July 30	6
A City Emptied by the Cholera Plague. August 20	7
The Corrupting Influence of the Bank. October 4	8
Jackson's Victory over Henry Clay. November 12	9
Mr. Van Buren's Return from England. November 22	11
South Carolina Must Yield. December 7	12
South Carolina Risking Ruin. December 21	13

1833

Some Poets. January 26	14
Andrew Jackson Visits New York. June 13	16
The Removal of the Deposits. September 23	17

1834

Three Opposition Leaders: Clay, Calhoun, and Webster. March 31	19

1836

How Abolitionists Are Made. April 21	22
Petitions Against Slavery. May 20	23
The Right to Strike and Journeymen Tailors. May 31	25
U.S. Consular Service and the Passport System. May 31	26

The Right to Strike and Journeymen Tailors. June 1	27
The Right to Strike & Journeymen Tailors. June 2	30
Right to Strike vs. Mob Intimidation. June 6	31
The Right to Combine and the Courts. June 11	33
Journeymen Tailors: Judge Edwards' Sentence. June 13	36
The Right of Workmen to Strike. June 13	37
Courts and Public Opinion. June 15	39
The Right to Combine vs. Forcible Intimidation. June 16	40
Native Americanism and the Rights of Foreigners. June 16	44
Credit System and Senator Tallmadge's Eulogy. June 17	45
Freedom of Speech. August 8	47
The Cincinnati Mob. August 10	49
Defense of the Loco-Foco, or Anti-Monopoly, Party. August 10	50
Slave-Catching. August 10	52
The Funeral of Aaron Burr. September 19	53
On Usury Laws. September 26	54
Copyright and Patent Right Are Natural Rights. September 27	57
Theatrical Riots. December 2	58
Henry Clay: His Reluctance to Retire. December 26	60

1837

The Pilot Monopoly. January 5	61
Negro Suffrage, New York State. February 7	62
The Approaching Retirement of Andrew Jackson. March 1	64
Copy-Rights. March 2	65
The Squatters. ca. March	67
The Proposed Annexation of Texas. August 4	68
The Wisdom of Our Ancestors. August 19	70
On Van Buren's Message. September 7	73
Calhoun's Diminished Stature. September 20	74
The Right of Suffrage. November 2	75
The Whig Victory in New York Elections. November 9	76
The Death of Lovejoy. November 18	78
Mr. Webster's Wit. November 20	80
Slam, Bang and Co. December 8	82

1838

Ride and Tie. June 12	83
New York Bird Catchers. June 27	84
Democracy Is Inextinguishable. July 13	85
Democratic Simplicity. August 7	87
Temperance Legislation. November 10	89

Contents

Old *vs.* New Federalists. November 22	90
Defense of Jackson Against Criticisms. December 3	92

1839

Sensitiveness to Foreign Opinion. January 11	93
The Death of William Leggett. May 30	95
Public Improvements. June 5	96
The Plea of the General Good. June 6	98
A Reply to Attacks. June 7	99
Politics and Literature. June 28	102
Banking Regulation. July 9	103
The Dangers of Centralization. July 27	105
The Bank of the United States and Nicholas Biddle. September 2	107
Schooner *Amistad* and Slave Mutiny. September 4	109
Bank of the United States *vs.* Independent Treasury. September 5	111
Henry Clay as Politician. September 11	112
Architecture and Taste. September 23	114
Federal Assumption of State Debts. November 21	117
Federal Assumption of State Debts Unconstitutional. November 23	119
Private *vs.* Corporate Banking. November 29	121
General Harrison: The Unwanted Candidate. December 14	122

1840

Loss of Steamer *Lexington.* January 18	123
The American Conservative. January 22	125
Rejection by Congress of Abolition Petitions. February 8	127
The Sub-Treasury and Farm Prices. February 20	128
Paternal Government: Its Degrading Effects. May 20	129
Campaign by Song. May 30	131
The Tippecanoe Clubs and Intemperance. June 1	133
The Political Creed of the *Evening Post.* July 1	135
The Kitchen Battery. July 2	136
The Parrot Tribe. July 31	138
Why Harrison Should Not Be Elected President. September 11	140
Daniel Webster, "Field Preacher." September 18	141
Daniel Webster: "Rankest" Member of the "Dangerous . . . Artistocracy of Wealth." September 24	143
The Election of William Henry Harrison: "The Contest Which Lies Before Us." November 9	146

The Intractibility of the Irish. November 10	148
The Law's Delay. November 14	150

1841

Defense of Newspaper Editors. January 14	153
Van Buren's Popularity. January 15	154
Daniel Webster—Secretary of State? January 27	157
Analysis of Webster, Continued. January 28	159
Tyler's First Veto of the Bank Bill. August 18	161
"Kiting" in Wall Street. August 19	163
Van Buren in Retirement. August 24	165
Bank of the United States: Final Demise. September 8	167
Daniel Defoe. November 15	169

1842

International Copyright. February 11	171
International Copy Right. May 9	173
Mother and Daughter. September 8	175
How to Destroy a Commercial Town. October 11	176
The Raccoon: Symbol of the Whigs. October 22	178

1843

The Tariff with Country People. March 2	180
John Quincy Adams. August 4	183
Names of Sects. August 14	184
The Corn Law Controversy. August 24	186
Cheap Postage and No Discontinuance of Post-Roads. December 18	188
The Presidency: "Neither To Be Sought Nor Declined." December 29	190

1844

De Mort[ui]s Nil Nisi *Verum*. February 28	191
A Friendly Word to the Manufacturers. March 12	192
The Convenience of an Average. March 20	194
Nathan Appleton's Letter of March 23 (Printed). March 25	196
Mr. Appleton's Letter. March 25	198
Mr. Franklin's Letter. April 6	200
Mr. Appleton's Second Letter. April 11	202
An Apology for the Tariff. April 11	208
The Remainder of the Apology for the Tariff. April 12	211
The Late "Whig" Victory. April 12	214

A Case of Delicacy. April 13	216
Political Ventriloquism. April 24	220
Friar Tuck Legislation. April 26	222
Disturbance of Public Meetings. May 27	223
A New Public Park. July 3	226
Blue Law Legislation. July 3	228
Industrial Feudalism. July 3	229
Texas. July 25	231
A Discovery. July 27	233
The New Texas Test. July 27	235
The Rhode Island and Philadelphia Cases. July 27	237
The Republic Newspaper. July 27	238
Manufacturing in a Pigstye. September 19	239
The Native American Party. November 12	241
The Charge of Fraud. November 13	243
Irishmen and Catholics. November 20	246

1845

The Police Magistrates. February 14	248
The Municipal Election. March 13	249
The Nativists and Our City Finances. March 13	250
The Day After the Election. April 9	252

1847

Pius IX—A Public Meeting. November 12	253
The Year 1847. December 31	255

1848

Mr. Webster's Speech. March 30	257
The Result of the Election. November 8	259

1850

Mr. Webster's Speech. March 8	261
A Recipe for the Extension of Slavery. March 9	263

1851

The Fugitive Slave Riots. October 4	265

1853

Public Parks. July 2	268
A Word for the *Evening Post*. July 14	269

1854

Backbones Wanted—A North. February 27	272
Touching It Off Softly. March 2	275
Japan and Japanese Expeditions. March 7	276
The Know-Nothing Movement. August 16	281

1855

Short Method with Disunionists. September 26	283
The Geography of Nativism. September 27	284
The Republican Convention. September 29	286

1856

Charity Made Easy. February 18	288
The Outrage on Mr. Sumner. May 23	289
Congressional Privilege. May 24	291
Brooks's Canada Song. July 24	293
Threats of Disunion from Head Quarters. October 6	294
The Conspiracy Against the Working Class. October 29	297
What May Happen in the Next Four Years. October 31	299
The Election of Yesterday. November 5	302
The Duty of the Republican Party. November 7	304

1857

Fate of Squatter Sovereignty. March 3	308
The New Federal Constitution. March 9	309
Judge Taney's Opinion in the Dred Scott Case. March 10	312
One or Two Results of the Late Change in the Constitution. March 11	315
The Cure for Dirty Streets. March 26	317

1858

Better Late Than Never. October 5	318
The Proposed Increase of Taxes. October 8	321
The Reaction in Pennsylvania. October 15	323
The Bible in the Public Schools. November 24	326
Changes in Asia. November 29	329

1859

The Direct Trade of the South with Europe. ca. January	331
Who Is the Intermeddler? January 17	333
Oysters and Letters. ca. April	335

Contents xiii

The Impending War. May 6 337
The Effect of the Sardinian War on American Travel. May 7 340
The European War. May 10 342
The Flight of the Duke of Tuscany. May 10 345
Nuisances on Railways. September 3 348
John Brown and a Slave Insurrection. October 18 350
The Execution and Its Effects. December 5 352
A Calm Word Respecting the Union—A Union Party at the
 South. December 23 355
Southern Literature. December 28 359
A Change of Tune. December 30 361
Benignity and Beneficence. December 31 363

1860

Who Is For a Coat of Tar and Feathers? January 9 365
Mr. Carey's Challenge. January 14 366
The Danger to the Union—The Cause and Remedy. January 17 368
Proof of Our Progress in Civilization. January 9 370
The Real Danger to the Union. January 20 373
Mr. Sumner on the Barbarism of Slavery. June 7 376
The Old-Line Whigs. June 7 377
Popular Sovereignty. ca. June 7 378
The Slave Interest Is a Spoiled Child. ca. October 379
The Election of Lincoln. November 7 380
A Moderate View of the South Carolina Question. November 15 383

1861

The Fifty-Ninth Anniversary of the *Evening Post*. ca. January 1 386

Index 389

Illustrations follow page 162.

ACKNOWLEDGMENTS

I should like to express my sincere gratitude to the many persons who have been supportive in various ways during the preparation of this work, among them Professors James T. Callow of the University of Detroit, Vincent Freimarck of the State University of New York at Binghamton, Norbert Krapf of C. W. Post College, Eric Lampard of the State University of New York at Stony Brook, Albert F. McLean of Park College, Andrew B. Myers of Fordham University, David Nordloh of Indiana University, Donald Ringe of the University of Kentucky, and Bernard Rosenthal of the State University of New York at Binghamton. I am indebted as well to Alexander Burnham, editor of the *Washington Book Review*, and Richard Newman, Manager of Publications at the New York Public Library. And I feel a sense of everlasting obligation to the memory of four scholars and gentlemen all, the late Tremaine McDowell, Allan Nevins, Norman Holmes Pearson, and Stanley T. Williams, who, from the outset of my studies in Bryant, have offered guidance, solace, and encouragement.

Finally, just as Bryant was never failing in his acknowledgment of gratitude to such of his editor-publishers as James Thomas Fields and George Palmer Putnam, I should like here to express unreserved gratitude to Loomis Mayer, and to Dr. Mary Beatrice Schulte who, throughout our long association, has been an editor, adviser, and friend *sans peur et sans reproche*.

FOREWORD

At his death in 1878, William Cullen Bryant had been, for fifty-one years, the chief editor and a principal owner of the New York *Evening Post*. The paper had been started in 1801 by another young lawyer, William Coleman, in association with the Federalist politician Alexander Hamilton. Coleman was still in effective control of the *Post* when he was disabled in a carriage accident in 1827, having the previous year hired Bryant as a reporter on his journal.

Though Coleman may have sought his services on the *Evening Post* in 1826 because of his distinction as a poet, Bryant was by then already a proficient writer for both magazines and newspapers. During the past eight years he had published more than fifty critical and familiar essays. He had been the editor of and chief writer for the *New York Review* and the *United States Review*, and was known as well for lectures on artistic subjects: one a series of four on poetry before the New York Athenaeum, and another of five on mythology to the students of the National Academy of Design. Before he wrote the first editorial in the present collection in 1829, he had proved himself, in three annual volumes of the holiday gift book *The Talisman*, proficient in wit and irony.

When Bryant began to define the *Evening Post*'s policies in 1829, he brought that staid journal to the support of the Democratic administration of President Andrew Jackson, and held it consistently thereafter to liberal principles, advocating free trade, free labor, and Free Soil.

Except for the years from 1829 to 1836, when he had as partner and assistant editor the ex-sailor and author of sea stories William Leggett, Bryant kept the editorial pen largely in his hands until after the Civil War. In 1848 he took into his firm as managing editor young John Bigelow. After Bigelow sold his shares in 1860 to Bryant's son-in-law, Parke Godwin, to become in 1861 the American consul general at Paris, Bryant engaged in succession several competent managing editors: William Sydney Thayer, a Harvard graduate who was later consul general in Cairo; Charles Nordhoff, like Leggett a former sailor and writer of sea tales who, after a decade on the *Post*, became Washington correspondent for the New York *Herald*; Charlton T. Lewis, a clergyman and classical scholar; Joshua Levitt, previously editor of the Congregational paper the *Independent*; Sydney Howard Gay, formerly an editor of the *American Anti-Slavery*

Standard, the New York *Tribune*, and the Chicago *Tribune*; and George Cary Eggleston, once a Confederate soldier, who was a popular storyteller and an historian of the Civil War.

There were others, whose writing on the arts, in particular, was notable, such as William J. Stillman, a founder in 1855 of the nation's first art journal, *The Crayon*; and John R. Thompson, a poet and former editor of the distinguished *Southern Literary Messenger*. Occasional contributors formed a representative roster of leaders in many fields: Charles Francis Adams, Edward Bellamy, Thomas Hart Benton, Francis P. Blair, Charles A. Briggs, Salmon P. Chase, Thomas Cole, James Fenimore Cooper, Hamilton Fish, Edwin L. Godkin, Parke Godwin, Bret Harte, William Kent, James K. Paulding, John Randolph, Theodore Sedgwick, Samuel J. Tilden, Martin Van Buren and John Van Buren, Artemus Ward, Gideon Welles, Walt Whitman, and Silas Wright. And now and then there were articles by British Parliamentarian Richard Cobden and artist–economist George Harvey, and the French critic Charles Sainte-Beuve.

During the Civil War, so steady was Bryant's support of the Union cause that in its crucial year 1864, on his seventieth birthday, he was hailed in verse by James Russell Lowell, in a reminder to five hundred guests at the Century Club, that "in our dark hour he manned our guns again; / Remanned ourselves from his own manhood's store." Another observer saw Bryant's editorials as "of more use to the Union than some of its armies." After Appomatox Bryant still kept key issues for his own pen. Among these were Reconstruction in the South, the treatment of former Confederate officials, and the tariff. As late as 1872 he struck off one of the most forceful leaders of his career, in denying New York *Tribune* editor Horace Greeley's fitness as a Presidential candidate.

Bryant's editorials after 1860 require separate treatment. The present volume traces the growth of his political and social maturity as he made over a conservative, parochial, small-city newspaper into a national organ which in 1850 Charles Francis Adams called "the best daily journal in the United States."

INTRODUCTION

THE DAY AFTER THE FUNERAL OF William Cullen Bryant on June 14, 1878, his son-in-law, Parke Godwin, wrote from Carlsbad, Germany, to the New York *Evening Post* a tribute to its editor-in-chief and principal owner, with whom he had from time to time been associated in its conduct: "No one of our journalists ever attained and preserved such uniform elevation, dignity and purity of manner."[1] Godwin's judgment anticipated the comments of many of his contemporaries in their appraisals of Bryant's editorial career.

At one of many memorials after Bryant's death, George William Curtis said, "'The fact is no such man ever sat before or since in the editorial chair.'"[2] John Bigelow extended the comparison. "It is doubtful," he wrote, "if so wise, comprehensive, and edifying a system of political ethics as might be compiled from Mr. Bryant's editorial contributions to the 'Evening Post' can be found elsewhere in the literature of our own or of any other country."[3]

Such encomia echo in the present century. William Ellery Leonard, an historian of American letters, thought that "in no other has there been such culture, scholarship, wisdom, dignity, moral idealism."[4] Allan Nevins, recounting Bryant's conduct of his paper, called his "stately, elevated style" a "model for American journalism," adding that "many of his editorial utterances display a grandeur of style, and a force and eloquence not to be matched in the press of the period."[5] Newspaper historian Frank Luther Mott saw Bryant as a "great liberal [who] has seldom been done full justice by modern writers." Mott proposed a reason for this neglect: contrasting Bryant with his erratic, colorful, and more easily recalled rival, *Tribune* editor Horace Greeley, Mott noted, "the one was relatively steadfast, far seeing; the other was tempestuous and eccentric."[6]

Of his sometime employer, Godwin remarked,

> Mr. Bryant could be trenchant, almost cruel at times—his hatred of pretence and wrong being most intense—but his prevailing moods were gentle, and he preferred to ridicule sham and injustice to denouncing them in bitter and truculent words.... His love of truth was so instinctive and controlling that he seldom indulged in an indirection of speech except in the indulgence of his wit, which often flashed like summer lightning through the dark clouds of debate.[7]

It was this "flashing wit," perhaps as much as the steady voice "ever defending free commerce, free speech, freesoil," which baffled

Bryant's critics. One of these could not decide whether he hated or admired Bryant's writings the more, for while he "detested" their "inculcations," he was charmed by the "beauty and vigor" of their style.[8] This reaction was not unlike the more friendly one expressed by a future Secretary of State, Hamilton Fish, who, thanking Bryant for his account of the *Evening Post*'s first half-century, commented, "I have a hereditary right to an attachment to the Evening Post [founded by his namesake Alexander Hamilton]. Although it has been my lot to differ in my views of many of the important questions which it has discussed [Fish was then a Whig, Bryant a Democrat], I have always admired the force, the ability & the fearlessness with which it has maintained its own views."[9]

An even more sympathetic reader, critic James Lawson, called Bryant's editorials "models of a manly, fearless, independent style," suggesting that their author had a "happy faculty in illustrating to the most careless reader a difficult argument by an apposite anecdote—and his extensive reading has filled his mind so full of 'various lore,' that he often introduces one, where, without it, he might not so easily carry conviction to ordinary minds."[10] Such "apposite anecdotes," graced by Bryant's "extensive reading," both teased and irritated his less widely read opponents; one complained that Bryant "began each editorial with a stale joke and ended it with a fresh lie." Bryant's Williams College classmate and Unitarian pastor, Orville Dewey, recorded in his *Autobiography*,

> When I went to New York [in 1835 or 1836] how many a fight I had for him with my Whig friends! . . . The "Evening Post" was a thorn in their sides. . . . When some keen editorial appeared in it, they used to say, "There! what do you say of that?" I always said the same thing: "Whether you and I like what he says or not, whether we think it fair or not, of one thing be sure—he is a man of perfect integrity; he is so almost to a fault, if that be possible, regarding neither feelings nor friendships, nor anything else, when justice and truth are in question."[11]

In 1842, appraising in the *North American Review* Bryant's *The Fountain and Other Poems*, Professor Cornelius Felton of Harvard marveled,

> "What a beautiful gift this is! Here is a man whose life is cast among the stern realities of the world, who has thrown himself into the foremost line of what he deems the battle for human rights, who wages a fierce war with political principles opposed to his own, who deals with wrath and dips his pen daily in bitterness and hate, who pours out from a mind, fertile in thought and glowing with passion, torrents of invective, in language eloquent with the deepest convictions of the

heart and keen as the blade of Damascus; yet able to turn at will from this storm and strife and agony to the smiling fields of poetry.... We gaze with wonder on the change, and can scarce believe the poet and politician to be the same man."[12]

In hostile critics such wonder provoked spleen. Commenting in 1844 on the death of United States Bank head Nicholas Biddle, under the caption *De Mortuis Nihil Nisi Verum* (thus substituting "truth" for "good" in the Latin apothegm "Say nothing of the dead if not good"), Bryant suggested that, after reducing thousands to poverty by his frauds, instead of spending his final years in luxury at his country seat Biddle should have died in the penitentiary.[13] Reading this, New York's crusty Whig ex-mayor Philip Hone spluttered to his *Diary,* "How such a black-hearted misanthrope as Bryant should possess an imagination teeming with beautiful poetic images astonishes me; one would as soon expect to extract drops of honey from the fangs of the rattlesnake!"[14]

While Bryant's taunts tormented opponents, his defense of minorities, and attacks on privilege, pitted him against conservatives in his own Democratic Party. One of these accused him of "prostituting his fine talents ... in the advocacy of doctrines ... injurious ... to the best interests of the country." His newspaper was "read out" of the party and denied public printing. In 1838 he wrote a friend, "I know very well that I am much railed at and that I pass with a very large class of well meaning persons as a man of no moral principles."[15] Even his wife and daughters were snubbed by "polite society." Reaching New York in 1842, Charles Dickens sought out Bryant as a fellow advocate of an international copyright law, only to be warned against association with him. "Freedom of opinion! Where is it?" Dickens complained to William Charles Macready; "I speak of [George] Bancroft, and am advised to be silent on that subject, for he is a 'black sheep—a Democrat.' I speak of Bryant, and am entreated to be more careful, for the same reason."[16] In the *Evening Post* Bryant charged that his forthrightness bared him to "efforts of the monopolists and more recently the bank conservatives to break down this paper."[17] He confessed to Richard Dana, "You cannot imagine how difficult it is to make the world go right."[18] In 1838 his former partner William Leggett appealed confidentially to President Martin Van Buren on behalf of his friend:

> I have recently learned [from Mr. Bryant] that the condition of the Evening Post is exceedingly straitened and perplexed, and that it is with the utmost difficulty he continues to keep it from falling to the ground. Indeed, he greatly fears that he shall not be able to do so much longer, unless strengthened by some extraordinary succour.

You can hardly be supposed to be aware of the extent of the efforts which, for a long time past, have been made by the political opponents of that paper to break it down.

Yet, Leggett cautioned, "anything bearing the appearance of a gratuity or not of such a nature as might be trumpeted to the world without raising a blush upon his cheek, would be rejected by Mr. Bryant without a moment's pause."[19]

At times Bryant confessed his fears for the future. As his income shrank in 1836–1838 to half that of the past three-year period, he told Dana that, while he longed to compose verses, "I have so much to do with my legs and hoofs, struggling and pulling and kicking, that if there is any thing of the Pegasus in me I am too much exhausted to use my wings. . . . I have several times been on the point of giving it up and going out into the world worse than penniless."[20] The only poem he managed to write in 1837, "The Battlefield," reflected his struggle:

> Soon rested those who fought; but thou
>   Who minglest in the harder strife
> For truths which men receive not now,
>   Thy warfare only ends with life.
>
> A friendless warfare! lingering long
>   Through weary day and weary year!
> A wild and many-weaponed throng
>   Hang on thy front, and flank, and rear.[21]

Yet, as his business improved slowly after the slump of 1837–1839, his spirits rebounded. With slow but steady growth in his paper's circulation, he wrote Dana, "Nothing but a disposition to look at the hopeful side of things prevented me [from giving up], and I now see reason to be glad I persevered."[22]

Visiting New York in 1837, the British reformer Harriet Martineau observed that the *Evening Post* gained honor by its "intrepidity" in speaking truth when it required great courage to combat popular opinion.[23] As the years passed, Bryant won growing approval for urging free trade, better public health and sanitation, and a just copyright law, and for opposing slavery and the denial of equal rights to labor and foreign and religious minorities. In 1848 he was an architect of the Free Soil Party, and in 1856 of its successor the Republican Party. His growing political stature was reflected in 1851 in a remark by Virginia anti-slavery leader John Curtis Underwood, "What a glory it would be to our country if it could elect this man to the Presidency— the country not he would be honored and elevated by such an event."[24] But Bryant scorned all proposals that he seek or accept public office, having made this clear as early as 1843, when he wrote in an editorial:

> it requires some firmness to receive the flattering notoriety which arises from being talked of for the first office in the nation; but so much more honor is due to him who voluntarily forgoes this notoriety. . . . the candidate who assents to the opinion that the office is not on any account to be declined, must act under the notion that nobody but himself is able to discharge its duties properly, which would be a prodigious mistake.[25]

He proved his conviction more than once thereafter. When, in 1861, a grateful President Lincoln showed his gratitude for Bryant's support by hinting that he would like to send the *Evening Post*'s editor as his envoy to Madrid, Bryant printed a paragraph stating:

> Those who are acquainted with Mr. Bryant know that there is no public office from that of President of the United States downwards which he would not regard it as a misfortune to be obliged to take. They know that not only has he asked for no office, but that he has not allowed others to ask for him—that he has expected no offer of any post under the government, and would take none if offered.[26]

When, a decade later, it was suggested that he run against the incumbent Ulysses Grant and his upstart opponent Horace Greeley for the Presidency, Bryant inserted a signed card in his paper:

> The idea is absurd enough, not only because of my advanced age [he was then in his seventy-eighth year!], but of my unfitness in various respects for the labor of so eminent a post. I do not, however, object to the discussion of my deficiencies on any other ground than that it is altogether superfluous, since it is impossible that I should receive any formal nomination, and equally impossible, if it were offered, that I should commit the folly of accepting it.[27]

As the threat of disunion grew with Southern efforts to intrude slavery into new states and territories, Bryant's Free-Soil convictions stiffened. After John Brown had been hanged in 1859 for his failed effort to arouse a slave rebellion, Bryant, while deploring its violence, foresaw that "A large part of the civilized public will, as a large part of the world does already, lay on his tomb the honors of martyrdom, and while those honors remain there, his memory will be more terrible to slaveholders than his living presence could ever have been. . . ."[28]

Earlier than most other observers, Bryant urged Lincoln's fitness for the Presidency. He initiated the successful effort to bring the Illinois lawyer to New York in February 1860 for a crucial speech at Cooper Union, presiding over the meeting and introducing the speaker as a "gallant soldier" in the "battle we are fighting for Freedom against Slavery; in behalf of civilization against barbarism."[29] After Lincoln's election in November as the first Republican President, Bryant called the result a vindication of principles for which he had himself fought during three decades. "It is most gratifying," he wrote,

> to see what we believe to be a righteous cause—the cause of justice and humanity—after a long and weary struggle, closed by a decisive triumph. . . . we take this occasion to congratulate the old friends of the EVENING POST, who have read it for the last score of years or thereabouts, on this new triumph of the principles which it maintains.[30]

In 1878 Parke Godwin said of Bryant, "His better discussions of current topics, if now collected, would form a most attractive and readable book, merely on account of the variety and aptness of the illustrations, and the delicacy of the humor."[31] Godwin did, in truth, include a few editorials in the six volumes of Bryant's life and writings he assembled in 1882–1883. Later biographers have added a scant handful more. But a far larger store have lain unnoticed in the files of the *Evening Post* for over a century.

This selection, although still only a substantial sample, preserves the best of his wit and humor, his cultivation, and the force of his convictions. One may wonder why these essays, for such they are, have not been gathered before this, for, in the strength and clarity of his prose style, Bryant was, as Vernon Louis Parrington assured us fifty years after Bryant's death, a "power for sanity in a scurrilous generation."[32]

NOTES

1. Godwin to *Evening Post*, Bryant Homestead, Cummington, Massachusetts.
2. Quoted in Allan Nevins, *The Evening Post: A Century of Journalism* (New York: Boni & Liveright [1922]), pp. 362–63.
3. Bigelow, *William Cullen Bryant* (Boston & New York, 1897), p. 83.
4. Leonard, in *The Cambridge History of American Literature* (New York: Macmillan, 1917–1921), I, 276.
5. Nevins, in "William Cullen Bryant," *DAB*.
6. Mott, *American Journalism* (New York: Macmillan, 1941), pp. 258, 344.
7. Godwin to *Evening Post*, June 15, 1878.
8. Mott, *American Journalism*, p. 258.
9. Fish to Bryant, November 29, 1851, Library of Congress.
10. Lawson, in *Southern Literary Messenger*, January 1840, p. 109.
11. Dewey, *Autobiography and Letters*, ed. Mary E. Dewey (Boston, 1884), pp. 85–86.

12. Felton, in *North American Review*, October 1842, quoted in Parke Godwin, *A Biography of William Cullen Bryant* (New York: D. Appleton, 1883), I, 400–401.
13. Bryant in *Evening Post*, February 28, 1844.
14. Hone, *Diary*, ed. Allan Nevins (New York: Dodd, Mead, 1927), II, 206.
15. Bryant to John Rand, August 13, 1838, *The Letters of William Cullen Bryant*, edd. William Cullen Bryant II and Thomas G. Voss (New York: Fordham University Press, 1975–1992), II, 100.
16. Dickens to Macready, March 22, 1842, *Letters of Charles Dickens* (London, 1880), I, 61.
17. Bryant in *Evening Post*, November 25, 1837.
18. Bryant to Dana, February 27, 1837, *Letters*, II, 64.
19. Leggett to Van Buren, March 7, 1838, Library of Congress.
20. Bryant to Dana, February 27, 1837, and June 28, 1838, *Letters*, II, 64, 97.
21. "The Battlefield," *Poems* (New York: D. Appleton, [1876]), p. 260.
22. Bryant to Dana, June 28, 1838, *Letters*, II, 97.
23. Martineau, *Society in America* (London, 1837), I, 113.
24. Underwood to Eli Thayer, March 11, 1857, Brown University Library.
25. Bryant in *Evening Post*, December 29, 1843.
26. Bryant in *Evening Post*, April 1, 1861.
27. Bryant in *Evening Post*, July 8, 1872.
28. Bryant in *Evening Post*, December 5, 1859.
29. *Evening Post*, February 28, 1860.
30. Bryant in *Evening Post*, November 7, 1860.
31. Godwin to *Evening Post*, June 15, 1878.
32. Parrington, *Main Currents in American Thought* (New York: Harcourt, 1954), II, 238–39.

EDITORIAL NOTE

Of the editorials gathered in this volume, all save a few have been reproduced from the files of the New York *Evening Post*, or from microfilms of its issues. In some cases, where a known editorial has not been located in the newspaper, it has been taken from such a printed source as Allan Nevins's *American Public Opinion*, or Parke Godwin's *Prose Writings of William Cullen Bryant*. In a few instances undated clippings from the *Evening Post* have been used and assigned a probable, or approximate, date. Spelling, capitalization, and punctuation are preserved as printed, except in the case of obvious typographical error.

EDITORIALS

John Quincy Adams Gives Way to Jackson
March 5, 1829

The New York American (1819–1845) was then a liberal semi-weekly paper supporting the Jacksonian wing of the Democratic Party. On the day preceding this editorial Andrew Jackson of Tennessee had succeeded John Quincy Adams of Massachusetts as President of the United States. As will be evident in his later tribute on August 4, 1843, Bryant had grown by then to admire Adams for his opposition to slavery and championship of free speech.

"The long agony is over," as the *American* says, and the new Administration, the strongest ever seen in this country since the days of Washington, has entered upon its career. Of the past we will not say much, since we can say no good. The country has been rendered contemptible abroad and distracted at home. Of Mr. Adams himself we must be permitted to state that his acts have all shown that we were not wide of the truth when we said, as may be seen in our files, that although not deficient in literary acquirements, he has certain defects of character that unfitted him for directing the affairs of a great empire; and that his prejudices against that nation, with which it more behooves us to be on good and amicable terms than with all Europe besides, were so blind and so inveterate that we ventured to predict that no satisfactory settlement could ever be effected with it during his Administration. The event has proved that our fears were not chimerical. As to his Cabinet friends and advisers, we shall dismiss them from our consideration at this time by congratulating the country on its escape from what was once called by an eminent English statesman "the worst of evils that could predominate in our country: men without popular confidence, public opinion, or general trust, invested with all the powers of government."

Effect of Climate on Age
March 1, 1832

The artist who had lived in Italy was probably Bryant's friend Robert Weir, whom in 1834 he would recommend successfully for the position of instructor in art at the United States Military Academy at West Point. The "distinguished Hollander" was probably Roger Gerard Van Polanen, a Dutch diplomat living in New York, whom Bryant had met in 1827. William Kitchener was a Scottish physician and scientific writer in Glasgow. The British poet George Crabbe is best remembered for The

Village *(1783)*. *The second verse quotation has not been identified. Louis XVIII was King of France, 1814–1824; George IV was the British monarch from 1820 to 1830.*

Notwithstanding the complaints made of our variable climate, there is no doubt that it has its advantages and its beauties. We have sometimes the frosts of a Siberian winter, and sometimes the continued heats of a West India summer; but we have days of the most delicious temperature, the clearest and bluest skies, the brightest sunshine, and the most inspiring airs. We have the word of an artist—who lived years in Italy, and who has as fine an eye for nature as ever looked upon her works—that he has seen as glorious evenings here as ever flushed the skies of that picturesque country; not so many of them, perhaps, but still to the full as beautiful. The praise which has been bestowed so lavishly on the beauty of the skies of Italy comes from those who were nurtured under the pale climate of England. Jefferson, it will be remembered, was glad to escape from the moist and clouded skies of Paris to the drier atmosphere and sunnier skies of Virginia. A distinguished and intelligent Hollander, who had resided in France, Switzerland, and England, and who reached his eightieth year in this country, always maintained that we have one of the best climates in the world. He was desirous of living in his native country, but, being subject to asthmatic affection, found the fogs of that country too dense for his lungs. We have heard him rail, in good-set terms, at the famed climate of Montpelier, for its easterly winds and raw, damp atmosphere. The towns of England do not experience the intense cold during winter that we do, but they are wrapt in almost perpetual fogs and wet with drizzling rains that scarcely cease. We have before us at this moment a letter from Dr. Burgess, of Leicestershire, to the editor of the *London Courier*, in which he is laboring to prove that the cholera will not be so fatal in the climate of England as it has been on the Continent, and among other reasons he mentions "the *quick succession and vicissitudes* of dry and wet—the utmost prevalence of the former scarcely ever continuing long enough to induce disease from that cause alone, and the long duration of the latter being timely succeeded by genial and favorable alternations." This is an equivocal compliment either to the beauty or steadiness of the climate of England. There is a prevailing notion that the period of decay in the human constitution arrives earlier here than in the mother country, and that the duration of human life is shorter in consequence of the climate. Let us see how this is. Dr. Kitchener dates the commencement of the decline of the physical faculties at the age of forty-two. Crabbe, in one of his tales, puts it four years later:

> "Six years had past, and forty ere the six,
> When time began to play his usual tricks."

And then he goes on, in his fine manner, to describe the circumstances which mark the abatement of bodily activity and the growing disinclination to exertion belonging to that time of life. We leave it to be decided by the experience of our countrymen, whether the period of decline in the animal powers arrives earlier than this; whether in this country men begin to feel the approaches of age before forty-six. We believe not. An Englishman of fifty may have as fair and fresh a complexion as an American at thirty; but this is the mere effect of a moist and shaded sky. We are a more spare and meagre race than the English—and, indeed, than most of the nations of Europe. Artists will tell you that the difference between Americans and the natives of Europe in the fleshy parts of the human frame is astonishing. The tendency to corpulency there is much greater than with us, and is distinguishable even in the hands, which with us are lean and bony, and with the Europeans plumper and fatter. This is no advantage, but it keeps the skin smooth and prevents the approach of wrinkles, which are looked upon as one of the signs of old age.

We remember once hearing an ingenious medical friend remark that the difference between people who grow old in England and those who grow old in this country is that the former bloat up and the latter dry up. Old age among us is less unwieldy. We can point to many a man,

> "adust and thin,
> In a dun night-gown of his own loose skin,"

who yet preserves all the vigor of mind and activity of body which distinguished his greener years. The same man in the climate of England would have been more round and rosy, with better teeth, perhaps, for they decay in this country sooner than there, with fewer wrinkles, but, after all, no younger in constitution and no farther from the close of life. There are no such prodigies of corpulence among us as Louis XVIII, who was obliged to be rolled in a go-cart, being too unwieldy to walk, and who finally burst with obesity. There are no cases like that of George IV, who perished, as was said, from a collection of fat about the heart, which prevented it from performing its functions. Whatever be the cause of the difference in the human frame on the two continents, whatever it be that makes our countrymen taller and more spare than the Europeans, whether it arises from the violent alternation of cold and heat, or from a difference in the electric state of the atmosphere, it is enough that it has no effect to shorten life. The same difference has been remarked in some kinds of animals; the climate is said to elongate their forms; and there are not wanting those who think they have observed it also in trees and plants. It is a physical variety, but not an unhealthy one, and is produced by causes equally friendly to the existence of the human species. It has been stated that of the population of London only *one in forty* arrives at the age of seventy. We have before us the bills of mortality for the city of New York for five years, commencing with 1826, from which it appears that the average number of deaths of persons over seventy years of age is *one in twenty-seven.*

As respects the moral effect of our climate, there is nothing to complain of. The inhabitants of lands blessed with a soft and equable temperature are apt to be voluptuous; the people of less genial regions have made the greatest advances in civilization, and carried the arts and sciences to their highest perfection. Labor is never loved for its own sake; men require severe necessity, or some desire, to sting them into activity. Our climate, while it presents many of the beautiful phenomena of those which are reckoned the finest, is yet (for the truth must be acknowledged) variable, capricious, and severe, and exacts more ingenuity and foresight in guarding against the extremes to which it is subject than almost any other.

A Leaf from Mrs. Trollope's Memorandum Book
July 9, 1832

In 1832 the English novelist Frances Trollope (1780–1863), who had spent three disappointing years trying to support her family as a merchant in Cincinnati, published in the United States as well as in Great Britain Domestic Manners of the Americans, *an ill-tempered and greatly exaggerated account of her experiences while here. Bryant's parody satirizes her account, to the point of absurdity. "Take the wall," that is, force to the muddy curbside. The English reformer William Wilberforce (1759–1833), a member of Parliament, had long been a persistent advocate of the abolition of slavery; his efforts had culminated in 1807, when the slave trade was abolished. The popular British comedian John Barnes was then the manager of the Richmond Hill Theatre. The English comic actress Blanche Keppel had just made her New York debut. Thomas Hilson was one of the city's most popular comedians; John Povey, veteran actor of minor parts, was anything but an opera singer; Henry Placide was the most notable comic actor of his day.*

(Found among some loose papers accidentally left at her lodgings)

New York is rather a charming little city, containing from 100,000 to 150,000 inhabitants, mostly black. The streets are altogether monopolized by these sons and daughters of Africa, who take the wall of you on all occasions; and it would be entirely useless, as well as extremely dangerous, to notice any insult which they may offer you, as they all carry long daggers concealed in their bosoms, and use them, too, with utter impunity, under the very nose of the public authorities. Indeed, I once saw a little black boy carried to Bridewell for stealing, and that very afternoon the whole negro male population turned out in a procession, consisting of twenty thousand, with banners which bore the words "Wilberforce Philanthropic Society." From this I presume the boy's name was Wilberforce; at all events, the Court of Sessions (which, by the way, is here held in a little grocery store in William Street, called Harmony Hall) acquitted the culprit, in consequence of the sensation his imprisonment had produced.

This took place in the month of August, and so great was the alarm that immense numbers fled from the city, fearing another *insurrection*. Whole families departed at once. The steamboats (of which there are two tolerable good ones, one plying to Albany, the other to New Orleans on Long Island) were every day crowded with trembling passengers, who sought refuge from the bloody and atrocious scenes which yearly disgrace the streets, and retired to Saratoga, Communipaw, Brooklyn in New Jersey, Charleston in North Carolina, and Greenwich Village on Lake George. Scarcely a night passes without the negroes setting two or three of the houses on fire with the view of destroying the inhabitants. As the best mansions are made of light pine wood, it may be easily imagined that they are universally combustible; but fortunately the city of New York has really a copious supply of water, which prevents much damage.

Their theatres are positively amusing, and I must say I laughed very heartily, although to confess the truth, it was only at their tragedies and their operas. The Park Theatre was originally an old barn; its outside is disgraceful, and its interior more so. It has been burnt down *fourteen times*, probably by the religious party, which form the majority, and have now elected Jackson to the Presidency. The establishment stands opposite the Roman Catholic Cathedral, and is under the management of Messrs. Pierson and Drurie. I am indebted to my kind friend for many of these particulars. He knows that I am writing a book of travels, and although himself only an American, has kindly volunteered his services to collect materials for me, giving me sketches of character and authentic anecdotes, and has corrected, with the most scrupulous care, all of my geographical and typographical illustrations, in which the reader may consequently repose the most implicit reliance. The theatres have, however, two or three decent performers. Mr. Barnes is the principal tragedian. I saw him one evening in Romeo to Mrs. Keppel's Juliet, and I must say I thought his conception of the character rather good. He is quite small, with large melancholy eyes, and features expressive of tenderness and passion. Mrs. Keppel, as Juliet, was not sufficiently poetic, but was nevertheless pretty well. This was, however, afterwards accounted for by the discovery that she was an English lady. I afterwards saw Mr. Hilson in Young Norval. The greatest attraction they have, however, is Mr. Povey, a distinguished vocalist. He plays the Prince in Cinderella, and Masaniello, quite delightfully; all the rest are not worth mentioning. A fellow by the name of H. Placide undertook to personate the Baron, but I was thoroughly disgusted.

There are some peculiar customs prevailing among the audience here, which are apt to provoke a smile on the lips of a rational stranger. All their ladies dress in the most tasteless and extravagant style, and yet betray the most incontrovertible evidences of vulgarity, sitting on the banisters with their backs to the stage, between the acts, eating Carolina potatoes, and drinking ginger pop. This is done every night at the Park Theatre, and some good society females smoke "long nines" with a degree of audacious ease and familiarity that are really shocking.

JACKSON'S VETO OF THE BANK RECHARTER
July 30, 1832

On July 10, 1832, President Jackson vetoed a Congressional bill which would have rechartered the Bank of the United States, which had been founded in 1816 as the privately run depository for government funds.

We want words to express our sympathy with our worthy friends of the opposition at discovering that the veto message of the President is likely to increase his popularity, instead of destroying it as they had intended it should. That the opposition meant to give him a bill which should produce a veto, there is no question; but now they have got the veto, they are puzzled what to do with it; and the majority of them, we have no doubt, repent the haste they were in to get it. Their first manoeuvre was an attempt to excite the people against it by all sorts of opprobrious epithets bestowed upon the document, the President, and his Administration. Unluckily this had no effect. The great meeting at Pittsburgh—the great meeting at Philadelphia, in which the course of the President was approved in the warmest terms—the public rejoicings in various places in the State of Ohio—the general voice of the press in favor of this act of the President—these circumstances together soon convinced them how different is the effect of the veto from what they had expected with so much confidence.

Now take one of the leading opposition papers, and see what are its principal topics. They are full of railing against the Jackson party for supporting, indiscriminately, all the acts of the Administration; they are in a transport of indignation at the blindness of the people; and they abuse, in the bitterest terms, the presses which uphold the Chief Magistrate in refusing his signature, styling them "slavish" and "pensioned." Then they set their "ready and exact calculators" to work to ascertain how many people the area which contained the great Jackson meeting at Philadelphia could hold, with a view to reducing the supposed number of persons present. What is the fair inference from all this? Why, that the opposition are disappointed, and that the veto is popular.

A City Emptied by the Cholera Plague
August 20, 1832

In the summer of 1832 New York City suffered an epidemic of cholera. Before leaving in May for a two-month visit to his brothers in Illinois, Bryant had moved his wife and two small daughters across the Hudson River to Hoboken, which was relatively free from infection. Many of New York's residents had fled from the congested streets of lower Manhattan to the then comparatively rural area Greenwich Village later comprised. Bryant himself commuted by ferry to his newspaper office in the city, as is reflected in the perspective in his editorial note.

The appearance which New York presents to one who views it at the present time from the midst of the Hudson or from the opposite shores of New Jersey is a spectacle scarcely less unusual and solemn than to one who visits what were two months since its crowded and noisy places of business. The number of persons who have left the city is estimated at upwards of one hundred thousand people, including all classes and occupations. So many domestic fires have been put out, and the furnaces of so many manufactories have been extinguished, that the dense cloud of smoke which always lay over the city, inclining in the direction of the wind, is now so thin as often to be scarcely discernible, and the buildings of the great metropolis appear with unusual clearness and distinctness. On a fair afternoon the corners of the houses, their eaves and roofs, appear as sharply defined as if the spectator stood close by their side, and from the walks of Hoboken you may count the dormer windows in any given block of buildings. The various colors of the edifices appear also with an astonishing vividness, while the usual murmur from the streets is scarcely heard.

The Corrupting Influence of the Bank
October 4, 1832

The "subtle and insinuating lender" whom Bryant castigates was doubtless Nicholas Biddle of Philadelphia, president since 1822 of the Bank of the United States, which, under the terms of its charter, paid no interest on the federal monies with which it made its loans, often, as Bryant charges, to secure political favors for its managers. The Washington Globe, *edited by Kentuckian Francis Preston Blair from 1830 to 1845, was the Jackson administration's organ. Joseph Gales and W. W. Seaton, newspaper publishers of Raleigh, North Carolina, compiled the* Debates and Proceedings of Congress, *published between 1834 and 1856.*

The election has now, we say it with feelings of the strongest regret, become little else than a battle between the United States Bank and the friends of the administration. Hitherto the warfare of elections has been carried on by the discussion of public measures and plans of policy, by the attack and defense of the characters and qualifications of the candidates, their acts, their opinions and their promises—by appeals to preconceived prejudices or partialities—but now, an element of a hitherto unknown and most dangerous nature is mingled with our party struggles. A monied institution, headed by an active, subtle and insinuating lender, has thrown itself with its capital of thirty millions, into the arena of political strife. What may be affected by such an institution, with such a means of influence, by the distribution of its favors among those from whom services are expected, of those whose enmity is feared, may be easily imagined. The Saviour of the world was betrayed for thirty pieces of silver. The influence of the "root of all evil" is not lessened by the lapse of eighteen hundred years, and the interests of the Union may be betrayed for thirty millions of dollars.

Sober and good men are alarmed at seeing the manner in which the Bank has intermeddled with the politics of the country. The regular organized system of corruption on which it has proceeded, the application it has made of pecuniary persuasion to men possessed of political influence—to members of Congress and conductors of the public press—while it has corrupted some enemies into friends, has caused hundreds of honest men who were its friends to become its enemies. We are yet, however, to see what will be the effect of all this upon public opinion. We are to see whether the detestation of corruption is strong enough among the mass of the people to cause them to rise in their might and prostrate, by a total and ignominious defeat, both the buyers and sellers engaged in the infamous traffic.

In the meantime, our readers may ask what the Bank is doing since the investigations of the Committee. We can assure them that it has intermitted none of its activity. The disgrace of exposure has had no influence upon its transactions. We take from the Washington *Globe* the following list of pecuniary favours distributed by it among those whose services are not to be undervalued. We have been assured from a respectable source that it is substantially correct. The accuracy of the statement that the Bank had *contracted* its loans may be judged of from this statement.

Innumerable *political* loans have been made by the principal Bank since the investigating Committee made their report.

To Gales and Seaton a new loan of $20,000 has been made, half covered up by a little indirection to give them a pretence for denial.

The faithless Senator from Mississippi has gotten at least $10,000, with mere nominal security.

About the sum of $14,000 was loaned to a member of the House of Representatives, supposed to be opposed to the Bank, who was not at his post to vote against the Bank.

Another member, always before opposed to the Bank, voted for the bill, and, with a friend who had taken care to be absent on the passage of the bill, went to Philadelphia shortly after, and the Bank loaned them on a mutual endorsement, $7,500.

After the veto, Daniel Webster, on his return home, got from the Bank about $10,000—swelling his debt to about $40,000.

Other loans have been made, even *recently*, to members of Congress and public officers, to a considerable amount.

Jackson's Victory over Henry Clay
November 12, 1832

In November 1832 President Jackson was re-elected over his principal rival, Henry Clay, by a margin of 219 electoral votes to 49, with 18 votes going to two minor candidates, John Floyd and William Wirt. In January 1832, by a margin of one vote, the Senate had refused to confirm Jackson's appointment of Martin Van Buren as minister to Great Britain, the deciding vote having been cast by Vice President John Calhoun, a bitter opponent of Van Buren, who was then chosen and elected Jackson's vice president. The discovery of gold in the Cherokee Indian country of Georgia in 1828 had led white settlers to disregard an earlier federal guarantee of independence to the tribe. This led to a decision by Chief Justice John Marshall that the laws of a state had no force in Indian territory. President Jackson, sympathetic to the Georgia claims, is reported to have commented, "John Marshall has made his decision. Now let him enforce it."

The question who is to be our President for the next four years is now universally allowed to be settled. Popular opinion has declared itself in a manner not to be misunderstood or explained away. The most obstinate and the most prejudiced of our adversaries no longer venture to question the fact that the present Chief Magistrate has, by some means or other, obtained a fast hold upon the affections and confidence of the people of the United States. They like his character, they like his manner of administrating the affairs of the nation, and they have made up their minds to have him for their President for another term. There has prevailed in the great mass of the people a deeply-rooted conviction that the principles of foreign and domestic policy adopted and avowed by him are essential to the peace and prosperity of the Union. This conviction did not manifest itself by any clamor, because there was no occasion for any; but when the time came for declaring itself through the ballot-boxes, it came forward with a strength which nothing could resist. The opposition were swept before it like stubble before the whirlwind. We look around us and wonder how so feeble a minority could have contrived to make so much noise, and by what means they could have inoculated themselves so universally—even to the shrewdest and most experienced in their ranks—with the delusion that they should prevail in the contest. . . .

For our own part, we rejoice at the result for manifold reasons independent of the ordinary pleasure attending the victory of one's own party. We rejoice because a man clear-minded, honest, and decided far beyond the majority of those who fill high political stations in the various States, is triumphantly sustained by the people against the malice of his enemies. We rejoice that the only man under whom there can exist a prospect of pacifying the discontents of the South, and of preserving the Union, is continued in power. We are glad that a pacific settlement of the Indian question is now certain, and that a civil war with Georgia, into which the declared policy of either of General Jackson's competitors would have inevitably plunged the nation, will be avoided. We congratulate the nation that so large a majority of its citizens have concurred with the President in placing the seal of reprobation on that folly which would have exhausted the resources of the nation in a series of wasteful and ill-considered projects of internal improvement, and which would have produced perhaps perpetual collisions between the national government and that of the States. We congratulate all honest men that the league between the opposition and the Bank, and the attempt to elect a President by pecuniary corruption, has been defeated in such a signal manner that it will serve as a fearful warning for the future. In the election of Mr. Van Buren to the Vice Presidency, we are gratified to see that the people have passed a solemn censure on that Senate which, listening only to the promptings of party hatred, endeavored to proscribe one of our ablest and most deserving citizens. Finally, we rejoice to witness with what an intelligent and fortunate unanimity the people have ratified the sound, wise, and healing principles of public policy adopted by the present Administration.

MR. VAN BUREN'S RETURN FROM ENGLAND
November 22, 1832

The Roman general Marcus Aemilius Lepidus, a member of the Second Triumvirate formed after the murder of Julius Caesar in 44 B.C., was forcefully retired to private life after his abortive revolt against his associate Octavius. Many years after Van Buren's failure of Senate confirmation as minister to Great Britain, Bryant recalled dining in Washington with his friend Congressman Gulian Verplanck when the vote was taken: "'There,' said Verplanck, 'that makes Van Buren President of the United States,'"—as it did indeed, with the expiration of Jackson's second term in 1837.

The compliment paid by our city authorities to Mr. Van Buren has been consummated at a moment when, from every quarter of the land, every mail brings to him the most gratifying assurances that his private virtues and public services, the moderation of his temper, the integrity of his heart, the fortitude of his mind, and the zeal of his patriotism, are justly estimated by the people. At such a moment, an avowal of regard from a single city can hardly be supposed to produce the deep effect upon his feelings which, a short while since, such an expression from the metropolis of his native State could not but have occasioned. But let it be remembered, in justice to the Corporation, that they are not timeservers in this respect. They have not waited till the sentiments of other cities and other States could be ascertained. They have not hesitated to act until a land's united cry should speak, with an emphasis not to be misunderstood, the sense of the whole people as to the character of Van Buren, and as to that proceeding of the United States Senate by which, without cause, and on the most unfounded pretence that was ever alleged against a statesman, he was called from a diplomatic mission which his talents promised to render of great value to the nation. New York was not so tardy to do honor to her insulted son. As long ago as March, 1829, the compliment yesterday paid was determined upon, as will be seen by the resolution which will be found in its place in the account below of the proceedings upon this interesting occasion. Why this resolution was not carried into effect immediately upon Mr. Van Buren's return from Europe, all our readers will remember; and the conduct of that gentleman then, in declining the ceremonial of a public reception, and the various honors which were intended him, gratifying as under the circumstances they must have been, was justly looked upon as another instance, added to the many he had before given, of his readiness at all times to sacrifice personal advantages to considerations of public good.

How significant, how beautiful, how fine a comment on the character of our people and the nature of our institutions, is the act of political retribution paid the Senate for their malignant course to Mr. Van Buren! Who now are the rebuked? To the same chair, lately occupied by the ambitious Lepidus when he dared to throw his casting vote into the political balance against a man his equal in acquirements, his superior in talents, and oh, how greatly his superior in honesty, in singleness of motive, in elevation of character, and in all those qualities which give the greatest value to talents and learning—to that high seat the rejected is raised! The rebuked of Clay and Calhoun is the honored of the people! The very act that was intended to prostrate him forever, has made him Vice-President of the United States! In contemplating such an act of retributive justice, one might almost be excused for exclaiming, "Vox populi, vox Dei!"

South Carolina Must Yield
December 7, 1832

In November 1832 a state convention in South Carolina adopted an Ordinance of Nullification which prohibited collection of tariff duties in the state after February 1, 1833. After alerting the garrisons of federal forts in Charleston harbor, and appointing General Winfield Scott commander of United States forces in South Carolina, President Jackson sent the Congress a mollifying proposal that tariff rates be reduced.

Letters from Washington assure us that notwithstanding the calm tone of the message in relation to South Carolina, the President, with his usual decision, is taking the *most efficient measures* to secure the due execution of the revenue laws in that State. No language has been employed the effect of which might be only to irritate, and it is not the manner of the President to bandy words with anyone. A course of legislation in relation to the tariff has been recommended which, if adopted, cannot fail to appease all discontentment in the South, and even to satisfy every man in South Carolina whose excitement on this question has not run away with his reason, or who has not suffered the views of a guilty ambition to make him forget his duty to the Federal Republic, and his regard to the welfare of his own State. This recommendation every true patriot must earnestly hope to see adopted—that it will be so, we cannot permit ourselves to doubt—if not by the present Congress, at least by the next. For our own part, we believe that the recommendation will of itself go a great way towards pacifying the excitement which exists in South Carolina, and that it will dispose the majority of her citizens to pause in the rash and violent career upon which they have entered. If it does not in good degree operate as a sedative upon the inflamed feelings of that State—if many of the leaders of the Nullification party, worthy by their talents and their previous standing in the councils of the nation to take the lead in a better cause, are not influenced by it to use their exertions in calming the storm they have raised, they will give the strongest confirmation of what has been laid to their charge, that they are guilty of a previous and deliberate design to dismember the Union.

In the meantime, however, while South Carolina remains a member of the Union, she must expect to obey its laws and contribute to support its burdens. The utter confusion into which the suspension of the revenue laws in one State, and that a State possessing one of our most important ports, would throw the affairs of the nation, the multiplied embarrassments in which it would involve the trade and revenue, make it a matter of imperious duty on the part of the government to see that those laws are strictly enforced.

South Carolina Risking Ruin
December 21, 1832

On December 10 Jackson had issued a "Proclamation to the People of South Carolina" warning them that "Disunion by force is treason." James Hamilton, governor of South Carolina, 1830–1832, had called the popular convention which passed the Ordinance of Nullification which stimulated Jackson's proclamation.

The Union party of South Carolina are no less ardent and determined in support of the execution of the laws of the Federal government, than the dominant party in taking measures to resist them. A letter from Columbia dated December 10, published in the Charleston *Courier*, says that "if there is any difference between the Unionists of Charleston and those of the interior, it is that the latter exceed the former in warmth and violence." The people of Greenville have raised the flag of the United States in the village, and declare that it shall remain flying while they have lives to defend it. Hamilton and Calhoun, it is said, have been hung and burnt in effigy in Spartansburg District. A similar spirit prevails in other quarters of the State, and the tyrannical decrees held over their heads by the majority seem to have inflamed the excitement which already existed into a feeling of fierce indignation. The resolutions already before the Union Convention in that State recognize most solemnly an undivided allegiance to the real government, and propose a military organization of the Union Party to defend, if necessary, their rights by force.

Should a civil war break out in consequence of resistance to the revenue laws, we have no doubt that it will first begin among the citizens of South Carolina. Any feeling of jealousy, animosity, or indignation with which the people of two portions of the Union may regard each other is complacency itself to that which subsists between the two parties in South Carolina. An attempt to carry the Ordinance of the convention into effect with the terrible array of penalties by which it is accompanied, much as it might be regretted for the sake of the Union at large, would be unutterably calamitous for the State itself.

Some Poets
January 26, 1833

The antiquary John Aubrey gathered in Brief Lives *"floating traditions" about Shakespeare and his contemporaries. Philosopher Thomas Hobbes has been called "the most hated writer of his times" for his "blasphemous book"* Leviathan, *but there is no evidence that he knew Shakespeare. Playright Ben Jonson, who did, left a sensitive appreciation of his friend. The acerbic satirist William Gifford reviewed Aubrey's book when it was published more than a century after its author's death. This tongue-in-cheek essay finds Bryant in the sportive mood seen earlier in his editorial on Mrs. Trollope (July 9, 1832).*

The circumstance that the two greatest authors of the present century, Lord Byron and Sir Walter Scott, were both lame of a foot, has several times given occasion for an exercise of memory and industry on the part of writers for magazines and other light works, and a long list of industrious individuals has been made out, all of whom labored under some similar personal defect. There is one name, however, not less illustrious than any that have been cited, which has not been given. No hunter up of lame poets has yet added the name of Shakespeare to the list; though, that among all his other claims to distinction, that of personal deformity of a kind not widely different from Byron's or Scott's was not wanting, we think may be shown from the tenor of certain passages in his own writings. And it is to his own writings that we must look for any light on a matter of this kind. . . .

We are aware that we are met on the very threshold by a sentence in old Aubrey, who, speaking of Shakespeare, says, "he was a handsome, well-shaped man; verie good companie, and of a very ready, pleasant and smooth wit"—a sentence which has been seized hold of by the biographers as conclusive on the subject, and the latter branch of which is so abundantly corroborated by the very best evidence in the world, that it is not strange readers have been led into the error of adopting the whole as equally true. But for our own parts, we question Aubrey's authority on several accounts. In the first place, he was not born until 1626, ten years after Shakespeare died, and of course could have had no other knowledge of his person than such as may have been derived from old Hobbes, or some similar source. His informant could hardly have been Ben Jonson, whose death took place while Aubrey was yet a child. In the second place, from whomsoever this blundering antiquary may have received his impression with respect to Shakespeare's appearance, there is no more reason to believe that he has accurately remembered and reported what was told him, than was the case in other instances; and we should remember that we have astute Gifford's authority for saying of Aubrey, that "he thought little, believed much, and confused everything"; and that "whoever expects a rational account of any fact, however trite, from him, will meet disappointment." But whether the assertion that Shakespeare was a handsome, well-shaped man is an error of Aubrey's own or arose from misinformation, we have the best authority for discrediting it. The Irishman who, wishing to get rid of his wife, wrote her that he was dead, thought it exceedingly hard that his own word should not be taken; and so we might complain of equal injustice to Shakespeare, if posterity should persist in believing him to have been well formed notwithstanding his own explicit assertion to the contrary.

But to the proof. Where shall we look for a plainer avowal of lameness than is contained in Shakespeare's thirty-seventh sonnet, which runs thus:

> 'As a decrepit father takes delight
> To see his active child do deeds of youth,
> So I, *made lame by fortune's dearest spite,*
> Take all my comfort of thy worth and truth,' etc.

And in a preceding sonnet, the 29th, we find a scarcely less ambiguous acknowledgment that he was halt:

> 'When, in disgrace with fortune *and men's eyes,*
> I all alone beweep my outcast state,
> And trouble deaf heaven with my bootless cries,
> *And look upon myself, and curse my fate,*
> Wishing me like to one more rich in hope,
> Featured like him,' etc.

Again, in the forty-fourth sonnet, we find him complaining of the difficulty which he experienced in moving from place to place as rapidly as he wished:

'If the dull substance of my flesh were thought,
Injurious distance should not stop my way,' etc.

These two lines by themselves, to be sure, would not pass for much, and we only adduce them as helping to thicken other proofs. . . .

But it is useless to go on this way, multiplying quotations, when those already given make it evident enough, if there is any confidence to be placed in Shakespeare's own assertions, that he was a lame man. Those who prefer the description of Aubrey to the bard's own story, ought at least to give some reason why he is not a creditable witness in the matter. The evidence we have adduced, at all events, whether it satisfies our readers or not, is quite as broad and solid, as that upon which many ingenious narratives of antiquaries, and a thousand improbable stories of historians are founded.

ANDREW JACKSON VISITS NEW YORK
June 13, 1833

The poet Walt Whitman recalled the picture "indelibly" fixed in his mind when, as a fourteen-year-old boy, he had seen the "fine old man, with his weatherbeaten face, snow-white hair and penetrating eyes, waving his big-brimmed beaver hat gravely to the throng." Even the crusty Whig ex-mayor Philip Hone recorded "ruefully" in his diary that the President was "certainly the most popular man we have ever known. Washington was not so much so."

The reception of the President yesterday was one of the most striking public ceremonies ever witnessed by the people of the city. It did not derive its interest from any splendour of preparation, though in this respect there was no deficiency, and the arrangements were made generally in good taste, and executed with admirable order, but from the spirit of cordial good-will and the enthusiasm of welcome which pervaded the vast population of the metropolis and the multitude of strangers assembled to witness his arrival, and which manifested itself in a thousand spontaneous demonstrations of personal kindness and respect. The inhabitants of the city seemed to have deserted all the other quarters for the Battery and Broadway. The approach of the steamboats and vessels in company made a noble and picturesque appearance from the shore, proceeding as they did, slowly and in beautiful order, decorated with coloured flags, and the decks covered so thickly with passengers that they seemed like vast animated masses, while the water around them was covered with smaller craft, which seemed with difficulty to subdue their speed to the deliberate and majestic progress of the steamers. The people stood waiting in the perfect silence on the Battery and the neighboring wharves until the moment he landed, when the salutes and the music were followed by deafening acclamations from the multitude. But the most striking part of the spectacle was the progress of the President through Broadway. The street from the Battery to the City Hall was thronged with spectators; the sidewalks were closely crowded; rows of carriages were drawn up on each side, and the narrow passage in the midst was less densely filled with a shifting multitude. Every perch that could sustain a spectator was occupied, the lamp posts, the trees, the awnings, the carriage tops,— every window showed a group of fair faces,—the house tops were also crowded with spectators wherever a footing could be obtained— men were seen sitting on the eaves and clinging to the chimneys. To those who looked from an elevated position on this vast and crowded aggregate of human life, the spectacle was inexpressibly imposing. The number of persons collected between the Park and the Battery has been estimated at a hundred thousand, but if we include those who occupied the windows and the house tops, the number must have been scarcely less than twice as great. As the President appeared, his white head uncovered, sitting easily on his horse and bowing gracefully on either side, the recollection of his military and civic service, of his manly virtues and chivalric character, rose in the minds of the people, and their enthusiasm was not to be restrained. They crowded about him so as often for a few minutes to impede his progress, they broke through the circle of armed cavalry that surrounded him, they rushed between the legs of his escorts' horses to touch his hand or some part of his person. The ladies waved their handkerchiefs from the windows, and his course was attended with perpetual acclamations.

The Removal of the Deposits
September 23, 1833

Soon after his re-election in 1832, President Jackson removed government funds from the Bank of the United States. For the verses heading this editorial, cf. the opening lines of Shakespeare's Henry VI, Part I. *"Olivier le Daim," Olivier Necker, was a French barber and a favorite of King Louis XI's who was hanged by the parliament after Louis's death. Walter Scott made le Daim a minor character in the novel* Quentin Durward. *The* National Gazette *was a conservative Philadelphia journal edited by Robert Walsh, the butt of many Bryant gibes. The Byron verses are from his "Stanzas to Augusta," his daughter. Trophonious, legendary builder of the Temple of Apollo at Delphi, Greece, was deified after his death and consulted as an oracle in a cave, whose awed visitors never smiled again. Thus, a melancholy or terrified man was said to have "visited the Cave of Trophonious."*

> Hung be the heavens with black! Yield day to night!
> Comets, importing change of time and states,

> Brandish your crystal tresses in the sky,
> And with them scourge the bad revolting stars,
> That let the public be removed
> From Biddle's bank—too famous to live long!

Of this tenor are the jeremiads of the Bank journals. It is heartrending to hear their doleful lamentations on the occasion of the removal of the deposits. They lift up their voices and weep aloud. From the depths of their affliction come sounds of sublime denunciation. They grieve with an exceeding great grief over the fallen glory of their temple, and refuse to be comforted. The tears which stream from their eyes seem to have cleared their mental vision, and they see future events as through a glass darkling. "A field of the dead rushes red on their sight." They foretell the ruin of their country, for "the Cabinet improper have triumphed!" and woe! woe! woe! is now the burden of their prediction. "The die is cast!" exlaims the *National Intelligencer*; "the evil counsellors by whom the President is surrounded have prevailed!" "The star of Olivier le Vain is in the ascendant!" "The evil consequences which we predicted *must* result from it to all the interests, public and private, of the country!" "If this be not tyranny—if this be not usurpation, what under heaven can constitute tyranny and usurpation?" "The law openly trampled on!" "its pernicious effects!"—"bankruptcy and ruin must result from it!" "Will the people stand by and calmly see their authority thus spurned?—We asked if the people will quietly witness the restraints of the law broken down, and trodden under feet by their own servants. Will the Secretary of the Treasury suffer the sanctity of the law to be violated in his person?"

The *National Gazette* is not less sublimely dolorous, nor less fearfully prophetic. But however great its patriotic grief for the evil that has befallen the country, the event does not excite its surprise. "It was to be expected," says that pure and single-minded journal, "that the scheme of profligate and rancorous hostility against the Bank would be implacably pursued"; and it added that "the case is fitted to awaken lively alarm and the gravest reflection." "To what does this lead?—to the result that the President of the United States will have usurped the command of the whole twenty-five millions of revenue! and the power of distributing that revenue to whomsoever he pleases, whether to Banks *or to individuals at Washington or elsewhere, as managers of a political game!*" "This affair is equal in fearful import to anything that has occurred in our country"; it is "outrageous law!" and is a "scheme of usurpation."

The rest of the purchased presses of the Bank are not less lachrymose and lugubrious, and all of them partake of a spirit of prescience. They all exclaim, almost in the words of Lord Byron,

> The day of our destiny's over,
> The star of our fate has declined!

—"the times are out of joint," they say—a disaster has befallen the country from which it can never recover—we are ruined, lost, utterly undone!—and like the misshapen dwarf in the "Lay of the Last Minstrel," they wave their lean arms on high and run to and fro, crying "lost! lost! lost!" Who can doubt the sincerity of their lamentations at the death-blow which has been given to the United States Bank, when it is remembered how munificent a patron that institution has been to them? Who can wonder that they appear at the head of the funeral train as chief mourners, and raise so loud their solemn wail, when he reflects how well their grief is paid for? No hired mourner at a New England funeral ever earned his wages by so energetic a wail, or so lachrymose an aspect. They seem as woebegone as pilgrims from the Cave of Trophonious, when

> —the sad sage, returning, smiled no more.

But their wailing is in vain—"vainly they heap the ashes on their heads"—the fate of the Bank is sealed; and we, who are not paid to wet our cheeks with artificial tears, who have no cause to be a mourner, must be permitted to congratulate the country that a monopoly which, in the corrupt exercise of its dangerous power threatened to sap the foundation of American independence, has by this firm and timely act of the general government been reduced to a state of feebleness which, we trust, is only the precursor of its final dissolution.

Three Opposition Leaders: Clay, Calhoun, and Webster
March 31, 1834

Henry Clay, John Calhoun, and Daniel Webster were then United States Senators, respectively, from Kentucky, South Carolina, and Massachusetts, all opponents of the Jackson administration, although for different reasons.

When an intelligent and rational people is called upon in a contest between two great political parties, it is proper for them to know who are their opponents and what they are fighting for; whether for something or nothing; principles or men. Although the question of restoring the deposits and perpetuating the monopoly of the Bank of the United States is inseparably associated with the result of the coming election, it is by no means the only point involved in the contest. The party we have to contend with is manifold; it is headed by the most discordant leaders, wielding the opposite weapons; each marching under his own banner, and each laboring in his own cause. Let us then pass in review their avowed principles and purposes, that the people may judge whether such discordant materials could possibly be kept together except by the strong cement of a common interest.

In the first place stands Henry Clay. He is the parent and champion of the tariff and internal improvements; of a system directly opposed to the interests and prosperity of every merchant in the United States, and devised for the purpose of organizing an extensive scheme through which the different portions of the United States might be bought up in detail. By assuming the power of dissipating the public revenue in local improvements, by which one portion of the community would be benefited at the expense of many others, Congress acquired the means of influencing and controlling the politics of every State in the Union, and of establishing a rigid, invincible consolidated government. By assuming the power of protecting any class or portion of the industry of this country, by bounties in the shape of high duties on foreign importations, they placed the labor and industry of the people entirely at their own disposal, and usurped the prerogative of dispensing all the blessings of Providence at pleasure. They could at any time decide what class of industry should be enriched, and what class impoverished; whether commerce should flourish or decay; whether the manufacturer of cotton, wool, or iron should become a king, while the common laborer sank into a pauper. Out of this system grew those great manufacturing establishments which have monopolized almost all the pursuits of simple mechanics, and converted them from independent men presiding over their own homes, masters of their own shops, and proprietors of their own earnings, into the pale, sickly, and half-starved slaves of companies and corporations.

It is against this great system of making the rich richer, the poor poorer, and thus creating those enormous disproportions of wealth which are always the forerunner of the loss of freedom; it is against this great plan of making the resources of the general government the means of obtaining the control of the States by an adroit specie of political bribery, that General Jackson has arrayed himself. He has arrested the one by his influence, the other by his veto.

In the second place stands John C. Calhoun. Reflecting and honest men may perhaps wonder to see this strange alliance between the man by whom the tariff was begotten, nurtured, and brought to a monstrous maturity, and him who carried his State to the verge of rebellion in opposition to that very system. By his means and influence, this great Union was all but dissolved, and in all probability would at this moment lie shattered into fragments had it not been for the energetic and prompt patriotism of the stern old man who then said, "The Union: it must be preserved!" Even at this moment Mr. Calhoun still threatens to separate South Carolina from the confederacy if she is not suffered to remain in it with the privilege of a *veto* on the laws of the Union. It is against these dangerous doctrines, which have been repudiated by every other State in the Union, which find no kindred or responsive feeling in the hearts of the people, that General Jackson stands arrayed, in behalf of the integrity of this great confederation. He appears as a champion of the Union, and appeals to the people to support him in the struggle for their happiness.

The third of the triumvirate of this strange confederacy of contradictions is Daniel Webster. Without firmness, consistency, or political courage to be a leader, except in one small section of the Union, he seems to crow to any good purpose only on his own dung-hill, and is a much greater fowl in his own barnyard than anywhere else. He is a good speaker at the bar and in the House; but he is a much greater lawyer than statesman, and far more expert in detailing old arguments than fruitful in inventing new ones. He is not what we should call a great man, much less a great politician; and we should go so far as to question the power of his intellect, did it not occasionally disclose itself in a rich exuberance of contradictory opinions. A man who can argue so well on both sides of a question cannot be totally destitute of genius.

And here these three gentlemen, who agree in no one single principle, who own no one single feeling in common, except that of hatred to the old hero of New Orleans, stand battling side by side. The author and champion of the tariff, and the man who on every occasion denounced it as a violation of the Constitution; the oracle of nullification and the oracle of consolidation; the trio of antipathies; the union of contradictions; the consistency of inconsistencies; the coalition of oil, vinegar, and mustard; the dressing in which the great political salad is to be served up to the people.

We must not deny, however, that these gentlemen have a sort of paternal, or maternal, influence watching over them and coöperating in the great cause of domestic industry and internal improvements; nullification and consolidation; State rights and Federal usurpations, thus inharmoniously jumbled together higgledy-piggledy. It is the Mother Bank, the Alma Mater, under whose petticoats they are fighting the great battle, every one for himself and Mother Bank for all. Nicholas Biddle, the paramour of the old lady, who has the sole management of her business, is connected with the partnership as a sort of Commissary-General of purchases. He holds the purse-strings, which are equivalent to both bridle and spur, arms and ammunition, in modern political warfare. To all these mighty powers and potentates the honest Democracy of this country have nothing to oppose but their ancient, invariable principles; their inflexible integrity of purpose; and their invincible old leader, Andrew Jackson. Is not this enough? We think it is, and await the issue without a single throb of apprehension.

How Abolitionists Are Made
April 21, 1836

Nathaniel P. Tallmadge was a conservative Senator from New York. In January 1836 Senator Calhoun had proposed that petitions to the Congress to abolish slavery in the District of Columbia be laid on the table without discussion as "foul slander on nearly one-half of the states of the Union."

Mr. Tallmadge has done well in vindicating the right of individuals to address Congress on any matter within its province—a right springing from the nature of our institutions, and never denied till now. For this we thank him. This is something, at a time when the Governor of one State demands of another that free discussion on a particular subject shall be made a crime by law, and when a Senator of the Republic, and a pretended champion of liberty, rises in his place and proposes a censorship of the press more servile, more tyrannical, more arbitrary than subsists in any other country. It is a prudent counsel also that Mr. Tallmadge gives to the South—to beware of increasing the zeal, of swelling the ranks and multiplying the friends, of the Abolitionists by attempting to exclude them from the common rights of citizens. For this counsel he deserves the thanks of the South. Yet it seems to us that Mr. Tallmadge, who, on other occasions, has shown himself not to be wanting in boldness and freedom of speech, might have gone a little further. It seems to us that the occasion demanded that he should have protested with somewhat more energy and zeal against the attempt to shackle the expression of opinion. It is no time to use honeyed words when the liberty of speech is endangered. In vindicating the North from the charge of sharing in the designs of the Abolitionists, he might have deplored and condemned, in the strongest terms, the excesses to which the people of the North have been led by a fanatical hatred of that party. He has shown how the rival parties eagerly sought to clear their skirts from the stain of abolitionism; but, instead of representing this spirit as in all respects laudable, he should have added with what a wolfish rage they fell upon a small association of benevolent and disinterested enthusiasts, and discharged the coarse fury of party spirit upon those whose only fault was to maintain and seek to propagate opinions which thousands of benevolent men had maintained and expressed before them, not only in our own, but in all countries of the globe. He might have added how, in this very city, the law had been violated by a postmaster erecting himself into a censor of the press, and refusing the aid of the mail in conveying publications which he deemed objectionable. He should have condemned those acts of violence and tumult which made the friends of despotism abroad to exult, and which covered with shame the faces of those who were looking to our country as a glorious example of the certainty with which good order and respect for personal rights are the fruits of free political institutions. There should be no compromise with those who deny the freedom of debate within or without the walls of Congress, in conversation, at public meetings, or by means of the press. If the tyrannical doctrines and measures of Mr. Calhoun can be carried into effect, there is an end of liberty in this country; but carried into effect they cannot be. It is too late an age to copy the policy of Henry VIII; we lie too far in the occident to imitate the despotic rule of Austria. The spirit of our people has been too long accustomed to freedom to bear the restraint which is sought to be put upon it. Discussion will be like the Greek fire, which blazed the fiercer for the water thrown to quench it. It will scorn the penalties of tyrannical laws; and if the stake be set and the faggots ready, there will be candidates for martyrdom.... the argument, which might otherwise have been carried on by inferiour talents ... has been invested with a new interest, and has forced itself upon those who were formerly indifferent.

PETITIONS AGAINST SLAVERY
May 20, 1836

In the House of Representatives on May 18 a committee under the direction of Henry Pinckney of South Carolina proposed that anti-slavery petitions be tabled without printing. This so-called "gag rule" brought from former President John Quincy Adams, now a Congressman, the charge that it was a "direct violation of the Constitution."

Our readers will find in another part of our paper a debate of no little interest which occurred on Wednesday, in the House of Representatives, on Mr. Pinckney's Report and Resolutions concerning the abolition of slavery in the District of Columbia. It appears that some of the Southern members opposed, with much warmth, the printing of the report. This is the more extraordinary, when it is considered that the report is drawn up by a Southern member, himself, we presume, a slaveholder, an enemy of the abolitionists, hostile to the emancipation of slaves in the District of Columbia, and desirous to hush all present discussion of the question. The report, as we understand, embodies the views which such a man would take of the question; the resolutions, which will be found in the proceedings of Congress, certainly do so. Yet some of the Southern members opposed its publication simply because it is not sufficiently *ultra*,— because it does not go the length of denying, what no unprejudiced person denies, the constitutional power of Congress to set free the slaves within the District of Columbia. The antipathy of these men to investigation, seems to have reached the highest pitch of fanaticism and intolerance. That they wished to gag the mouths of those who desired the abolition of slavery in that district we well knew; but we had no idea, 'til now, that they denied even to the resolute enemies of abolitionism the right of being less violent and fanatical than themselves.

We feel it the more our duty to notice these indications of intolerance on the part of certain of our legislators, because they form part of a plan for breaking down the liberty of speech and of the press by a most odious, tyrannical and intolerable censorship. The freedom of discussion is the guard and bulwark of our other liberties, and the slightest attack upon it ought to be met and resisted as an attack upon all the rest. There never was a country in which political freedom existed for an hour without the right of discussion, and no nation, so long as that right is permitted, can be deprived of its liberties. An avowal of monarchical principles of government may be smiled at, because there is no danger that a people educated under institutions like ours will adopt them; but an attempt to fetter the expression of opinion should be repelled with indignation, because it is the first sure and fatal step in the change from free to despotick institutions.

The resolutions offered by Mr. Pinckney appear to us open to objection on this very account. The first, which purports that Congress has no right to interfere with the institution of slavery in any of the states, will be universally assented to. The second, that Congress ought not to interfere with slavery in the District of Columbia, involves a question of expediency which it is not within our present purpose to discuss. The third, which is to the effect that all future memorials relating in any way or to any extent whatever to the subject of slavery or its abolition, shall be neither printed [n]or referred, but laid on the table in silence, and never called up again, is a resolution which, if its effect be intended to extend beyond the present session of Congress, is bad as a measure and dangerous as a precedent. If it was intended only to have effect during the present session it is scarcely worth disputing about, as the session is so near its end. Even in that case the resolution should have been expressly limited to the present session. But we protest against any attempt to tie up the hands of the members of any succeeding session; and we look with something more than distrust upon a resolution of Congress to treat with utter disregard and contemptuous silence any memorials, expressed in the language of decency, respecting any matter upon which Congress has power to legislate. If this precedent be allowed, and if it pass into a maxim that Congress may so neglect any set of representations which may be presented to it, the right of addressing that body by memorials is at an end. The Congress of 1832, which was friendly to the Bank of the United States, might, by the same rule, have tossed under its table all the representations addressed to it against that institution. It may, at any time, make a selection of those subjects on which it is determined to pursue a certain policy, and then refuse to look at the remonstrances which the people address to it. If this resolution passes, depend upon it that we shall hear next session that it was a compromise, that it gives the slaveholding states a vested right to perpetual silence on the topick of slavery within the District. Against this we feel it our duty to enter an earnest and solemn protest beforehand, in the name of all those who value the right of free discussion, who hold that the people are entitled to make known their views to their representa[t]ives, and who believe that the proper sphere of a legislature is circumscribed by its present duties, and does not extend to putting restraints upon its successors.

THE RIGHT TO STRIKE AND JOURNEYMEN TAILORS
May 31, 1836

In the fall of 1835 a newly formed Society of Journeymen Tailors increased its rates, and won its demand after a short strike. When, a few months later, their employers combined to rescind this increase, the tailors struck again, resulting in bitter fights with strike breakers. On May 30, 1836, twenty-one journeymen tailors were convicted in a New York court of "conspiring injurious to trade and commerce," in refusing to work unless given higher wages. Bryant continued his objections to their conviction in a series of editorials between May 31 and June 16. Judge Ogden Edwards of Staten Island, New York, was a grandson of the Congregational minister Jonathan Edwards, and a cousin of both Aaron Burr, formerly Vice President of the United States (1801–1804) under Thomas Jefferson, and a practicing attorney in New York since 1812, and the Reverend Timothy Dwight, president of Yale College from 1795 to 1817.

The twenty-one journeymen taylors indicted for a conspiracy injurious to trade and commerce, were last night, after a trial of three days in the Court of Oyer and Terminer, and after an elaborate charge from Judge Edwards, found guilty of the offence laid to their charge. The jury, however, seem to have had some misgivings as to what they were doing, since they recommended them to the mercy of the Court. If the report of the charge, as given in a morning paper, be a correct one, Judge Edwards takes the ground that any combination not to work for less than certain rates of wages, is a conspiracy, injurious to trade and commerce, and therefore punishable by law. We do not admit, until we have further examined the question, that the law is as laid down by the Judge; but if it be, the sooner such a tyrannical and wicked law is abrogated the better. His doctrine has, it is true, a decision of the Supreme Court in its favour; but the reasoning by which he attempts to show the propriety of that decision is of the weakest possible texture. The idea that arrangements and combinations for certain rates of wages are injurious to trade and commerce, is as absurd as the idea that the current prices of the markets, which are always the result of understandings and combinations, are injurious to trade and commerce. Any temporary inconvenience which results from such combinations works its own cure. We shall publish the report of the Judge's charge, and examine its positions more particularly.

U.S. Consular Service and the Passport System
May 31, 1836

On March 26, 1836, Bryant returned from a residence of nearly two years in Europe, during which he had traveled through France, Italy, Austria, and Germany. Thomas Appleton of Massachusets was American consul at Leghorn, Italy, from 1798 until his death in 1840.

Do such of our countrymen as remain at home know that our government are laying, in various cities of Europe, a vexatious tax upon those who go abroad? It arises in the following way.

The persons who hold the office of Consul in foreign cities perform various duties, for which they receive no direct compensation. They are expected to assist American citizens in distress; they look into the circumstances of their case, do what is necessary to be done for their protection, and furnish them with opportunities to return to their country. To do them justice, they generally render these services with great cheerfulness, though they must, of course, take some trouble and give to them a considerable portion of their time. In certain places, as at Rome and Naples, the principal, in fact the only compensation which the Consul receives for these services, is a fee of two dollars for examining and endorsing the passport of every American citizen who arrives and departs. In some places the endorsement of the Consul on the passport is not necessary, but in most it is required by the government of the country, and wherever it is so, the American who holds the passport is obliged to pay his Consul two dollars. If he travels far, he will find that he has paid in this way a considerable sum, before his journey is ended. No travellers of any other country are taxed in this manner. The publick agents of every other government endorse the passports of their own countrymen gratuitously—the American agent only exacts a fee. The passport system on the continent of Europe is certainly troublesome and vexatious enough in itself, without our government interfering to render it more so by making it an occasion of extorting money from its own citizens. It is enough in all conscience to be detained a day or two, and to be sent from office to office for the authorizations of half a dozen different officers of the police, and half a dozen different foreign ministers, without being mulcted into the bargain, by our own government, for no other offence but that of being an American citizen.

The want of a compensation for services for which the Consul ought to be paid, tempts him in some instances to demand the fee in cases where his endorsement of the passport is not necessary. Our Consul at Leghorn whose name is APPLETON, is in the practice of telling American citizens who come in his way, that his indorsement of their passport is necessary, to enable them to proceed to Rome or Naples. This man knows better, but the temptation of the paltry fee to be obtained in this way is too great for his honesty. As Leghorn is a place which our countrymen frequently visit in their way to the south of Italy, he picks up a pretty sum in this manner annually, to which he has no more right than a bandit of the Appenines.

The remedy for this evil is to grant salaries to our Consuls abroad, proportioned to the services they are obliged to render, and abolish the practice of taking money for looking at passports. Our treasury is in a state to pay these salaries; and there is no reason for obliging a few Amerian travellers, who receive but a slight service from the Consuls, to pay for important services rendered to others.

THE RIGHT TO STRIKE AND JOURNEYMEN TAILORS
June 1, 1836

Bryant's reference to Samuel Butler's verse satire Hudibras *(1663–1678) is doubtless to the lines "For what is Worth in any thing, / But so much Money as 'twill bring" (I, 465).*

We copy from the *Journal of Commerce* of yesterday, what purports to be a statement of Judge Edwards's opinion in the recent combination case, with a pretended exposition of the arguments in support of that opinion. It is easy to see that the writer has either blundered most egregiously in reporting the justification of the charge, or has ventured upon the reprehensible step of dressing up the arguments of the Court in a travesty, intended to betray what the sly reporter has regarded as illiberal or unsound. We have too much charity to hesitate in this alternative; but we must be pardoned if we make it appear that the most ingenious reduction to the absurd, could not have been more fatal to the Judge's reasoning, than the want of skill which has been shown in telling us what it was.

The danger of giving a report as inaccurate as we take this to be, may be best exemplified by supposing a plain man to fall into the mistake of regarding the published arguments as the actual dicta of the Judge. Would he not deal with them something after the following fashion?

"The Judge puts it to the Jury to suppose that a number of persons engaged in the trade or manufacture of this city, would from time to time enter into combinations of this sort, and determine not to work under certain rates, and carry their resolutions into effect at times when their services were most necessary, and he asks what sort of a state would society be reduced to?

"Why, is the Court so uninformed as not to know that these very combinations have been entered into, year after year, time out of mind, with every revolving sun, and that trade and manufactures instead of being injured, seem to run on, like a trundled hoop, all the steadier and merrier for the strikes? If Trades' Unions could reduce society to a sort of a state too horrid to be mentioned, the catastrophe would have happened long ago. In spite of these conspiracies to injure commerce, ships are built and houses are tenanted, our backs and our feet are covered and cared for, as well now as during the reign of the greatest of the Guilds.

"But the Court has modern instances for all its saws. Suppose all the carpenters and bricklayers should at the commencement of next May, determine not to work unless their wages were raised, and demanded ten times more than they ought, and could succeed in doing so, what would become of the citizens or who would occupy their houses?

"If carpenters and bricklayers demand[ed?] ten times more than they ought, they would not get what they demanded. Carpenters and bricklayers cannot do the thing that can't be done. More than they ought! And who is to set the assize of just what they ought to ask? What they can get, that they ought to have, and 'the citizens' might do a more manly thing than say "what shall become of us?" If carpenters and bricklayers are so much sought for and so hard to find, that they can ask and get fifty times what they are getting now, why, in the name of common sense, should they not agree to take as much as men that have money are willing to give.

"But what would become of the men of the money bags? Poor souls! they would have to pay for labour what labour was worth; and the value of a thing is just what it will bring, now as in the days of Hudibras.

"But the Court has another instance. Or suppose that the produce of this country bore the highest price in the foreign market, and that every one was anxious to export it; and that, at that moment, all the stevedores, shipwrights, and other mechanicks whose services were necessary to fit out ships, insisted upon having ten times the value of their services; such conduct must bring commerce to a stand, and would be well calculated to destroy the trade of the city altogether.

"Painful as it would be to put a damper on this interesting 'anxiety to export,' disagreeable as the alternative might be, the necessary services would certainly have to be paid for, or the pleasing 'high price in the foreign market' would never be touched. If the mechanicks insisted on no more than they could get, they would get it; and so much they have always been able to get, without bringing commerce to a stand. If they insisted on more than they could get, they would not get it, and never have got it, combination or no combination, for this plainest of reasons, that

"What's impossible can't be,
And never comes to pass."

"But to get all they can would destroy the trade of the city altogether. Just the reverse. A strike for higher wages is a notice to all the world that more hands are wanted at the striking place, and is, besides, the very best way of getting a supply of them. Strikes are the self-acting alarm bells of trade; and the knife that would cut the cords of this machinery is not the sword of justice, but the dagger of folly and of suicide.

"But if such a system were tolerated, the constitutional controul [*sic*] over our affairs would pass away from the people at large, and become vested in the hands of conspirators. Not so. If such a system be *not* tolerated, all this and something worse will happen. For all this and something worse did happen, precisely where, and simply because, this right to combine was denied to those who owned it first and claimed it last—the honest and hard-working poor."

It is needless to multiply proofs that the Court gave better reasons for the charge than the reporter has preserved. A charge so imperfectly sustained could never have convinced the jury, and yet the jury were convinced, that the laws of the free State of New York have made it *criminal* for the working classes to settle among themselves the price of their own property, and to promise each other they they will not part with it for less than they believe it to be worth!

The Right to Strike & Journeymen Tailors
June 2, 1836

There is not an association of any sort for the purposes of business, the members of which may not be prosecuted and sent to the penitentiary, if the doctrine laid down in Judge Edwards's charge, published yesterday, be law. According to his position, a combination to take a settled price and no less, for any thing to be sold, is a conspiracy injurious to trade and commerce, and is punishable. Then the owners of our packet-ships, who demand a hundred and forty dol-[l]ars for a passage to Liverpool, are conspirators. Go to them and see if you can obtain a passage for less—they will answer you in the negative—and if you ask the reason, you will be told that it is a fixed price, *agreed* upon by the proprietors. Here is a criminal combination; for suppose with Judge Edwards, that all the packet owners should ask more than the citizens were able to give, who would find his way across the Atlantic, and what would become of our commerce? Two or three owners of a merchant vessel agree that they will not take less than a certain rate of freight—this is a conspiracy—for suppose that all the ship owners should demand exorbitant prices, our trade would be at an end. Our respectable neighbours at the next corner have fixed prices for their dry goods—the partners have put a fair profit on the first cost of their goods, and they will not take less—they are conspirators. The daily papers have certain rates agreed upon among them—they require ten dollars to be paid by yearly subscribers—and they have established in concert certain rates of charge for their advertisements which they will not depart from—we are all conspirators. The proprietors of a hotel agree upon the rates to be charged the guests—here is another conspiracy. The proprietors of a stage coach do the same thing with respect to their passengers—another conspiracy. The directors of an Insurance Company fix their rates of insurance—another conspiracy. The butchers have an understanding as to the prices of their meat; the bakers as to the prices of their bread; the very price current is the witness to a vast and general conspiracy through the whole world of commerce, for it shows what people have agreed to sell their commodities for. Now suppose—after the fashion of reasoning which finds so much favour with certain people—suppose that all the hotel-keepers, and all the stage coach offices, and all the publishers of newspapers, and all the dry goods' merchants, and all the bakers, and all the butchers, and all the grocers, and all the vendors of every kind of commodity, should demand prices which nobody could pay, what would become of the world in such a case? The result would be that nobody would buy, nobody would sell, news would not circulate, nobody would travel,—the merchant would go to sleep on his bales, and the shopkeeper on his counter; the hotels and insurance offices and stage offices would be shut up, and the whole community be brought to universal nakedness and starvation. What a frightful idea! The misfortune of the supposition, however, is, that the state it contemplates cannot by any possibility come to pass.

What a crowd of delinquents might not be picked up by the officers of the law, if every man who has offended by a conspiracy of this sort were to be brought before the Court of Oyer and Terminer. Pearl-street and Broad-street, William-street and Pine-street, and half the streets in the city would be depopulated, and the criminals could not be crammed into a penitentiary as large as St. Peters.

Yet hurtful as these combinations are to trade and commerce, we see trade and commerce constantly flourishing by their means. They have been entered into in one shape and another ever since commodities were bought and sold and wages were given.

Is any thing further necessary to show the absurdity of the doctrine in the reported charge of Judge Edwards? Or will it be allowed that the law would be unjust and oppressive if enforced against the opulent and prosperous, while it is contended that it is just and equitable, when those who depend only on the labour of their hands are made its victims?

RIGHT TO STRIKE *VS.* MOB INTIMIDATION
June 6, 1836

At the Park Theatre in New York on May 27 the British actors Mr. and Mrs. Joseph Wood had been driven from the stage during a performance, for having declined to act in a benefit that evening for a minor actress named Mrs. Conduit. For Bryant's quotation of the lines beginning with "Hence linen things," cf. Macbeth, V, *iii, 15–17; for the quotation "ancient and fishlike," see* The Tempest, II, *ii, [27–30].*

A foolish handbill was posted up yesterday in various parts of the city, animadverting in strong terms upon the recent charge of Judge Edwards in the case of the twenty-one journeymen, and calling in very inflammatory language on the working men to turn out in a body this morning, filling the Court room, the Hall, and the Park itself, in order to witness the sentence passed upon the persons convicted. Such a call is nothing more nor less than an invitation to a riot. A crowd brought together in such numbers as the handbill contemplates, and animated by such feelings as it was calculated to excite, could not have demeaned themselves peaceably, to say nothing of the outrage which would be committed in endeavouring to influence the deliberations of justice by a popular assemblage. The local authorities of the city may take to itself the credit of this invitation. It had its encouragement in their conduct with respect to the late disturbances in the Park Theatre, which they might have prevented by binding over the instigators to keep the peace, and guarding the building with a strong force.—Our city authorities are too timid, procrastinating, and dawdling for the times. If they can[n]ot prevent riots, let them give place to better men—and if they will not, then let the people say to the whole troop of them—

> Hence linen things! your lily-livered cheeks
> Are counsellors of fear—

and supply their places with men whose characters are cast in a robuster mould, who will take boldly, promptly and effectually the few previous steps by which a threatened outbreak of popular violence may be always prevented. We are glad, however, to know that the handbill failed of its effect—and that the peace of the city is not likely to be disturbed. Sentence has not been passed this morning as was expected, upon the journeymen; and the crowd of people who gathered about the Hall seemed drawn only by curiosity to witness the trial of Robinson. The working men doubtless have had the penetration to see the hand of an enemy in the handbill, and therefore staid away.

The riot however, had it taken place, would have been a godsend to the enemies of the Trades Union. We should then have had the question of the right of combination prettily mixed up with two illegalities that have nothing to do with the matter. In the dust that would have been raised, not one in a hundred would at first do the strike-men the justice to distinguish between the right to stand out, the right of conspiring to intimidate those who will not, and the right of overawing, by a tumultuous show of resistance, the arbitrary sentence of a court.

When we say that the riot would have been a godsend, we are unnecessarily charitable in the suggestion of the cause. There is little reason to doubt that the author of all mischief was the instigator, that the enemies of the people were the principal agents, and that the catspaws in this miserable force were some of the sufferers themselves. 'Tis the old trick of tyranny. She goads the poor devils into violence, and takes this opportunity to throw them off their guard, to frighten off the timid and the temporizing, and then to clap on the fetter and the handcuff. But the strategy, though ingenious in its day, and still carrying a point now and then, has grown too "ancient and fish like" to serve much longer the purpose of a trap. In spite of the opposite example of their adversaries, the disfranchised are fast learning that a resort to brute force will ruin the best cause that ever good man embraced; that the enemy of order, if honest is a fool, and a foul traitor if disguised; that the most culpable connivance of the magistrates at the riots of the "mob genteel" is never to entice the oppressed into the use of a machine, which cannot but recoil upon the hands that direct it, and which is the very worst weapon that, in a country like ours, Right can bring to bear against Power.

Let the questions now before the community be kept carefully distinct. Let the weight of a just indignation fall heavily upon those who would sully their own cause, by a frenzy so absurd as an attack upon the independence, or an outrage upon the privileges of the Bench. Let the peace-breaker and the rioter, wherever they be found, be made to feel the presence of the law; whether they be gentle or simple, rich or poor, learned or untaught; whether arrayed against the enemies of Slavery, or in arms against the champions of Privilege; setting the fire-brand to the dwelling of the zealot, or the cord to the throat of the bravo; plundering the palace of the bankrupt, or invading the closet of the miser; bullying the mountebank upon his platform, or bearding Justice in her Hall. Let this be done, and sternly. But in the name of honor and manliness and truth, let not the equity of the outcast's claim be prejudiced by the violence into which the arts and aggressions of his oppressors may betray him. And above all, let not the friends of the working man bate a jot of heart or hope, for any little hour's advantage that the friends of his opponents may yet filch from the blindness of his allies. Let them press straight onward—neither deterred by threats on one side, nor disheartened by folly on the other. The people will be true to themselves, and whatever wrong may have been done in the struggle will be sure to be set right in the end.

THE RIGHT TO COMBINE AND THE COURTS
June 11, 1836

The previous year at Geneva, New York, journeymen shoemakers who had refused to work unless a non-union shoemaker was discharged were indicted for criminal conspiracy. When the case was appealed to the State Supreme Court, its Chief Justice, Savage, upheld their conviction, declaring that their act was injurious to trade. We are reminded by Bryant's reference to Coke, Littleton, and Blackstone that during his preparation for law practice in Massachusetts he had studied their authoritative works. The other legal authorities to whom Bryant refers were, perhaps, Sir Matthew Hale (1609–1676), Lord Chief Justice of the King's Bench in England, and William Hawkins (1673–1746), Sergeant-at-law, of the Inner Temple.

The monstrous doctrine that any two persons may be sent to prison for agreeing together what price they shall set upon their labour, finds less and less favour the more it is examined. Its friends tell us that the Supreme Court has decided that such is the law. We can only say, so much the worse for the Supreme Court. This is one of the cases in which a law tribunal might easily err—in which the mere lawyer would be almost certain to go wrong. The sole foundation of this decision is a law of our state which declares a combination to do any act injurious to trade and commerce to be an offence, and prescribes its punishment. Now whether an agreement not to work under certain wages be an act injurious to trade and commerce is a question of political economy which any well informed man can decide as well as the Supreme Court. It is a question not to be settled by a reference to the opinions of English jurists and books of English reports, but by an enlarged survey of the occupations of society, and with a judicious reference to our free political institutions. This is a matter with which Coke on Littleton, and even the more modern commentator Blackstone, have nothing to do. American legislators have made the law, and it is the duty of our judges to expound the law like men of sense and American citizens. The mere lawyer, however, is apt to sit down and fumble at his Hale and Hawkins, and turn over the pages of his books of Criminal Reports, instead of asking his practical neighbours what is the universal custom of the commercial world, and interrogating his own good sense as to the intent of the law and its proper application to that custom. We can account for the decision of the Supreme Court in no other way than ascribing it to a blind deference paid to the big-wigged gentlemen of the English bench.

It is unnecessary for us to repeat here the arguments already made use of in this paper, to show that combinations to regulate prices are the daily and universal practice of the commercial world. That they are so is a proof that they are inherent in the nature of commerce; if they were not found necessary or useful, they would not be practised. Commerce not only subsists, but flourishes in the midst of these combinations; they are a part of the soil in which the tree, whose branches overshadow so many lands, grows, and from which it derives its nutriment. The judges of our courts have certainly heard of the maxim, that trade prospers best by being let alone. *Laissez nous faire*, we should think was a maxim old enough for their taste—it was pronounced long enough ago to be in blackletter, and it is in Norman French too, or in French that is still better. Trade has no need of the paternal fussing of law-givers, and the officious protection of tribunals; leave it to itself, and it will take care of itself—it ever has and ever will. It is as presumptuous and foolish to interpose these petty regulations in the great course of trade, as it would be to undertake to interfere with the rains of heaven; you may, it is true, keep a portion of the ground dry by stretching a blanket above it, but the result will be barrenness.

We have spoken of the English law—it is stated in an eastern gazette that the laws against combinations to fix prices were abolished in England in 1824. If so, what a wretched figure does the democratick [*sic*] State of New York, which allows such a tyrannical law to subsist, make by the side of monarchical England. A fine theme of declamation might this be for those who mention that there is more liberty after all in Britain than in America. In the neighbouring State of Connecticut there is no law against combinations to settle the rate of wages. We have before us the case of the Thompsonville Carpet Manufacturing Company against William Taylor and two others, who were charged with a conspiracy for being concerned in a strike for wages, and who were tried before the Superior Court for Hartford County. The defendants in that case though proved to have been concerned in a strike, were acquitted of a conspiracy. Chief Justice Williams, in giving his charge to the jury, said: "The act charged upon the defendants in this case is a conspiracy to interrupt and destroy the plaintiff's business. The defendants claim that there was no agreement or concert on their part, except an agreement not to labour below certain prices. If that was the real nature of the agreement between the defendants, or between the defendants and other workmen, it has been determined in this court that such as agreement is not by law an indictable offence, nor the subject of a civil action." Either the law-givers or the judges of Connecticut are immensely in advance of those of New York, on this point at least.

We do not by these observations intend to pronounce an opinion as to the justice or propriety of any particular combination to raise wages—we simply contend for the legal right to combine. That right may be either injuriously or beneficially exercised according to circumstances. It has been said that strikes are bad things, and ought not to be encouraged—this is true—strikes are bad for workmen, and bad for employers; they stop the wages of the former and the business of the latter, so that both parties are the losers, whichever may succeed at last. Going to law is also bad for both parties, and no prudent man will have any thing to do either with a strike or a lawsuit, unless driven to it by absolute necessity. But as lawsuits may sometimes be necessary, so also may strikes, and the necessity must be judged of by the peculiar circumstances of the case. They may, it is true, and doubtless sometimes are made without good grounds, and in that case the strikers must be the greatest sufferers.

Journeymen Tailors: Judge Edwards' Sentence
June 13, 1836

". . . Associations of this description are of recent origin in this country. . . . Every American knows, or ought to know, that he has no better friend than the laws, and that he needs no artificial combination for his protection. Our experience never manifested their necessity, and I may confidently say that they were not the offspring of necessity. They are of foreign origin, and I am led to believe, are mainly upheld by foreigners. If such is the fact, I would say to them, that they mistake the character of the American people, if they indulge a hope that they can accomplish their ends in that way. No matter how crafty may be their devices, nor how extensive may be their combinations, or violent may be their conduct, yet such is the energy of the law, and such the fidelity of the people to the government, that they will soon find their efforts as unavailing as the beating of frothy surges against a rock. It is a sentiment deeply engrafted in the bosom of every American, that he ought and must submit to the laws, and that to its mandates all stubborn necks must yield.

"Self-created societies are unknown to the constitution and laws, and will not be permitted to rear their crest and extend their baneful influence over any portion of the community.

"In fixing your punishment, we have duly considered the recommendations of the jury, for we are under an impression that you acted in ignorance of the law, and we the more incline to this opinion, as we understand that you are almost all foreigners. . . ."

A meeting of the Mechanics of New York is to be held in the Park this evening to express their opinion as to the law under which the twenty journeymen have been convicted and sentenced. We have no doubt from what we are assured of their intentions, that the proceedings of the meeting will be peaceful and orderly, and we have as little that any attempt to lead them into disturbance will fail. It is somewhat remarkable that Judge Edwards should have supposed that the only persons who dissent from the doctrine he was laying down were a few emigrants from other countries, when the fact is that the Trades Union comprises thousands of native born Americans. But this is not extraordinary in one who in addressing twenty men, of whom eleven were native Americans, told them that they were almost all foreigners.

THE RIGHT OF WORKMEN TO STRIKE
June 13, 1836

Sentence was passed on Saturday on the twenty "men who had determined not to work." The punishment selected, on due consideration, by the judge, was that officers appointed for the purpose should immediately demand from each of the delinquents a sum of money which was named in the sentence of the court. The amount demanded would not have fallen short of the savings of many years. Either the offenders had not parted with these savings, or their brother workmen raised the ransom money for them on the spot. The fine was paid over as required. All is now well; justice has been satisfied. But if the expenses of their families had anticipated the law, and left nothing in their hands, or if friends had not been ready to buy the freedom of their comrades, they would have been sent to prison, and there they would have staid, until their wives and children, besides earning their own bread, had saved enough to redeem the captives from their cells. Such has been their punishment. What was their offence? They had committed the crime of unanimously declining to go to work at the wages offered to them by their masters. They had said to one another, "Let us come out from the meanness and misery of our caste. Let us begin to do what every order more privileged and more honoured is doing everyday. By the means which we believe to be the best let us raise ourselves and our families above the humbleness of our condition. We may be wrong, but we cannot help believing that we might do much if we were true brothers to each other, and would resolve not to sell the only thing which is our own, the cunning of our hands, for less than it is worth." What other things they may have done is nothing to the purpose: it was for this they were condemned; it is for this they are to endure the penalty of the law.

We call upon a candid and generous community to mark that the punishment inflicted upon these twenty "men who had determined not to work" is not directed against the offence of conspiring to prevent others by force from working at low wages, but expressly against the offence of settling by pre-concert the compensation which they thought they were entitled to obtain. It is certainly superfluous to repeat, that this journal would be the very last to oppose a law levelled at any attempt to molest the labourer who chooses to work for less than the prices settled by the union. We have said, and to cut off cavil, we say it now again, that a conspiracy to deter, by threats of violence, a fellow workman from arranging his own terms with his employers, is a conspiracy to commit a felony—a conspiracy which, being a crime against liberty, we should be the first to condemn—a conspiracy which no strike should, for its own sake, countenance for a moment—a conspiracy already punishable by the statute, and far easier to reach than the one of which "the twenty" stood accused; but a conspiracy, we must add, that has not a single feature in common with the base and barbarous prohibition under which the offenders were indicted and condemned.

They were condemned because they had determined not to work for the wages that were offered them! Can any thing be imagined more abhorrent to every sentiment of generosity or justice, than the law which arms the rich with the legal right to fix, by assize, the wages of the poor? If this is not SLAVERY, we have forgotten its definition. Strike the right of associating for the sale of labour from the privileges of a freeman, and you may as well at once bind him to a master, or ascribe him to the soil. If it be not in the colour of his skin, and in the poor franchise of naming his own terms in a contract for his work, what advantage has the labourer of the north over the bondman of the south? Punish by human laws a "determination not to work," make it penal by any other penalty than idleness inflicts, and it matters little whether the task-masters be one or many, an individual or an order, the hateful scheme of slavery will have gained a foothold in the land. And then the meanness of this law, which visits with its malice those who cling to it for protection, and shelters with all its fences those who are raised above its threats. A late solicitation for its aid against employers, is treated with derision and contempt, but the moment the "masters" invoked its intervention, it came down from its high place with most indecent haste, and has now discharged its fury upon the naked heads of wretches so forlorn, that their worst faults multiply their titles to a liberty which they must learn to win from livelier sensibilities than the barren benevolence of Wealth, or the tardy magnanimity of Power. . . .

"Self-created societies," says Judge Edwards, "are unknown to the constitution and laws, and will not be permitted to rear their crest and extend their baneful influence over any portion of the community." If there is any sense in this passage it means that self-created societies are unlawful, and must be put down by the courts. Down then with every literary, every religious, and every charitable association not incorporated! What nonsense is this! Self-created societies *are* known to the constitution and laws, for they are not prohibited, and the laws which allow them will, if justly administered, protect them. But suppose in charity that the reporter has put this absurdity into the mouth of Judge Edwards, and that he meant only those self-created societies which have an effect upon trade and commerce. Gather up then and sweep to the penitentiary all those who are confederated to carry on any business or trade in concert, by fixed rules, and see how many men you would leave at large in this city. The members of every partnership in the place will come under the penalties of the law, and not only these, but every person pursuing any occupation whatever, who governs himself by a mutual understanding with others that follow the same occupation. . . .

Courts and Public Opinion
June 15, 1836

A few weeks after this assertion of faith in the justice of a public opinion in favor of labor's rights the acquittal of eight shoemakers at Hudson, New York, on similar charges led Bryant to welcome the verdict, writing on July 2, "What but a general revolt of all the labouring classes is to be gained by these wanton and unprovoked attacks upon their rights?"

Certain prints are trying to revive the old doctrine of the infallibility of courts of law. It may be a convenient doctrine for those who wish to keep the working classes from ascertaining and asserting their rights; but unfortunately it is a little too stale for the present day. Judges may direct the conviction of those who are brought before them, or they may interpose in behalf of the guilty, but after this there is another tribunal to which they are themselves responsible—the tribunal of publick [sic] opinion. In this court must the judicial magistrate himself be tried, whether he consent or not. It is as much the right of a free people, and a free press, to examine, discuss and pronounce upon the judgments of a court, as it is upon the acts of a legislature or a Chief Magistrate. The effect is not to produce a disrespect for the laws—on the contrary it increases that respect—for it is by the standard of the law that the decisions of the judge must be tried. If he have pronounced according to the law, he has done his duty and must be acquitted; if otherwise, he must be condemned. He must submit to the same salutary ordeal with other publick men, and cannot expect to shield himself in the blind veneration of the people from the blame of errour or partiality.

Those who, for present convenience, maintain the infallibility of courts, talk of an attempt to question their decisions "as an offence against the majesty of the laws." They style a meeting to protest against one of these decisions, a MOB, a RABBLE, denounce their proceedings as disorderly and disgraceful, and heap upon them every epithet of scorn. Go on gentlemen; the cause which calls forth your frothy vituperation needs an impulse like that which you are giving it. Show that you mean not only to oppress, but to insult the oppressed, and the business is done to your hands; the law which you uphold, if law it be, is repealed. A few more such attempts to heap contumely and contempt upon those who live by the labour of their hands, and we pledge our word that Judge Edwards's law does not survive another session of our legislature. Nor will this be effected by the labouring classes merely—men of just and generous feelings in every situation of life will be found on their side.

The Right to Combine vs. Forcible Intimidation
June 16, 1836

A writer in the *American* of yesterday, whose strictures under the signatures of Vindex, are adopted by that print, attempts a justification of the late enforcement of the law against conspiracies to injure trade and commerce. In reply to the arguments we urged on Monday last against what struck us as the glaring disproportion between the punishment selected by the judge and the offence as stated in the charge, Vindex, (in a tone, however, which we could wish to see more frequently imitated in the discussion of great principles,) taxes us with misconception of facts, and with negligence in ascertaining them. He contends that we have inaccurately stated the offence for which the journeymen were punished, and he insists that the misdemeanour which was proved against the accused, and for which chastisement was inflicted by the court, consisted not in "combining not to work," but "in conspiring to prevent others, by force and intimidation, from working at low wages or any wages."

Let us see how far this charge of misconception is sustained. Our attention was first particularly called to the merits of this case on the day after the verdict was rendered by the jury. A morning paper gave what purported to be, and for aught that has yet been stated to the contrary, appears to have been, an accurate report of the charge of the Judge. In that report, occupying nearly a column of our journal, (we call the attention of Vindex to the fact) the offence of having conspired *by force and intimidation* to prevent others from working, the offence for which it is now alleged the mechanicks were condemned, *is not so much as mentioned from one end to the other of the charge*. So far from being presented by the court as the basis of a verdict, there is not the slightest allusion to any thing of the kind. The whole argument for the conviction of the accused is founded on the injury which commerce is supposed to sustain by concerted "refusals to work." With this one idea the charge begins, with this one idea the charge continues, with this one idea the charge reaches its foregone conclusion, and goes from the Bench to the box. The court sets out by citing the decision of Judge Savage, and treats it exclusively as a case where shoemakers conspired to prevent each other from *working below certain prices* under one dollar fine, where they *made a regulation that they would not work* for any Boss who gave less than the price fixed on, where they *refused to work* for Mr. Lunn, and where they *agreed not to work* for certain others. The Judge quotes no other offence, and approves of the opinion that "this conduct was a violation of the statute."

We might stop here, for here is the doctrine we denounced. Even if the tailors were charged with something more, the broad ground is boldly taken that the offence of conspiring not to work is sufficient to convict; the startling conclusion is distinctly maintained that mechanicks may be punished by imprisonment for simply agreeing not to work. As long as this is held to be law, it is of very little consequence what the tailors did or what they were condemned for. The difference between Vindex and ourselves would not be worth the trouble of a thought.

The Judge proceeds. For fear the jury might not readily conceive how a conspiracy not to work was the conspiracy intended by the statute, he argues in the following strain:

"Suppose that a number of persons engaged in the trade or manufactures of this city would from time to time enter into combinations of that sort and *determine not to work* under certain rates, and carry their resolution into effect at times when their services were most necessary, what sort of a state would society be reduced to? For instance, suppose all the carpenters and bricklayers would, at the commencement of next May, *determine not to work* unless their wages [were] raised, and demanded ten times more than they ought, and could succeed in doing so, what would become of the citizens, or who would occupy their houses? Or suppose that the produce of this country bore the highest price in the foreign market, and every one was anxious to export it; and that, at that moment, all the stevedores, shipwrights, and other mechanicks, whose services were necessary to fit out ships, insisted upon having ten times the value of their services, such conduct must bring commerce to a stand, and would be well calculated to destroy the trade of the city altogether. If such a system was tolerated, the constitutional controul over our affairs would pass away from the people at large, and become vested in the hands of conspirators."

If this extraordinary language does not mean that a determination by carpenters, &c. not to work when their services are necessary, will not be tolerated by our laws, what in the name of common sense does it mean? If it does not mean that mechanicks may be punished for agreeing not to work will Vindex favour us with his theory of explanation.

The Court then proceeds to the offence alleged against the tailors:

"Amongst other things charged against them was that they entered into a conspiracy, and agreed not to work for any master who did not give them certain rates which they demanded, or for any master who employed men who worked for a less rate, or for any master who employed men who were not members of their society. They also made various other rules to secure the objects they had in view, which was to place thereby both the master and journeymen tailors under the domination of a few individuals. It would be for the jury to say, whether any body of men could raise their crests in this land of law, and controul others by self-organized combination."

We should have been recreant to the trust we have assumed of watching the least encroachment upon the limits of Civil Liberty, had we not entered our early protest against a doctrine so repugnant to the rights of industry, to the principles of freedom, and we are compelled to add, to the intelligence and humanity of the age. We accordingly inserted an immediate remonstrance, and republished on the following day from the *Journal of Commerce* the report of the trial, and in particular the charge of the Judge, repeating our dissent, with additional emphasis, from the reported language of the Court.

It is not pretended by Vindex that the publication of the Judge's charge was incorrect. But even if it were, our remarks were expressly confined to the hypothesis of its correctness, and that no one has yet undertaken to deny. If the published report contained substantially the language of the Judge, then our assertion that the mechanicks were found guilty of a conspiracy to injure trade and commerce, without reference to the acts of violence with which they had been charged, and of which, for aught we know, they have been guilty, is abundantly made out. What mattered it to us what other things they had done besides determining not to work, if the court held the doctrine that such a refusal by preconcert was sufficient to convict?

But, says Vindex, the opening counsel disclaimed expressly that the defendants were indicted for conspiring to raise their wages. It was explicitly admitted that they had the right singly or by dozens, to fix the price of their own labour; but it was denied that they had the right to interfere with the labour or price of labour of others;

and more especially was it denied that they had the right to prevent by force or intimidation, others from working, who were willing and anxious to work.

What sound doctrine the able counsel may have laid down in his opening, is no vindication of the court. Vindex has not charged us with misrepresenting the language of the opening counsel, and until he does, his disclaimer of the opinion we have imputed to the Judge exculpates a party against whom nothing has been charged, but leaves the court as naked as before.

Vindex refers us to the Address before the sentence in proof that a determination not to work was not regarded by the judge as sufficient ground for a conviction. On an attentive reperusal we find nothing in the address which nullifies the law so emphatically expounded in the charge. It is true that the rebuke after conviction, by an unfortunate transposition, contains matter of reprehension apparently never thought of in the charge. But surely it will not be asserted that the mechanicks were tried for one offense, convicted for a second, and punished for a third. The charge was studiously silent on the subject of a conspiracy to terrify or assault—a subject on which the address was rather eloquent. But though other offences are enumerated in the address, the only one presented to the jury is still held sufficient to convict.

Either the address is consistent with the charge, or it is not. If consistent, then it is law that mechanicks may be punished for agreeing not to work. If not consistent, the Judge has stultified his charge. Vindex is welcome to the choice.

In the charge, the offence consisted simply and purely in determining by preconcert not to work. In the address, a variety of misbehaviours are mingled up together. But, nevertheless, the judge reiterates the dogma that a club to refuse work is injurious to trade, and as such simply, may be punished. He again repeats his approbation of the decision of the Supreme Court. He declares that we have re-enacted with an additional provision, the common law on the subject, and we all know what the English statute undertook, in its odious life time, to forbid. He again takes the distinction, that an individual may work or not as meets his pleasure, but that a confederacy shall not have the same liberty. He states in terms, that the rules of a Trades Union, though not countenancing violence, are illegal if craftily devised so as to endanger the throwing journeymen or masters out of employment, a dictum pregnant with all the perils of construction, and leading to measures more high handed than the worst assumptions of the Unions. He lays down the extraordinary doctrine that self-created societies—and therefore, if the sentence means any thing, bible, tract, and temperance societies—are illegal, and will not be permitted to rear their crests and extend their baneful influence over any portion of the community. But here, as we have said before, we feel sure the address has been misreported. And we take this opportunity to add that we have not for a moment ascribed to any unworthy motive the extraordinary doctrine of the Court.

On one point Vindex may dismiss his fears. We have ever been most earnest to inculcate that the admixture of the principle of force is sure to poison and destroy the best intended institutions. Vindex may rest assured that he will find us with him among the foremost in denouncing every attempt to molest the labourer who chooses to secede from the tyranny of an unjustly constituted strike. It is for this very reason that we resolutely oppose the exercise of power in the suppression of even injurious combinations, where they aim at nothing hurtful to life, limb, property or reputation. We believe, that much of the bitterness of these unprofitable feuds, may be attributed directly to political or popular attempts to put them down by force. We contend that all that is really illegal in the strikes may be put down by other statutory remedies, more effectual than the Strike-law, and free from its tyrannical pretensions. In the application of these remedies, we pledge ourselves to be where we have always been, among the foremost friends of law and order. But we should sink with shame, on every recollection of our weakness, if we could be tempted, by the turbulence of individual fanaticism to play foul, the noble cause of the Liberty of Associated Effort.

Native Americanism and the Rights of Foreigners
June 16, 1836

The conservative New York Journal of Commerce *was an organ of the Whig Party. "The Park" was then what is now City Hall Park, between Broadway and Park Row.*

The *Journal of Commerce* attempts to make its readers believe that a person went through the vast multitude assembled in the Park on Monday evening, "and *ascertained* that *almost all* were foreigners." Why, the *Journal* cannot believe this story itself! The man who professed to have made this important discovery could not have had time during the meeting to interrogate one sixth part of the six or seven thousand whom the *Journal* admits to have been present, and ask them where they were born. Does the *Journal* expect that its readers will bolt down a misstatement so monstrous and mountainous that the old illustration of swallowing a camel is nothing to it? That print should pay some little regard to the understandings of its readers. Credulity, like an over-bent bow, will crack if strained too unmercifully.

But suppose they were foreigners—have they no rights? Has not a labouring man a right to set the price to his labour, because he is a foreigner—has he not a right to agree on that price with his brother labourer, because he is a foreigner? Has he not as much a right to do this as if he was a native American? A foreign merchant who brings his merchandize to our shores is permitted to fix, whether individually, or in concert with others, just what price he pleases upon it. By what rule is the labourer from abroad, the strength and skill of whose hands is his only stock, prevented from doing the same thing? But they shall not, says the *Journal,* be permitted "to dictate to others for whom and for what wages they shall labour, under penalty of being waylaid, assaulted, beaten or murdered." Who claims for them the right to do this? Not we—we have condemned in the strongest terms, all violence and threats of violence in the workmen. Not the mechanicks assembled in the Park—their resolutions simply assert the right of associating to determine the price of their labour. Who then claims such a right? Nobody—the *Journal* wilfully puts the case upon a false issue. Judge Edwards, in his charge to the jury, in the case of the twenty journeymen, laid it down as the law of the land, that journeymen had no right to agree among each other, that they would work for a certain price and no less. Let the *Journal* justify that decision if it can; let it "produce its strong reasons"; we should be glad to see the utmost that can be said for the outrageous and tyrannical doctrine which we are charged with "villifying."

Credit System and Senator Tallmadge's Eulogy
June 17, 1836

Earlier, in the Senate, Tallmadge, leader of the pro-bank, conservative faction of the New York Democratic Party, had defended inflation, declaring that "political economists" were blind to "the cause which makes us, above all others, a happy, great, and prosperous people, . . . our CREDIT SYSTEM." *The once–German immigrant John Jacob Astor had by this time gained a twenty-million-dollar fortune through the northwest fur trade, New York real estate, and lending money at exorbitant rates to the government.*

When Senator Tallmadge pronounced his memorable eulogy on the credit system which he affirmed had been brought to its maturity and perfection in the United States, he was hardly aware of the full extent of the benefits it was destined to confer upon the nation. Since that time the system has reached a more transcendent ripeness. How would he have rejoiced if, at the moment he pronounced his speech, he could have seen in beatific vision the happy consequences it is now dispensing so abundantly among all who are engaged in the pursuits of commerce!

It is false to say, as some have done, that the democratic party are the enemies of credit. It has no better and truer friends.—Their entire creed, their whole course of policy are favorable to the fair, steady, regular use of credit. Their principles forbid them to make laws in favour of one species of credit and against another. He is the friend of man who vindicates man's natural freedom and equality; he is in like manner the friend of credit who refuses his approbation to laws enabling the credit of one class to overpower and swallow up the credit of another. The democrat makes war against the monopoly of credit, which by the help of unjust legislation, usurps the place of the true. Let us illustrate our meaning by a familiar example.

A labouring man goes to market with a note of a bank authorized by one of the state governments. It is issued by nobody knows who, and is perhaps never to be paid, but it bears on its face the stamp of state superintendence. With this he can purchase any thing that is to be sold; the receiver is satisfied when he knows that the government of the state in which the bank was issued, has taken care of the matter. But let the same man go to market with one of the notes of John Jacob Astor, whose title to credit is sounder and more stable than that of any bank in the republic, and he cannot buy with it a bunch of greens.

Is not this a proof that the credit system stands upon a false foundation; does it not show that for the natural and genuine credit which is founded upon the well known possession of property and sure resources, we have substituted something very different, a factitious credit growing out of imperfect knowledge and imperfect vigilance, a credit which rests upon the official license of men appointed to relieve the community from the task of exercising their own better sagacity? Is there any reason to be surprised that a system so faulty and so false should be ruinous in its effects?

The credit system is erroneous on two accounts. It is erroneous because it interferes with commerce, which is always better and more safely conducted when let alone. It is erroneous again because it interferes with opinion. We reject the regulation of religion by law as tyrannical and mischievous; we find that a church established by law is the parent of false professions and hypocritical observances. Yet we regulate credit, which, equally with religious belief, depends upon opinion; we make laws defining who are worthy of credit; our state governments take upon themselves to instruct us whose promises are to be trusted. The same effect follows as in other cases where the public authorities tamper with opinion. We have insolvency in the disguise of licensed credit, and the licensed few wield their powers to the disadvantage of the unlicensed many. The real enemies of credit are they who support this narrow, tyrannical, and as it now fully appears, fatally pernicious system.

Freedom of Speech
August 8, 1836

The meeting to which Bryant refers was a large one held in the Market House on July 23, presided over by the Cincinnati postmaster William Burke, and attended by most of the prominent members of the city's commercial interests.

A meeting of the people of Cincinnati have proclaimed the right of silencing the expression of unpopular opinions by violence. We refer our readers to the proceedings of an anti-abolition meeting lately held in that city. They will be found in another part of this paper.

If the meeting had contented itself with declaring its disapprobation of the tenets of the abolitionists, we should have had nothing to say. They might have exhausted the resources of rhetorick and of language—they might have indulged in the very extravagance and wantonness of vehement condemnation, for aught we cared; they would still have been in the exercise of a right which the constitution and the laws secure to them. But when they go further, and declare that they have not only a right to condemn certain opinions in others, but the right to coerce those who hold them to silence, it is time to make an immediate and decided stand, and to meet the threat of coercion with defiance.

The Cincinnati meeting, in the concluding resolution offered by Wilson N. Brown, and adopted with the rest, declare in so many words that if they cannot put down the abolitionist press by fair means they will do it by foul; if they cannot silence it by remonstrance, they will silence it by violence; if they cannot persuade it to desist, they will stir up mobs against it, inflame them to madness, and turn their brutal rage against the dwellings, the property, the persons, the lives of the wretched abolitionists and their families. In announcing that they will put them down by force all this is included. Fire, robbery, bloodshed, are the common excesses of an enraged mob. There is no extreme of cruelty and destruction to which in the drunkenness and delirium of its fury it may not proceed. The commotions of the elements can as easily be appeased by appeals to the quality of mercy as these commotions of the human mind; the whirlwind and the lighning might as well be expected to pause and turn aside to spare the helpless and innocent, as an infuriated multitude.

If the abolitionists *must* be put down, and if the community are of that opinion, there is no necessity of violence to effect the object. The community have the power in their own hands; the majority may make a law declaring the discussion of slavery in a certain manner to be a crime, and imposing penalties. The law may then be put in force against the offenders, and their mouths may be gagged in due form, and with all the solemnities of justice.

What is the reason this is not done? The answer is ready. The community are for leaving the liberty of the press untrammelled—there is not a committee that can be raised in any of the State legislatures north of the Potomac who will report in favour of imposing penalties on those who declaim against slavery—there is not a legislature who would sanction such a report—and there is not a single free state the people of which would sustain a legislature in so doing. These are facts, and the advocates of mob law know them to be so.

Who then are the men that issue this invitation to silence the press by violence? Who but an insolent brawling minority, a few noisy fanatics who claim that their own opinions shall be the measure of freedom for the rest of the community, and who undertake to overawe a vast pacific majority by threats of wanton outrage and plunder? These men are for erecting an oligarchy of their own and riding rough shod over the people and the people's rights. They claim a right to repeal the laws established by the majority in favor of the freedom of the press. They make new laws of their own to which they require that the rest of the community shall submit, and in case of a refusal, they threaten to execute them by the ministry of a mob. There is no tyranny or oppression exercised in any part of the world more absolute or more frightful than that which they would establish.

So far as we are concerned we are determined that this despotism shall neither be submitted to nor encouraged. In whatever form it makes its appearance we shall raise our voice against it. We are resolved that the subject of slavery shall be as it ever has been, as free a subject of discussion and argument and declamation, as the difference between whiggism and democracy, or as the difference between the Arminians and the Calvinists. If the press chooses to be silent on the subject it shall be the silence of perfect free will, and not the silence of fear. We hold that this combination of the few to govern the many by the terror of illegal violence, is as wicked and indefensible as a conspiracy to rob on the highway. We hold it to be the duty of good citizens to protest against it whenever and wherever it shows itself, and to resist it if necessary to the death.

One piece of justice must be done to the South. Thousands there are of persons in that quarter of the country who disapprove, as heartily as any citizen of the North can do, the employment of violence against the presses or the preachers of the anti-slavery party. There are great numbers also, as we are well informed, who think that only harm could result from directing the penalties of the law against those who discuss the question of slavery. They are for leaving the mode of discussing this question solely to the calm and considerate good sense of the North, satisfied that the least show of a determination to abridge the liberty of speech in this matter is but throwing oil on the flames.

The Cincinnati Mob
August 10, 1836

In January 1836 a former Alabama slave-owner-turned-Abolitionist, James G. Birney, had established in Cincinnati the Philanthropist, *a newspaper sponsored by the Ohio Anti-Slavery Society. Earlier attacks on this journal culminated on July 30 when, in Birney's absence, a mob attacked its printshop, destroyed the press, and scattered its type. Subsequent attacks were made on Negro homes, and Birney's own home escaped from incendiaries only after a brave appeal from Birney's young son.*

The Cincinnati Mob.—The *Cincinnati Whig* has an account of the late disgraceful riot got up at that place ten days since. The *Whig* allows that the outrages which occurred were of a most unfortunate and disreputable character, but says:

"The incendiary Abolitionists among us have been the wicked cause of a reproach to our city that every man must lament. Those heartless fanaticks have sinned with their eyes open, and after having been appealed to by every consideration of patriotism and good order, and warned of the inevitable consequences of their mad and diabolical determination to persist in the publication of their loathsome power, they yet had the hardihood and effrontery, in their manifesto in reply to the citizens committee, to insult our southern brethren, contemn the proceedings of the great Anti-Abolition meeting recently held in the Market House, and unblushingly, in defiance of the almost unanimous voices of people here, to proclaim the most disgusting and revolutionary sentiments."

If such arguments as these are a justification of the Cincinnati riot, there is no outrage and no violence which cannot be excused by similar considerations. Suppose the Whigs should take into their heads to suppress the Evening Post for supporting Mr. Van Buren, suppose they should call a meeting on the subject, and pass resolutions appointing a committee to remonstrate with us, and to tell us that if we persisted they would not be answerable for the consequences, and suppose in their concluding resolutions, they should threaten that if we did not abandon the cause of democracy, they would compel us to do it by violence. What answer should we naturally give, what answer should we be bound to give to such remonstrances and such threats? The answer of defiance, open, unshrinking defiance. If we did otherwise, we should confess ourselves to be cowards and slaves. Suppose then, the Whigs in their just indignation, should assemble a mob and break into our office, destroy our papers, burn our books, scatter our types, heave out our press, drag it to the East River, break it in pieces, and throw it into the dock, and not content with this, should search the city for the conductors and their friends to commit violence on their persons. Would any single print in this city venture to disgrace itself by speaking of such an outrage in the terms used by the *Cincinnati Whig*? Would it venture to say:

"The incendiary Van Burenites among us have been the wicked cause of a reproach to our city that every man must lament. These heartless fanaticks have sinned with their eyes open, and after having been appealed to by every consideration of patriotism and good order, and warned of the inevitable consequences of their mad and diabolical determination to per[s]ist in the publication of their loathsome paper, &c. &c."

We will not pursue the parallel any further; the supreme ridiculousness of treating the question in this manner is too evident. It was the folly and madness of the mob and their leaders which have brought this reproach on Cincinnati, and not the conduct of those who simply persisted in the exercise of a liberty secured to them by law. The tyranny of Austria might as well say to those whom it imprisons for talking politicks, that the fault was their own and not that of the government, which imprisoned them only to make them silent. The press in our country is free from legal tyranny; it must be free, also, from the more terrible tyranny of mobs.

Defense of the Loco-Foco, or Anti-Monopoly, Party
August 10, 1836

The Anti-Monopoly, or Equal Rights, Party earned its nichname "Loco Foco" when, after conservatives adjourned a meeting in Tammany Hall and turned off the gas, radicals lit candles with the new friction matches, or "loco-focos," and named their own candidates. The Albany Argus *was the voice of the state Democratic organization. The short-lived* Times *was a predecessor of its later namesake, founded in 1851. Shays's Rebellion, led by a former Revolutionary officer, Daniel Shays*

(1747?–1825), was an uprising in 1786–1787 against western Massachusetts courts for their foreclosure on the property of debtors.

The Spanish nurses have a goblin with horns, goggling eyes, a long tail, and sharp claws, bearing the terrifick name of Coco, with which they use to frighten their children. If the urchins under their care show any disposition to "set up for themselves"; if they squall too loud, or want what they should not have, or straggle beyond their prescribed bounds, or indulge in any other naughtiness of the sort, their skinny guardian has only to croak out Coco! Coco! and straightway the children gather about her skirts and become as mute and passive and obedient as she could wish.

The *Albany Argus* has also its goblin with which it tries to keep its followers in order; and it is somewhat remarkable that it bears, with a slight difference, the Spanish name. Whenever there are symptoms of insubordination, the *Argus* calls out Loco Foco!, an evident corruption of the cry of the Spanish nurses. The *Argus* endeavours to frighten the community by describing the length of the horns, and tail, and claws of its monster. It tells us that the Loco Foco party is one "whose aims are selfish, if not dangerous to the publick weal," whose "designs" are "mischievous and disorganizing," and who "run their candidates with active and unscrupulous zeal against the regularly nominated democratick tickets." Frightful words these—selfishness, danger to the publick weal, mischief, disorganization, running of candidates, activity, and unscrupulousness! We perceive that the nurse has succeeded in alarming the children; for the *Times* of this morning echoes the cry with its usual alacrity, and barks most loudly against the imagined goblin. Suppose we enquire a little into the nature of these alarms. The Spanish boys, when they grow up, learn to laugh at the terrour with which they on[c]e heard the cry of Coco Coco. Perhaps the community, when it becomes wiser, will see how ridiculous are the fears with which the *Argus* seeks to inspire it by the call of Loco Foco.

In this city both the profession and practice of the "anti-monopoly party," sometimes called the "Loco Foco party," are beginning to be pretty well understood. Their principles have been set forth in various letters to distinguished men, which have been recently published. They are expressed in passages selected from the writings of Thomas Jefferson, who we believe was a pretty good democrat. They have been countersigned by Colonel Richard M. Johnson, who is the democratick candidate for Vice President, and who has thus formally acceded to the Loco Foco party. So much for their principles which, we think, will be allowed to be unexceptionable, even by the *Argus*.

Now as to the practices of the same party: the charge of selfishness and dishonesty is here known to be as absurd as it is insulting, where their very adversaries look upon them in no worse light than that of honest enthusiasts. They may want prudence; they may want the art of management; they may be sometimes hasty and sometimes in errour; but they are disinterested and honest. What is the proof of their dishonesty? Why, simply that they do not vote for the regularly nominated ticket; a rogue is one who votes for somebody else. Is that the standard by which the *Argus* measures morality? We remember to have heard a man in the western part of Massachusetts, who brought a prosecution against his neighbour for killing his horse, and to prove it produced a witness who swore that the defendant had been heard to call out "Hurrah for Shays." The *Argus* appears to have adopted this worthy man's mode of reasoning.

In conclusion, we would observe that although we question the propriety of some of the steps taken by the "anti-monopoly party" in this city, to remedy abuses of which they justly and not too loudly complain, we give them credit for excellent principles, upright intentions, and disinterested conduct. These qualities make them respectable, and, let us add, these qualities, if they are trifled with, will make them formidable.

Slave-Catching
August 10, 1836

When, in 1830, the Evening Post *had been "violently assailed" as "libelous" for printing an advertisement for domestic help by a country gentleman which included the stipulation that "No Irish need apply," Bryant had dismissed the criticism as "poor drivel" which should simply awaken "disgust or pity." But here, six years later, he sets forth a deliberate rationale for his paper's advertising policy.*

In a copy of a paper called *The Emancipator* sent to this office we find an attack upon the EVENING POST for publishing the following advertisement:

"TEN DOLLARS REWARD.—Left the City Hotel, on Sunday the 10th instant, a small *Mulatto* Boy, named Marcellus, aged about twelve years. Had on a fur cap, roundabout thin jacket, striped cotton pantaloons, and wears no handkerchief about his neck. The above reward will be paid to any person who will leave said boy at the *Post Office* in this city."

The Emancipator goes on with some indecencies which are wholly gratuitous, and which we shall not copy, to state that this boy is a slave, and asks us whether we are going to turn slave-catchers. We must inform the *Emancipator* that we wholly decline its superintendence of our advertising columns. They are open to the entire community, and will continue to be so, for the publication of notices relating to all transactions which the laws allow. They contain advertisements of quack medicines, and sales of West India rum, and Monongahela whiskey, and the vanities of the toilet, and yet we are neither quacks, nor distillers, nor wet grocers, nor milliners. The advertisement in question neither states that the boy in question was a slave, nor asks the exercise of any illegal violence to reclaim him. If in fact the boy was a slave, of which we know nothing, it is most natural for the master to desire to recover him, and as long as the master, of whom we also know nothing, contents himself with gentle means, or even with the legal means of doing so, we shall lay no obstruction in his way.

We shall always esteem ourselves fortunate if there is nothing to condemn in our paper but the advertisements, and the responsibility for the advertisements we leave to those who send them, taking care however, that by their publications we do not transgress the law. We do not read one in ten of them, and they are never brought to us for inspection except when some doubt arises as to the legality of publishing them. This is a fixed rule, and if another advertisement like the one we have quoted were brought to us to-morrow, we should allow its insertion. In this matter we will not submit to the slightest dictation of others, as we have already taken more than one occasion to declare.

In the mean time we would remind the *Emancipator* that slave holders, although members of a state of society embracing an institution which we believe to be contrary to natural rights, and pernicious in its consequences, are yet entitled to courteous treatment and fair construction in whatever relates to their personal character and conduct.

The Funeral of Aaron Burr
September 19, 1836

Aaron Burr, an officer on George Washington's Revolutionary staff and Vice President under Thomas Jefferson, died at Port Richmond on Staten Island, New York. Both the Reverend Jonathan Edwards and Burr's father had been presidents of The College of New Jersey, later Princeton College. The "adventures" and "intrigues" to which Bryant refers include the killing of Alexander Hamilton in a politically motivated duel, and various filibustering attempts for which Burr was four times tried and acquitted of treason.

The remains of Aaron Burr were on Friday committed to the earth at Princeton, New Jersey, beside the graves of President Edwards and President Burr, his father and grandfather. It was natural enough that the relatives of this man should wish to perform his obsequies with decency and propriety, but we protest against the puffery of which he is made the object in the public prints, the effect of which is to confound all moral distinctions. When we read of "admiration for his greatness," "respect for his memory," and "condolence for his loss," we are tempted to ask ourselves if the community have ceased to discriminate between the good and bad actions of men. The truth is, nobody is to be condoled with for his loss; no respect is entertained for the memory of one so profligate in private and public life; and, though Colonel Burr was a man of acute and active mind, he did not rise to the measure of intellectual greatness, as he certainly was at a deplorable distance from moral greatness. We would willingly have passed by this subject in silence, but these remarks have been forced from us by what we must regard as a shameful prostitution of the voice of the press.

Some of the public prints are indulging in anticipations of the publication of a posthumous record of Colonel Burr's political and personal adventures, prepared under his direction for the press; and they are essaying to awaken a prurient curiosity concerning them by the intimation that they contain disclosures of things which ought never to be revealed. We have no expectation of advantage to the cause of truth or of morals from the appearance of such a work. It were better that the memory of his intrigues should die with him.

On Usury Laws
September 26, 1836

At first the Jewish and Christian religions forbade the charging of interest, then the equivalent of usury; later, only high interest was considered usurious. In 1545 England fixed a maximum interest charge, and much later the United States followed suit. In early England, "usurer's chains" were worn by wealthy bankers and money-lenders—thus Shakespeare's "Shylock the usurer." Legend has it that Danish king Canute of England (1016–1035) commanded the waves to stand still as a proof of his power.

The fact that the usury laws, arbitrary, unjust, and oppressive as they are, and unsupported by a single substantial reason, should have been suffered to exist to the present time, can only be accounted for on the ground of the general and singular ignorance which has prevailed as to the true nature and character of money. If men would but learn to look upon the medium of exchange, not as a mere sign of value, but as value itself, as a commodity governed by precisely the same laws which affect other kinds of property, the absurdity and tyranny of legislative interference to regulate the extent of profit which, under any circumstances, may be charged for it, would at once become apparent.

The laws do not pretend to dictate to a landlord how much rent he may charge for his house; or to a merchant what price he shall put upon his cloth; or to a mechanic at what rate he shall sell the products of his skill; or to a farmer the maximum he shall demand for his hay or grain. Yet money is but another form into which all these commodities are transmuted, and there is no reason why the owner of it shall be forbidden to ask exactly the rate of profit for the use of it which its abundance or scarcity makes it worth—no reason why the laws of supply and demand, which regulate the value of all other articles, should be suspended by legislative enactment in relation to this, and their place supplied by the clumsy substitute of feudal ignorance and worse than feudal tyranny.

The value of iron and copper and lead consists of exactly the same elements as the value of gold and silver. The labor employed in digging them, the quantity in which they are found, and the extent of their application in the useful arts, or, in other words, the relation of the demand to the supply, are the circumstances which fix their market price. Should some great manufacture be undertaken in which a vast additional amount of iron or copper or lead would be used, a sudden and considerable rise of price would be the inevitable consequence. Should this increased demand lead to any valuable improvement in the mining art, or to investigations which should discover new and prolific beds of ore, a corresponding fall of prices would occur. These fluctuations are continually taking place, and an attempt to prevent them by state legislation would be about as effectual as the command of the barbarian king that the ocean should not overpass a certain bound. Silver and gold, though in a less degree, are liable to precisely the same fluctuations of intrinsic value, and to seek to confine them to a fixed point is an attempt marked by equal folly.

If, then, the intrinsic value of money cannot be established by law, the value of its use is no less beyond the proper compass of legislation. Though a certain per centum is established as the rate which may be demanded for the use of money, we find, when the article is relatively abundant, that, notwithstanding the law, a much lower rate is received; and why, on the other hand, when money is scarce, should an attempt be made to prevent it from rising to its natural level?

Such attempts have always been, and always will be, worse than fruitless. They not only do not answer the ostensible object, but they accomplish the reverse. They operate, like all restrictions on trade, to the injury of the very class they are framed to protect; they oppress the borrower for the advantage of the lender; they take from the poor to give to the rich. How is this result produced? Simply by diminishing the amount of capital, which, in the shape of money, would be lent to the community at its fair value, did no restriction exist, and placing what is left in the most extortionate hands. By attaching a stigma and a penalty to the innocent act of asking for money what money is worth, when that value rises above seven per cent, the scrupulous and reputable money-lenders are driven from the market and forced to employ their funds in other modes of investment. The supply, the inadequacy of which in the first place caused the increase in the rate of usance, is thus still further diminished, and the rate of usance necessarily rises still higher. The loanable funds, too, are held only by those who do not scruple to tax their loans with another grievous charge as security against the penalty imposed by an unwise law; and thus our Legislature, instead of assisting the poor man, but makes his necessities the occasion of sorely augmenting his burden.

But usury laws operate most hardly in many cases, even when the general rate of money is below their arbitrary standard. There is an intrinsic and obvious difference between borrowers, which not only justifies but absolutely demands, on the part of a prudent man disposed to relieve the wants of applicants, a very different rate of interest. Two persons can hardly present themselves, in precisely equal circumstances, to solicit a loan. One man is cautious; another is rash. One is a close calculator, sober in his views, and unexcitable in his temperament; another is visionary and enthusiastic. One has tangible security to offer; another nothing but the airy one of a promise. Who shall say that to lend money to these several persons is worth in each case an equal premium?

Should a person come to us with a project which, if successful, will yield an immense return, but, if unsuccessful, leave him wholly destitute, shall we not charge him for the risk we run in advancing his views? The advocates of usury laws may answer that we have it at our option either to take seven per cent or wholly refuse to grant the required aid. True; but suppose the project one which is calculated, if successful, to confer a vast benefit on mankind. Is it wise in the Legislature in such a case to bar the door against ingenuity, except the money-lender turns philanthropist and jeopards his property, not for a fair equivalent, but out of mere love to his fellow-man?

The community begins to answer these questions aright, and there is ground for hope that they will ere long insist upon their legislative agents repealing the entire code of barbarous laws by which the trade in money has hitherto been fettered.

Copyright and Patent Right are Natural Rights
September 27, 1836

Some of the newspapers, we perceive, are treating the subject of a copy-right law, as if such laws were grants of monopolies, and rested on precisely the same principles with enactments conferring exclusive trading privileges, as banks, insurance companies, and the like. This is a very erroneous view of the matter. A copy-right law instead of being a monopoly, is the very reverse. A monopoly is a legislative grant, to an individual or association, of exclusive or peculiar privileges or immunities denied to the rest of the community. A copyright law, on the other hand, confers no new privilege or immunity, but absolutely takes away a portion of an author's right of property in a work of his own creation, and renders no equivalent, except the mere guarding the remainder with some special provisions.

It would be far more proper to call the laws securing to men their rights of property in land monopolies, than those which protect authors and inventors in the productions of their intellectual industry and ingenuity. The rights of property in land are not natural rights. By nature, we are all heirs in common of the earth, as well as of the air and ocean. The origin of individual rights of territory may all be traced, either to the lawless rapacity of might, or the arbitrary enactments of incompetent legislative authorities. The letters patent of an ignorant monarch have granted away a whole continent to the discoverers, though that continent was already in the occupation of numerous tribes of human beings. Such grants may with some propriety be called monopolies.

But an author's right of property in his productions rests on a juster basis. In all ages and all nations of the world, the rights of an individual to the creations of his own labour or skill have always been considered sacred. Even the Indians, who hold their hunting grounds in common, and admit of no arbitrary divisions or appropriations of territory among the members of their tribes, respect each other's exclusive claim to the creations of their own efforts, to that species of property which owes its value to individual labour and skill. Thus the red hunter, who ranges free over the face of the earth, who would spurn the idea of being shut in by fences, and mock the claims of personal possession, yet respects the rights of his fellows in their bows and arrows, which they shape from the reeds and saplings; in their wigwams, which they construct of the trees of the forest; and in the wampum and moccasins, which are woven by their own ingenuity. On the same basis rests an author's right of property in the book which he draws from the resources of his mind, and prepares with labour both of the hand and the head. On the same basis, also, rests the right of the inventor to the productions of his ingenuity. These are natural rights, not rights created by law; not rights growing out of kingly grants, or the preponderance of might over justice.

But society, to promote the benefit of the mass, deprives the individual of this inherent natural and perpetual right, after a limited period of time; and the only consideration which it renders in return for usurpation, is to guard him in the exclusive possession and advantages of his property for the short space he is permitted to retain it. In doing this, however, it does no more for the author, than it is its duty to do for the possessor of every species of property, the grand object for which all government is framed being to protect men in the peaceful enjoyment of life, limb and property. To the author and inventor, then, the law grants no exclusive privilege, but curtails them of a natural right—limits them to a few years in the possession of property wholly created by themselves, to which, without such limitation, their claim would be of the same enduring character, as the mechanic's is to the results of his skill, or the farmer's to the products of his industry. Such being the facts, is it not manifestly absurd to call the copy-right law or the patent-law a monopoly?

Theatrical Riots
December 2, 1836

Note Bryant's earlier reference on June 6, 1836 to this theatrical "disturbance." Bryant refers in passing to the landscape painter Thomas Cole, and the visiting British artist and archeologist Frederick Catherwood, later known for his illustrations of the Mayan ruins.

Several of the journals are earnestly engaged in the controversy whether Mr. and Mrs. Wood shall be mobbed in case they return to perform at any of the theatres in this city. We take little interest in the question of their reappearance; but in case any of the managers of our theatres should think fit to engage them, we hope that the civil authorities will see that the rights of individuals are protected. We hope that any violence threatened either to the theatre, or its performers, will be prevented by a proper array of force, and that if any disturbance should manifest itself it will be repelled and chastised. The custom of theatrical rows, the practice of turning theatres into places of riot, of visiting them for the very purpose of driving from the stage, by violence and uproar, performers whom a part of the audience have come purposely to hear, is a piece of brutality which we have copied from English manners, and which we should do well to lay aside with all expedition. If a sense of shame be not enough to make a part of the community desist from so barbarous and uncivilized a custom, from such a wanton, inexcusable aggression on the rights and the quiet of others, the law should interfere firmly, deliberately, and with a show of strength to quell the brawlers who lead or the brawlers who follow in these outrages. Our city has too long been the scene of shameful disturbances, directed now against a political party, now against teachers of unpopular doctrines, and now against a singer on the stage. It is time that those who "bear the sword of the law" should learn that they are not expected to bear it "in vain." We appoint magistrates and organize a police to preserve order, and not to shrink and tremble, and stand aside when the rioters are a little better dressed, or more numerous than usual.

We have had a succession of mobs in this city, and we believe one of them was actually put down by a display of military strength; but then it was a mob of friendless journeymen, whom nobody cared for. It will be remembered, also, that when Judge Edwards was about to pass sentence upon the journeymen tailors, the Park bristled with preparations to subdue a disturbance that probably was never meditated. We do not complain of this; we only want the laws to be enforced against the genteel mob as well as against the forlorn mob. It is not the business of Justice and Law to swell and look big, and frown, when three ragamuffins are amusing themselves with getting up their little riot, and at the same time to smile, and bow, and give the wall to a score of swaggerers, strikers and window-breakers in swallow-tailed coats.

The barbarous and brutal practice of theatrical rows is unknown in every country but England and America. It is a custom for which, unless when it is excited by some unexpected outrage upon publick feeling committed by the manager or the actors, there is not the slightest excuse. A premeditated row is a crime which should rank next to house-breaking. If the audience were turned into the theatre every night like sheep into a pen, and the doors shut and barred upon them, they might with good reason become uproarious if they did not like the entertainment or the actors. But no law compels them to resort nightly to the theatre. If they do not happen to like a performer, they can show their dislike most expressively by not going near him. They can stay at home with their wives and children, or attend the lectures of the Mercantile Library Association or the Mechanicks' Institute, or go to the Tabernacle, or Catherwood's lectures, or look at Cole's pictures, or amuse themselves in any of the thousand ways that a great city offers. They have no more right to disturb the amusement of others, or to outrage the person who is amusing them, than they have to enter a church and disturb the devotions of the congregation with whooping and pelting the clergyman with rotten eggs.

Henry Clay: His Reluctance to Retire
December 26, 1836

Kentucky Senator Henry Clay had been in and out of the Congress since 1806. Long an aspirant for the Presidency, he had failed of that office in 1824 and 1836. Vice President Martin Van Buren was elected in November 1836 to succeed President Andrew Jackson. As Bryant hints, Clay was susceptible to fleshly temptations. Ashland was his Kentucky estate. The Athenian statesman Demosthenes was considered the greatest Greek orator.

We remember an old lawyer who at one of the terms of the Court in which he practised, declared his intention of retiring from the profession, and bade his brethren of the bar an affectionate farewell in writing. As they on their part were glad to get rid of him they reciprocated his farewell in a very civil answer full of flourishes about their esteem for his character and respect for his learning. The old barrister was so delighted with these unwonted compliments, and so fond moreover of the gains of his practice, that he appeared again at the bar the very next term, and at the close of it sent in another valedictory.

Mr. Clay, who, a short time since, announced his intention of retiring to private life, for the third or fourth time, we believe, and who received the compliments and regrets of the whig journals on that occasion, is re-elected to the United States Senate from Kentucky. His friends may now dry their eyes and put up their white pocket handkerchiefs, for the great champion of the Bank, of internal improvements, of high tariffs and of surplus revenues, is persuaded to remain a little longer in public life. He has been convinced by their farewell eulogiums how strongly they are attached to him, and he cannot find it in his heart to desert such good friends. He will remain to save the country, to uphold the constitution and to resist the reign of corruption under Mr. Van Buren, all which is to be done by a national bank, a large surplus revenue, and its distribution among the States.

An old and practised politician, particularly if he have looked upon politics as a mere game of skill, which Mr. Clay appears to do, never goes willingly into private life. He keeps his seat at the table till the cards are taken from his hand. He wields the cue till the keeper of the billiard-room disengages it from his fingers and tells him that it is another gentleman's turn to play. He forswears the dice-box, as many a gamester has done before him, and the next hour he is seen rattling it as eagerly as ever. The alternate successes and defeats of political warfare, the laying and managing the plot of a political campaign, the pleasure of foiling the designs of the other party, of robbing it of its due credit for good measures, of aggravating the effect of its mistakes, the hope of beating it at last out of winning and wearing the spoils of public office—these are things which hold the mind of the veteran politician with as strong a spell as the most fascinating game holds its habitual votary. Politics are to such a man his daily stimulus, his alcohol, his opium, without which he is in the depths of wretchedness. The father of the American system would be miserable enough walking with his hands in his pockets over his fields at Ashland and whistling to himself. When Mr. Clay's name is no longer in the newspapers as the proposer of this or that measure, as toasted at this and that dinner, as the author of this or that speech in which he outshone Demosthenes, when other men spout in Congress and at public banquets, and are toasted and bepraised, and drive to and fro with loud outcries the shuttlecock of politics, what will be his reflections in his retirement and obscurity? He would hardly revert for consolation to the acts of his own past life, to his scheme of high duties which had well nigh caused a separation of the southern from the northern states, to his support of the mischievous and now exploded internal improvement system, to his support of a corrupt and dangerous moneyed institution, to his wicked scheme of revenging himself on a political rival, by procuring the censure of the Senate to be passed on his conduct, or finally to his compromise act which now loads the nation with a burden of unnecessary taxation. These recollections would be but a sad compensation for the loss of that notoriety and excitement which have been to him the breath of life for thirty years past. The time is not come for Mr. Clay to retire to Ashland. He prefers, we doubt not, to drown any unpleasant reflections on his past political course, in the tumult of political strifes, and to avoid retrospection, by keeping his attention fixed on the game he has so long been playing—a mere game for political mastery.

The Pilot Monopoly
January 5, 1837

As recently as at the outset of World War II, a maritime historian has noted, the professional pilots licensed by New York and New Jersey to guide ships into and out of the Port of New York were "organized into powerful guilds that dated back to the age of sail" and stringently limited their membership. On the day following this editorial the Evening Post *reported that two ships which could not secure pilots the previous Saturday night had run aground; the next day Bryant returned to the subject with a leader on the disastrous consequences of pilot monopoly.*

Our coast is strewn with wrecks and dead bodies in consequence of the detestable regulations of the law which directs the licensing of the pilots, and prescribes their duties. Bitter and accursed are always the fruits of the unjust principle of monopoly; but in this instance, most bitter and most accursed. The pilot law is in effect a sweeping statute of assassination; it destroys men, not singly or in small bands, but by companies and ship loads; it does not, like war, spare the wom[e]n and the tender children, and the infirm aged; but like the pestilence, it sweeps to a common death, victims of every age and every sex. If clumsy law-givers, deeming themselves wiser than Providence, had never intermeddled with the business of pilotage, our coasts would have swarmed with enterprising and hardy guides through the intricacies of the entrance to our harbour; the Bristol and the Mexico would have been at this moment riding quietly and safely at our wharves, and the multitudes whom the sea swallowed up, when its waves broke over those ill fated vessels, would have yet breathed the air, and rejoiced in the light of day.

But if the consequences of the pilot law are thus shocking to the sense of humanity, they are otherwise disgraceful and hurtful to us as a community. The port of New York will, if the evil be not instantly redressed, be avoided like some inhospitable shore without harbour or shelter for ships, beaten with perpetual storm, and white with the bones of mariners. The merchant will direct his cargoes to another mart, and the visitor from foreign countries will take passage for a port the avenues to which are not like the gates of death. Not only humanity, but self-interest, therefore, demand of us all to use our exertions to change the present cruel, fatal, and infamous system. A cry should go forth from this city that shall shake the walls of the legislative palace. Our legislators should repeal this statute of murder before the week ends. The lives of those who may perish in consequence of further delay will be required at their hands.

Negro Suffrage, New York State
February 7, 1837

A provision of the New York State Constitution of 1821 required of free Negroes a higher property qualification for the right to vote than it did of white citizens.

The rejection of the petition of the coloured men of Troy, addressed to the legislature of this State, praying to be put on the same footing with whites, as respects the right of suffrage, has set certain journals to sounding a note of triumph over the abolitionists.

It appears to us that it is very unwise to connect this question with that of the principal object of the abolitionists, which is to do away [with] slavery in the Southern states. The great objection brought against their course hitherto, has been that they were intermeddling with a matter with which they had no concern, and which their interference might make worse for both master and slave.

There is not the least ground for either of these objections in the case of the petition in question. The removal of the disabilities of the blacks within our own limits, no body will deny to be a proper subject for our legislature to discuss and act upon. We recognize them as citizens and we have a perfect right to say how easy we will make the conditions of their citizenship. The moment we allow ourselves to be restrained in legislating on this subject, by a regard to what is or may be said at the south, or any where else, we submit to external interference, we allow a power from without to dictate what shall be the qualifications of our voters.

For our own part, we hesitate not to say that the prayer of the petition was just. If the House of Assembly were not prepared immediately to adopt it, it should have been referred to a committee for consideration. As the law now stands, a coloured man is not entitled to vote unless he be the owner of a freehold estate worth two hundred and fifty dollars. If the ownership of a freehold estate gives a man a greater interest in his own happiness, or makes him a better judge of what is better for the happiness of the community, why not require that every white voter shall possess that qualification? If, on the other hand, the capacity for self-government depends on the colour, why not exclude the African race altogether? Why allow a black man of the full blood, with his two hundred and fifty dollars, to vote, while you exclude the man who is three-quarters white, and who, according to your theory of colour, must be three times as capable of voting intelligently as the full-blooded African? The law, as it now stands, is pregnant with absurdities.

By this attempt to throw the odium of abolitionism upon measures which, in themselves, are proper subjects of state legislation, if not just measures of state policy, an increase of respectability, power and numbers is given to that sect. It gradually changes its position, and becomes the champion of projects not within its original scope. Numbers who did not come into original views of the abolitionists, are insensibly drawn into its ranks by a community of opinion on collateral measures. In this view, the cry of abolitionism raised against the harmless and very proper petition from Troy, is as grossly impolitick as it is unjust.

The Approaching Retirement of Andrew Jackson
March 1, 1837

The approaching retirement of President Jackson has called forth numerous testimonies of respect both at home and abroad. It is in vain that his enemies seek to gainsay it; the sagacious, right-minded, just and fearless old man, who for eight years has been our Chief Magistrate, has already taken his place among the most illustrious of those who have ever stood at the head of nations. Defects of character he may have had, and we never sought to deny or disguise them a hot and hasty temper—an attachment to his friends which sometimes led him into mistakes concerning their real character— but these have been redeemed by so many nobler qualities, by so much rectitude of purpose, so much ingen[u]ousness, so much practical wisdom, so much moral courage, such perspicacity in discerning his duty, and such inflexible firmness in performing it, as to have fitted him in a singular manner for the high and responsible station he has occupied. There prevails a general conviction, that under the administration of no other man would the perplexities of our foreign relations have been so happily disentangled, or the difficulties of our domestic politics so promptly and fortunately adjusted.

The demonstrations of esteem which President Jackson now receives cannot be accused of proceeding from mercenary motives. He has no longer any offices to bestow—no rewards for simulated attachment, or clamorous patriotism. His personal merits and public services are now his only titles to homage, and desiring, as he does, no other reward than a candid appreciation of what he has done, he will have no reason to repeat the old complaint of the ingratitude of republics.— The approbation of his constituents will follow him to his retirement, and the applauses which his well acted part has called forth will penetrate the shades of the Hermitage.

We have lying before us a correspondence between the citizens of Albemarle County, in Virginia, and the President. The citizens of Albemarle County desirous of manifesting their high sense of his character and services, have invited him to a public dinner to be given on his way from Washington to his estate in Tennessee. After alluding to the difficult duties which General Jackson was called to perform, and the tempest of opposition with which he was assailed, the letter of invitation proceeds thus:

"It was our pleasure, as it was our duty to our country then, to sustain you and your measures throughout those trying scenes, regardless of the idle charges of 'man-worship, office-seeking, corruption and subserviency,' heaped upon us, and of 'tyranny, usurpation, and despotism,' so liberally bestowed upon you, by those whose minds could not conceive of power without oppression, or praise without a price.

"In a few days you will have ended your career of active usefulness, and retired to your own home covered with years and with honors. We now desire to meet you as you pass, as plain Andrew Jackson, stripped of the insig[nia] of office, and divested of power, that we may pay to the man and the patriot, without suspicion, that voluntary homage of respect and gratitude, which the heartless and corrupt have affected to think a free people paid to [p]ower and patronage."

Copy-Rights
March 2, 1837

From the outset of his journalistic career Bryant had urged a fair international copyright law, calling it in 1831 "the only link required to complete the chain of reciprocity between nations." Terming it in 1836 a "natural right," he was urged by fifty-six British writers to join their petition through Henry Clay to the American Congress for a fair law. This failing, again in 1842 he supported a like appeal brought him by Charles Dickens. In 1843 Bryant was an organizer and first president of the American Copyright Club, publishing an address on the subject. The Plaindealer *was a forthright liberal journal conducted briefly in New York in 1836–1837 by Bryant's former associate editor and partner William Leggett.*

COPY-RIGHTS.—The report of Mr. Clay on the subject of granting copy-rights to foreign authors, which has been excluded for several days past by other matter, will be found in our columns of today. We agree with the conclusions of the report, but we wish that it had entered more deeply into the question.

The report speaks of the right of literary property as incontestable, yet it has been very ably contested. The question has been well argued pro and con in the *Plaindealer,* and the argument in favor of extending the copy-right to foreigners has turned principally on the preliminary question, whether there is any natural right of literary property.

All agree that the right of property arose originally from the peculiar form given by the labor of the individual to any object which was previously the common property of all. This idea is illustrated in the following manner.

In a state of nature the forests are common property. The earth produces its plants and trees for the service of all. A savage cuts off a sapling, shapes it into a bow, and fits to it the sinew of an animal slain by him in the chase. What was before common property now becomes private. The savage in altering the shape of the sapling has combined with the material object his own labor and ingenuity. He has imparted to it something of his own, his intelligent industry; and the rudest state of human existence acknowledges his exclusive right to what is thus, in some sort, his own creation. As an illustration of the idea of property acquired in this manner, it may be mentioned that the backwoodsmen, who consider the forests on the public lands as common property, never make use of the timber felled by another, considering that the act of cutting transfers the exclusive right of possession to the individual.

Let us see how this doctrine applies to literary productions. Language is a common possession. The author arranges the words and phrases of which language is composed into a moral, political or scientific treatise, an oration or a poem. In so doing he gives a new form to a material which is common property. The new arrangement is the result of his own intelligent labor. He has combined something of his own with what he has taken from the common stock; he has filled the mass of lifeless words with the light of his own reason, the energy of his own feeling, the glow of his own imagination; he has breathed into it the breath of life, infused into it a portion of his own mind. We give it a name which signifies how peculiarly it is his; we call it his "work," his "production"; if in verse, we call it his "poem," which is derived from a Greek word signifying a making or creation. The work of the author may be even considered more exclusively his than the bow of the savage; since the savage, by cutting the sapling, withdraws something from the common stock, while the author leaves the treasury of language as full as ever. The right of property, therefore, which the author has to his own productions, seems to be as complete to say the least, as that of the artizan to the implement he has shaped.

Subtle reasoners have raised difficulties about the application of this doctrine in particular instances, but the general principle appears to us to rest on firm grounds, and with respect to the practical application, experience has shown that there is in ordinary cases no difficulty in identifying literary property.

If we admit the right of literary property on the grounds we have laid down, and at the same time, refuse the enjoyment of it to foreigners, we set our faces against the rules of natural justice, and place ourselves on a level with the inhabitants of those islands of the Pacific which steal from vessels arriving at their shores every thing they can lay their hands on.

The mischiefs which arise from leaving the law as it now stands, allowing a copy-right to persons residing in this country, and refusing it to persons residing abroad, are sufficiently obvious to make it unnecessary to dwell upon them here. The principal ones are these—that it promotes the circulation of works of English origin in this country to the exclusion of our own, and to the discouragement of our authors—and that it leads to the ignorant and injurious mutilation of foreign works republished here.

The Squatters
ca. March 1837

In 1830 a temporary pre-emption law was passed in Congress over the opposition of Eastern interests who feared that the availability of cheap land in the Ohio and Mississippi valleys would draw away needed labor from the East. Not until 1841 did a permanent statute permit settlers to claim, after fourteen months' residence, 160 acres of land for $1.25 an acre. In 1832 Bryant had visited his youngest brother, John, the first of four brothers to settle on the prairie, at Jacksonville, Illinois.

We see pretty frequently in the party prints, expressions of scorn concerning the squatters of the western country, and attempts to scout the notion of passing a general pre-emption law for their benefit. We know well what class of persons are designated by this title, for we have seen them amid the broad prairies, where they raise their harvests, and beside the noble woods where they hunt their game, and we have shared the hospitality of their cabins. They are our old friends and neighbors; men who have emigrated from the Atlantic States, men who are perhaps a little more adventurous and restless, but quite as moral and intelligent, as those they have left behind; nay, if we take into the estimate the inhabitants of the larger towns, more moral and intelligent. We have known among these squatters some of the best and purest men it has ever been our fortune to be acquainted with. No man who has once visited the West, scruples, if his convenience should lead him, to seat himself upon the unoccupied territory belonging to Government, the sale of which is not yet permitted. Here he builds his log cabin, in the edge of a grove, splits his trees into rails, fences in a portion of the wide and rich prairie, turns up the virgin soil, which yields a hundred fold for the seeds which he casts upon it, and pastures his herd upon the vast, unenclosed, flowery champaign before his dwelling. One emigrant arrives after another, and in this way neighborhoods are formed, communities of honest, kind, and religious people, with their schools and places of worship, before a single inch is offered for sale. This is the universal and well understood custom of the

West—not a custom of yesterday, but of a century's growth; a custom which dates back to the time when the first hunter raised his cabin in the rich natural meadows of Kentucky. It is a custom which the government itself has tolerated; we may use a still stronger term—it is a custom which the government has recognised and sanctioned, by passing from time to time pre-emption laws giving the settler the first right to purchase the soil he has occupied.

And these laws are consonant with natural equity. The cabin of the settler is the work of his own hands; and he has made the prairie valuable by surrounding it with fences, and breaking up the green sward. The neighborhoods formed by squatters give a value to the unclaimed lands around them which they otherwise would not have. The speculator and the newcomer both reap the benefit of a settlement already formed, instead of selling or settling upon lands in the midst of a wilderness. It is just that they who founded the colonies from which the lands derive their subsequent value should be compensated in some way or other for the hardships and inconveniences they have undergone.

If local and temporary pre-emption laws are just in principle, then is also a general pre-emption law. What is right in one case is right in all.

The Proposed Annexation of Texas
August 4, 1837

On this date, the "Republic of Texas," so declared a year earlier by American settlers in territory taken forcefully from Mexico, petitioned the United States government for annexation to the Union. Three weeks later this request was denied by the Van Buren administration, and not until 1845 was it granted by joint action of the American Congress.

The Rhode Island candidates for the office of Representative in Congress have been interrogated as to their opinions concerning the annexation of Texas to the American Union. We have before us a Providence paper containing the answers of the four gentlemen nominated by the two opposite political parties. They all declare themselves decidedly adverse to the admission of Texas into the confederacy. This affords a strong presumption of the state of public opinion on that question in Rhode Island.

It has been intimated in some of the southern papers that the question of receiving the Texan republic into our confederacy would be brought up at the extra session of Congress in September. If it should be so, the members will have enough to occupy them until the ordinary time of opening the winter session. Whoever broaches that question awakens a long and vehement controversy. If that firebrand be tossed into the hall of legislation, and be not immediately thrown out again, it will kindle a flame which all the storms of next winter will not quench.

Yet the question is to be decided, and we should be ready to meet it whenever it comes up. We care not, for our part, how soon it is met and settled.

The project is to annex to the Union a territory in which slavery is an established political institution—a territory so ample that half a dozen states as large as Kentucky might be carved out of it—a territory rapidly filling up with adventurers from this country, who have just wrested it from the hands of the Mexicans, and but the other day obtained the recognition of its national independence by the United States.

The question will immediately arise whether we shall not violate the obligations of neutrality with Mexico by annexing Texas to the republic. On this point there can be no doubt. We break our treaty with Mexico the instant we do this. We adopt the quarrel of the new member of the confederacy; we must fight her battles and protect her frontier. We have a Mexican war on our hands at once.

But, suppose that while we are agitating the question of annexing the Texan republic, Mexico, alarmed at the probable success of the project, and certain to be beaten in a contest with the United States, relinquishes her claim to the territory. Will that put a better face on the matter? Let us see how this will tell in history.

It will be related that the people of the United States overflowed into the territory belonging to Mexico. They quarrelled with Mexico, declared themselves independent, and de[fi?]ed her power. The people of the United States at home, hastened, while the war was yet unfinished and before any other nation, to recognize the political independence of the people of the United States in Texas. It will be related, that as soon as this was done, a compact was formed between the emigrants in Texas and their friends at home, transferring to their native country the territory of which they had taken possession. Mexico, conscious of her weakness, saw that it was prudent to acquiesce.

This would be the story of a high handed public robbery. Yet this, in our view, is precisely the part we are called upon to act, by the numerous speculators who have purchased large tracts of Texas Lands, and now expect the nation will forfeit its honor to enable them to make their fortunes.

But there are yet other considerations connected with this question of great, and eventually perhaps, of still higher importance to the welfare of the nation. If the independence of Texas had been acknowledged by Mexico herself ten years ago, we should still oppose her annexation to the republic.

The question how long an empire so widely extended as ours can be kept together by means of our form of government is yet to be decided. That this form of government is admirably calculated for a large territory and a numerous population we have no doubt, but there is a probable limit to this advantage. Extended beyond a certain distance, and a certain number of states it would become inconvenient and undesirable, and a tendency would be felt to break up into smaller nations. If the Union of these states is destined to be broken by such a cause, the annexation of Texas to the Union would precipitate the event, perhaps, by a whole century. It is better to carry out the experiment with the territory we now possess.

The slaveholding states, by the Constitution of the Union, are disproportionately represented in Congress. While other states are represented only according to their free population, the slaveholding states are allowed an additional number of representatives for a certain species of property, their slaves. This we hold to be an unjust partition of the political power, and utterly contrary to the spirit of our democratic institutions. It was, however, the original compact, and we are not disposed to disturb it. But Texas, if she comes into the Union with her slaves, must come in under this very compact, and we protest vehemently against extending it to a new territory. A territory so broad and fertile, promising so soon to be filled with inhabitants, electing its members on this aristocratic basis, would produce a prodigious inequality in our representation in Congress.

The extension and corroboration of the institution of slavery within our republic, is also another objection to the annexation of Texas. Holding, as we do, its existence among us to be a great evil, a great misfortune, and a monstrous anomaly in our institutions, we cannot but regard with the strongest alarm the project of adding to the nation a vast territory which holds that evil within its bosom. We have enough of it as the republic is now constituted. Its difficulties, its dangers, the dissensions to which it gives rise among ourselves, its mischiefs "moral, social and political," are already sufficiently great, without the reinforcement which they would derive from the addition to the Union of a vast and populous slaveholding territory.

THE WISDOM OF OUR ANCESTORS
August 19, 1837

THE WISDOM OF OUR ANCESTORS.—It is too late to ask whether Benjamin Franklin was a wise man. Even those who are disposed to detract from his well earned fame, allow that in all matters relating to economy, whether public or private, he was wonderfully sagacious and clear-sighted. His unerring common sense taught him, before Adam Smith published his Wealth of Nations, that restrictions of the intercourse between nations are always hurtful to the interest of the great whole. The same faculty showed him the folly of all attempts on the part of government to regulate the exchanges between different parts of the country. Listen to the voice of this great man speaking to us from the grave.

Doctor FRANKLIN'S *opinion of the ability of Government to regulate currency, and give stability to trade, published in 1774.*

"It is impossible for Government to circumscribe or fix the extent of paper credit, which must of course fluctuate. Government may as well pretend to lay down rules for the operations or the confidence of every individual, in the course of his trade. Any seeming temporary evil arising must naturally work its own cure.

"*Exchange* by bills between one country or city and another, we conceive to be this: One person wants to get a sum from any country or city, consequently has his bill to sell: another wants to send a sum thither, and therefore agrees to pay such bill or draft. He has it at an agreed price, which is the course of the exchange. It is with this price for bills as with merchandise—when there is a scarcity of bills in the market they are dear; when plenty they are cheap. We think it necessary to offer a few words, to destroy an erroneous principle that has misled some and confused others; which is, that by authority, a certain *par*, or fixed price of exchange, should be settled between each respective country, thereby rendering the currency of exchange as fixed as the standard of coin. We have before hinted that plenty and scarcity must govern the course of exchange; which principle, duly considered, would suffice on the subject; but we will add that no human foresight can absolutely judge of the almost numberless fluctuations of trade, which vary, sometimes directly, sometimes indirectly, between countries; consequently, no state or potentate can by authority any more pretend to settle the currency of the several sorts of merchandise sent to and from their respective dominions, than they can a par of exchange. That the wisdom of government should weigh and nicely consider any proposed regulation on these principles, we humbly judge to be self-evident, whereby may be seen that it coincides with the general good. Solomon adviseth *not to counsel with a merchant for gain*. This, we presume, relates to the merchant's own particular profit, which, we repeat, must ever be the spring of his actions.

"Perhaps, in general, it would be better if government meddled no further with trade than to protect it, and let it take its own course. Most of the statutes, or acts, edicts, arrets, and placards, of Parliaments, Princes, and States, for regulating, directing, or restraining of traders, have, we think, been either political blunders, or jobs obtained by artful men for private advantage, under pretence of public good."

We must go back to the wisdom of our ancestors—the wisdom of Benjamin Franklin. Since his time, legislation has fallen into the hands of visionaries and theorists, who are as much wiser than Providence as a quack doctor is wiser than nature. They have had their schemes for regulating the exchanges and adjusting banking facilities to the business wants of the community; they have had their national banks and their safety fund systems and their boards of commissioners, and their minute and painful regulations tie down the banks to a safe business. What have we gained by all these innovations? What is the fruit of all this fussing and discussing and legislating, this proposing of fresh schemes and patching up of schemes already in use, this hard work at the artificial banking system at which we have been kept like galley slaves for forty years? We will answer the question. These pernicious novelties, sown broadcast over the land, have sprung up in a harvest of mischief more plenteous than all the wheat fields which wave between the Gulf of Mexico and the lakes of the north. The fiercest political quarrels, the most shameless corruption of the press, the buying and selling of members of congress and the state legislative halls with a crowd of unprincipled and greedy lobby members, are but general terms for a host of evils. Add to these, selfish intrigues innumerable for nominations and at elections—add to these, perpetual fluctuations in commerce, distempered activity at one time, death-like stagnation at another—add the wild career of modern speculation, wilder than a hurricane—add the distress and ruin which are the "maturity and perfection" of this system, like the maturity and perfection of a Congreve rocket, exploding, stunning, suffocating and slaying all whom it reaches. Is there any one in the community who is willing to own that he has not had enough of all this?

Let us then return to the good old paths; let us go back to the simplicity of natural credit, the only safe and stable condition in which the business of banking can be left. Let us have no more nostrums for the cure of a disease which has been caused by taking medicine. It is true there are more specifics for the regulation of the currency and the adjustment of exchanges than for the cure of corns. Let us [have?] none of them. Let us toss the gallipots out of the window, and the state doctors after them, divest the patient of the bandages with which ignorant nurses have tied him to his bed, open the doors and allow him to walk out in the blessed air, in his ancient liberty, and recover his health and strength by free exercise and abstinence from physic.

On Van Buren's Message
September 7, 1837

On this date President Van Buren proposed that Congress set up an independent treasury to replace private banks as depositories for federal funds. Democrats backed his plan, but Whigs reacted furiously against it. The verse quotation is from Dante's Divine Comedy; The Inferno.

If one might judge of the vexation suffered by the opposition party, at the tenor of the President's message, by the noise they make, it must be infinite. The cries of the wounded wild beast prove the vigor and just aim of the arm which dealt the blow. It is not mere blame, it is not simple dissent and disapprobation with which the message is greeted; it is met with shouts of fury, bellowings of rage, gnashing of teeth, howls and shrieks of agony;—an uproar like that which saluted the ears of Dante when he entered the City of Pain.

"Voci alte e fioche, e suon di man' con elle."
Loud cries and hoarse, and sound of smitten hands.

The whig presses in this matter afford an example of the too common misfortune of persons repeating a falsehood till at last they come to believe it. By dint of perpetually asserting that Mr. Van Buren was not a man to declare an opinion, or recommend a measure, that he was "of the noncommittal school," as they styled it in their slang, and would never assume the responsibility of urging any reform, they at length brought themselves to believe that the calumny they had tried so hard to pass current was actually true. They have reaped the reward of persevering falsehood; they have deluded and deceived themselves. They actually imagined, we have no doubt, that they should not find Mr. Van Buren in their way. They had no idea that he would give the sanction of his authority to the wholesome reforms which the times demand, and they thought to carry their own schemes by the mere effect of his indecision.

The recent Message, in which the Chief Magistrate comes forward with a noble frankness, stating his views with the clearest unreserve, putting them forward in various lights, vindicating them from objections in the most satisfactory manner, and grounding upon them a series of practical recommendations, has utterly thrown the tactics of these gentry into confusion. Their calumnies, their expectations, and their plan of operations explode together. It is like a volley of grape shot among a crowd of naked cannibals who had just after much talking, convinced each other that the enemy was unarmed. Who can then wonder at the savage howl that has been set up?

Calhoun's Diminished Stature
September 20, 1837

John Calhoun of South Carolina, Vice President during Jackson's first term, was now in the Senate. In John Milton's epic poem Paradise Lost, *God's messenger, the angel Ithuriel, caught the "arch-fiend" Satan "squat like a toad, close at the ear of Eve," tempting her with "Vain hopes, vain aims." Satan rose up, and "His stature reached the sky." In 1837 independent Calhoun ceased his earlier cooperation with Whig associates to back Van Buren's plan to replace the private United States Bank as a repository for government funds with a United States subtreasury. James Boswell had written of Milton that he "was a genius that could cut a Colossus from a rock."*

It is surprising how suddenly the dimensions of Mr. Calhoun's intellectual stature are reduced in the estimation of certain persons. The other day he towered to a height like that of Milton's arch-fiend when he prepared to do battle with Ithuriel. At present, since he has declared himself in favor of the divorce of bank and state, he is shrunk to a size no larger than that of the same personage when he lay "squat at the ear of Eve." Hear the *Journal of Commerce,* speaking of Mr. Calhoun's speech, in which he declares himself hostile to renewing the connexion of the government with the banks:

> "Every body will be disappointed. There are no footprints of a giant here; and we think it will be the general feeling, that Mr. Calhoun has seldom done himself so little credit, as in his speech on Monday."

The colossus, whose footprints the other day were like the broad tracks on the Rock of the Giants, now leaves a vestige as minute as that of a sparrow on the sand.

It is told of a country fellow who had caught a rabbit, that he broke out in praise of the excellent properties of the animal's flesh. "You are good broiled," said he, "you are good roasted, you are good stewed, you are good fried, you are good fricaseed; you are good any way." At this moment the rabbit sprang from his arms and disappeared among the brush wood. "Go to pot," said the man, "you are a good-for-nothing dry-meated beast, to make the best of you."

Mr. Calhoun, the other day, was one of those men at whose greatness the whig prints were lost in astonishment; he was good in a speech, good at a report, good in defence, particularly good in an attack; in short, he was good any way. He is now unlucky enough to agree with the administration in an important measure; he slips from the arms of the whigs, and runs off by himself; and becomes a good-for-nothing dry-meated animal on the instant.

The Right of Suffrage
November 2, 1837

Englishman John Rolfe settled in Virginia about 1609. The first child of English parents in New England was Peregrine White, born on the Mayflower in Plymouth Harbor in 1620. Descendants of the Dutch who settled New York, then New Amsterdam, in 1609 acquired their nicknames after Washington Irving's fictional author of his A History of New York *(1809), "Diedrich Knickerbocker." A fusing of Whig and Nativist (anti-foreign) parties had elected a mayor of New York in March 1837.*

For which ticket will the citizens of foreign birth give their votes in the election which is at hand?

It is not our design to flatter adopted citizens, but to reason with them. We pay them a higher compliment by doing so. We detest the practice of appealing to the vanity or the self-love of any set of men at the eve of an election. Not long since we remember an attempt was made to coax the Irish to vote for the whig ticket, and the "generous natives of the Emerald Isle," as they were called, were deluged with a flood of soft words and compliments from quarters whence they had been previously habitually pelted with abuse. It was as if the great conduit of Canal Street should take to discharging Eau de Cologne into the North river, instead of its usual feculence.

Persons of foreign birth are found among all classes of our citizens; they employ themselves in all the various occupations of which this mixed community is composed; they acquire property here, marry among us, and their children are natives of our soil. Those who have chosen our country for their permanent residence, have as deep an interest in the laws under which they are to live as if the accident of their birth had occurred within our own domain. Their interests of every nature are as much affected by the laws as the interests of the descendants of Rolfe or Peregrine White or the first of the Knickerbockers. It is clearly just, then, that they should have a voice in the framing of those regulations which dispose of their rights.

The principle which we have stated is that which has governed the practice of the democratic party. They do not ask on which side of the Atlantic the individual was born, but only whether he is a member of the community. Regarding all men as equal, and as beings endowed with the common faculty of reason for their guidance, they would allow them all to protect their rights by the exercise of suffrage.

Not so is the practice, nor are such the principles of the whig party. They are for circumscribing, restricting and rendering difficult and rare the right of suffrage. It was that party which clung to a property qualification as long as they were able. It is that party which would now set up a qualification of birth. Some of their journals have gone so far as to declare that they would deny all political rights to the natives of foreign countries. This narrow jealousy has shown itself in a deplorable manner during the past season, when a whig Mayor has rendered the New York coast famous for its barbarous inhospitality to strangers.

Are the citizens of foreign birth prepared to support a party which seeks to disenfranchise them; a party which would deprive them of all voice in agreeing on the laws under which they are to live; a party which holds them to be incapable of judging of their own rights, and would place them under a perpetual political guardianship; a party which seeks to prevent the entrance of their brethren upon our territories, by the exaction of an exorbitant tax; a party which brands them as the refuse of poor-houses, prisons and hospitals—the importers of both moral and physical pestilence?

There is no need of our indicating the natural and proper reply to these questions. We are all aware that there are citizens of foreign birth whose partialities are strong in favor of the whig party—but we can hardly imagine that with all these partialities, they can submit placidly to this proscription, and record their solemn assent to these calumnies by giving their vote for the whig ticket.

On the other hand we know that there are men whose feelings have been stung to the quick, by seeing what a few years ago was the mere smothered flame of jealousy and dislike, now blazing out in open persecution. Under a whig chief magistrate of the city, they have had a foretaste of what is prepared for them if the whigs gain the ascendency in the State. They will attend at the polls and give their votes for the democratic ticket.

The Whig Victory in New York Elections
November 9, 1837

The verses quoted are the opening lines of Shakespeare's Macbeth, Act III. *"The love of money is the root of all evil."—Philippians 4:8. The year 1837 was one of financial depression and widespread unemployment. Baal was the Canaanites' dissolute god before whom the Israelites "bowed down."*

> "Thou hast it now, King, Cawdor, Glamis, all
> As the weird women promised; and, I fear,
> Thou playedst most foully for it."

The whig ticket has succeeded, at the election in this city which terminated last evening, by a considerable majority. It is the fashion, we know, for the beaten party on such occasions to charge their adversaries with profligate practices. Yet in the present instance we entertain the most solemn belief that such charges are deserved by the whig party, and that the most impartial and indifferent chronicler, while he recorded their victory, would say,

They played most foully for it.

It has been affirmed again and again, and not denied by the whigs, that immense sums have been contributed by them to this week's election. Beyond the payment of certain necessary expenses incident to all elections, such as the printing of votes and handbills, procuring their distribution, &c., all use of money in elections is corrupt. Large sums cannot be expended otherwise than profligately and for purposes of mischief. With whatever intention the money may be given, it goes into the hands of the venal creatures who act as electioneering agents, men indifferent to morals, subtle, impudent, active, intent only on increasing, by whatever means, the vote of their party, and who will be sure to employ it corruptly, because that is the only way left of employing it at all. So far as a party raises more money than is required for the expenses we have already indicated, it is guilty of corruption. Where there is so much of the Root of Evil there must be some of the branches. If a venal vote has been given at this election, it has been bought for the whig ticket.

Besides the power of gold, the power of slander has been invoked in aid of the whig party. The democrats have been charged, day after day, in the face of their most solemn denials, and in utter disregard of what their calumniators knew to be true, with maintaining doctrines the very opposite of what they actually maintain. The cry of agrarianism and infidelity has been raised by those who knew that they were bringing a false accusation. Never was a party more foully, more remorselessly, more shamelessly, more ceaselessly libelled than ours has been. The daily press, including almost every newspaper in the city, has pelted us morning and evening with its putridity, as if all the sinks and sewers of the city had been endued with the power of ejecting their accumulated filth into the air. These wicked arts have had their effect. Many worthy people have been deceived by them. Falsehood has triumphed for a time, but the reign of falsehood is short.

Another profligate method which has been adopted to a considerable extent by the whigs in this election, has been the coercion of persons in their employment. The greater number of employers are whigs—and the candidates for employment at the present moment in this city are more numerous than the opportunities. This advantage the whigs have used—cruelly and wickedly used. It was a frightful dilemma in which to place the labourer—the choice of voting against his own conscience or seeing his family deprived of their daily bread.

Yet, with all these difficulties to contend against, we stand [not alone], but nearly seventeen thousand freemen of New York have been found "who have not bowed the knee to Baal." We have had the satisfaction of seeing a ticket, framed wholly of men professing those great and salutary principles of equal rights and equal laws which we have maintained so long through good report and evil report, selected and presented to the people, welcomed with enthusiasm, and supported at the polls by more than sixteen thousand votes. We have seen our party purged of [those] who filled it with contention, who seized hold of its organization, directed it to the furtherance of their own selfish purposes, brought scandal on the name of democrat, and finally landed us in a minority. With a party thus circumstanced, just cleared of its aristocratic incumbrances, and starting anew in the career of democratic principles, we have done well. We have formed a nucleus around which will soon gather the majority.

THE DEATH OF LOVEJOY
November 18, 1837

In 1836 the Reverend Elijah Lovejoy, editor of a temperance and anti-slavery newspaper in Saint Louis, moved it across the Mississippi River to Alton, Illinois, renaming it the Alton Observer. *There his press was destroyed several times by pro-slavery mobs, who on November 7, 1837, shot and killed him. The New York merchant Lewis Tappan was a founder of the American and Foreign Abolition Society, whose Ohio branch had supported Lovejoy's operation.*

We have received by this morning's mail a slip from the *Missouri Argus*, printed at St. Louis, containing intelligence which has filled us with surprise and horror. A mob, in making an attack upon an abolition press established at Alton, in Illinois, murdered two persons, wounded several others, and triumphing over the objects of their fury by this atrocious violence, destroyed the press which these men had defended at the cost of their blood and their lives.

We give the slip from the *Missouri Argus* as we received it, but we cannot forbear expressing in the strongest language our condemnation of the manner in which it speaks of this bloody event. The right to discuss freely and openly, by speech, by the pen, by the press, all political questions, and to examine and animadvert upon all political institutions, is a right so clear and certain, so interwoven with our other liberties, so necessary, in fact, to their existence, that without it we must fall at once into despotism or anarchy. To say that he who holds unpopular opinions must hold them at the peril of his life, and that, if he expresses them in public, he has only himself to blame if they who disagree with him should rise and put him to death, is to strike at all rights, all liberties, all protection of law, and to justify or extenuate all crimes.

We regard not this as a question connected with the abolition of slavery in the South, but as a question vital to the liberties of the entire Union. We may have different opinions concerning the propriety of the measures which the abolitionists desire to recommend, but we marvel and we deplore that any difference can exist as to the freedom of discussion. We are astonished that even a single journal can be found, so forgetful of its own rights, to say nothing of its duties to the community, as to countenance, even indirectly, the idea of muzzling the press by the fear of violence.

For our own part we approve, we applaud, we would consecrate, if we could, to universal honor, the conduct of those who bled in this gallant defence of the freedom of the press. Whether they erred or not in their opinions, they did not err in the conviction of their right as citizens of a democratic government, to express them, nor did they err in defending this right with an obstinacy which yielded only to death and the uttermost violence. With these remarks we lay before our readers the brief narrative with which we are furnished of this bloody outrage.

Office of the *Missouri Argus*,
St. Louis, Nov. 9, 1837.

Mob at Alton, Illinois—The Rev. E. P. Lovejoy killed, and his Abolition press destroyed!!

The infatuated editor of the *Alton Observer* has at length fallen a victim to his obstinacy in the cause of the Abolitionists. Disregarding the known and expressed sentiments of a large portion of the citizens of Alton, in relation to his incendiary publications, and, as it would seem, bent upon his own destruction, he formed the determination to establish another press for the propagation of the odious and disorganizing principles of Tappan and his eastern confederates. But his temerity has received an awful retribution from the hands of an infuriated and lawless mob.—The following particulars of the tragical outrage is [sic] contained in a postscript to the *Alton Telegraph* of the 8th inst.:

LAMENTABLE OCCURRENCE.—It is with the deepest regret that we stop the press in order to state that, at a late hour last night, an attack was made by a large number of persons on the warehouse of Messrs. Godfrey, Gilman & Co., for the purpose of destroying a press intended for the revival of the *Alton Observer,* which, shocking to relate, resulted in the death of two individuals—the Rev. E. P. Lovejoy, late editor of the Observer, and a man named—BISHOP. Seven others were wounded, two severely, and the others slightly. We can add no more at this time, than that the assailants succeeded in effecting their object.

MR. WEBSTER'S WIT
November 20, 1837

Massachusetts Senator Daniel Webster, like his fellow-Whig and rival, Henry Clay, often coveted the Presidency. The Italian Giambattista Casti (1724–1803) and the Frenchmen Paul Scarron (1610–1660) and Paul Louis Courier (1772–1825) were poets and political pamphleteers. John Ward Fenno, like his father before him, had edited the Federalist Gazette of the United States. *Austin was a prominent Boston Whig, as was Fenno. Levi Woodbury of Massachusetts was the Democratic Secretary of the Treasury under Jackson and Van Buren, and a strong supporter of the subtreasury plan.*

That men of some wit and humor have lived before the present age is not, we believe, contested. Not to speak of the Greeks and Romans, there is wit in Boccaccio, and wit in Ariosto, and wit in Casti. Witty was Rabelais, and witty was Scarron, and witty, in another way, was Paul Courier. There are things in Cervantes which will make the reader laugh in spite of himself; Molière has been known to coax a grin from the most splenetic, and some passages in Shakespeare no man can read or hear without acknowledging that they are quite droll.

These authors were very well in their time, and some of their works are passable even now. We must not speak disparagingly of what made our fathers and mothers laugh. It would be irreverent.

But the age for wit is decidedly the present age, and the wittiest man of the time, beyond all question is Mr. Webster, the gentleman spoken of last summer as the whig candidate for the Presidency. Wit has hitherto been only in the bud,—Mr. Webster is the full blown flower; wit has till now remained in the clumsy chrysalis state,— Mr. Webster is the broad-winged butterfly. We have had indeed the promise of wit, but Mr. Webster is its fulfilment and perfection.

On Tuesday evening last a brilliant festival was given at East Boston, by John W. Fenno, Esquire, in honor of the recent glorious whig victories in New-York. It was held in Maverick House, the largest hotel in the city, gorgeously illuminated for the occasion. The festivity is duly chronicled in the columns of the Boston *Centinel.* Elbridge G. Austin presided at the dinner, and at his right placed the witty Mr. Webster. Mr. Austin gave a toast in compliment to Mr.

Webster, and Mr. Webster responded. We give his speech in the words of the Boston *Centinel,* cautioning our readers to look well to their diaphragms, and to hold their sides with both hands, for the drollery of this Mr. Webster is irresistible.

"Mr. Webster rose and pronounced a most eloquent and agreeable speech, which occupied the profound attention of his audience for three quarters of an hour. He touched happily on the great questions before the nation, and enlarged on the glorious results of the present and past week, and although now and then he spoke in the most serious and impressive tones, yet at other times he was sportive and humorous to admiration, and [kept] the company in roars of laughter. He remarked pleasantly that at the approaching session, when he should go to Washington, and call on the President, he should probably have occasion to say—'How do you do, Mr. Van Buren? How go the times? What news from New York?'

"The effect of this frank colloquy was irresistible; the room was convulsed with laughter. It was all uttered with so much pleasantry and respect, and with such perfect good humor and *naiveté* of manner, that had Mr. Van Buren himself been present, he would have forgotten his own reverses, and joined heartily in the laughing all round the board. Mr. W. then added, that when he should see the Secretary of the Treasury, he might have occasion to say—'How is Mr. Woodbury? What are the exact financial statements and plans that you propose to report for our consideration? What do the people say of your *sub-Treasury system?*' These words were accompanied by appropriate action, and the effect was such as may be imagined, but cannot be described."

Ah the wag! We are tempted to say to Mr. Webster as the negro boy said to Garrick when the great actor had stolen into the back yard and was personating the cock-turkey for his entertainment: "Massa Webster, you make-a me die wid laffin."

"How do you do, Mr. Van Buren? What news from New York?" "How is Mr. Woodbury? What do the people say of your sub-Treasury system?" Is there any mortal whose gravity is stern enough to stand any thing so superlatively comic as this? Why, it would have drawn a horse laugh from the lungs of the weeping philosopher.

We take it upon us to say that there is not so irresistible a jest in the works of all the wits who ever wrote, from Lucian down to the last number of the Pickwick papers by Boz.

In his True History of New York, Diedrich Knickerbocker relates the fate of a fat little Schepen who died of a Burgomaster's joke. If a mere Burgomaster's joke, a hundred and fifty years since, when wit was in its infancy, could do such execution, what must be the effect of the joke of so accomplished a wag as Mr. Webster? We have, however, looked carefully over the account given by the Boston *Centinel,* and we find no return of the killed. How is this? Is there no concealment of the consequences of Mr. Webster's waggery?

SLAM, BANG, & CO.
December 8, 1837

According to Bryant's biographer Parke Godwin, "At this time the Democratic Party in New York numbered among its leaders gentlemen of the not euphonious names of Slamm, Bangs, and Ming, which, furnishing the opposition with a good deal of amusement, provoked this reply." In his Dunciad *(1728) Alexander Pope had satirized some of his contemporary writers. "Whilome" is an archaic term for "formerly."*

Short work is made in certain quarters with the President of the United States. Mr. Van Buren has issued his message, and the Whig journalists have answered it with the phrase "Slam, Bang & Co."

It is wonderful how much the Whigs make of the combination of these little words, Slam, Bang & Co. Those who are not in the habit of reading the journals of that party cannot imagine to what a degree they have illuminated and enlivened their columns by this happy invention. Slam, Bang & Co. stands them in place of wit—it stands them in place of reason—it is their resort in all emergencies—it is their answer to all arguments. With Slam, Bang & Co. they attack their enemies; with Slam, Bang & Co. they protect themselves against attacks; it is their weapon, offensive and defensive.

Pope, in his "Dunciad," speaks of certain affectors of obsolete phraseology

"Who live upon a *whilome* for a week."

But this is a trivial feat in comparison with what has been done by certain modern Whig journalists. We know one or two who have lived upon Slam, Bang & Co. for a twelvemonth. We know some who set up with Slam, Bang & Co. as their whole stock in trade, and have carried on a flourishing business of editorials on no other capital.

One of Shakespeare's clowns boasts of having invented an answer to fit every question—using always the simple phrase, O Lord, Sir. But the phrase Slam, Bang & Co. will not only answer but ask all questions; it will serve as a commentary to all texts, or a text to all commentaries; it will furnish matter for a squib of three lines, or may be beaten out into a political disquisition of two columns. Reader, if you are the conductor of a Whig newspaper, learn this mystery at once; it will save you all expense of thinking. If you wish to find fault with a public measure, or attack a public candidate, or censure a public document, or condemn a political doctrine, print the words Slam, Bang & Co., and it will answer your purpose without any further trouble. Pepper your articles well with Slam, Bang & Co., and you may be sure they will be swallowed.

Useful inventions are sometimes long in being adopted, but they are sure to make their way at last. One or two grave journals, which were slow in learning the trick of using Slam, Bang & Co., now begin to employ them with a praiseworthy diligence, and in time they may possibly be brought to utter them with as much flippancy as the inventors of the phrase.

But, after all, Slam, Bang & Co. is not the superlative degree. If you would goad your enemies with the utmost keenness of sarcasm, if you would wield the lightnings of the most brilliant wit, and crush, confound, and annihilate the Democracy with the thunders of the most potent argument, you must go a step farther and utter the magic words Slam, Bang, Ming & Co.

Ride and Tie
June 12, 1838

Joseph Andrews (1742) was British novelist Henry Fielding's first novel. Legend has it that in the thirteenth century angels transported the Holy House of the Virgin Mary from Nazareth to the central Italy town of Loretto, thus making it an object of pilgrimage. General William Henry Harrison, hero of the War of 1812 and briefly President before his death in 1841, had a farm in North Bend, Ohio. Martin Van Buren had gained the nickname "The Little Magician" as leader of the New York Democratic Party.

"Ride and Tie."—Fielding, in his Joseph Andrews, refers to a practice prevailing in England at that time, from which Messrs. Clay and Webster seem to have borrowed the hint for conducting the Presidential Campaign. It was called "Ride and Tie," and consisted in the following arrangement:

When two men were inclined to ride and had but one horse to ride upon, they drew lots who should first mount, and he that won proceeded onwards a certain distance, dismounted, tied his steed to a fence and then footed it away as fast as he could. In the meantime the other would come up, get into the saddle, pass his companion the like distance, tie his horse to the fence, and take his spell on "Shanks's mare." By these means they got on right merrily without overtiring themselves or their horse.

It is thus with the two great available candidates; they are both going the same pilgrimage to the White House of Loretto, and have but one horse between them. Mr. Webster mounts first, skirts along through highways and byeways, making speeches, skimming the cream of all the taverns by the road side, and eating his way to the White House, like a mouse in a cheese. Having done this, he dismounts, and with great magnanimity permits his rival, or associate, to scour the country, make speeches, eat dinners, and reap all the glory left behind by the "godlike man." This will do well enough until they come to the last stage of the pilgrimage, and the White House is full in view. In that crisis it is probable there will be some jockeying, and if this should be the case, we think Kentucky Lad will prove an overmatch for the Down Easter, though both have their eye-teeth cut. Should a third rider appear in the person of the "old Farmer of the North Bend," as seems not improbable, there is reason to believe there will be a great squabbling, and that the horse, like Aladdin's lamp, will become the prize of some arch "MAGICIAN."

NEW YORK BIRD CATCHERS
June 27, 1838

William Hone's Table Book *(1827–1838) was a compendium of "curious learning on miscellaneous subjects." The New York* Express, *started in 1836, was a prominent Whig paper. The Scottish reformer Frances ("Fanny") Wright visited New York several times and became a target of frequent journalistic taunts; John ("Jack") Cade, an Irish rebel, was killed in 1450 during a raid on London. A* kite *was both a bird and a person who preyed on others, or passed a bad check. Bryant's friend the tragedian Edwin Forrest was, in addition, a popular Democratic orator.*

In the first volume of Hone's Table Book is an engraving of a London Bird Catcher in the year 1827, and under it are printed the calls, or *jerks,* as they are technically called,—the peculiar sounds and articulations of voice, by which the people of this profession allure wild birds within their reach. Our readers will perhaps be amused with a sample of these *jerks.*

"Tuck—Tuck—Fear.
Tuck, Tuck, Fear—Ic, Ic, Ic.
Tuck, Tuck, Fear—Ic quake-e weet.
          (This is a *finished jerk.*)
Tolloc, Ejup, R—weet, weet, weet.
Tolloc, Tolloc, cha—Ic, Ic, Ic.
Lug, Lug, G—cha, cha.
Lug, Lug—Orchee, weet.

New York has its bird catchers as well as London. One of these goes under the name of the *Express.* He has established himself at the corner of Wall and Water streets, where he practises his jerks diligently every morning, for the catching of such foolish birds as he finds in that neighborhood. Here is a sample of his jerks:

"Slam Bang—Slam Bang—Slam Bang & Co.
Slam Bang—Slam Bang—Slam Bang Ming & Co.
                              (This is a *finished jerk.*)
Loco foco, Loco foco—I quacky, mob—Eli.
Loco foco, Loco foco—Eli Har's flour sotre—
   Flour riot, Flour riot.
Agrarians, Agrarians—Fanny Wright, Fanny Wright.
Levellers, Levellers, Levellers—Jack Cade, Jack Cade, &c. &c.

The birds allured and taken by means of these calls are chiefly of the kinds called gulls, boobies, noodles, doddrels, and geese, which do mostly affect maritime places.—Plenty of lame ducks, which haunt the neighborhood where the bird catcher has stationed himself, are also taken, being more easily made prisoners on account of their disabled state; and that fiercer fowl, that bird of prey, the kite, which delights to hover and swoop his victims in the atmosphere of Wall street, is often by these calls decoyed into the net. When caught, the birds are made to practise the jerks which we have given, until they become quite perfect in their parts, when you will hear the boobies, lame ducks, noodles, geese, kites, &c. call out "Slam Bang, Slam Bang—Jack Cade, Jack Cade," all at once, with astonishing energy and correctness of accent. A friend of ours heard the words Slam, Bang, Ming & Co. pronounced by one of these birds the other day in Broadway, not far from Leonard street, as distinctly as the bird catcher himself could have uttered it. A great black and white bird, called the *Journal of Commerce*, from its coming out every morning and hovering over the shipping, was once caught, and for two or three mornings together uttered the words Slam, Bang & Co. as distinctly as a human being, of which there are at present several living witnesses.

Those who are curious in these matters will find most of the jerks we have quoted in the leading article of the *Express* of yesterday morning, attacking Mr. Forrest's fourth of July oration before its delivery.

Democracy Is Inextinguishable
July 13, 1838

We hear that the ancient supporters of aristocratical principles in the city of Boston are horror-struck at having discovered the progress which democratic opinions are making among the younger class. Not a few intelligent, well educated, and full of the enthusiasm of youth and genius, have lately avowed their attachment to these opinions—an attachment arising from a strong conviction of their conformity with the great principles of benevolence and justice—an attachment, too, which they cherish the more ardently on account of the unjust prejudices of which they are the object. Some of these young men, we are told, are even the scions of families in which a belief of the necessity of a privileged class has been the hereditary creed. Their seniors deplore the delusion into which they have fallen, and reflect with alarm on the danger of their becoming the ancestors of a posterity of loco focos.

We say to these young men, *macte virtute*! go on in the noble career on which you have entered—pursue it with all the ardor of your age, while yet your hopes are fresh, your candor unwarped, your generous feelings unsoured by wrongs from your fellow men, the impulses of your philanthropy unchecked by the whispers of private interest, We know well how quickly the blossoms of human virtue wither. We have seen in more than one instance the politician who began his career with the most fervent and apparently disinterested devotion to the principles of democratic liberty, gradually become changed into the selfish intriguer, in whose mouth the phrases of his early creed are mere cant, and who lends his powers to assist in encroachments upon the rights which he formerly vindicated. We have seen others treating the doctrines of equal rights which they formerly professed, as an abstract theory, beautiful in itself, a pardonable dream of young men, but not reducible to practice. We have seen others, democrats at one time of their life, becoming aristocrats by the mere possession of riches, which is as fatal a corruption of political as of personal morals.

If there were not in the doctrines of democracy something which commends them to the disinterested reason of mankind, to the conscience, and the uncorrupted sense of justice, it must have become extinct ere this, on account of the multitude of its champions whom ambition and interest and misanthropy are perpetually taking from its side to swell the ranks of its enemies. They depart, and their places are immediately supplied by men whose opinions were formed aloof from those corrupting influences. It is this perpetual supply of strength which renders democracy inextinguishable while thought and the expression of thought are free, and which, under institutions like ours, must render it almost always victorious in the contest with its enemies.

Democratic Simplicity
August 7, 1838

Victoria had succeeded to the British throne the previous year. The Virginia Congressman Andrew Stevenson was United States minister to Great Britain from 1834 to 1841. Appearing at the French court as the American diplomatic agent in 1778, Benjamin Franklin took off his wig and donned a coonskin cap, endearing him to the people as personifying Jean-Jacques Rousseau's "noble savage" and the American Revolutionary cause. Prince Pál Antal Esterházy was a wealthy and distinguished Austrian diplomat; Marshal Jean de Dieu Soult had been one of Napoleon's chief lieutenants.

The following article appears in the Baltimore *American*:

> "Fault has frequently been found with the appearance made by our Ministers at foreign courts, and blame has often been attached to the individual representing our country, for the want of a proper degree of display. The plain truth of the matter is, that our diplomatists are so miserably paid that they cannot afford to make the appearance which belongs to their station. It has been remarked that the American minister rode at the late coronation of the Queen of England, in a plain, very plain two horse carriage, and that the plainness of the equipage had attracted general observation. How could it be otherwise, when that dignitary receives but $9000, or less than two thousand sterling a year, independently of his outfit, which is as much more for the first year, and is brought in contact with persons the incomes of some of whom are from one to two hundred times as great. We neither desire nor expect to see the representatives of our Republic able to cope with such persons in point of expense, but they might at least be enabled to appear as private gentlemen of moderate fortune. . . . The salaries of our diplomatists should be so graduated as to enable them to maintain at least the expense incident to their dignity at the Court near which they are stationed."

If fault has been found with the unostentatious appearance of our ministers abroad, the complaint appears to us a very idle one. Such an appearance is certainly most comfortable to the simplicity of our government. We do not despatch agents to the European courts to vie in their mode of living with the foreign nobility or the ambassadors of crowned heads.

Let the minister of a monarchical or aristocratical form of government dazzle all eyes, if he will, with magnificent carriages, trains of liveried servants, costly entertainments, splendid dresses. These things in him are proper perhaps—they certainly harmonize with the character of his government, one of the great elements of which is pomp and display.

But the representative of a plain, simple, economical government like ours, a government which rejects show and ceremony, ought, we think, to appear with a corresponding simplicity abroad—at least, if his tastes be otherwise, his own government ought not, surely, to furnish him with the means of departing from that simplicity. If Mr. Stevenson's equipage was the plainest that was seen at the coronation of the Queen of England, there was an admirable propriety in its being so—he represented the plainest government.

The Baltimore print appears to suppose, that display on the part of our ministers is necessary to maintain the dignity of the nation abroad. We are of opinion that the dignity of the nation abroad is best maintained by its behaviour at home, and by the character and talents of those that represent it in foreign countries. When Franklin appeared at the brilliant court of Louis the Sixteenth, was he, or the youthful and gallant republic whose cause he pleaded, less regarded or less honored, on account of the extreme plainness with which the philosopher presented himself?

At the late coronation of the British Queen, when equipage after equipage passed by, each more gorgeous than the last—a procession of the proudest and richest peerage of the world, and of the representatives of the proudest and most puissant monarchs—a train never perhaps equalled in magnificence—who was it that bore away the palm of dignity? On whom were the regards of the admiring multitude fixed, and whose name was on their tongues, when they broke into involuntary cheers? Was it the Prince Esterhazy with his diamonds? his horses, and their glittering trappings? his lackeys, and their gorgeous livery? By no means.

On the contrary, the eyes of all were attracted and their cheers called forth by a war-worn, weather-beaten man who came in an equipage comparatively plain—by Marshal Soult, already eminent in history, and renowned both as a statesman and a warrior. It was to the man and not to the equipage that this honor was paid; it was in the man and not in his carriage and servants that the essential dignity was acknowledged to reside.

It will be time enough to say that the compensation we allow our ministers to foreign countries is inadequate when the offer of the appointment will not command the services which are wanted. At present there appears to be no difficulty on that score. The emoluments or the honor of the post, one or the other, are in the eyes of our ablest men a sufficient recompense for its labours. Increase the salary and you only increase the eagerness of intrigue and the opportunity of corruption.

Temperance Legislation
November 10, 1838

In Bryant's boyhood public occasions such as militia musters, and even the installation of a new clergyman, were often accompanied by the consumption of large quantities of rum. His reaction here to the 1838 Massachusetts law seems to anticipate by nearly a century the fate of Prohibition in the country as a whole.

A blacksmith attempting, with his pincers and sledge hammer, to improve the delicate mechanism of a watch, is no unapt type of the legislature of Massachusetts interfering in the temperance question. Scarcely any folly, however, can be committed in legislation which shall not find its ready apologists. The absurd sumptuary law passed last winter by the legislature of Massachusetts, the fifteen gallon law, as it is called, has been defended in some of the public journals here, and it is not improbable that our own legislature may be asked next winter to transcribe it into the New York statute book.

Nothing could be more worthy of admiration and respect than the change of habits in regard to the consumption of intoxicating liquors which has lately taken place in New England. From a race of tiplers and hard drinkers, the people of that region have become in the short space of ten years one of the most temperate races of men on the entire globe. The deplorable vice, the sin against man's physical and moral nature, which annually swept to the grave, or gave over to infamy, so many young men, the flower of the rising generation, is almost hunted out of society, and obliged to hide itself in holes and corners.

All this was the fruit of voluntary effort, without any aid from the awkward processes of legislation. Indeed, if the laws and the lawmakers had interfered in the matter, it is likely that the reformation would never have taken place. The community would not have been driven to be virtuous. Compulsion on the one side would have produced resistance on the other; and the question whether it was better to be a nation of sober men or a nation of drunkards would have been forgotten in the question of the propriety and justice of the laws enacted. On the contrary, the reform which had taken place was the sole effect of persuasion—of appeals to reason and conscience. The statistics of drunkenness were collected, its deplorable consequences were set down in particulars and numbers, like the muster roll of a regiment—a frightful catalogue of crimes, diseases, poverty and death; the people became convinced that a reform was indispensable, and by a great moral effort they broke loose from the slavery of a pernicious habit. Individual exceptions there might be to the general reform of manners; but they were persons whose way of life had been formed under the ancient customs of the country, which had now grown obsolete. The new generation were growing up a race of water drinkers.

The legislature of Massachusetts, at this stage of the matter, thought proper to intermeddle. The bull could no longer be restrained from entering the china shop.— Instead of leaving the matter in the hands of public opinion, which began the reform, and brought it to so beautiful and happy a conclusion, they resolved to take it into the hands of the law. They passed a statute which showed neither a regard for individual rights, nor any knowledge of the motives of human action. They ordained that no sale should be made of wines and spirits in smaller quantities than fifteen gallons at a time—thus making an invidious distinction between different classes of men, allowing him who could command the cash or credit to purchase fifteen gallons of spirits to indulge his appetite without limit, while he who has the means of purchasing only a gill or a quart is compelled to abstinence. This nonsensical law, we fear, is the first symptom of a reaction. Already has it brought not a little scandal on the friends of abstinence by its manifest injustice. The best that can be said for it is, that it is unnecessary, and unnecessary laws are always mischievous. When matters of this kind are regulated by law, public opinion goes to sleep, under an idea that the thing is cared for, and that voluntary effort is no longer necessary. The best mode to prevent the mischief is for the legislature of Massachusetts to repeal the obnoxious law without delay.

OLD vs. NEW FEDERALISTS
November 22, 1838

Daniel Webster, the "old gentleman," had begun his political career as a Federalist in the party of Washington and Hamilton, and in opposition to the high tariff forces led by Henry Clay. But when Clay became leader of the new Whig Party in the late 1830s and early 1840s, a party largely made up of conservative former Democrats, Webster joined the new coalition. The Madisonian, *founded at Washington in 1837 in opposition to Van Buren by disgruntled Democrats, soon became a Whig organ. The New York* American *(c1820–1845), edited earlier by Bryant's friend and literary collaborator Gulian Verplanck and later by Charles King, subsequently president of Columbia College, was a respected adversary of Bryant's newspaper. James Tallmadge was a former congressman and lieutenant governor of New York and an anti-slavery advocate. During the War of 1812 so many American prisoners died under mistreatment in the British prison on Dartmoor that after the peace an Anglo-American commission compensated their families. The* Natural History of Selborne *(1789) by Gilbert White is a classic account of the habits of birds and animals near his home in southern England.*

A great scandal has recently taken place in a certain political party. The adopted son who was a few months since installed in the whig family, with such ceremonies of welcome and rejoicing, has lately taken to horsewhipping the old gentleman every morning before breakfast, by way of procuring an appetite. We had thoughts of addressing a remonstrance to the young fellow on the subject of this irreverent and parricidal amusement, but knowing that the whigs and conservatives never take our advice, we abstained.

The conservatives having become regular members of the whig party, are determined to have every thing their own way. With the help of such of their friends as deserted from the democratic ranks a few years before them, they lord it in high style over the ancient, veteran, immemorial members of the party they have joined. They even go so far as to revile them for being "old federalists," as if it were not better to be old federalists than new federalists.

The old federalists numbered many men of extraordinary talent, energy and honor of character. Their doctrines were erroneous and dangerous, but they were maintained with frankness and boldness. That distrust of the people which they really felt they freely proclaimed. The new federalists are of a different stamp; subtle, intriguing, indirect, pretending a respect for the people at the same time they are pursuing measures which strike at the root of popular rights, and if carried out, would transform our democratic government into an oligarchy of capitalism. We have had too much of this leaven in our state politics—too much of it in our own party. These new federalists, under the name of democrats, corrupted the course of our state legislation, brought scandal on the cause we support, betrayed the party into improper measures, and lost us the ascendancy in the State. That they have now annexed themselves to the whig party is occasion for rejoicing. We shall be delivered from their intrigues, and shall be able to bring the practices of the democratic party to conform rigidly to its doctrines.

Hear how the conservative print, the *Madisonian*, now received into full fellowship with the whig party, taunts the *American*, a journal which represents the opinions of the old federalists:

> "THE NEW YORK AMERICAN.—Now that the election has terminated in the success of the anti-Sub Treasury party, this paper, which professes to be opposed to the administration, has undertaken to proscribe Mr. Tallmadge, to whom the opposition are mainly indebted for their overwhelming majorities."
>
> "We are not surprised at this, nor do we regret it. It is the natural ebullition of its malignant fanaticism, ultra federalism, abolitionism, and its organic disease of impracticability. We do not regret it, because it will hasten the termination of what little remnant of political influ-

ence that paper before possessed. It will bring it to its proper level of political contempt," &c.

"While on the subject of reminiscences of the past, it might as well have extended its recollection to the Dartmoor prison massacre, and refreshed itself with a home example of the pertinency and propriety of reminiscences. If it has discovered one instance of 'misfortune, synonymous with crime,' it would then have discovered another, synonymous with inhumanity and treason. But we leave it to the mercy and justice of its city contemporaries."

WHITE, in his Natural History of Selborne, gives an account of a cuckoo, hatched in the nest of a titlark where the egg had been laid by the parent bird, which was very fierce and pugnacious; and having shoved out all the young titlarks, was making perpetual and clamorous demands on the old one for provisions. The conservatives and new federalists are expert imitators of the cuckoo. They are fierce and pugnacious; they shove out all the brood of titlarks, the true and ancient possessors, with Daniel Webster at their head, and clamour for every thing the officious dam can provide. The new federalists are adherents of Henry Clay, himself formerly a democrat, and are determined to force the party to support Mr. Tallmadge as Senator in Congress from this State. They have acquired the entire ascendancy in the whig party in this State, and struggle as violently as they may, the older members must submit to their domination.

DEFENSE OF JACKSON AGAINST CRITICISMS
December 3, 1838

"Veto" was Bryant's young friend and occasional contributor to the Evening Post *Theodore Sedgwick III (1811–1859). In the November 1838 gubernatorial election the Whig candidate William H. Seward had defeated the Democratic incumbent William L. Marcy by ten thousand votes. Zeno was the Cypriot founder in the fourth century B.C. of the Stoic school of philosophy.*

An article from our correspondent "Veto" will be found below, which we give precisely as we received it, because it is drawn up in a sincere and friendly spirit, and because we were not willing, by any pruning of our own, to diminish the interest with which it will be read. At the same time we dissent from many of its positions.

That the defeat of the democratic party in New York is an overbalance for the successes which that party have obtained elsewhere in the recent elections, is, we think, a great mistake. Our successes in Maine, in Ohio, in Maryland, in Delaware, and we may add New Jersey, are far more than a compensation for the reverse we have met with in New York, when we consider that the whig majority has been considerably diminished from what it was in the election of 1837.

The faults of General Jackson's character and course are also overstated by our correspondent. Faults he had undoubtedly—such faults as often belong to a generous, ardent and sincere nature—such weeds as grow in a rich soil. He was hasty in his temper, and though generally sagacious in his estimate of human character, was led by the warmth of his friendships into some great mistakes, and appointed men in several instances to places for which they were quite unf[i]t. Notwithstanding this, he was precisely the man for the period in which he filled the Presidenti[a]l chair, and well and nobly did he fulfil the duty which the times demanded of him. If he was brought into collision with the mercantile class, it was more their fault than his. No man, even the most discreet and prudent, could, under the same circumstances, have done his duty without exasperating them against him. The immediate and apparent interests, though not the permanent and true interests of trade, were involved in the continuance of the national bank, and as men are apt to look principally to the interests and convenience of the moment, it was impossible to attack the national bank without offending the mercantile class. Artful party leaders exaggerated the cause of offence, until the commercial class were almost entirely alienated from the administration. This, and not the haste of General Jackson's temper, is the true cause. Had Zeno himself been president, the result would have been the same.

There are one or two other passages in the article of "Veto" on which we might advert, but we prefer submitting it to the judgment of our readers.

Sensitiveness to Foreign Opinion
January 11, 1839

Returning in 1833 from a seven-year residence in Europe, the novelist James Fenimore Cooper criticized in his fiction what he thought to be shortcomings in American society. In Homeward Bound *and* Home as Found, *both published in 1838, he was especially critical of journalistic practices, bringing repeated attacks upon him for which he took their publishers to court. Bryant wrote later that, although he had thought "Leviathan is not so [easily] tamed," nevertheless Cooper "put a hook into the nose of this huge monster, wallowing in his inky pool and bespattering the passerby: he dragged him to the land and made him tractable" by winning suit after suit for libel.*

Cooper's last work, "Home as Found," has been fiercely attacked, in more than one quarter, for its supposed tendency to convey to the people of other countries a bad idea of our national character. Without staying to examine whether all Mr. Cooper's animadversions on American manners are perfectly just, we seize the occasion to protest against this excessive sensibility to the opinion of other nations. It is no matter what they think of us. We constitute a community large enough to form a great moral tribunal for the trial of any question which may arise among ourselves. There is no occasion for this perpetual appeal to the opinions of Europe. We are competent to apply the rules of right and wrong boldly and firmly, without asking in what light the superior judgment of the Old World may regard our decisions.

It has been said of Americans that they are vainglorious, boastful, fond of talking of the greatness and the advantages of their country, and of the excellence of their national character. They have this foible in common with other nations; but they have another habit which shows that, with all their national vanity, they are not so confident of their own greatness, or of their own capacity to estimate it properly, as their boasts would imply. They are perpetually asking, What do they think of us in Europe? How are we regarded abroad? If a foreigner publishes an account of his travels in this country, we are instantly on the alert to know what notion of our character he has communicated to his countrymen; if an American author publishes a book, we are eager to know how it is received abroad, that we may know how to judge it ourselves. So far has this humor been carried that we have seen an extract, from a third- or fourth-rate critical work in England, condemning some American work, copied into all our newspapers one after another, as if it determined the character of the work beyond appeal or question.

For our part, we admire and honor a fearless accuser of the faults of so thin-skinned a nation as ours, always supposing him to be sincere and well-intentioned. He may be certain that where he has sowed animadversion he will reap an abundant harvest of censure and obloquy. We will have one consolation, however, that if his book be written with ability it will be read; that the attacks which are made upon it will draw it to the public attention; and that it may thus do good even to those who recalcitrate most violently against it.

If every man who writes a book, instead of asking himself the question what good it will do at home, were first held to inquire what notions it conveys of Americans to persons abroad, we should pull the sinews out of our literature. There is much want of free-speaking as things stand at present, but this rule will abolish it altogether. It is bad enough to stand in fear of public opinion at home, but, if we are to superadd the fear of public opinion abroad, we submit to a double despotism. Great reformers, preachers of righteousness, eminent satirists in different ages of the world—did they, before entering on the work they were appointed to do, ask what other nations might think of their countrymen if they gave utterance to the voice of salutary reproof?

THE DEATH OF WILLIAM LEGGETT
May 30, 1839

Leggett had been Bryant's associate on the Evening Post *from 1829 to 1836. In verses published in the* Democratic Review *the following November, Bryant wrote of his friend, "The words of fire that from his pen / Were flung upon the fervid page / Still move, still shake the hearts of men, / Amid a cold and coward age."*

It is with sorrow that we announce the death of William Leggett, formerly one of the editors and proprietors of this paper.— He expired at his residence in New Rochelle at nine o'clock last evening, in the thirty-ninth year of his age.

As a political writer, Mr. Leggett attained, within a brief period, a high rank and an extensive and enviable reputation. He wrote with great fluency and extraordinary vigor; he saw the strong points of a question at a glance, and had the skill to place them before his readers with a force, clearness and amplitude of statement rarely to be found in the writings of any journalist that ever lived. When he became warmed with his subject, which was not unfrequently the case, his discussions had all the stirring power of extemporaneous eloquence.

His fine endowments he wielded for worthy purposes. He espoused the cause of the largest liberty and the most comprehensive equality of rights among the human race, and warred against those principles which inculcate distrust of the people, and those schemes of legislation which tend to create an artificial inequality in the conditions of men. He was wholly free—and, in this respect his example ought to be held up to journalists as a model to contemplate and copy—he was wholly free from the besetting sin of their profession, a mercenary and time-serving disposition. He was a sincere lover and follower of truth, and never allowed any of those specious reasons for inconsistency, which disguise themselves under the name of expediency, to seduce him for a moment from the support of the opinions which he deemed right, and the measures which he was convinced were just. What he would not yield to the dictates of interest he was still less disposed to yield to the suggestions of fear.

We sorrow that such a man, so clear-sighted, strong minded and magnanimous has passed away, and that his aid is no more to be given in the conflict which truth and liberty maintain with their numerous and powerful enemies. . . .

Public Improvements
June 5, 1839

In 1835 work had been begun by the New York and Erie Railroad Company, enfranchised by the State, on a line to connect the mouth of the Hudson River with the Great Lakes region.

The *American* of last evening seeks to create the impression that the Evening Post is hostile to rail-roads and canals. In some journals we might forgive such an attack on account of the confusion of ideas under which the writers of political paragraphs often labour, but in the *American* it is disingenuous.

The *American* expatiates grandiloquently on the benefits of such undertakings, the immense amount of the products they bring to a speedy market, the quantities of merchandize they scatter in return over the land, the industry they animate and reward, and the augmentation they give to the value of real estate. All this is very fine, and very true; we gainsay it not, we extenuate it not. Canals and rail-roads are excellent things wherever the transportation of goods or the conveyance of passengers will pay for their construction. The question is, however, in what manner they shall be constructed, and this question the *American* does not touch or even approach.

Suppose a project were to be laid before the legislature of this state to fit out a flotilla of ships, at the public expense, for making voyages to the northwest coast, and bringing home cargoes of whale oil and spermaceti. Suppose the Evening Post should object to such a violation of the true principles of legislation. Would it be any answer to our objections to say that whale oil and spermaceti are indispensable articles, that when kindled in lamps and candle-sticks they light our streets and dwellings at night, that they shed their rays on the toils of the artizan and the studies of the scholar, and that without them we should be reduced to gas and tallow candles? A very fine declamation could be composed on the subject, but, like the declamation of the *American* about internal improvements, it would be nothing to the purpose. The real objection would not be touched; which is, that the fitting out of vessels at the expense of the state is not the proper way to supply the community with oil and spermaceti.

There is no more controversy concerning the convenience and utility of canals and rail-roads, than concerning the utility and convenience of light, but it does not follow because we admit their advantages, that we are therefore ready to consent to their construction on the worst possible system. Such a system we hold their construction by the state to be—the most wasteful, the most improvident, the most likely to produce signal failures, the most exposed to be managed by intrigue and corrupt bargaining, and the most opposite in spirit to our democratic institutions. These are the objections to the execution of such enterprises by the government of the state, and these the *American* passes by, to declaim in general terms on the advantages of rail-roads and canals.

Doubtless the time is not far distant when the whole surface of this state, as it becomes populous and assiduously cultivated, will be intersected with rail-roads meeting at all the considerable towns like threads at the knots of a net. If one of them is to be undertaken by the state government there is no reason why the rest should not be. The project of the New York and Erie rail-road, which last winter was so zealously urged upon the state, would naturally draw after it this mighty scheme with all its train of commissioners, superintendents, agents and clerks, its jobs contracts—a vast array of officers, employments and emoluments to be dispensed among partisans and favorites.

The utility of highways and bridges is questioned by nobody, yet our political system jealously excludes the state government from directing their construction. They are built by the towns and counties which have occasion for them, the inhabitants of which are willing to assume the expense and watch with the greatest attention the economical expenditure of the funds they have provided. This arrangement, which refers these works to the judgment and direction of the smallest divisions of the community, has been looked upon as an admirable peculiarity in our institutions, and as in perfect harmony with the general spirit. What would be thought of a proposition to surrender this power, so long exercised by the towns and counties, to the state government? Would it not be instantly condemned on all sides as a plain departure from the democratic principle—as a scheme to bestow upon public officers the power and consequence which it would subtract from the people, as opening a door to waste, negligence, extravagant projects, jobbing and corruption? Yet there is no difference, that we can see, between such a proposal, and the proposal to construct our rail-roads at the expense of the state.

We must make our choice between the method of building our rail-roads as we do our highways and bridges, or leave them to private enterprise altogether. Their construction under the direction and at the expense of the state government is exposed to objections which in our opinion are altogether insuperable.

The Plea of the General Good
June 6, 1839

The first great National Road was begun under federal government contract in 1815 to connect the East Coast with the Mississippi Valley, from Maryland to Missouri. The initial section was completed from Cumberland, Maryland, to Wheeling, [later West] Virginia, in 1818. Largely through the influence of Henry Clay, by 1833 it had crossed Ohio. By that time, the earlier section was badly in need of repair.

The plea of the general good has been advanced by the New York *American* in favor of making railways under the direction and superintendence of the state government. This pretext of the general good has been used as the apology of every kind of misgovernment, and every abuse of legislation. No change in the laws was ever yet made for the worse, without the general good being urged as the motive. No innovation upon the rights of the mass was ever made but upon considerations connected with the public good. No speculator, or projector, or seeker of jobs, ever approached Congress or a state legislature to request to be employed and paid, without the pretence of a concern for the general good upon his lips.

Railways and canals contribute to the general good, but it does not therefore follow that they must be made by the state. Commerce is for the general good, but it does not follow that the state is to fit our packets to trade with Europe, or purchase teams and wagons to carry on a land intercourse with Pennsylvania and Ohio. The exercise of a thousand arts, trades and professions, is for the general good, but it is not therefore to be inferred that the state is to provide the community with artizans and tradesmen. We want milk for our coffee every morning, but it is not the business of the government to establish dairies.

Our great national roads have been, for the most part, signal examples of the wastefulness of this kind of government expenditure. The Cumberland road, for instance, has swallowed up one vast appropriation after another, yet it has been for the greater part of its existence in a state of scandalous disrepair. We remember that in 1832, travelling in Maryland, we came upon this road. Our way had been along a road kept in excellent order by a turnpike company, but the moment we arrived at this great national work, upon which such enormous sums had been expended, every thing bore witness to the difference between a public and a voluntary enterprise. The road was full of inequalities, loose stones, sloughs, and gullies formed by the rains. Yet there were at the same time tokens of the cost at which the road had been constructed, in the bridges of hewn stone, often out of repair it is true, but built for the most part in a most ostentatious style of masonry.

The negligent and improvident execution of these works by the government is not the only nor the principal reason why, in the case of highways and bridges, they have been made matters of local regulation. By placing them under the direction and care of government, the effect is to accumulate power and influence in the hands of a few, and to remove their superintendence to a distance from the people. By committing them to the direction of the smaller divisions of the community, on the other hand, the power is kept nearer to the people, where they can watch, check, control, or resume it at their pleasure. The first method is contrary to the general spirit of our political institutions, which are jealous of the accumulation of power and influence. The second is in perfect accordance with it, since it retains the power among those from whom it is derived.

If this system of employing the state government to project, execute and keep in repair the railways with which our state is to be traversed, goes into effect, who will direct and control them? Who will mark out the channels of communication for us across our broad and fertile country? Not the people certainly—neither they, nor yet the projectors of voluntary enterprises set on foot to meet the wants of the people. On the contrary, the routes of our rail roads will be traced by selfish schemers, and speculators, by men who have lands to sell or who want profitable contracts; our plans of internal improvement will be decided in the lobbies of the capitol, and executed by lobby members or their principals; the legislative floor will be a perpetual theatre of intrigue and bargains, and the people will be in effect as much excluded from any agency in the matter, as if it was no concern of theirs.

A Reply to Attacks
June 7, 1839

The German poet Gottfried August Bürger (1747–1794) was also a satirical journalist. The New York Gazette and General Advertiser *was a commercial newspaper supporting the Whig Party. The former Democratic—now Whig— Congressman from Virginia, Henry A. Wise, was a rather intemperate defender of slavery. Jean Baptiste Louis Gresset (1709–1777), French poet and playwright, published* Vert-Vert, Histoire d'un perroquet de Nevers, *the tale of a malicious and indiscreet parrot, in 1734.* Vert *(green) also has the connotation in literature of "spicy" or "risky." Bryant's anecdote of the Naples shoemaker reminds us that he had passed nearly a month in that city in 1835 with his family.*

We are sometimes inquired of why we do not oftener answer the attacks so frequently made upon the EVENING POST in other journals. Bürger, the German poet, shall answer for us:

> "A plain man," says Bürger, "on a fine morning, passed in his walk the door of an ale-house. A dog, whose collar was hung round with little bells, sprung out, tinkling his bells and barking at him with the greatest fury. The plain man paid him no attention, and, without even lifting his cane at the animal, walked quietly away from the noise. The next moment a well-dressed young man passed the ale-house; the dog was out again in an instant; the bells tinkled and the barking was terrible. The young man was nettled, and thought to quiet the cur by stoning him; but the dog growled furiously at every stone that was thrown, and, coming nearer, barking louder than ever, took liberties with the flap of the young fellow's coat, and finally began to snap at his legs. Half a dozen other dogs, roused by the yelping of their brother, joined in the chorus; windows were thrown up, doors were opened on every side, the business of the neighborhood was suspended to look at the battle, and the boys clapped their hands and shouted to encourage the combatants, till the young man was ready to sink into the earth with shame."

Besides the inconveniences so well set forth by Bürger, we have another reason for not indulging very deeply in these quarrels with newspapers. We must have time for better things. There are graver questions to be settled than those which are generally raised by the journalists who attack us. When we find any of their arguments worth answering, we are not backward to engage in controversy; when we find a misrepresentation which is likely to do mischief if not corrected, we correct it; but to mere scolding we are quite indifferent. It is evident that, if we were to answer every assault of this kind, we should be obliged to give up our whole time and the whole space of our columns to the answers we might make. There are two evening papers, and twice as many morning papers, in this city belonging to the Whig party; and we have sometimes had all of them, or nearly all, in full cry upon us at once, to say nothing of the attacks made upon us by the journals we receive by the mails.

There are a few prints which would be sadly puzzled for matter out of which to concoct the excellent speculations with which they daily edify their readers were it not for the EVENING POST. But for the opportunity afforded them by our journal, their facility of abuse might unfortunately be lost for want of exercise. To such the EVENING POST is their stock in trade, the capital with which they carry on business. The *New York Gazette*, we believe, is one of that class. We do not often see the paper, by reason of which we doubtless escape many sleepless nights; but we have "good-natured friends" who often insist upon telling us how cruelly we are cut up in it. The *New*

York Gazette has not been, we believe, once alluded to, either for good or for evil, in the EVENING POST for two years past or more, until the other day a Southern correspondent deprecated its defence of Southern rights as doing more harm than good; yet we hear that it rails at us daily with the eloquence of ten fish-women.

There is an honest shoemaker living on the Mergellina, at Naples, on the right hand as you go toward Pozzuoli, whose little dog comes out every morning and barks at Vesuvius.

Some of the prints to which we refer occasionally indulge in personal allusions to persons concerned, or supposed to be concerned, in the management of this paper. With such prints it is manifest we cannot enter into controversy.

Three or four of the New York daily journals, among which are the *Courier* and *Gazette*, have adopted a style of political writing which seems to be copied from the speeches of Mr. Wise and his imitators. It consists of running off at the end of the quill a set of opprobrious epithets which answer for all occasions. These words are profligacy, hypocrisy, perjury, robbery, rascality, and other names of vices and crimes that end in *y*—meanness, obsequiousness, perverseness, and the names of all other bad qualities that end in *ness*—corruption, degradation, assassination, and every name of evil that ends in *tion*, with every other possible epithet of vituperation, of whatever ending, are put together, like pieces of colored glass into a kaleidoscope, and shaken up into as many different forms as they will make. Arithmeticians can tell by calculation into how many thousand different forms of abuse a hundred different epithets may be combined. With these presses, which turn out railing accusations to order, as a button-machine turns out buttons, it is evident that it would be folly to engage in dispute. In the words of Pope,

"We wage no war with Bedlam,"

we cannot dispute with those who never reason.

It is a great mistake in these writers to suppose that calling names without discrimination or selection is strong writing. The sing-song of abuse is as easily learned as any other sing-song. A parrot can be taught to curse and swear as easily as to say "Pretty Poll." Gresset, in his work entitled "Vert-Vert," gives the history of one of these birds who was educated in a nunnery, and who said his *Ave Maria* and his *Pater Noster* with an appearance of devotion which edified everybody. The inmates of a distant convent were desirous to see the wonderful parrot, and, accordingly, he was sent to them on board a coasting schooner. But during the voyage the bird learned other accomplishments, and on his arrival the good sisters were struck with horror on hearing him swear like a boatswain.

Politics and Literature
June 28, 1839

In 1836 British poet Walter Savage Landor, whom Bryant had met at Florence in 1834, prefaced the second volume of his Pericles and Aspasia *with an ode to Andrew Jackson. The Italian journalist and politician Antonio Gallenga had been exiled in 1830. Adopting the name Luigi Mariotti, he settled in London, where he taught Italian at University College. Bryant's friend the historian George Bancroft was an active Democrat.*

There are some indications that the literature of this country will have ere long to contend with a new obstruction, and a new cause of debasement, the intrusion of party prejudice. We are not by any means of those who desire that there should be no connection between literature and politics in the nobler sense of the latter term. The exposition of great political truths, and the consideration of their application to legislation and government are tasks worthy to engage minds of the highest culture and the noblest intellectual endowments. We hope yet to see a literature tinctured throughout its whole essence with the free principles of our institutions—a democratic literature—arise in our land and utter itself to all parts of the earth where our language is spoken or read.

But we refer now to the wretched illiberality of spirit which will not see any literary merit in the writings of a political adversary, but on the contrary seeks to blast the fame and undervalue the writings of men whose genius fair criticism cannot question.

Something of this disposition, unless it be watched and checked, will grow up in all parties—it is the natural fruit of the dislike with which [two] great divisions arrayed in fierce mutual opposition regard each other. Among the democratic party in this country, however, it can hardly be said to have had an existence. The greater number of distinguished authors and scholars have hitherto been found on the other side of the question, among those who are friendly to artificial distinctions among men, and who regard the people with distrust. There have been no symptoms of a desire in the democratic party to detract from the honors to which these men might fairly lay claim.—Their literary distinction was freely and cheerfully allowed. The time has now arrived when the democratic party numbers among its active supporters many persons of unquestionable and extraordinary merit as authors. A disposition to deny their merit and to lessen their reputation begins to manifest itself in their political adversaries. We do not mean to be understood—we know very well that this disposition is not yet universal, that there are noble exceptions to it—that there are yet readers and writers who can award the meed of deserved praise even to authors who do not vote as they do—but the evil of which we speak is a growing one, and instances of illiberality of literary judgment in consequence of political prejudices occur more and more frequently. Every body remembers with what ferocity the literary character of Cooper was assailed immediately after he published a political pamphlet. The other day a work of modern English literature was mutilated in its republication here by the booksellers—the dedication to General Jackson was omitted from Landor's Pericles and Aspasia; a noble tribute from a man of genius to a great captain and illustrious statesman was suppressed, in compliment to the prejudices of whig readers. In the last number of the North American Review in an article written by a learned and eloquent foreigner, Mariotti, an Italian exile, the writer had inserted a compliment to our distinguished historian Bancroft, and the editor of the review struck it out. The indulgence of such narrow prejudices, the practice of such suppressions and mutilations, this whig censorship of the press, cannot but degrade and corrupt the literature on which they are exercised, cannot but tend to crush its naturally frank and magnanimous spirit and discourage those who make it their pursuit. We have thought it necessary on our part to enter an early and earnest protest against this wretched illiberality, and to call upon the community to prevent its growth, by turning against it the power to which all other power in this country yields, that of public opinion.

Banking Regulation
July 9, 1839

If the legislature of the state of New York and those of the other states, were solicited to grant to certain petitioners the exclusive right of purchasing and selling the harvests of the earth and the herds of the pastures, the petitioners would ask in vain. The selfishness of the demand would be too barefaced; the violation of natural equality would be too evident and enormous to be favored even by those who might see their own profit in it. The petition would be unceremoniously rejected; the devil would be kicked out of doors for coming with his long tail and cloven foot, and without his mask.

But who does not see that every provision of law which tends to confine the trade in money, or in other words the business of banking, to a few hands, has the same effect? Whether it be by a system of special charters or by restrictive provisions in a general banking law, it matters not; whatever tends to check competition and the trade in money, and to concentrate that trade within a small compass, gives to it a certain control over all other trade. Such a course of legislation is in effect a contrivance for accumulating prodigiously the facilities of speculation, and for protecting those by whom they are wielded against disturbance by competition.

The results of this policy are already before us. While we imagined that we were only legislating in regard to the trade in money, we find that we were in fact legislating in regard to all commerce. We thought that we were only constituting a class of Lords of the Money Market, but we discover that we have created a nobility of the cotton market, of the flour market, of the cattle market. We have been legislating the harvests of earth into their lap. For the bankers, and those associated with them, the blacks have toiled in the cotton fields of the south, for them the glebe has been broken by the plough in the western prairies, for them the steer is fattened on the herbage of the hills of Vermont, and the porker on the mast of the western forests.

We know very well that in any state of things men will speculate more or less in commodities. Whenever any commodity which belongs to the class of necessaries is produced in diminished quantity, it is immediately an object of speculation. It is bought up with the view of being sold at a higher price. In a healthy state of the money market, there is no great evil arising from such practices. There is a difficulty in combining and concentrating the means of carrying them on to any great extent and for any great length of time, and the temporary scarcity they create is balanced by the subsequent plenty which high prices, encouraging production, inevitably cause. But with the help of our restrictive banking system, which collects the means of speculation into vast masses, managed by a favored few, and which ties the hands of the rest of the community, there is no difficulty in organizing a speculation with as much precision as you organize a party in favor of a candidate for the presidency. The persons who have it in their power to engage in these speculations are known throughout the country; they are in fact designated by law, and they are easily found, an understanding grows up between them, a permanent plan of operations is agreed upon, and a scale of prices fixed. It is no answer to say that all such schemes must be disastrous in the end to those who engage in them; we allow that they often are so; but speculators always expect to make their escape from the mine before it explodes. In the mean time the artificial scarcity which has been produced is too extreme, too greatly prolonged, and the final revulsion to another state of things too sudden for the public welfare. In the end it turns out that these speculators have stimulated human industry excessively in a particular direction to the neglect of others; the fair proportion which should exist between the different occupations of men is destroyed—an artificial scarcity is followed by an artificial superabundance; and the commodity which at the time bore an exorbitant price is produced in such excess as not to remunerate the labour and cost of the production.

Such is the effect of regulating, as it is called, the occupations of society by provisions of law. Such is the wisdom of those legislators who fancy that they can manage these things better than Providence.

THE DANGERS OF CENTRALIZATION
July 27, 1839

In the discussions of the tariff, internal improvements, the independent treasury, and other topics in which we have indulged at various times, allusion has been made to the dangers of centralization. Let it be understood what is meant by this term.

We take it to be desirable, as the condition of socie[t]y in this country, to preserve as much power as possible in individual hands. If it be a good thing to enjoy liberty at all, it is a better thing to enjoy it in the largest measure compatible with general safety. Whatever advantages there may be in freedom, they are certainly increased as that freedom becomes perfect and secure. Personal dignity, domestic comfort, social order and happiness, may be proved to be the inevitable results of a removal of the restraints imposed upon the free actions of men. To lessen the number of these restraints then, is to assist in many ways the advancement of society.

The great enemy to enlarged freedom is the accumulation of power, is the limiting it to one place, confining it to single hands, whether they be those of a government or a class of men. It is quite too obvious for remark that to invest one person with the whole power of the community is liable to abuse, yet all the objections that apply to a procedure of this sort pertain in some degree to any centralization of authority. Power is safe only when it is distributed, when its exercise is divided among many, in other words, when it [is] broken up into small bits.

The institutions of the United States, both of the federal and state governments, were organized in accordance with this thought. As much power as was thought consistent with due energy in the respective governments was reserved either to the whole body of the people or to local administrations. Even that which was conferred was dispersed through different departments, adjusted as mutual checks. Nothing was granted to the national government for instance, which was not necessary to an efficient national existence. All else was jealously retained by the states. And so in the states themselves, the institution of townships and counties, each in certain respects distinct and independent has divided public power, and rendered its use at all times effectual, yet at all times harmless.

There is such wisdom in this doctrine of division that it becomes a duty to apply it in the most unlimited practicable extent. The advantages lent by it to the practical workings of the general government are s[o] apparent as to have forced a conviction almost universal. All men begin to confess the danger of expanding the federal powers,—the necessity of confining their action, or narrowing as far as feasible the sphere of their operation. If the people of the United States were strictly one people, with one constitution, one destiny, which is made a rallying cry by some, all the beauty and peculiar force manifested in the structure of their government would be lost. Its vitality would not be sap[p]ed but it would grow into monstrous and despotic vigor, becoming a huge giant of government, crushing every smaller sovereignty with equal ease and indifference. Yet the principle of federation intelligently viewed is susceptible of the widest application. Whilst it admits of strength in the head, it gives life and freedom to the members; its centre may be a point whilst its circumference spans the world.

If the utility of dispersing political power has not been so generally recognized in state constitutions, it is not because it is less necessary. A more important matter cannot be well conceived than restricting power as far as possible, in the first place, to local magistrates or officers, and in the second place to individuals. To enlarge the authority of counties and towns, and to expand the sphere of individual action, should be a leading object in state legislation. There has scarcely been a more frui[t]ful source of evil, than the concentration of many functions in one agent, or, in other words, the conferring a vast political jurisdiction on a central government. It withers the public spirit of a people by diminishing their interest in, and, of course, their attachment to, their institutions. Local duties, duties imposed by local relations, are to them daily recu[rr]ing remembrances of their privileges and rights. They create a perpetual attention to public concerns, they keep alive patriotic vigilance, they infuse into men the sense of dignity and worth, and either train the citizen to acuteness and sagacity in estimating public measures, or fit him for personal exertion on a larger field. Besides the action of a great central power is perpetually attended by injustice. Where the interests to be effected are scattered over a wide space, it is difficult to adjudicate among conflicting claims without the commission of gross wrongs. An equality of administration becomes impossible, one part of the country is sacrificed to another, and unjust burdens are ever[y]where imposed for objects either impracticable or wicked. Local jealousies, fostered by avarice, excite bitter and unrelenting strife, and political contests which should be the conflict of great principles, degenerate into mean and miserable struggles for spoils. Public bodies are besieged by innumerable armies clamoring for favors, schemers of every hue, crazy projectors, office seekers contemptible to the last degree, and speculators not a whit better, cluster around them and then such a scene of wicked solicitation and bargaining ensues that good men shrink from the sight. Every legislature of the union could illustrate practically what is here uttered in general remarks. Instances of rank corruption, of the foulest plannings, and the basest [co]mpliances, might be gathered in abundance,—[al]l springing from the abuse which is inevitable of the enormous discretion that it has been our policy to commit to a single instrument. There could be none of this, if that discretion was parcelled among separated administrations. Both the corruption it engenders, and the patronage it confers would cease, together with the strong tendency to despotism which is its inseparable attendant.

THE BANK OF THE UNITED STATES AND NICHOLAS BIDDLE
September 2, 1839

The phrenologist Orson Squire Fowler was a popular writer and lecturer on a combination of scientific fact and popular superstition. From his offices at 131 Nassau Street he published an annual Phrenological Journal. *The popularity of this craze in the 1840s Bryant recognized, as he deplored it, in a letter to Orville Dewey on January 11, 1842: "New York is by no means dull. . . . Firstly, There is animal magnetism which . . . has made great progress in America. . . . It is quite the fashion for people to paw each other into a magnetic sleep. . . . A Dr. Buchanan, at Louisville, mixes up phrenology and animal magnetism, puts certain faculties to sleep and excites others, operates on alimentiveness and makes people hungry, upon destructiveness and makes them choleric, upon ideality and makes them talk poetically, upon mirthfulness and makes them pleasant, upon love of approbation and makes them put on airs; or paralyzes one of those organs after the other, and makes the choleric man imperturbably good-natured, the funny man as stupid as an oyster, etc."*

Dr. Caius' comment is made in Shakespeare's Merry Wives of Windsor, *II, iii, 71–72 (clapper-claw, i.e., maul, thrash).*

In his poem on the Vanity of Human Wishes, Dr. [Samuel] Johnson enumerates the calamities which men bring upon themselves.

> When VENGEANCE listens to the FOOL's request—

when their ill-judged prayers are heard and their preposterous desires granted.— An occurrence has recently taken place in this city, which illustrates the vanity of human wishes as remarkably as any instance related or alluded to in the Doctor's poem.

More than a year ago, a deputation of our most respectable merchants left this city for Philadelphia. Among them were men of mature age, long experience and much reputation for commercial sagacity; men who had grown grey in harness, and on whose brows the cares and complicated transactions of trade were written almost as plainly as the accounts in their ledgers. Surely such men should have known what they wanted.

Their embassy was to that eminent banker, whose broad and bland countenance in plaster may be commonly seen, adorning a pedestal and looking complacently on the passers by, in front of Fowler's phrenological rooms in Nassau street. They were instructed to lay before him the depressed and languishing state of commerce in New York, and to pray that he would be pleased to take it into consideration, and apply the remedy by establishing a branch of his bank in our city. They were graciously received, they delivered their message, and Mr. [Nicholas] Biddle kindly promised to consider of it, but dismissed them without any positive answer. Not long afterwards, however, they were gratified with the news that an association was to be organized in New York under the general banking law to act as a branch of the Pennsylvania United States Bank in Philadelphia. The intelligence was received with joy, the branch was established, and the mercantile world stood waiting to see the happy transformation which it was to effect in the state of their affairs.

A transformation has taken place, it is true, but a very different one from what was anticipated—a change from bad to worse.—New York now rings with a hubbub of complaints against the branch and its parent.—The merchants complain that the accommodations of the branch here, instead of being properly distributed, are made in large single loans, after the example of its parent. They look at the last returns; they find that the United States bank in New York has on hand $1,524,587 in deposites, and 532,706 in [sp]ecie, while its circulation is but $124,000; and they complain that its loans and discounts, amounting only to $1,408,999, are less in proportion to its resources than those of any other bank in the state. They quarrel with the parent bank for disturbing the natural course of commerce by embarking in the cotton trade to the exclusion of regular merchants, and they quarrel with the bank here for acting as its instrument.—They exclaim against the base currency of post notes which these institutions are throwing into the market, a kind of paper which those who deal with the bank are obliged to receive at par, and which immediately falls to a discount of one per cent and a half, or more, per month. They accuse them of selling bills of exchange on

England, with a view of obtaining balances against the New York banks, and then demanding these balances in specie, by which operation the banks of our city are cramped in their resources and obliged to reduce their discounts. In short the outcry is as great, to say the least, as that which ascended from the marshes, in the ancient fable when Jupiter, having been implored by the frogs to grant them a monarch of some spirit and activity sent a stork, who entered upon his reign by picking up his subjects with his beak from among the rushes, and swallowing them alive for his breakfast.

The worst of these complaints is that they are true. The worthy gentlemen who went to Philadelphia on the embassy of which we have spoken, have received an instructive lesson on the vanity of human wishes. They find that they knew as little what they really wanted as the frogs when they asked for a monarch of spirit. They see at last that associations of capitalists, wielding vast resources, and armed, by law, with peculiar powers and prerogatives, make wild work with trade. They are the upper and nether millstone between which whatever comes, is ground to powder.

The time has been, we admit, when the mercantile class knew well what they wanted—reliance on their own skill and industry, and the absence of interference from without. The answer they gave to the French government, when they were asked what could be done for them—"LET US ALONE," was an answer in the wisdom and self-reliance of which there is a kind of moral sublimity. The same class now cry out with Dr. Caius in the Merry Wives of Windsor,

"*By* gar, he *shall* clapper-de-claw me";

and they have been clapperclawed with a vengeance by those on whom they blindly relied to befriend them. We can only explain this fatal mistake, made by a class who are commonly so sagacious in discerning their own interests, by imputing it to a kind of epidemic alienation of reason.— Whole classes of men sometimes go mad together. There is an old story of a party of Greeks drinking together in a house, who suddenly became possessed with the idea that they were on ship board in a storm, and began throwing the tables, couches and wine jars out of the windows, to lighten the vessel.

SCHOONER *AMISTAD* AND SLAVE MUTINY
September 4, 1839

As recommended in 1806 by President Thomas Jefferson, the Congress had prohibited the importation of slaves into the United States after January 1, 1808, with a penalty of forfeiture of vessel and cargo, and disposition of the seized slaves to be decided by the state where the vessel was condemned. Taken in the mutiny Bryant describes, this ship was misguided by a captive white crew member into American waters where it was in turn seized by a United States warship, and the mutineers turned over to a Connecticut court. Bryant engaged his friend Theodore Sedgwick III to prepare briefs in their defense. Two years later they were released upon appeal after their stirring defense by ex-President John Quincy Adams.

The question in what manner the negroes in the *Amistad*, who rose on the captain and crew and took possession of the vessel, are to be disposed of, is not without difficulties. These men it appears were not born in slavery, but were captives newly deprived of their liberty and brought to the island of Cuba, from the coast of Africa. After remaining a few days in Havana, they were purchased in the slave market by a planter and shipped on board the *Amistad*, for his estates on the same island. On the passage they killed the captain and took possession of the vessel, in which they were endeavoring to regain their native country, when they were captured by Captain Gedney.

Two points present themselves for discussion—first, whether the courts of the United States have jurisdiction in this matter—and, secondly, whether in case the slaves are claimed by the Spanish authorities, they should be given up. In regard to the former of these questions, we doubt very much the right of jurisdiction in our courts. The vessel was a Spanish one, passing from one Spanish port to another. The offence for which they would be tried was therefore committed within Spanish jurisdiction, and by and against persons subject to that jurisdiction. Unless our courts mean to take cognizance generally of all crimes committed on board of the vessels of other nations on the high seas, we do not see how they can extend their jurisdiction to this.

In regard to the second question, there would have been no difficulty had not the captives been landed and sold at Havana. The importation of slaves from Africa is piracy by our laws, and by the common consent of the civilized world is justly regarded as a heinous crime,—as an encouragement to unprovoked wars among the black tribes, to manstealing, to the cruel separation of members of families, and to the most horribly barbarous treatment in their transportation from their native country to America. In short, aside from the wrong done in the exchange of liberty for servitude, there are reasons enough for regarding it as one of the worst of crimes. If the *Amistad* had been a slave vessel on her way to Havana there could have been no hesitation whatever in refusing to deliver up the captives who were on board of her. Their attempt to recover the liberty of which they had been forcibly deprived, was a natural and rightful action, and no scruple would have been felt in allowing them to go free.

But the planter, who was conveying these men to his estate, became possessed of them by a regular purchase according to the laws and customs of his country. He was not concerned, for aught that appears, in their introduction into Cuba; he found them slaves already, and he bought them. This does not, we admit, make any difference in the moral character of the attempt on their part to regain their liberty, in which they acted precisely as so many Americans carried into slavery on the Barbary coast would have acted; but it may make a difference in regard to the disposition of the question in a country, the constitution of which recognizes the institution of slavery in a part of the republic. It has struck us, on a hasty view of the case, that both the vessel and those on board, upon a competent demand and ample proof on the part of the Spanish authorities, must be delivered up, though we confess that this view of the subject in regard to the blacks is not one which we are willing to entertain. The question, as we think it should be, is likely to be fully discussed, before any step in regard to it is taken.

BANK OF THE UNITED STATES vs. INDEPENDENT TREASURY
September 5, 1839

[If] the merchants of this country do not shortly become reconciled to the independent treasury scheme, if they do not come to regard it as a necessary restraint upon those gigantic monied institutions which the state legislatures are creating, it will be because the lessons of experience are lost upon them. We expect for our part to hear them, ere long, as loud in praise of the most obnoxious part of that scheme, the "specie clause" as it is called, as they ever were in favor of a national bank.

It is hardly possible to describe the exasperation against the bank with the long name, the United States Bank of Pennsylvania, which now prevails among the mercantile part of our population. Every body understands and declares that the operations of which that bank is the source and centre, are the cause of the present paroxysm of pressure. Every body sees that it regulates currency and credit, to be sure, but regulates them with a view to its own profits in the cotton trade from which it has elbowed every individual merchant. It regulates the currency by throwing out a debased issue of post notes; it regulates credit by bestowing it in large proportions upon its favorite customers, and by compelling the smaller banks, by a run upon their vaults, to contract their discounts and withhold their usual accommodations. If a storm of execrations could blow down the bank, not a stone of its walls would be left upon another.

Hard words, however, have no effect; the bank keeps on the even tenure of the way; its managers, to use the simile which one of its friends once applied to its former president, are as "calm as a summer morning." Neither the cursing and swearing of some, nor the more measured and more significant condemnation of others, will prevent them from using their power in the manner most conducive to their private interests. If those interests require that some few hundred of the merchants in this city and elsewhere should be ruined, they will be ruined; there is no alternative. Already we hear of failures which are indulgently concealed by the creditors, in consideration of the emergency of the times occasioned by the unexpected measures of the United States Bank.

It is time that a net was thrown about this Leviathan and that his propensity to mischief was restrained. Let the merchants take their choice between the capricious tyranny of these great banks on the one hand, and the independent treasury and the specie clause on the other.

Henry Clay as Politician
September 11, 1839

Captain Bobadill was a boastful, cowardly soldier in Ben Jonson's comedy Every Man in His Humour *(1598).*

In an article respecting the Vermont election, the *American* has attempted to account for the increased democratic vote in that State, by ascribing it to the disaffection of the whig party with Mr. Clay, or, in the words of that journal, to "the dislike of a particular and prominent candidate for the presidency."

We have seen no evidence of any such disaffection in Vermont. Mr. Clay is a perfectly fair and competent representative of the party of which he is so distinguished a leader. He holds to all their notions of special legislation, and a strong and complicated government. His maxims are "legislate—legislate—legislate; govern—govern—govern"; and he has proved his fidelity to these maxims through the whole course of the controversies concerning internal improvements, the tariff, the national bank, and the distribution of the public moneys among the States. He is a dexterous and impressive debator, an experienced and skilful political manager, a man of courteous and winning manners. It was very early in life that he sat down to the game of politics, and he has remained at the table, with the cards in his hand, till his temples are white with age.—He knows every trick, resource, shift and surprise of the game, as well as Bobadil[1] knew every motion of fence. He has studied more deeply than any of our public men the *mollia tempora fandi*, the art of holding his opinions in reserve till the time arrives of proclaiming them with effect—the art of driving bargains with a political adversary by keeping up a fierce controversy after further resistance is hopeless, and then suddenly proposing a concession short of what he would be obliged to yield had the battle been fairly fought out. It is true that he sometimes overreaches himself, and that he is sometimes embarrassed with the unforeseen consequences of his own arts, but this is a misfortune common to all cunning men.

It would be strange if the whig party were disaffected with such a man—a man holding all their opinions, infected with their distrust of the popular sovereignty, yet endowed with popular manners, and favoured by kindly reminiscences of the time when he proclaimed and defended democratic opinions—a man fitted to conciliate personal friendship and skilful to give that friendship a political direc[ti]on—a leader under whom the whig party have a better chance of success than under any other, since it is only by ingenious stratagems, by the dextrous use of sudden emergencies, and by covering the doctrines hostile to liberty by artful disguises, that the antidemocratic party can hope to obtain the ascendency in this country.

It may be said, however, that the abolitionists are numerous in Vermont, and that Mr. Clay's speech of last winter, on the abolition question, in which they and their schemes were treated harshly enough, has cooled their attachment to him. This may be true in some degree but not to the extent which might at first be supposed.—There were numbers who before the publication of that speech favoured the views of the abolitionists, with a view of obtaining their votes against the adminstration.—They cannot do so any longer with consistency. Mr. Clay's speech has made a vast many converts from this class. It has also made many converts among that numerous class, who take their opinions upon trust, and conform their notions of right and wrong as nearly as they can to those which are entertained by great men. Numbers who answer to each of these descriptions, are to be found in Vermont, we are sure, as well as here.

But granting that some of the Vermont whigs have grown a little cool towards Mr. Clay, it does not follow that they are ready to go into minority. Mr. Clay is not yet nominated as candidate for the presidency.—The question in Vermont was, whether the whigs should be kept in power, whether Mr. Jenison should be re-elected, and whether the whigs should have a majority in both houses of the legislature. These questions had no necessary relation to Mr. Clay's nomination.

We can tell the *American* what was the principal cause of the diminution of the whig vote in Vermont, as we have it from a conversation with an intelligent citizen of that state. The question of the connection of government with the banks has been much discussed in that quarter, and the people are coming to just conclusions. The credit system, so ruinous even to many of those who extol it so much, is growing every day more and more unpopular in Vermont, and every day adds to the number of those who approve the policy of the federal administration in regard to it. Let who will be nominated as the whig candidate for President, the vote of Vermont will be given at the next election for the candidate of the democracy.

Architecture and Taste
September 23, 1839

The New York Society Library, established in 1754, is one of the oldest subscription libraries in the country. Priapus, the mythological son of Bacchus and Venus, so deformed that he was abandoned by his mother, was worshiped by the Romans as the god of orchards and gardens, and of licentiousness.

On Wednesday we published what we thought an innocent paragraph, expressing our opinion concerning the front of the new building in Broadway, intended to contain the New York Library. To our surprise, we find in Saturday's *American* a severe reprimand for what we have done, accompanied by a lecture upon the science of architecture. The following is our paragraph:

"The front of the new building in Broadway, near Leonard street, erected to contain the New York Library, will do no honor to the architectural taste of this city. The row of red sandstone columns which stand close to the wall and support nothing, are useless as members of the building, and preposterous as ornaments. Columns should never be employed but to support a roof, their original purpose. In this way the effect is grand and noble; but stuck against the wall, as in this instance, they are as awkward an appendage as an extra pair of legs dangling from a man's shoulders. If a portico had been wanted, the use of the columns would have been proper to stand under the entablature, but the new building has no portico, and the columns, adding nothing to the support of the roof, are simply an encumbrance."

To this the *American* replied thus:

"We take up the gauntlet thrown down with even less than the usual courtesy of the Post, to defend what, in the above paragraph, is called 'the architectural taste of this city,' meaning thereby the taste of those who have been mainly instrumental in deciding whether the city should have an efficient public library and reading room, confined to no class, pursuit or profession, but adapted to the wants of all. We cannot persuade ourselves that this attack is really the result of the judgment and conviction of the editor of the Post, who, upon subjects unconnected with politics, and especially in the fine arts, has a claim to be heard. We rather suspect it to be the rankling of some disappointed hope, which has only procured his endorsement to the calumny. It is a serious matter to commit a crime against property, more heinous to assault the person—but to impeach the taste, is confessedly the most atrocious attack that can possibly be made upon one. Of the unmitigated ferocity of the above paragraph, there can be but one opinion. Assault and burglary are mere cheese cakes in comparison. It is written in an *ad captandum* style, and is put forth with that dictatorial authoritativeness, which Dr. Johnson recommended as an infallible mode of securing the confidence and support of the ignorant. It is wisely written, too, in the present tense, and is, in that respect, strictly true. The columns certainly support nothing. No unfinished columns ever do. More may be said when the entablature, cornice and pediment, are placed upon them. The 'original purpose' of columns may have been to 'support a roof,' but they are often employed, and with much taste, for other purposes. Sometimes they support statues, as the columns of Trajan and Antonine at Rome, and of the Place Vendome at Paris; and sometimes they, with their proper architraves and cornices, form gate-ways.

"The walls of a building also, aid somewhat in the support of the roof even when encircled by a peristyle. A projecting portico was forbidden by a just economy in the present case, but the charge that the columns are 'simply an encumbrance,' is simply absurd. As to their partial projection, its strangeness and disfavor among us is one of the results of a want of information. If antiquity—whence we draw all our best examples of Grecian architecture—has any claim to respect, and is worthy to establish a precedent, we may mention, as a case in point, the temple of Jupiter Olympus at Arigentum, second in magnificence to no structure of the kind ever erected, not excepting those of Diana, at Ephesus, or of Minerva, upon the Acropolis. There, the columns are bonded with the wall, and present a semi-cylindrical projection, fluted and carped as if they stood apart from the building.

"To this we may add the temple known as the Erectheum, at Athens, one of the most exquisitely finished specimens of architecture extant; and that known as the *Maison Carré*, at Nismes, the side[s] of which are also finished with half columns. The beautiful figure of 'an extra pair of legs dangling from a man's shoulders,' is what Talleyrand called *le bon mot pour le peuple*, and was, no doubt, used as a spice wherewith to flavor the morsel for the palate of the reader, and to assist the memory to retain the subject;—in which same way, we may quote a proverb—'Only children and fools judge of unfinished work.' So we would advise all of sound mind and mature age, particularly the subscribers to the Library, to wait and see the building when finished; assertain its cost, scrutinize the expenditure, compare the end with the means; and, if the comparison is sustained by the fitness of things, be not ashamed to think so, and to say so, in spite of dictatorial assertion, and abuse without argument; with which advice, we take leave of the subject."

Before proceeding to answer the architectural criticisms of the *American* we must say a word in regard to the discourtesy and abuse with which the EVENING POST is charged. It seems that we have insulted brick and mortar and treated old red sandstone with disrespect. For brick and mortar we solemnly declare that we have the highest regard, and towards our venerable friend, old red sandstone, we aver that we never entertained any other than the sentiment of profound deference due to years and usefulness. If in aught we have exceeded the proprieties of a respectful behavior towards them we humbly beg their pardon. As to the rankling of a disappointed hope, of which the *American* speaks, we are conscious of none except the hope that the exterior of the building would prove an ornament to our city, a hope which we confess is disappointed. The calumny, as that print calls it, which we have uttered in questioning the taste of that exterior is wholly our own, and was published without knowing by whom the design of the building was drawn, and by whom it was approved, and was simply suggested by looking at it the day before.

That columns may be properly enough employed to support statues or to sustain the entablature of gateways we did not intend to deny, and we crave leave to amend our paragraph by inserting these cases. But that they are properly placed, as in the new building, against the side of a wall where they cannot be necessary to sustain the roof or the entablature, we deny, notwithstanding the example of the temple of Jupiter at Agrigentum, the Erectheum at Athens, and the *Maison Carrée,* at Nismes. The Maison Carrée was a Roman work, and architecture was notoriously degenerate among the Romans. The manifest good sense of the Greeks in their architecture makes it no improbable conjecture that the original buildings were finished with columns only, and that the walls were a subsequent addition in which taste was sacrificed to convenience.

But even if this were not so, as is very possible, we appeal to any man's instinctive feelings to say whether the effect of columns in a portico, or in the nave of a church supporting the interior of a roof has not in it an impressive air of grandeur, and whether their appearance on the side of a wall when they are not wanted, does not strike him as poor and meagre, and as an effort to produce effect without understanding the true principles of architectural effect. You may talk of Jupiter Olympus and of the Erectheum as long as you please without doing away [with?] this impression.

It was the business of the committee who directed the design for this building to copy the beauties and not the deformities of ancient architecture. Every thing that is antique is not beautiful. Who would think of setting up Priapi in his gardens as the Romans did?

Federal Assumption of State Debts
November 21, 1839

A plan has been formed among the speculators to seize upon the government of the United States, and wield its powers and its credit to the advantage of their own interests and their own projects. It is said to have been first conceived in the inventive brains of certain English stockjobbers in London, and having been imported into this country, under the auspices of the Bank of the United States, is now canvassing for advocates and supporters both in and out of Congress.

The plan is, that the general government shall pay the debts of the several states; that it shall take upon itself the issue of all their extravagances, their unfortunate speculations, their wild and abortive enterprises, or rather shall shift the mighty burden from those who have madly incurred it, upon the great mass of citizens of the United States. To secure the acquiscense of those states which have not run into similar extravagances, they are to be offered the means and temptation of doing so as quickly as they please. They are to be allowed a share in this plunder of the public treasury in proportion to their population; they are to receive back a part of the funds they must be taxed to supply; they are to be bribed with their own money, and instructed to squander it like their neighbors.

The declining prices of the state stocks have alarmed those who hold them, and those to whom they are pledged to raise money, both here and in Europe. It is now clear that many of the states will be obliged to abandon their great schemes of internal improvement already begun; that they will be left without a public revenue, and, it is feared, that their citizens will not bear the enormous burden of a direct tax to repay the loans they have imprudently negotiated.—We hear that considerable amounts of the stock of Michigan and Indiana have, by the mismanagement of corporations entrusted with them, been disposed of in such a manner as to yield no returns to those states, and we may be assured that the people will not consent to repay what they have never received. To avoid these consequences, the federal government is to be called in with its greate[r] resources, its undoubted credit, and its facility of extracting money from the people by indirect taxation. It is proposed that the federal government shall issue its stock to such an amount as shall cover all the public debts of the states, amounting, it is estimated, to *two hundred millions of dollars*, and that the stock so issued shall be handed over to the delighted holders of the state stocks, who in turn, are to hand over their trash to the federal government.

There are two or three objections to this clever stockjobbing scheme; which present themselves to us, and which we will briefly state.

In the first place, there is no power given to the general government by the constitution to assume or pay the debts of the states. The general government has a right to incur debts for certain specific purposes, and to raise a tax for defraying them, but there is no clause in the constitution which confers upon it the pretence of an authority to distribute among its citizens the burden of paying the debts of an insolvent state. This single objection is sufficient, until the constitution is altered.

But, even if the constitution permitted it, the measure would be in the highest degree unjust. It would make those states which have run into no folly of speculation—and there are several states in this fortunate condition—and incurred no public debt, responsible for the extravagance of others. It would be as gross a violation of rights as if a court, after having received evidence that a debtor had no means of satisfying his creditor, should order his next door neighbor to pay the debt. It is no answer to this to say that the states which are not in debt shall receive their proportion of stock along with the rest, to expend in the same manner as the others have done. They have no occasion for such a present of their own money. If they had thought such expenditures justifiable or expedient, they would doubtless have incurred them in the time when speculation was most active and men's views of the advantage of any given project were most sanguine. But we go further—we affirm that even were a majority in every legislature of the Union to assent to the plan of which we speak, it would be none the less unjust to the citizens who do not assent. It would be an act of tyranny, the tyranny of the majority, the tyranny of unnecessary and oppressive taxation; for all this waste must at last be reimbursed from the pockets of the people.

In the third place, even if the measure were not unjust, it would be impolitic. It is impolitic to encourage extravagance. It is impolitic to interfere between the folly of rash speculation and those consequences by which Providence has decreed that it shall be punished and restrained. If a state has plunged madly into speculation and lost her credit, or if people in New York or in London have indiscreetly involved themselves in her concerns, let their case stand as a warning to others; let the state remain bankrupt till it retrieve itself by its own exertions; let the imprudent creditor wait, like other creditors, till he can get his money, and the lesson will prove a whol[e]some one. If the general government interfere, it will remove the principal check upon the improvidence of the state legislatures, and their auxiliaries. If folly is always to be protected against its own natural and just consequences, where will be the end of it? In a very few years we should have another brood of extravagant projects, another batch of state debts, another interference of the general government, and new burdens upon the people.

We have argued this question the more at length, because, clear as it seems to us, palpable as is the fraud it contemplates upon the constitution, gross as is the injustice of the measure, and manifest as is its impolicy, we have no doubt that it will be warmly urged in the next Congress. All the corporations and individuals concerned in state stocks, and they are numerous, comprising the Bank of the United States, and the free banks, as they are called, of this State, will undoubtedly support and press a measure which so greatly favors their interests. All the speculators along the lines of unfinished state rail roads and canals will forward the measure with all the intrigue and influence which they can bring to bear upon it. It will be zealously supported by the politicians who have procured extravagant schemes of internal improvements to be adopted by the states, inasmuch as it will shift the consequences of their folly upon other shoulders. Against these influences we have nothing to oppose but the constitution and the sacred principles of justice.

Federal Assumption of State Debts Unconstitutional
November 23, 1839

Baring Brothers was a banking firm based in London. In 1845, when Bryant and Charles Leupp were traveling in England, its head, an American merchant from Boston named Joshua Bates, entertained them for the night at his home on the Thames near Twickenham.

Those who demand that the debts of the states shall be paid by the general government; those who hold depreciated state stock and desire that the loss they have suffered shall be made good, those who own lands along the courses of rail roads and canals laid out through wildernesses, which they fear will never be made, admit that unluckily the constitution of the United States appears to stand in the way of the project. The stockholders and speculators, however, propose to obviate the difficulty by the following expedient. They suggest that a land bill should be passed, dividing the money arising from the sales of the public lands among the several states, and in the mean time that the general government shall issue its stocks to be exchanged for the stocks of the states and finally to be redeemed by proceeds of the public lands.— Thus by that ingenious polic[y] which is commonly called "whipping the devil round a stump," they think to circumvent the constitution. Stockjobbers and speculators, we know, make short work with constitutional objections. When Baring, Brothers & Co. are called in to expound the American constitution they do not allow themselves to be embarrassed by petty scruples.

But even supposing a land bill to be constitutional, which we do not admit, the issues of stock by the general government in behalf of the states, which is only a mode of borrowing money for them, is clearly unconstitutional. The constitution allows the federal government to borrow for its own absolute wants and purposes, but it no where allows it to borrow money for the states. It no where constitutes it general stockjobber and loan agent for the states which form the confederacy. That certainly is not among the offices which the general government is authorized to discharge.

For our part, if the government is to be called upon to pay debts and to relieve apprehensive or unlucky creditors, we see no reason why it should confine its charity to the states. It is better that it should pay the debts of individuals, which occasion much greater embarrassment and suffering. It is even more consonant with the aspect of the constitution that it should deal directly with its own citizens, who elect the principal officers of the general government rather than with the states, who move in a sphere independent of the general government. Let us, then, if we are to make a loan agent of the general government for the benefit of those who are in debt come down at once to the people.— If stock is to be issued for such a purpose let it be equally distributed among the individual inhabitants of the Union, and if the proceeds of the public lands are to be divided, let other people share in benefits of the division as well as stockjobbers and speculators. We know of numbers whose debts are as pressing as those of the states; we know hundreds of creditors who would be [as] glad to get their pay of individual debtors as any holder of state stock or state bonds can be. There are multitudes of enterprising people who have more rational projects on hand than rail roads through deserts, which they might be able to execute with a little help from the government, projects of humble but useful industry and activity. Let these classes receive assistance rather than the states. You will find such persons in every state, but you will not find every state in debt.

Private vs. Corporate Banking
November 29, 1839

How much safer is private than corporate banking, we endeavored the other day to show by examples drawn from this country. The doctrine is illustrated with equal force by what is now happening abroad.

We often hear it said that something like the American banking system, confining the business to few hands, and keeping it under the special direction of the legislature, is necessary to the protection of the community against the frauds of those who issue bank notes. The failure of the American banks twice in two years, and the enormous frauds of some of the largest of them, show that this is a mistake, and that the more a government tampers with banking the more its citizens are cheated.

While this important truth is becoming established by experience on this side of the Atlantic, we see on the other, that the most powerful institutions are doing homage to the superior safety and skill of private banking. The Bank of England itself, which is trembling on the verge of insolvency, has applied for aid to the private bankers Hottinguer & Co. The Bank of the United States, in the extremity of its distress, sends its agent as a suitor to borrow money from the private bankers Hope & Co., of Amsterdam. The greatest bank in the world, with the parliament of the greatest maritime and commercial nation on the earth to back it, is shaken to its foundations by a convulsion which itself helped to raise, but which leaves the private banker unharmed. The greatest bank in America, chartered by one of the most populous and richest states in the Union, is compelled to employ its agents to go like mendicants from door to door of the private bankers of Europe, soliciting assistance to extricate it from the consequences in which its own folly has involved it.

These are results at which no one should be astonished. Build your corporations on as broad a basis as you please, grant them the greatest imaginable privileges, protect them from competition by the most rigorous restraints on others, and subject them to the visitation and inspection of as many officers and boards of officers as you will, you cannot be sure of their good conduct and discretion. The private banker deals with his own capital and at his own proper peril.—The directors of corporations, and banking associations under government superintendence, deal with the capital of stockholders. The private banker knows that if he mismanages his ruin is inevitable. The banking association created by law, relies on the indulgence of the legislature. The private banker is watched by the community and by the thousand jealous eyes of the money market.

The association created by law is watched only by the officers of the government, to whom this task is delegated by the community. Where then is the wonder that private bankers are prosperous when corporations fail, and that the agents of corporations stand cap in hand, as humble solicitors, at the counters of the private bankers.

General Harrison: The Unwanted Candidate
December 14, 1839

In 1836 William Henry Harrison had lost his bid for the Presidency to Martin Van Buren. The British political satirist John Wolcot, writing under the pen name Peter Pindar, took as targets Samuel Johnson, William Pitt, and particularly King George III.

It is remarkable what a transformation can be effected in the character of an individual by making him a candidate for the presidency. A few days since General Harrison was looked upon and spoken of by almost every body in these parts, whig and democrat, as a tiresome, stupid old gentleman. The whigs had tried him as a candidate for the presidency, they had been beaten with him as they deserved, and they hoped that they were now fairly and forever rid of him. Nothing could exceed their surprise when they saw him, with all the bruises of his defeat upon him, come up a second time as a candidate, like a cat which you thought you saw killed yesterday, looking in at your window with a bloody head, to scare you as you wake in the morning.

As soon, however, as they could recover from their astonishment, it is wonderful what new excellencies they began to discover in the character of General Harrison. The whig journals all at once resound with his praises; the tiresome, stupid old gentleman has suddenly started into one of the most illustrious warriors, civilians, and legislators of the age; the unfit candidate with whom they deserved to be beaten, becomes the best candidate that could have been pitched upon; the man whom they hoped they had got rid of forever, is on the whole the very man whose nomination they ought to have demanded. The Harrisburg Convention have done all this—they have applied the philosopher's stone, which turns all this dross into gold.

Those who have amused themselves with turning over the pages of Peter Pindar may possibly remember the anecdote of Alderman Skinner, who being informed that somebody had arrived at Fleet Market with a quantity of unwholesome mutton, went to the spot in great wrath and ordered the man with his cart and carrion out of the market. The man, for answer, pointed to the top of his cart, where was an inscription signifying that it belonged to King George the Third and came from his estates at Kew. The Alderman's eyes were opened, the quality of the mutton was changed in an instant, and he broke forth in these words:

> "I've made a great mistake—oh, sad!
> The sheep are really not so bad.
> Whoever says the mutton is not good
> Knows nothing, Mr. Robinson, of food.
> I verily believe I could turn glutton
> On such sweet, wholesome, pretty looking mutton.
> Pray, Mr. Robinson, the mutton sell;
> I hope sir that his majesty is well."

The Harrison Mutton has wonderfully improved in quality since the cart that carries it has received the inscription of the Harrisburg Convention, that is certain.

Your whig journalist, after all, is your true optimist. He makes the best of the most untoward dispensation. He improves a bad nomination as a good Christian improves a personal calamity, deeming it the fittest and wisest thing that could be done in his case, and submitting to it, not only with acquiescence and resignation, but with praise and thankfulness.

Let the whigs be grateful that matters are no worse. Let them call to mind the philosophy of the honest Dutchman, who, having broken his leg, told the bystanders that it was a mercy that he had not broken his neck. The Harrisburg Convention had the party in their power, and might have nominated a baboon, or made the whigs vote for the big bear at the show of beasts in the Bowery.— They have exercised their authority on the whole with great moderation; they have been reasonable enough to nominate a thing in human shape, though by no means, so far as intellect is concerned, a favorable specimen of the human species.

Loss of Steamer *Lexington*
January 18, 1840

On January 13, 1840, the Long Island Sound steamer Lexington, *sailing from New York City to Providence, Rhode Island, caught fire and burned, with only one of its 113 passengers surviving. Among those lost was the Bryant's friend Dr. Charles Follen, a Unitarian clergyman and author of German textbooks the Bryants had used to study that language. Follen was a former Harvard professor who had lost his position through his radical anti-slavery activities.*

One of the daily prints has made this excuse for the criminal carelessness which occasioned the loss of the *Lexington,* that they who piled the cotton about the smoke pipe were willing to take the risk, that if the lives of the passengers were in danger on that account, their own lives were in danger also, and that they exposed others to no greater peril than they were willing to expose themselves.

This will not do. Rash and fool-hardy men, who do not hesitate to take any hazard upon themselves, have no right to put the same hazard upon others without their concurrence. They must at their peril take notice of the common rules of caution, the common notions of danger and safety, which govern mankind, and must conform to these strictly in all things which concern the interests of their fellow-creatures. If they do not they are criminal. He who throws away his own life in a dangerous experiment takes the consequence of his own folly, but if he throws away the lives of others, also, whom he decoyed into the danger without apprising them of it, he is little better than a murderer. A soldier who should carry his youngest child into battle in his knapsack would deserve to be hanged if the child was killed and he escaped.

The other night a person in another steam boat, in passing the *Lexington*, observed a portion of the smoke pipe red hot. If the passengers, on going on board the vessel, had been properly apprised of the danger they were about to incur, not one of them would have set foot on the deck. If the captain had stationed a man at the gang way to say to them as they arrived, "we are going to load the deck with cotton, which you know is a kind of tinder; we intend to pile it against the wooden box which encloses the smoke pipe, and the smoke pipe is often red hot; if the cotton should take fire, as is likely enough, we have no immediate means of extinguishing it, so that if you go with us you understand the risk you run"—if he had given this kind of notice, and the passengers had persisted in going with him, we could have only said that they had paid the penalty of their own rashness. But now they have suffered from the rashness and criminal carelessness of others. They went on board unconscious of the danger, in the confidence that all proper precautions were taken; timid women went passengers without suspicion of the danger that hung over them; men trusted on board their dearest friends, husbands their wives, and parents their little children, who, if the real condition of the boat had been known to them, would as soon have trusted them in the power of a madman with a drawn knife. And yet we are coolly told, that because the captain and the hands on board were willing to take the same risk nobody was to blame.

We are credibly informed that when the *Lexington* failed to arrive at Providence at the due time, it was commonly said that she must have been burned; so general was the conviction that she was unsafe, and that she must be destroyed by fire at some time or other. What was so well known at Providence must have been still better known to the company who owned the *Lexington*. It was their duty to employ careful and prudent men to take care of the boat; it was their duty to allow no combustible materials to be placed in an exposed situation; it was their duty to provide proper and instant means for quenching the fire, as soon as it should break out. In all these respects, we believe, but in the two last most certainly, they have failed to do what common humanity required of them, and are without excuse. It is idle to ask of the public to suspend its judgment in this matter; the fact of the cotton piled about the smoke-pipe is admitted, and the fact that adequate means were wanting to put out the fire is manifest. The guilt of the proprietors is as evident as the loss of the *Lexington*.

Not that there can be any objection to a further investigation of the matter; the more it is investigated and agitated the better. The question ought not to be allowed to rest until a thorough reform is brought about in the arrangements made by the boats which navigate the Sound for the safety of their passengers.

The American Conservative
January 22, 1840

David Rittenhouse Porter, an iron manufacturer, was the Democratic governor of Pennsylvania from 1839 to 1845.

Some of the whig prints commend Governor Porter's message to the Pennsylvania legislature, because as they say, its recommendations are "conservative." The journalists which use this expression, it must be recollected, attach to it a peculiar sense. By conservative they do not mean conservative of our political institutions, of the principle of equal rights which forms their basis, and of the great objects of their founders, a simple and impartial government under which men in the pursuit of happiness might be shackled by no restraints except such as the rights of others render indispensable. On the contrary, by conservative they mean conservative of new abuses, mischievous innovations, diseased excrescences on our institutions. They simply mean conservative of the banks which were chartered the other day, and which having first inflamed speculation to madness, and corrupted the public morals, have violated their charters and broken their faith with the community. This is the extent of the meaning they give to the term conservative.

The British conservative, whether he be in the right or in the wrong, espouses a cause, which has in it a certain dignity, which enlists his feelings of reverence and of attachment to the practices of his fathers. He upholds forms of government made glorious in his eyes by historical associations, and he finds them connected with much that is kindly and pleasant in manners, customs, and affections, which he fears to lose by a change. He supports a monarchy which antiquity has made venerable, and under which his country has risen to power and splendor; he strives to preserve a nobility which, if it has no other recommendation, has that of hereditary elegance of manners. The American conservative, on the other hand, merely seeks to preserve certain modern devices of money-making, convenient to speculators, and odious to the people, smuggled but the other day through the state legislatures, and found to be as mischievous to the community at large as they are profitable to those who employ them. The American conservative calls his speculations by the name of institutions, and claims that his innovations and experiments shall be held sacred; he demands that the ancient rules of honesty shall be set aside in his favor, and that the standing laws of the country shall be abrogated so far as he is concerned. He is a conservative not of good faith, nor of public morals, nor of law, nor of democratic institutions, but of expedients of fraud, stratagems for levying a tribute from the community for the benefit of the banks, practices which affront and defy both law and honesty. Such is the length and breadth of American conservatism.

The party which supports our present banking system is conservative in the same sense i[n] which a physician is conservative who cherishes a disease by medicines, who irritates the ulcer which he should cure, administers drugs to exasperate a cancer, and skillfully prolongs an intermittent from year to year. We have had enough of this preservation of abuses, this keeping alive of mischiefs. It is time to begin to be conservative in a better sense, it is time to look to keeping sacred the obligations of honesty, and the enforcement of law against corporations with the same rigor as against individuals.

Some of the whig journals are beginning to express themselves in favor of a general bankrupt law. We have already, sometime since, given our opinion on this subject; but if we are to have a general bankrupt law let it be such a one as was recommended by Mr. Van Buren in his message to Congress at the special session of the winter of 1837,—a general bankrupt law which shall include corporations as well as individuals, and which shall be enforced without remorse or delay against all banks that fail to perform their promises.

Rejection by Congress of Abolition Petitions
February 8, 1840

It is to be hoped that the resolutions read in the Assembly of this state, condemning the action of Congress on the memorials relating to the abolition of slavery, will meet the concurrence of every member of the legislature. It seems to us a matter of little consequence what may be the object of these petitions, so long as they are couched in respectful terms, and express the deep and earnest convictions of a portion of the people. The duty of a representative is to listen to the wishes of his constituents. When he undertakes to reject their complaints without regard to their import, he is transcending his authority, and tranforms his character as a mere agent into that of a master and despot. He is placed where he is to give expression to the feelings of the community to which he is indebted for his distinction; and not only to the feelings of that community in the aggregate, but to those of every class and member of that community. We hold that every man, when he feels aggrieved in an important particular, has a right to be heard in the councils of the nation. He has the right to set forth the causes of his complaint, and is entitled to a deferential consideration. Must Congress open its ears to every private claim for mere pecuniary redress, and yet exclude the petitions of thousands of men, directed against what they esteem a most flagrant and crying abuse?

Nothing can be simpler than the course which reason and equity prescribe in relation to this subject.—Let the suggestions of the petitioners be candidly investigated and discussed. If their requests have no foundation in justice and in truth, it is easy enough to establish that point and dismiss the plaintiffs with the satisfactory knowledge that their decl[a]rations have been at least heard. Or, if they have raised a question in the face of the constitution and laws, give them the evidence of their error that they may retire from a contest which must be utterly hopeless. Whether right or wrong, there will be no end to their remonstrances so long as they shall be treated with cavalier or cold contempt. The very fact that they are served in this manner can only strengthen their determination and add fresh zeal to their perseverance. Will it not excite the suspicion that there are other causes for this abrupt procedure beside the bare impracticability of what they demand? None shrink from discussion but those who are afraid of the truth, and none seek to veil their deeds in profound darkness and silence unless apprehensive that the light will reveal some wickedness.

Abolitionism, at this day, cannot be put down by coercion. It is altogether idle to expect that a movement which appeals to such strong feelings can be defeated either by legislative chicanery or despotism. The late decision of Congress has only imparted to it an additional impetus. It has mingled with the original question, other questions of moment, questions which touch the sincerest convictions of the people, and which must inevitably array them on the side which it is the object of that decision to vanquish. Abide by the decision, and hereafter the dispute will involve not the freedom of the blacks, but the freedom of the whites. Already, we believe, the abolition cause has acquired strength from the absurd and tyrannical course pursued at Washington. The attempt to suppress debate is regarded as a gross infringement of a most sacred right, an arbitrary assumption of power, an outrage to common sense, and a palpable violation of the spirit of o[ur] government and laws to which men will not tamely submit.

The Sub-Treasury and Farm Prices
February 20, 1840

Cela [va] sans dire: That goes without saying; That is understood.

The assertion which certain journalists are so fond of repeating that it is the *sub-treasury* which prevents the farmers from obtaining a liberal price for their wheat, reminds us of an incident which occurred in one of the western counties of Massachusetts, about the time of the disturbances commonly called the Shays war.

A man who had found his horse dead in the field, set on foot a prosecution against another, for maliciously killing the animal. On the trial he proved that the defendant on a certain day had been seen at the distance of about half a mile from the pasture in which the horse was, and had been heard to cry "hurrah for Shays." Here the counsel for the prosecution rested the cause. The counsel on the other side, a shrewd old gentleman, addressed the jury in this short speech: "Gentlemen, if crying hurrah for Shays can kill a horse at the distance of half a mile then I acknowledge that my client is guilty." The jury laughed and returned a verdict of not guilty without leaving their seats.

We make a similar acknowledgement for the democratic party. If it was the independent treasury bill which caused the late enormous issues of paper money, extravagant speculations, and exhorbitant prices, out of which the present contraction of credit, stagnation of business, and decline of prices proceeds—if it had this effect, not only years before it was passed, but years before it was thought of— then we acknowledge that it is the sub-treasury which has reduced the price of wheat. But unless this can be made out—unless it can be shown to be a natural consequence that crying "hurrah for Shays!" will kill a horse half a mile off, and that a proposal to dissolve the dependence of the government upon the banks will fill the whole country with overbanking and overtrading years before such a proposal is spoken of—then we claim that the administration and its friends shall be acquitted.

Most true it is that the administration and their friends are to be taken to task for every thing that goes wrong. If wheat is too dear, it is the fault of the administration; if the community or any class of men suffer any possible inconvenience, it is the administration that is to blame; these are matters of course with the whig party; *cela sans dire* as the French say.

But although it is the trade of the whig journalists to charge all these things on the administration, yet we submit the question to their cooler judgment, whether the thing may not be overdone, and the effect of it greatly injured, if not destroyed altogether. For example, when they attempt to show *how* the administration have brought about a particular mischief, they may ascribe it to measures which it is evident to the dullest capacity had no tendency to produce it, as they are now doing in endeavoring to connect the low price of wheat with the independent treasury scheme. They may become as much the objects of laughter and derision as the unlucky prosecutor, who thought that the jury would presume that the exclamation "hurrah for Shays!" would kill a horse at the distance of half a mile.

Would it not be policy therefore in these journalists to avoid mentioning any particular measure of the democratic party as the cause of any particular mischief, and to deal only in general assertion? Let them lump together every thing that goes wrong in our commerce at home or abroad, in the grain market, the money market and the other markets, in our domestic and our foreign relations, and put them all to the account of the administration, without troubling themselves to show how the administration is in fault, lest they should make themselves ridiculous in the attempt. Let them leave that to be discovered by the ingenuity of their readers.

Paternal Government: Its Degrading Effects
May 20, 1840

It is a sensible remark which we find in a German paper, that the riots which have taken place in France on account of the dearness of grain, are owing to the perpetual interference of the government in affairs which ought to be left to regulate themselves. That government, like too many others, is continually governing, administering, putting things in order; it is a paternal government, always fussing over its grown up children. The classes whom it regulates, remind us of the story of the gentleman of sixty, who was found by a traveller in a neighborhood famous for longevity, crying because he had just been whipped by his grandfather.

They who enjoy this paternal government, repay its cares for the most part, by grumbling. The more legislation, the more discontent. The old gentleman of sixty, when whipped by his grandfather, pipes his eye; he kicks while the rod is applied; after the flogging is finished, he petitions that his younger brother may be whipped also, and when the venerable ancestor deals out his supper, the scarcely less venerable grandchild criticizes the size of his bread and butter, and complains that it is not large enough. A people that is taught to depend upon the government for every thing, is always ready to ascribe to the government the blame of every thing that goes wrong. When the crops are bad, and the land is visited with scarcity, as is now the case in France, the inhabitants of such a country call upon the government, and say, "You who profess to set every thing right by regulation—you who believe in the omnipotence of laws and ordinances to secure the welfare of the people, exert your power now that it is needed; lower the price of grain, and give cheap bread to our hungry families, or we will pull down your custom houses."

Such is the natural effect of too much legislation. It makes the people restless and disorderly. A government that leaves nothing to its natural course, a government that is perpetually interfering with the laws of trade, will inevitably be called upon to remedy evils that are wholly above its reach, and will suffer censure, incur hatred, and perhaps be convulsed by riot and disorder because it cannot. In a country like France the insurrection of the multitude may be put down by the bayonet, and tranquility, as they call it, may be preserved, but the only method by which a republic like ours can preserve internal peace, is by making its laws as few, as simple, and as equal in their operation as possible. The people, accustomed to rely on individual foresight and exertion, and not on the interference of the government, will then submit to any inevitable calamity with all the patience of which they are capable; they will see that the evil neither arises from the law nor is to be remedied by law, and they will neither ask the interposition of the government nor rise in violence against it.

We have seen in this country an effect similar to that which we have noticed in France. The creation of a national bank by the general government, and the elaborate banking systems of the several states, made a large class of our citizens suppose at one time that it was in the power of the government to keep money plenty and commerce prosperous, by simply passing laws from time to time; in short that the government could prevent hard times, the horror of the trading class, from ever occurring to trouble them. When therefore by the aid of overbanking and overtrading, thousands of persons found themselves involved in debts that they could not pay, [they] called loudly on the government to come to their aid. Their case was past all remedy, and every body now sees that it was so; but at that time the delusion was exceedingly general that it was in the power of Congress by some legerdemain of legislation to make rich men of bankrupts, without injustice to the rest of the community. Both the mischief, [and] the delusion were the fruit of legislation operating beyond its proper province. The federal government is disposed to profit by the lesson taught by this circumstance; whether or not it will be lost on the state governments remains to be seen.

Campaign by Song
May 30, 1840

Andrew Aguecheek is a comic character in Shakespeare's comedy Twelfth Night. *The* Evening Star *(1833–1840) was a Whig paper. The Whig campaign clubs of 1840 drew their name from the battle in Indiana on November 8, 1811, during the War of 1812 in which General Harrison had defeated a force of Shawnee Indians under Chief Tecumseh.* Di tanti palpiti *(Ital.), "with many throbs or palpitations." The Congreve rocket was a weapon invented by Sir William Congreve in 1808. In the many doggerel Whig campaign songs directed at President Van Buren in 1840 a typical refrain was "Van, Van, is a used-up man." While completing his* Requiem *at Vienna in 1791 Mozart died of rheumatic fever. The poet Tennyson wrote in* Tithonus, *"After many a summer dies the swan," reflecting the belief in fable that the swan's song signals its imminent death. Bryant was unwittingly prophetic; President Harrison died one month after taking office.*

A new political danger has lately arisen which we confess gives us some anxiety, although we are little inclined to despondency. The enemies of the democratic party threaten to put it down by singing. They have pointed at it the whole artillery of the gamut. We are all to undergo solmization; we are to be destroyed by "the sweet and contagious breath," as Sir Andrew Aguecheek has it, of our adversaries. Here is a sample of the preparations which the friends of Harrison are making for our defeat. This which follows is from the *Evening Star.*

"Seventeenth Ward. —There will be a rousing meeting this evening, at the Tippecanoe Club of the 17th. Music, public speaking, *good singing and hard cider.* Several eminent persons are expected to speak."

The next is from the *American.*

"FIFTH WARD TIPPECANOES. —There will be a great gathering of the 'Tippecanoes' at the Log Cabin, No. 165 Chapel street, *to-night*. Good speaking and *spirited singing* may be expected, as several distinguished members of the party, from New Jersey and elsewhere, will be present."

So it seems that the two divisions of the whig party are united in the determination to destroy the democrats with music as we exterminate vermin with ratsbane. The readers of the *American* and the readers of the *Star*, the drawing room and the tap room, are united on this point; while the one set trill their Tippecanoe ballads to the air of *di tanti palpiti*, the other thunders them out to the tune of *come let us all be jolly*. A regular organization has been set on foot for this purpose; Tippecanoe Clubs are forming not only in the various wards of this city, but throughout the country, to drink hard cider and sing songs in praise of Harrison. Stores of ballads have been provided to serve as heavy ordnance for the political campaign; glees and catches are ready to throw into our camp like hand grenadoes and Congreve rockets; the whig poets are at work like armourers and gunsmiths, fabricating election rhymes, and we scarcely open a whig newspaper, without finding one or two Harrison songs. The plan is to exterminate us chromatically, to cut us to pieces with A sharp and lay us prostrate with G flat, to hunt us down with fugues, overrun us with choruses, and bring in Harrison by a grand diapason.

We could meet the whigs on the field of argument and beat them without effort; if the question were of principles and measures, we should make short work with them; in that contest we have the people fully on our side. But when they lay down the weapons of argument and attack us with musical notes, what can we do? We can refute their reasonings, but how can we stand against their minims, their crotchets and their volleys of demisemiquavers linked together like chain shot? We care not for their orators and their journalists, their speeches and their paragraphs, but how shall we resist their counterpoint?

There is a certain beauty of correspondence in these musical arrangements of the whigs. Men whose brains are muddled at the Tippecanoe clubs with drinking hard cider, qualified with a little brandy, to prevent it, as the Highlander says in one of Scott's novels, from being "owre cauld for the stamach," can neither reason nor understand reason. They cannot reason, but they can shout, and they feel a strong propensity to lift up their voices. By providing them with glees and catches and choruses, two important ends are attained: they both gratify their inclination for making noise, and do infinite mischief to the party they oppose.

It is said that Mr. Van Buren is so ill-informed on this subject, that he actually expects to be re-elected President of the United States. We admit, as all the world does, his shrewdness and sagacity, and his usual exemption from the delusion of false hopes, but we fear he has not a musical ear. We fear he has not read the ballads written against him, and does not know the tunes to which they are set.

We had written thus far, when the thought struck us that we had heard of persons who had died of their own music. Mozart, for example, died of his own Requiem. We somewhere read the other day, an account of a young lady who actually sang and played herself to death. The swan, as the ancient poets said, after screaming horribly all his life, expires in singing, and who knows but this may be the euthanasia of the whig party? The idea is very probable. As we approach the November election, and as the indications of the final issue grow clearer and clearer, the whig party, we are suspicious, will begin, as the cant phrase has it, to "sing small," until its strains shall die away gradually into complete silence; unless, like the boy in one of Chaucer's tales, who chaunted loudly with his throat cut from ear to ear, it continues to sing after it is fairly dead. It is perhaps presumptuous in us to make the suggestion to persons so well skilled in music as the whigs, but we cannot help thinking, that by way of preparing for the worst, it would be well for them to set a portion of the Harrison ballads to "the tune the old cow died on."

The Tippecanoe Clubs and Intemperance
June 1, 1840

The Reverend Leonard Bacon was a Congregational minister and lecturer at the Yale University Divinity School.

If any of our grave and sober citizens who are the fathers of young men belonging to the Tippecanoe clubs in this city should find themselves perfectly at leisure of a fine evening, when the clubs are advertised to assemble, perhaps they could not better employ their time than by walking out and dropping in at the meetings, which are public, in order just to satisfy themselves what their sons are about. They will then be able to judge for themselves whether these promiscuous convivial associations are proper things to encourage, and whether the newspapers perform their duty in commending them and counselling their readers to attend. We have heard that the number of young men who are seen at these places in a state of intoxication is so great as to excite alarm even in many who at first saw with satisfaction the establishment of the Tippecanoe clubs as a party engine.

At the Annual Temperance Convention of the state of Connecticut, held at New-Haven a few days since, Mr. Leonard Bacon, a clergyman, and we infer from his language a whig, after alluding to some other causes which had led to backsliding in temperance, said:

> "There is another reason why the cause of temperance is retrograding. It is (and I say it with no wish to offend any person) it is owing in a great measure to causes of recent occurrence: Within three or four months, *Intemperance has become the badge of a political party!*—The hard money humbug was hard enough—but the *hard cider* humbug, will prove more disastrous to the country, and more degrading to those concerned in it. Yes, intelligent men—men who have enjoyed the benefits of Christian teachings—and who live in a land of gospel light—are called upon to exhibit their enthusiasm in a political strife, by drinking *hard cider*, made harder by hard *brandy*, for the glory of General Harrison! Yes—at these conventions and committee-rooms, many a young man will take his first lessons in drunkenness, which will bring him to the almshouse or the prison, and the drunkard's grave!—More than ten thousand men will be made drunkards in one year, by this hard cider enthusiasm."

From all that we can learn we have reason to believe that Mr. Bacon has neither overstated the fact, nor overestimated the danger. Whatever may be thought of the prudence and the propriety of some of the measures resorted to by the zealous friends of temperance, there can be no question with any man, that it is most desirable to preserve all that the community has gained in the general prevalence of temperate habits, and that any relapse towards that vice which is the parent of so many crimes, so much poverty and so many diseases, would be most deplorable. The relapse, however, is going on; going on rapidly, contagiously; spreading with all the fury of a new fashion, under the auspices of a party which pretends to the exclusive possession of good manners and good morals. If there are among the whigs any who value the moral and physical well-being of their fellow citizens, we counsel them to look to it, lest by their encouragement or their acquiescence they bring upon the community a greater and more permanent evil than any which, even according to their own notions, could arise from keeping the present administration in power.

Relapses in disorders of the human frame are the most difficult of all maladies to cure; and the same thing is true of relapses into bad habits. They who have established those nurseries of drunkenness, the log cabins, will find too late that the fire they have kindled will not go out at their bidding. If Harrison should be successful, the triumph will be celebrated by drunken revels; if he should be beaten, his adherents will, as the saying is, drink to drown sorrow. The log cabins may be razed to the earth, but the habit which has once taken root will survive and increase in strength.

It is certainly a remarkable fact in the political history of this country, that a party which makes such boasts of its lofty aims, and of the virtue and intelligence of its members, should at once lay aside all the common methods of persuasion, all discussion of political principles and public policy, and forming an alliance with a degrading vice, should establish schools of intoxication, take a drunken cry for its watchword, and rely upon gaining the majority by such expedients. If these methods succeed, we shall not hesitate to confess that our opinion of the intelligence and the moral condition of the Amerian people has been far higher than it ought to be.

The Political Creed of the *Evening Post*
July 1, 1840

On August 19, 1841, a Second Federal Bankrupt Law would pass the Congress, allowing, with some exceptions, anyone to become a voluntary bankrupt; this law was repealed five years later.

Our correspondent who signs himself "One who knows," is no doubt friendly in his intentions, but his arguments are not of a kind that have any weight with us. When we consider a public measure, it is our habit to inquire whether it is right or wrong—not whether it will benefit or injure the party to which we belong; if it is right, we always feel quite certain that it will be for the benefit of the party; if it is wrong, we are equally sure that it will ultimately be to its injury. We shall not, therefore, say a syllable more or less, either for or against the bankrupt bill, for the reason that it may gain or lose votes to the democratic party.

When General Jackson was addressed by one of his friends in regard to a certain measure, and asked whether it was expedient, he answered, "Sir, the word expediency is not to be found in my vocabulary. Is the measure right and just? That is the only question with which I concern myself." General Jackson was one of the most successful politicians that the country has ever produced.

It was the happiness of that eminent man's moral constitution, that without studying to be popular, he was led by it in the true path to the approbation of his fellow men. The doublings and shiftings of most professed politicians, their perpetual anxiety as to what people will say, their constant reference to the opinions or what they think are the opinions of the day, and their trimming and tacking to catch the wind of the moment, involve them in endless embarrassment, and finally in odium. It is the conduct of such men that causes some author, we do not recollect who, to speak of "the rascally virtue of prudence." Rascally it is, as these men understand it, in every sense of the word, mean in its practice, beggarly and unsatisfactory in its results.— True prudence in political life is only shown when a man of sound mind and well balanced faculties quietly follows the promptings of his own conscience.

What is often mistaken for public opinion is merely an effervescence on the surface, a gust of mistaken feeling that passes away as soon as men have had time calmly to examine the question that raised it; or else a clamour among the journalists who, like frogs in a marsh, are fond of croaking in chorus; or perhaps a noise got up by bustling and intriguing men, with whose proceedings the people have no real sympathy. But deeper than all these, and indestructible by them, lies the sacred feeling of justice and the reverence for the right, by which the statesman must finally be tried and judged. He who has not this feeling and this reverence in his own bosom, must prove in the end a wretched politician, inasmuch as he has not the true standard of public approbation in himself, and the greatest exercise of human sagacity cannot always discern it in those circumstances, which are usually taken as indications of public opinion.

In conclusion, we must say to such of our correspondents as solicit us to favor this or that scheme, because it will be likely to bring votes to the democratic candidates, or because certain friends of the administration will fall off to Harrison if it be not adopted, that we are insensible to all such motives, except to despise them.

The Kitchen Battery
July 2, 1840

The Italian physicist Count Alessandro Volta (1745–1827) lent his name to a unit of electrical force. Venetian playwright Carlo Goldoni was a writer of comedies in the manner of Molière. The appeal of Pope Urban II at a conclave of French bishops and princes in 1095 brought about the first of eight crusades during the ensuing two centuries to liberate Jerusalem from Persian conquests. In 1830, and again in 1835–1837, a French force captured Algiers and disposed its ruler.

The French, who have almost exalted the art of cooking into a science, call the apparatus of pots and pans and other utensils, by the help of which they get up their varied and flavorous repasts, "a kitchen battery." The term is admirably well chosen, as any person will acknowledge who has seen the formidable array of implements which garnishes the hearth and walls of a French kitchen.

But if any of our readers are whigs, enemies of the administration, and want to see a BATTERY that will do their hearts good, let them look in at one of the log-cabins recently erected by their party in this city. A friend of ours who ventured, the other evening, into one of these places just opened, has given us a description of the fearful preparations for the overthrow of the democratic party, which met his eyes. On the bar—an entrenchment more formidable than any thing in military fortification, than any bastion or curtain, or counterscarp or glacis—stood twenty-one decanters, flaming with all the various alcoholic fluids. At each end they were flanked with a barrel of cider and an enormous punch bowl, while a beer fountain was playing in the middle like a shower of rockets. Under the stair case was a huge pile of champagne baskets, which had been emptied of their contents by the heroes who are actively engaged in carrying on the war. Alarmed at the terrible magnificence of these preparations, our friend, who is a democrat, made haste to leave the spot before he should be descried by any of the engineers on the ramparts.

Our readers will judge for themselves whether any electromagnetic battery invented by Volta or Goldoni and improved by their followers, though able to make a dead man utter a groan; whether the array of catapults and battering rams with which the crusaders beat down the walls of Jerusalem; or whether the battery with which the French bombarded Algiers, can compare in potency with this apparatus for demolishing the democratic party. So well satisfied are the whigs of its efficacy, that, it is said, the plan is entertained of erecting one in every ward of New York, with a view of attacking and capturing the town in detail.

In the histories of European wars we sometimes read of the nobility, and even the ladies of a besieged place, working in the trenches and tending the mortars and howitzers. These, however, are examples of defence, not of attack; we do not read of their submitting to these labours in the attempt to storm and capture a city or fortress. But in this community of ours, heroism is carried to a higher pitch. The most effeminate of our populations magnanimously take their turn in tending the log cabin batteries with which it is expected to overthrow the strong holds of the administration. The drawing-room whigs, the youths particularly, smitten with the love of glory and of cider, withdraw for a time from the soft task of curling and perfuming their mustachios and assist in discharging the decanters, draining the punch bowls, and letting off the champagne bottles, of which so ample a provision is made in the log-cabin magazines.— True it is, that now and then a youthful warrior is disabled in the battle and carried home in that state to his mother; but, such is the fortune of war; it strikes down young and old alike, and he is but a cool sort of patriot who is not willing to sacrifice himself in that manner for the good of his country. The *American* newspaper in the mean time raises its voice and thus cheers them to the charge:

> "That the adoption of 'hard cider' as a RALLYING CRY, *any more than* ITS GENERAL ADOPTION BY THE PEOPLE AS A DRINK, is fraught with danger to the human or to the political constitution, is a thing yet to be proved. We suppose it to be conceded that of all liquors used by any people, hard cider, as a matter of fact, is about the healthiest, and least intoxicating—and to make it a complaint, therefore, on behalf of the cause of temperance, that the people *are addicting themselves to such a drink*, in preference to whiskey, rum, and like fiery mixtures, seems to be very preposterous indeed."

Golden words these, worthy to be chalked on the head of every cider barrel, and attached in silver labels to the neck of every gin bottle in the bar of every log cabin in the United States. Your log cabin bar-room is your only general lounge, and hard cider, nominally at least, for there is a vast class of liquors that come under this appellation, is the only beverage of your man of fashion.

Unluckily, it may possibly happen that this kind of battery as well as others, will do most execution to those who set them up. The French *batterie de cuisine* has often destroyed its owner, who fell a victim to good eating. Many an operator has been knocked down by his own electrical battery. We shall not be surprised if some accident of this kind happens to those who are engaged in the attempt to put down the admininstration by hard drinking.

The Parrot Tribe
July 31, 1840

Alexander Pope's Martinus Scriblerus *(1741) was a verse satire on several of his now-forgotten contemporary poets.*

> "There's a parrot at New Orleans which, captivated by the popular music, cries constantly, 'Hurra for Harrison and hard cider!' 'Go it Tip, Tip, Tip-pecanoe!'"—*Evening Star.*

New Orleans is not the only place which can pride itself on the possession of this wonderful breed of parrots. Here, at the north, they are as plenty as canaries.

There is a parrot at the office of the *Evening Star* who articulates the words "Hurra for Harrison and Hard Cider" so distinctly, that you would be astonished to hear him. He has also, we are told, been heard to utter the additional words "Go it, Tip, Tip, Tippecanoe."

This bird talks only in the afternoon; he is silent o' mornings, but after two o'clock, when his cage is hung out in the street, he is surprisingly loquacious.

The parrot at the office of the *New York American* was some time in training, and showed himself a little awkward at first, like the bird that Gresset tells of, who having belonged to a convent of nuns, and being accustomed only to say *Ave Maria* and such like ejaculations, was somewhat slow in acquiring the accomplishment of swearing under the teaching of the sailors. The parrot of the *American* has now, however, after sufficiently long discipline, learned to pronounce the words Harrison and Hard Cider as trippingly as any of its species. The learned Martinus Scriblerus tells of certain parrots who repeat the words of others "in such a hoarse odd voice that they seem their own." The parrot of the *American* has the same peculiarity. It rattles off the catch-words we have mentioned, in such sulky and lugubrious tones, that they seem like nothing one has heard before. This also is an afternoon bird; and when it is hung out in its cage in Wall Street, the purlieus of that cheerful region catch the infection of sadness, and even the stockjobbers, although the most placid of men, become fretful.

The parrot whose cage hangs at the office of the *Express* newspaper, is a remarkably lively and noisy bird; it learned its lesson sooner than any of its fellows in this quarter, and will jerk you out the cries, "Hurrah for Harrison and Hard Cider," and "Go it Tip, Tip, Tippecanoe" faster than any other creature of its kind. It sometimes boasts of having drunk cider out of the mug of old Tippecanoe himself. It is a morning bird; it begins its notes very early, and may be heard chattering before breakfast like ten magpies.

There are several other parrots equally apt in the same lesson, who are kept in cages at the offices of the other political newspapers, some of them as foul harpies; who intersperse their cries of "tip" and "hard cider" with plenty of hard swearing, and throw the filth of their cages on the passers by, so that the best thing a clean man can do is always to take the other side of the street.

Besides these, there are cages built in different parts of the city, under the name of "log cabins," large enough to contain whole flocks of parrots and parroquets, who are brought thither from different parts of the city, as into a kind of seminary, and taught to pronounce the words "Harrison and hard cider," by the example of older and more expert birds of the parrot tribe. So pleased are the friends of General Harrison with this device, that they have no doubt of effecting a political revolution of the entire republic by the aid of Poor Poll.

Let not New Orleans, therefore, fondly plume herself upon possessing the only parrot that can shout "hurrah for Harrison and hard cider."

WHY HARRISON SHOULD NOT BE ELECTED PRESIDENT
September 11, 1840

Major George Croghan, a nephew of explorer George Rogers Clark, had distinguished himself under the command of General Harrison at the Battle of Tippecanoe in 1811 against Indians under Chief Tecumseh, although Harrison was later criticized for heavy losses in gaining the victory. Two years later, when in command at Fort Meigs, Croghan ignored an order from Harrison to withdraw and successfully fought off a British attack. As a result, Harrison became involved in unpleasant arguments and recriminations. The independent-minded Democrat Littleton Tazewell was the governor of Virginia from 1834 to 1836.

We promised yesterday to explain in what respect we differed from our correspondent Veto, when he said that "General Harrison has been all his life a brave, well-meaning, and honest man."

Animal courage we will not deny General Harrison to possess. He would probably at any time of his life, if engaged in a contest of physical force, stand his ground like most other men. This is a very common and not a very exalted kind of merit. So far Veto is right. The higher kind of courage, moral courage, we see no ground for ascribing to him. He is not the man who will boldly avow an unpopular opinion. He is too fond of being on good terms with everybody, too desirous of getting everybody's good word, and when he is a candidate, of obtaining every man's vote, to have any of that sort of boldness. His attempt to secure the votes of the Northern abolitionists, by writing letters representing himself favorable to their cause, while he was endeavoring to obtain the support of the Southern States by making different representations in that quarter, is an act of the grossest moral cowardice.

"Well-meaning" in certain respects Harrison may be. He is not, we believe, very select in his morals; it would not do to compile a code of ethics from his example. Yet he is hospitable, and probably in the main friendly in his dealings with mankind. He has good nature we doubt not, but his very good nature, being accompanied with a weak intellect, only makes him the easier tool of others. The most convenient and supple instruments of profligate politicians are often good natured. In a higher sense, that of governing his conduct by a steady and rigid conscientiousness, he is not well-meaning, as is evident from the course he has pursued towards Colonel Croghan, of which an account has already been published in this paper; and the same remark may be made on the course he has pursued in regard to the abolition question.

"Honest" in some respects, probably Harrison is. We hope he would not attempt to cheat anybody in driving a bargain, and that he punctually pays such debts as he contracts. He is probably a man who, if he had never been thought of for any place of honor or trust, might have passed through the world with the reputation of average honesty. But his conduct in the case of Croghan, to which we have alluded, and his concealment and double-dealing in regard to his political opinions since he was last nominated for the Presidency, are at variance with every principle of honesty. When his incapacity for places of high responsibility is threatened with exposure, as in Croghan's case, or when his popularity is concerned, as in the present canvass for the Presidency, he is neither brave enough nor well-meaning enough to be honest. His pliancy of temper and dullness of moral perception are such that when advised to play the knave by those who are about him, he does so without much hesitation.

We take no pleasure in discussing these matters. We have spoken of Harrison's personal character in this article in as mild terms as conscience would allow us to use, and we should not have written it had not the words of our correspondent been falsely imputed to us. The great objection, after all, to General Harrison is that he is set up by a party who are governed by pernicious maxims of government and who propose pernicious measures, and that his election is their victory. Another objection which certainly deserves great consideration is that made by Governor Tazewell, that even allowing him to be "brave, well-meaning and honest," he is "both physically and intellectually incompetent to the duties of the Presidency."

Daniel Webster, "Field Preacher"
September 18, 1840

The town of Ellsworth lies in south central Maine, a short distance from the coastal resort of Bar Harbor.

The eminent Massachusetts barrister who has lately turned political field preacher, who has held forth at Saratoga, in this state, and at Warren County in New Jersey, and who is now going to Patchogue, on Long Island, to convert the democrats of Suffolk County to the support of Harrison, has better reasons for his enmity to the democratic party than some people imagine. Mr. Webster has had some magnificent projects of money-making unluckily overset by the perversity of Mr. Van Buren and his friends. Yet with a beautiful and becoming unwillingness to make himself the hero of his own complaints, he suppresses all mention of his personal wrongs, and confines himself to general lamentations concerning the ruin brought by the administration upon the country.

This modesty diminishes both the interest and clearness of Mr. Webster's harangues by making them vague. Field preachers of another class, individualize their instructions; they enliven and enforce them by pithy instances. Let us do for Mr. Webster what his magnanimity will not allow him to do for himself; let us give an example of the pernicious doings of the administration which the people of Patchogue may read as a practical commentary upon Mr. Webster's speech. In doing this, we draw our materials from a pamphlet published about four years since under the auspices of Mr. Webster.

About the time that so many persons were busy in laying out cities as large as Paris and London, all along our sea coast, and on the banks of our great rivers, the idea was entertained of hewing down the forests of Maine, to build houses for the immense multitudes that were to inhabit the new towns. A company was formed under the auspices of Daniel Webster, called the Ellsworth Land and Lumber Company. Daniel Webster was the president of the association, and the first on its list of directors.— The plan was to purchase some eight townships of land lying on the Union River, a bargain for which had already been made by David Webster, a relative of the Massachusetts Senator. This tract was well wooded and by cutting down, sawing and bringing to market the trees with which it was covered, immense sums were to be realized.

The capital stock of the company was two millions, and for this sum the company was to be put in possession of property estimated at nearly eleven millions. In less than four years the stockholders were to be the possessors of this broad domain of forest, which was to be fully paid for by the mere income of that period, and the timber of which would not be exhausted in less than thirty years. The following is the conclusion of the statements in the pamphlet now before us:

> Estimated surplus dividends in 1841, after paying all assessments for which the stock is liable:
>
> $145,811.50
>
> Thus by the above estimate the stockholders will in less than four years, that is, on the 1st of January, 1841, hold stock paid up in full, by the yearly income derived from the manufacturing operations of the company.

Such was the splendid scheme of Mr. Webster, according to which more than eight million dollars were to be gained by the payment of two millions, and those two millions were to be paid by the yearly income of the enterprise. But the commercial troubles of 1837 came.

The cities that had been laid out, could not find either builders or inhabitants, and the Ellsworth Land and Lumber Company, with all its magnificent arrangements, and its hopes of princely revenues to the stockholders, passed to the limbo where lie all things lost on earth.

This was clearly the fault of the administration. The "Declaration of Whig *Principles*" as it is humorously styled, read by Mr. Webster to the late meeting at Bunker Hill, charges against the present national administration, as its great transgression, that when the crisis of 1837 came, it "abandoned all care of the currency," and thus "renounced its constitutional duty." Mr. Webster in his Saratoga speech also insisted upon the duty of the general government to keep the paper money in circulation on a par with specie. If this could have been done in 1837; if the government could by any possibility have kept the immense amount of paper money, which was already in circulation in 1836 and 1837, upon a par with specie, Mr. Webster's speculation might have gone on until the original speculators had sold out at an immense advance upon the first prices of their stock. If the establishment of a national bank, or if receiving the money of the broken state banks at the Treasury could have had the effect to give this artificial value to paper, the government ought to have tried it. Why should so promising an enterprise as that of the Ellsworth Land and Lumber Company be blown away like a summer cloud in consequence of the perversity of the administration?

It is no answer to say that even if the government could have kept up the great credit system a little longer by the measures asked for by Mr. Webster and his friends, the explosion would have been only more violent at last. It is no answer to say that false values, like stones thrown into the air, must come down at last, and that when the time for the collapse of the bubble of false credit has finally arrived Eolus with all his winds cannot keep it inflated. The government should have done what it could; it should not have abandoned the cause of the currency; it should have stood by Mr. Webster and his friends in their speculations. It should have done its best to put money in his pocket, and then it could not have been blamed for "renouncing its constitutional duty."

Daniel Webster: "Rankest" Member of the "Dangerous ... Aristocracy of Wealth"
September 24, 1840

At Patchogue, Long Island, New York, on September 22 Webster had attacked in harsh words Democratic Senator Silas Wright of New York, who had charged Webster with catering to "moneyed aristocrats." In refutation, Webster had boasted of his frontier background.

Mr. Webster, to use the words employed by him on another occasion, "has come out a democrat died in the wool." He is not only a democrat, but a most pugnacious democrat; he pronounces the man who calls him an aristocrat a liar, and promises to flog him if he will only come to him for the purpose.

Such is the principal purport of the speech delivered the other day at Patchogue. When we read the report of it yesterday morning, we thought that the journal in which it appeared was quizzing its readers, and therefore abstained from taking notice of it. But as it has been copied into the *Commercial Advertiser,* and other organs of the whig party, some of which accompany it with expressions of strong approbation, we can no longer refuse to look upon it as authentic, and shall therefore regale our readers with a few quotations. Mr. Webster, near the commencement of his speech, after complaining that some people had called him, or would call him "an old aristocrat," says:

"Now my friends, it would be very strange if I, who have grown up among the people, and as it were, of the people, should at any time of life take a fancy to aristocracy. I have ploughed, and sowed, and reaped the acres that were my father's, and that now are mine. By the aid of those valuable institutions, public schools, and the guidance and assistance of the best of parents, I was enabled to get such an education as fitted me to come to the bar; I have been some time in public life; I never held an [offic]e in the course of my life except such a one [as co]mes directly from the bestowment of the people[; I ha]ve had no money out of the public treasury, exce[pt in] pay as a member of Congress; I have no fami[ly or r]elations—no one in any way or shape—nothing [w]ith blood of mine flowing in their veins that ever held an office or touched a cent of the public money. (*Cheers.*)

"After all this I shall be told that I am an aristocrat. Very well. Prove it. If I am one I am quite false to my origin and connexions, as well as to my nature. But I ask for the proof. Look at my votes in Congress. What right of the people have I voted away? By what vote of mine in the public councils of the country am I to be proved an aristocrat?"

Again, as to the flogging he will give to any body who shall call him an aristocrat:

"I claim no more patriotism than others—but I claim just as much. Have I no stake in this fair inheritance of our common country? Don't I wish to go down to my grave with my full share of its honors and its glories? Have I no int[e]rest or desire to protect what I have, that it may descend unblemished to my children and my children's children? (Here Mr. Webster's voice changed very perceptibly, and he was much [a]ffected, and labored with strong feelings.) The man that says that I am an aristocrat—IS A LIAR! (Tremendous cheering.)

"I may be mistaken. I may err. I submit to the judgment of those who can see more clearly than myself when I am at fault. But the man who will not meet me fairly with argument, and uses idle and abusive declamation instead—*and then will not come within the reach of my arm*, is not only a liar, but *a coward!*"

It may be said, we know, that even granting Mr. Webster not to be an aristocrat it may possibly turn out that he is a monarchist, and that if he is not in favor of the dominion of the few, he may desire to bring the nation under the rule of one. But Mr. Webster, who it is whispered is to be General Harrison's Secretary of State, and whose opinions, it is highly important that the public should know, provides against this supposition also. Not only is he not an aristocrat, according to his own account of the matter, but he is a democrat, and not only is he a democrat, but a democrat of the genuine Jeffersonian school, a Virginia democrat, a democrat of the school of '98. He says very emphatically:

"I desire to put it upon that issue—that if the measures of the present administration have been democratic, support them; if not do not so. But do not take names for things, and professions for principles. By democratic measures, I mean such as the good old democrats of past times would have supported. Such measures as Chancellor Livingston would have supported—such as Mr. Jefferson would have supported—such as Virginia, the old pure school of democracy, would have supported, *Such measures I advise you to support*. But examine and enquire well for yourselves, and decide as you find."

There is a story written by a wit of this city, now no more, entitled "The Height of Impudence." It was a narrative of a man who intruded himself into other people's parlours, made free with their letters over the fire place, and thrust his feet into their slippers; but it related nothing so impudent as this intrusion of Mr. Webster among the Jeffersonian democrats.

Mr. Webster seems to suppose that there is no aristocracy but the aristocracy of birth, and overlooks the fact that there is a more narrow-minded, and in this country, more dangerous aristocracy, that of wealth. Of this aristocracy, we take leave to say, in spite of Mr. Webster's vulgar epithets and brutal threats, that he is a most ser[v]ile and thorough-paced champion, and that his whole public course has been an attempt to reduce the people of the United States under its dominion. Whoever would give by law peculiar privileges to associated wealth, whether in the shape of a Bank of the United States, or any other institution; whoever would impose a law for the benefit of a particular class to the injury of others, whether that law be a protective tariff or any other; whoever would accumulate patronage and concentrate power in the government, whether it be by a splendid system of what are called internal improvements, or by any other method, that man is an aristocrat, an adversary of the political rights of the mass; and such Mr. Webster has proved himself to be by a long series of public acts. Among the great leaders of the aristocratic party to which he belongs, we believe we make no mistake when we say that Mr. Webster, the future head of General Harrison's cabinet, is the rankest aristocrat of all. Struggle as violently and angrily as he may, the imputation will still cling to him; he might as well disown his name.

In another part of his speech Mr. Webster says that if he had sided with the friends of nullification, when that question came up in Congress, HE "might have CRUSHED GENERAL JACKSON'S ADMINISTRATION IN AN HOUR." We would call the attention of our readers to the enormous egotism of this passage. If Mr. Webster had at that time taken part with the nullifiers, he would have earned only the indignation of those whom he represented. Their opinions on the subject were fixed, and their feelings strongly excited, and if he had betrayed their cause by deserting to the other side, they would have driven him forth from his high post with shouts of wrath and hisses of scorn.

We publish all of Mr. Webster's speech that appears in the *Commercial* of last evening. The whigs seem to be ashamed of it, and we hear it spoken of by them as unworthy of the powers of its author, but as well adapted to the understandings of the audience he was addressing. What idea must Mr. Webster entertain of the people of Suffolk County? Read the speech, observe its puerilities, its coarseness, its egotism, and draw your own conclusion.

THE ELECTION OF WILLIAM HENRY HARRISON:
"THE CONTEST WHICH LIES BEFORE US"
November 9, 1840

In the Presidential election in November 1840 Harrison defeated the Democratic incumbent Van Buren by a decisive majority of electoral votes, 234 to 60, although out of nearly two and a half million popular votes cast Harrison's margin was only about 146,000.

General Harrison is the President elect of the United States; the returns from the western counties of New York have decided that question. The time for a "change" has at last arrived; the time when the people, in order to be convinced of the benefits of a democratic policy, must try a taste of its opposite.

There is no teacher like experience. No man values the blessing of health like him who has just risen from a sick bed—no man enjoys the sweets of liberty like him who has tasted the bitterness of oppression. We suppose that it is just so with nations;—to keep up their attachment to a wise and liberal government, which respects the rights and liberties of all alike, it may be necessary that now and then they should submit to see their affairs administered on principles which exalt the few at the expense of the many.

The democratic party will watch the conduct of the new administration, we hope, in a spirit of fairness, but with a determination to contest every inch of ground, in the attempt which will doubtless be made to revive exploded principles and pernicious measures. If they succeed in forcing a national bank upon us, we shall never cease to call for a repeal of its charter. If they return to the policy of internal improvements which prevailed under the younger Adams, we shall demand that they be abandoned, the moment the democratic party is again in the ascendancy. If they revive a protective tariff we shall claim that it be rescinded. Every step that is taken in violation of the constitution and the principles of equal rights will be retraced the moment their brief hour of authority is past.

The first step will undoubtedly be to propose a national bank. They see that the commerce of the country is rapidly reviving, and the money market gradually recovering from the state of confusion into which it was thrown by the failure of our banking system, and they will be in haste to apply their grand remedy, in order that it may have the credit of bringing about the favorable results which must infallibly take place, and in fact, are now taking place without it. Let them create their national bank, and let those subscribe in its stock who are willing to contribute their capital to an institution which has only four years at most to live. Its charter will scarcely out live the period prescribed for filling up its stock.

We enter upon the contest which lies before us, not only with a firm resolution, but with the most cheerful hopes of the issue. Democratic principles have taken deep root in the hearts even of many who have been led, by a popular delusion, to assist in the overthrow of the present administration.—The young men of the country, with no very numerous exceptions, are indoctrinated in democratic principles, friends to the freedom of trade, inclined to those plans of legislation which interfere least with men's employments, which create fewest offices, and which are founded on an honest and rigid construction of the constitution. The moment the whig party begin to move in those projects which their leaders have darkly hinted at, but which they dared not distinctly proclaim, because they knew them to be unpopular, we shall have this class of young men instantly upon our side.

The dispute which has now been decided against the democratic party, has been conducted by them in a manner highly to their honor, with a frank avowal of their doctrines and intentions, and for the most part with the weapons of fair controversy. Their adversaries on the contrary, keeping their own future policy out of sight, and taking advantage of the embarrassments of the times, which they artfully and unjustly laid to the door of the administration, have gained the majority by the propagation of a gross delusion. If our party has fallen, it has fallen with honor.

If our adversaries have triumphed, their triumph is their disgrace, inasmuch as it is the fruit of a fraud. It will be short too; for the fraud is sure to be detected, and all delusion is but for a time.

We have heard people say that they are sorry for Mr. Van Buren, who has been defeated in the canvas for a re-election. For our part we envy Mr. Van Buren. We envy him for the high moral standing to which he is raised by this very defeat;—we envy him for the honorable place his name will hold in history. He is defeated because he would not betray the trust which the people had reposed in him; because he would concede nothing to expediency; because he would not join with those, by whose fraud the majority has now been changed, in their conspiracy against the people and the constitution. He has been defeated simply because of his integrity and his inflexibility, and because he would not swerve from the principles upon which the welfare of his country depended, for the sake of securing the present ascendancy of his party.

The Intractibility of the Irish
November 10, 1840

Job 5:7: "Who has let the wild ass go free? . . . He scorns the tumult of the city; / he hears not the shouts of the driver." As governor of New York between 1839 and 1843, William Henry Seward twice proposed separate but equal schools for immigrant children staffed by teachers of their native languages and religious faiths.

It is surprising how intractable the Irish are. The *Troy Morning Mail* of the 5th instant, a whig paper, gives the following instance in point:

> "IRISH VOTERS.—Almost the entire Irish vote in Albany, this city and the neighboring country, has been cast against the whigs. In many instances, where they have professed to act with their employers, and been kindly aided by them, *with special reference to the election*, when

the contest came on they have gone to the polls and voted the locofoco ticket. There is method, system in this, —not merely here, but doubtless in other portions of the state."

In saying that the Irish naturalized citizens generally voted against the whig ticket, and that even in cases where they had been "kindly aided by the whigs with special reference to the election," they were so insensible to the obligations of gratitude as to persist in voting according to their honest opinions, we believe that the Troy print is not guilty of the least exaggeration. Think of a genteel whig, his eyes glistening with affection, grasping the hard hand of an Irish laborer, inquiring with the most anxious tenderness concerning the health of his family, telling him what a fine race of men his country people are, and what valuable citizens they make, and offering him employment and good wages, with a "special reference to the next election," as the *Troy Mail* says, in other words with a gentle hint that as a return for all this civility and kindness he is expected to vote for Harrison! Think of the Paddy turning off the hint in his merry way, accepting the employment, pocketing the wages, and then on the day of the election making a democratic ticket, and in the coolest, most impudent and most ungrateful manner in the world depositing it at the polls!

We have sometimes heard the Irish called "wild Irish." We no longer wonder at the epithet—they are like "the wild ass who regardeth not the crying of the driver"; they can be neither coaxed nor driven to vote against their consciences. They can neither be tamed by bribes nor blows. They have been discharged from employment, "with a special reference to the next election," but without any effect; they have been "kindly aided with a special reference to the next election," with no better success; they are untamed still, and as wild as ever. Nothing can ever be hoped from them by the whig party; their native democratic instinct is too strong. The only method left for the whigs, is that to which they resorted in 1838, namely, to import their voters from the highly civilized city of Philadelphia. They can do nothing with the Irish.

Even Governor Seward's appeal to the religious attachments of our Irish population, "with special reference to the next election" failed of success, although he approached them on the side on which they were most sensitive. When he recommended an appropriation of public money to the Catholic schools he, no doubt, expected the Irish votes in return. Yet did the ungrateful Irish vote against him almost to a man. They seem to be particularly shy of any bait thrown out "with special reference to the next election." No wonder that the whigs begin to talk, as we hear they do, of calling a public meeting to denounce the interference of naturalized citizens in our elections.

We fear that this practice of "kindly aiding men with special reference to the next election," has been too common among the whig party. Translated into plain English it is BRIBERY. It is the bestowment of an advantage upon an individual with a view of buying his vote. We record the confession of the Troy print that the attempt has been made by men of its party, and take this occasion to express our satisfaction that by their own admission it has not succeeded with our Irish population.

THE LAW'S DELAY
November 14, 1840

In reading the following editorial, we may recall that, after practicing law for ten years in Massachusetts before taking up editorial work in New York City, Bryant had confessed himself disgusted with "legal chicanery," and called his late profession a "shabby business," one for which his dislike had been "augmenting daily."

THE LAW'S DELAY.—Some time since the lawyers of this city had a meeting, at which they passed a set of resolutions complaining of certain matters in the practice of the Superior Court of this city. For our part, we are not among those who expect much from the lawyers in the way of improving our legal practice. Their prejudices, particularly after they have arrived at a certain age, and have acquired a certain degree of reputation, are, in general, strongly attached to the forms to which they have been accustomed, however objectionable they may be.

There are certain formalities of legal practice, not in the Superior Court only, but in all the civil courts of the city, which are exceedingly inconvenient to suitors, however convenient they may be to lawyers, and which work delay, expense and absolute injustice. The members of the legislature of this state who brought forward last year, their plans of legal reform, seem to have understood as little what they had to do as how to do it.

We will give an instance of the obstructions to justice to which we allude. A suit is commenced in the Superior Court of this city, the defendant is summoned in the beginning of August to appear on the first Monday in September. A person not acqu[a]inted with the practice of our law, would naturally suppose that when the process was served on the defendant, he would receive, at the same time, a written and specific statement of the nature of the claim or charge brought against him, a "declaration," as the lawyers call it, so that he may be prepared to defend himself. But it is not so; he is only served with a summons or held to bail, and he finds on inquiry, that he cannot obtain a statement of the nature of the suit, or "the declaration," until the court sits, nor even then, unless he employs a lawyer, to give the lawyer on the other side a "notice of retainer," as it is called.

The first Monday in September arrives; the Court is in session, the plaintiff neglects to file his declaration containing a statement of the nature of his claims. The defendant then naturally supposes that the suit will be dismissed, and that without any additional ceremony he shall be relieved from further trouble and uncertainty. He applies to his counsel and finds that he is mistaken. He is caught in the net of the law, and must be kept floundering and struggling in it for the benefit of the profession. His counsel must move the court for a rule upon the plaintiff's counsel to file his declaration, and inform the defendant why he has called him into court.

Behold then the defendant, who has been dragged into a law suit against his will, obliged to commence a suit in his turn against the plaintiff, in order to discover for what cause he is brought into court and kept there. His counsel moves the court, obtains the rule, and it is served upon the counsel of the plaintiff. He then finds he must submit to a further delay, and that the plaintiff is not compelled to file his declaration till the next term of the court, which is at the end of October.

At the next term of the court therefore, the defendant calls again upon his counsel and asks to see the declaration. He finds that it is not yet made out; that the plaintiff's counsel has been busy with other matters, travelling in the country, or occupied with weighty duties as a member of an election committee, or travelling agent of a party, and could not have the declaration ready. He learns also that a practice has grown up among the lawyers of allowing counsel further time in such cases, and that the declaration is promised in about a fortnight.—At last about the middle of November the declaration is made out, and then for the first time the defendant is permitted to know for what he is sued and to prepare for his defence.

Here are more than three months wasted in delays and formalities which do not advance the cause of justice a single step, but on the contrary have only the effect of harrassing the defendant's patience and picking his pocket. When the three months and a half are over, he is but just upon the threshhold of the lawsuit. He is just where he ought to have been the day when the writ was served upon him.

We do not see why the practice in this respect should not be as simple and direct here as in Massachusetts or other New England states. There the declaration goes out with the writ, the defendant is immediately acquainted with the nature of the suit, and can make up his mind at once whether he will allow the suit to go against him by default, or contest it, or seek an accommodation with the plaintiff. If he contests it, he may begin immediately to prepare his defence.

We know it is answered to this, that the defendant might be on the point of going out of town, and that in such cases there would not be time to frame a declaration properly, before serving it upon him. Well, then; let the plaintiff wait till the defendant comes back— he must be unreasonable indeed in his absence, if he should not return before a declaration, in the present state of the practice, is ready for him. Or suppose he should not come back at all, the mischief is not very great—the world would not revert to chaos because there is one law suit the less. But if the circumstances of the case require great haste and the declaration is imperfectly drawn in consequence, let it be afterwards amended and cast upon payment of costs. It is better that some inconvenience of this kind should be incurred in one law suit out of five hundred, than that all suits should be subject to unreasonable delays.

Why the evil we have pointed out has not been remedied before is not very surprising. The greater part of the community live in a happy exemption from law suits.—Those who are unfortunate enough to be engaged in them meet with little sympathy. They are generally looked upon, too often unjustly, as a quarrelsome race who might live in peace if they would, and who deserve by their litigious temper the losses they meet with. Besides, the ceremonials of practice are so intricate and wrapped up in such strange and unintelligible phrases that they are Greek to the greater part of suitors, and it requires more than common perspicacity of intellect, on their part, to understand in the first place what the attorneys are about, and in the second place, how much of what they do might better be dispensed with. Of the members of the legislature, those who are not lawyers, for the most part know nothing of the evil on which we are animadverting and those who are, do not look upon it as an evil.

We hope the attention of the members of the legislature from this city will be directed to this matter, in the session which is soon to open. It is certainly agreeable to justice that he who is prosecuted at law should immediately be allowed to know for wh[at] cause. It is an enormous, a horrible perve[r]sion of justice, that he who is dragged into court by a prosecutor should not be allowed to escape from the meshes of litigation, without himself turning plaintiff, and employing counsel to institute legal proceedings for the purpose of discovering why he is sued.

Defense of Newspaper Editors
January 14, 1841

Mordecai Noah, playwright, journalist, and pioneer Zionist, edited several New York newspapers, including that with the largest circulation in the city, the Courier and Enquirer. *This was a political paper, the principal rival of the mercantile* Journal of Commerce. *Noah had held consular posts in Tunis and Algiers, as well as the office of sheriff in New York County. John Davis, Whig governor of Massachusetts, was a conservative tariff protectionist; James Buchanan, later President of the United States, was in 1841 a Democratic Senator from Pennsylvania. In April 1840 the Pennsylvania Whig Congressman Charles Ogle had proposed to the Congress that $3,665 be denied President Van Buren for repair of the White House, accusing him of spending public money lavishly, while hoarding his own with "sordid parsimony." Ogle's diatribe was credited with help in the Whig election victory later that year.*

The *Journal of Commerce*, in censuring the appointment of M. M. Noah to a judicial station, pronounces the editors of political journals to be a class "from whom all moral rectitude is thoroughly extracted." This is a most extravagant and unjust denunciation.

Editors of political newspapers are bad enough we admit; we have no desire to palliate their wrong doings; but they are not worse than some other classes of men, and we are inclined to think that they possess the average honesty of the community. They have as much virtue, as much integrity, as much fairness of purpose as there is any demand for. If the community were not as bad as they, their journals could not find support and circulation. Let other classes of men call for newspapers of a higher character, a more rigid respect for truth, a more candid construction of motives, a more conscientious regard to the public morals and public welfare, and they would be supplied. Let the community discountenance dishonest and malignant journals and they will go out of publication. If newspapers are not what they ought to be it is because the public will not allow them to be so.

Their morals are on a level with the morals of their readers. If they are unprincipled and flagitious, it is because their conductors are encouraged and rewarded by the public for making them so. The public is the principal, the instigator in this matter. The newspaper editor is but the accessory; it is the public who instruct, educate and form the newspaper editor; his sheet is simply the reflection of their own moral qualities.

Compare the newspaper editor with other classes which you can fairly bring into comparison with him, and see whether they have the advantage of him in point of a mor[a]l rectitude. The makers of poli[tical] speeches in and out of Congress, the managers of elections, and the framers of political addresses and resolutions, are they more fair and just than the political editor? Was Mr. Ogle, whose lying speech about the furniture of the President's House was so widely circulated by the whigs previous to the late election, a newspaper editor? Was John Davis, now Governor of Massachusetts, and author of the gross misrepresentation concerning Mr. Buchanan's doctrine of low wages, was he a journalist?

When the merchants of this city all turned whig politicians in 1834, and took the management of the elections in that year, and several of the succeeding years, did they not in unfairness, immoral means, and party ferocity, leave the journalists at an immense distance behind them? Who planned the scheme of bringing on spurious voters from Philadelphia in the fall of 1838, to change the majority in this city? Who paid the blackguards their hire, and who gratified their leader with one of the most lucrative offices in the state? Were they journalists?

We protest therefore against making the journalists the scapegoats who are to bear the reproach of all the dishonesty and ferocity of party. The journalist has the misfortune of always being before the public—his mistakes, his prejudices, his bad temper, his weakness, his want of veracity and disregard of justice are always in sight—yet he is in almost every case the mere index of what other men are doing. He is but a straw swimming on the surface of the stream, which, though it attracts the eye, is not the cause of the current, but is merely borne along by it, and shows its direction.

Besides, the journalist who is tolerably conscientious in the exercise of his vocation, is in a state of constant resistance to the influences by which he is surrounded; he is exposed to perpetual solicitations from selfish and unprincipled men,—men who have [their own?] interest in view, or a malignant [curiosity?] to gratify, or whose motives of political expediency admit of the practice of political dishonesty. He finds in fact that a large part of the community are in a plot to make him a rogue, and where is the wonder if the plot should sometimes succeed?

No, the community must become better itself, before it can expect to have better newspapers, so far at least, as concerns moral honesty and decency.

Van Buren's Popularity
January 15, 1841

The prescient congressman Bryant cites as having foreseen Van Buren's presidency was Gulian Crommelyn Verplanck of New York, a close friend and literary associate of Bryant's (see the headnote to "Mr. Van Buren's Return from England," November

22, 1832). Bryant had reported this incident in a letter to his wife from Washington in January 1832. Van Buren had been nominated for President on the first ballot at the Democratic convention of 1835, and elected in 1836 by a margin of 170 electoral votes over 124 for his Whig opponent, General Harrison.

The *Boston Quarterly Review* for January has come to hand. It is full of its usua[l] spirit and talent, with much of its usual inconsiderateness and extravagance. In the article entitled "Our Future Policy," we find a passage on the character of Mr. Van Buren, in which great, we might say gross injustice is done him. The writer says:

> "He has f[ai]led in his re-election, not because he has lost in popularity, but because he never was the choice of the people. The people never willed his elevation to the presidential chair. He was elevated to that chair, not by his own popularity, but by the popularity of his predecessor, and by the management of party leaders."

These are the rash assertions of one who has not given himself the trouble to understand the subject. If ever a president was raised to the chair by the sober, deliberate choice of the American people, it was Mr. Van Buren. We recollect being at Washington when Mr. Van Buren's nomination as minister to England was under consideration, and the Senate determined upon his rejection. Thousands of people were waiting with intense suspense for the decision of the Senate, and when it was at length announced,—"that act," said an intelligent member of Congress, then of our party, but now a whig, "that act of the Senate has made Mr. Van Buren president of the United States." Whatever were the motives of those who voted for rejecting Mr. Van Buren's nomination, it is certain that it gave an immediate and strong impulse to his personal popularity. The people believed him injured and espoused his cause with enthusiasm. He returned from England and immediately was chosen Vice President of the United States; and when the t[i]me arrived that General Jackson was to retire from office, he was fixed upon, not through the management of political leaders, but by the voluntary act of the great party which elected and supported General Jackson, to be his successor. He was nominated because the p[e]ople demanded his nomination; because no other nomination would have fully satisfied them; he was chosen not because of the popularity of his predecessor, but because he was looked upon as a fitting representative of the democratic party, holding its principles in their purity, and in sincerity of heart, and resolute not to forsake them in the most discouraging emergencies.

The confidence of those who called him to the chair of state has been fully, no[b]ly, we may even say gloriously justified. He has disappointed the fears of his lukewarm friends, and won a higher admiration from those who expected the most from his administration. Under the greatest discouragements, amidst the strongest temptations to backsliding which ever assailed a President of the United States, he has steadily maintained the principles which his calmer judgment approved, turning neither to the right nor the left, despising any temporary advantage which might result to himself or to his party, and looking confidently to the final approbation of his countrymen.

Nor was it for the want of popularity that Mr. Van Buren failed in his re-election. There have been within a few years past many extraordinary fluctuations of public opinion. If the election of President had taken place in the autumn of 1834, amidst the artificial panic, got up by the friends of the United States Bank, Mr. Van Buren would not have been elected. Afterwards the tide of public opinion took another direction, and in 1836, he was chosen by a prodigious majority.

In 1837, the state elections showed that the whigs were rising to the ascendancy, and if Mr. Van Buren, or any other democratic candidate had been before the people at that time, he must have lost his election. In 1838 the democratic party began to recover its old majorities, and if the vote had been taken in 1839, Mr. Van Buren would have been carried into office by a majority like that which he had in 1836. In 1840 the elections again went in favor of the whig party, and Mr. Van Buren's friends were overpowered.

It is not therefore on account of Mr. Van Buren's deficient popularity, it is not because his supporters have lost any of the confidence which they placed in him, it is not because he has not shown himself equal in talents and courage to the high eme[r]gencie[s] by which he has been tried, that he has lost his election. The question of low prices, coming suddenly upon the people, staggered their confidence in the great public measures, to which only the year previous they had given their sanction, and the foul arts of the whig party coming in aid of this hesitation, turned the scale against the democratic candidate.—This is the true solution of the late election. No personal popularity could have withstood the influences which gave a majority to Harrison.

It is said in the *Boston Quarterly* that Mr. Van Buren wants enthusiasm. He is the better fitted on that account for a Chief Magistrate in the difficult times through which we have passed. We needed a man capable not only of the firmest, but the calmest resistance, and to the exercise of this important quality will be owing much of the honor which will yet crown the memory of Martin Van Buren.

Daniel Webster—Secretary of State?
January 27, 1841

Webster became Secretary of State in March 1841. The non-Semitic Philistines, chief rivals of the Israelites, occupied approximately what is now known as the Gaza Strip. The quotation is from Macbeth, *III, i, 56–57. A dispute between Maine and New Brunswick led to the "Aroostook County War" of 1838–1839, in which open hostilities were avoided by an agreement brought about by General Winfield Scott. Thomas Hart Benton was a Democratic Senator from Missouri.*

"It is understood that Mr. Webster will resign his seat in the Senate, preparatory to entering upon his duties in the new cabinet, on the 15th of February."

We quote this from the *Commercial* of last evening. It seems to be admitted on all hands that Mr. Webster is to be the Secretary of State under Harrison's administration. Let us take him in hand for a few moments, and satisfy ourselves, if we can, what sort of prime minister he is likely to make.

Mr. Webster is a man of extraordinary ability in certain respects; if we were to say that he is not we should be guilty of gross injustice, and should moreover imitate a very bad example, that of the whigs when they speak of eminent men of the democratic party. Give Mr. Webster a brief, and nobody would make you a better argument. He will state his positions clearly, illustrate them ingeniously and enforce them impressively. Let him know that it is his business to produce a speech in favour of free trade or against free trade, for a hard money currency or against it, for a national bank or against it, and you will be pretty sure to have an able speech, and most likely, if he happens to be on the right side, a capital one.

This is a great merit, perhaps, but this is all. In certain other respects, Mr. Webster is not an able man; nay, he is a weak man, and an unsafe man. He wants foresight, he wants decision, he wants persistency in right purposes, three things indispensable to the principal minister in an executive cabinet. Some men have a knack of talking plausibly, others have the gift of acting wisely, and Mr. Webster unfortunately belongs to the former class. In defending a course of conduct already determined upon, he has great talent; in choosing a course of conduct he is helpless, hesitating, uncertain; and when he breaks loose from the trammels of his hesitation, he is rash and imprudent. Not fully able to decide for himself which course to take, he chooses desperately and chooses wrong.

It is therefore that Mr. Webster has been always governed by men about him; he has ground corn at the mill of the Philistines ever since he came to his strength. His early speeches—the best he ever made—in favor of free trade, were in the defence of the interests of his patrons, the Boston merchants; his subsequent speeches against free trade, were in defence of the interests of the same class of men, now become holders of shares in manufacturing corporations.—His old opposition to a national bank was abandoned when that class insisted that a bank was necessary to their purposes, and his ancient doctrine that hard money was the only proper and constitutional currency, was given up when they voted it a humbug. In Congress he was never a leader of his party; he had never any measures of his own to propose; in the presence of Henry Clay,

> "His genius was rebuked; as it is said
> Antony's was by Caesar's—"

and he was content to leave the practical direction of his party to that more shrewd and skilful manager, while he took his station in the ranks and followed where he led. In fact throughout his whole political life he has shown himself a man to be led, and not a man to lead.

Yet when occasionally he is indiscreet enough to judge for himself he does very unwise things. Two years since, at the close of the session of Congress, he startled the country with a sudden proposal that the government should cut short the negociations about the disputed portion of Maine, by taking military possession of it on the fourth of July. The country would have been plunged into a profitless war without preparation, if such a proposal had been listened to, and his friends made him explain it away. Last summer he made a speech at Patchogue, in which he claimed to be a Jefferson democrat, and threatened to flog the man who said that Daniel Webster was an aristocrat. Some of the whig journals published a part of the speech, but it being immediately seen that it was a very foolish thing, they dropped the matter instantly, and nothing more was said about Daniel Webster's democracy.

Nor has Mr. Webster the firmness to follow out a right course in the face of other men's disapprobation. After making his tour, in the summer of 1837, through the western states, in which he skilfully managed to lose popularity in proportion to the number of speeches he made, he took his seat in Congress and declared himself a zealous champion of the policy of allowing those who settle on the unsold lands a liberal right of pre-emption. For this Mr. Clay rebuked him fiercely and rudely on the spot, and since that time his zeal in favor of the squatters has slept. Mr. Benton's pre-emption bill is now before the Senate; Mr. Clay's distribution bill is before the Senate, also; Mr. Webster puts aside the question of pre-emption, and gives his support to the project of Mr. Clay. The whig journals this very day are publishing this new proof of Mr. Webster's want of decision and consistency.

This man is to be made Secretary of State, a principal counsellor of the President, and is to be entrusted with the charge of our foreign relations. How ill suited he is to such a post we have seen. The settlement of our relations with foreign nations on favorable terms requires either perfect frankness and decision, or consummate art.— Webster has neither—frank and resolute he is not, neither is he fitted for artifice; his cunning is awkward, and his expedients unskilful. He must be watched or he will spice his despatches with something like the indiscretions of his speech about the north eastern boundary, or the extravagances of his harrangue at Patchogue, or haply allow himself to be driven from a just position, by a little dexterous blustering, just as he was forced to abandon his doctrine concerning pre-emption, to which, without consulting Mr. Clay, he had prematurely given utterance.

We say therefore to the whigs, if you make Mr. Webster Secretary of State, you must watch him well; you must assist him with good counsel; you must put "a viceroy over him," to stiffen him when he is weak, and to hold him back from indiscretions. Nobody we suppose will pretend that Harrison will be capable of directing what shall be done in our intercourse with foreign governments. The poor old gentleman with Mr. Webster at his side will be in the situation of a blind commander steering his vessel with the aid of a blind helmsman.

ANALYSIS OF WEBSTER, CONTINUED
January 28, 1841

The boundary between the state of Maine and the province of New Brunswick in Canada had been in dispute ever since the end of the Revolution in 1783. It was not finally settled until August 1842 in negotiations between Great Britain and the United States, with the Webster–Ashburton Treaty.

In remarking yesterday upon the alternate indecision and rashness of the per[so]nage who is selected as Mr. Harrison's Secretary of State, we had not [room?] to [speak] of the great interests [which] lie at his mercy.—Whether [the] condition of the country shall [be war or] peace; whether its just claims upon foreign governments shall be promptly and honorably satisfied; whether it shall become entangled in the quarrels of kingdoms of the old world or keep clear of them,—these are questions which for the next four years may depend much upon the manner in which Mr. Webster manages the department charged with the direction of our foreign negotiations.

One great interest of the American republic is peace—unbroken, perpetual peace.—War crushes commerce; diverts the labor of man from the cultivation of the better arts; taints the public morals; familiarizes a community to acts of violence; sets up a complete despotism within its immediate sphere, and leads to gradual encroachments on the public liberties. The great endeavor of our Executive should be so to conduct our intercourse with foreign nations as to obtain at their hands strict and immediate justice, yet never to involve the nation in war.

No man who well understands Mr. Webster's character can help feeling concern and apprehension at seeing this great responsibility pass into his hands. In our dealings with foreign governments greater circumspection and foresight are necessary than in the transaction of domestic affairs. In the latter case a false step may be easily retraced, in the former it cannot. Once make an indiscreet concession to a foreign power, and it will never be forgotten; it will be flourished in your face through long years of negotiation, and made the foundation of as many unreasonable demands [as it? can] possibl[y] become. Offend the pride of a powerful nation by an unnecessary insult, and you are plunged in a war at once, unless you avoid it by an humiliating apology. Carry into your negotiations the unthinking rashness which dictated the proposal to take possession of the disputed portion of Maine on the fourth of July, and the foreign commerce of the nation would in a very few weeks be the prey of war. Or conduct your negotiations with the same spirit of indecision which made Mr. Webster return from the ground he had taken on the pre-emption bill, at the stern reproof of Mr. Clay, and you may negociate unsuccessfully for centuries.

It is therefore, we repeat, that the whigs, if they will have Mr. Webster for Secretary of State, must do something more than give him the office; they must give him an adviser, unless they mean that he shall involve our foreign affairs in the same embarrassment and confusion in which, notwithstanding his splendid talents as an advocate, and the large emoluments they bring him, he has always kept his own private affairs. He will probably not be found very unmanageable. Indeed it is one of the peculiarities of his public course, that he has allowed himself to be managed by men of inferior minds, for their own purposes. His pliancy in the hands of one of the members of Congress from this city has caused him to be compared to the great Malabar elephant, led about by the little East Indian who came over as his keeper.

Tyler's First Veto of the Bank Bill
August 18, 1841

Upon the death of President Harrison a month after his inauguration, his successor Vice President John Tyler, a former Virginia congressman long opposed to the United States Bank, promptly vetoed a bill which would have revived the bank.

Mr. Tyler has put a torch to the web which has been years in weaving, and it lies in ashes. The intrigues of many seasons are frustrated by his message rejecting the bank bill. He has broken up the whole plan of the late presidential campaign, which consisted in studiously concealing the true designs of the whig leaders until a majority should be obtained in Congress, and then proclaiming a national bank as the great remedial measure of the day, and seizing the earliest opportunity to impose it upon the nation. All that art and patience, all that ingenious pretences, dexterous concealments, and a skilful organization could do, to carry this plan into effect, has been done, and one thing only remained, the signature of the President, to perfect the scheme. A Virginia politician, nominated as Vice-President, with the very purpose of hiding the true object of the whig leaders from the people, becomes by accident the Chief Executive. He refuses to do what those leaders expected from the pliant temper of General Harrison; he refuses his signature to the bill, and the work of years is undone in a moment.

It becomes the democratic party to rejoice at this event for more reasons than one.

In the first place, it puts an end to our apprehensions of a national bank. We know it is said that if the bank bill had passed, the stock would not have been taken up by capitalists, and this is in a great measure true. But the bill anticipates this difficulty, and after directing that the United States shall subscribe for one-third of the whole stock of the bank, and a third of the remainder if necessary, it authorizes the bank to open for business as soon as six millions and a half of the stock shall be taken up. There is no doubt that a shift would have been made to procure subscriptions for this six millions and a half, by some of the various expedients of the money market; men whose political prejudices overpower their prudence would be made to take stock; more wary men would be tempted by the offer of preferences and peculiar advantages as soon as the bank should go into operation, and money would be raised in other quarters by the future managers of the bank, on condition of repaying it as soon as the control of the capital should come into their hands. Thus furnished, the bank would have gone into operation at Washington, a party engine. A board of directors, the tools of the party who established the bank, would have been formed; the means of corruption would have been tried upon public men, too open—it is the fault of this sordid age—too open to corrupt influences; and a fierce struggle would have again taken place, a long and weary struggle, we fear, between the bank and the people. To have escaped from this impending danger takes a weight from the minds of all well-intending and well-jud[g]ing men.

In the second place it is matter of rejoicing that treachery has met with its due reward. Perhaps no severer punishment for fraud can be devised, than when, after an immense expense of pains and stratagem, after coming nearer and nearer to its object by the most artful approaches, it beholds its prey rescued from the grasp which was just ready to close over it, and placed at an inaccessible distance. Such is the punishment which has overtaken the conspirators who sought to establish a bank without consulting the will of the people—covering them alike with chagrin and shame, and reading the political world a pregnant moral lesson.

In the third place, it is a subject of congratulations, that the least scrupulous and most sordid of all political parties which ever existed in this country, is broken up, prostrated, and scattered by this blow from the hand of one who assisted to place it in the ascendancy. The Vice President of their own choice has publicly rebuked their fraud, and they stand abashed and dispirited in his presence, and behold the power passing out of their hands, not to return. An immense majority of the people of the United States are at this moment congratulating each other on the failure of that act of treachery so subtly planned, and carried forward with such mingled art and audacity to the very moment of its consummation, and they rejoice at the downfal[l] of the party under whose auspices it was all but successful.

We hear, it is true, of another scheme of a national bank which is to be presented to Mr. Tyler by the whigs, and in which discounts are to be masked under the name of exchanges. Mr. Tyler, however, has declared himself utterly opposed to any bank of discounts, and we have no doubt that when he gives his attention to this part of the subject, he will see that it will be necessary to confine the exchanges of the bank to the simple transfer of the funds of the government from place to place—in other words to render it a sort of sub-treasury.

Bryant's 1832 pencil sketch of a cabin where he stayed on the Illinois prairie. Trustees of Reservations, Massachusetts.

"The Rejected Minister," depicting Martin Van Buren on the back of Andrew Jackson. See editorials of November 12 and 22, 1832. Collection of The New-York Historical Society, New York City.

"King Andrew the First," 1832. Collection of The New-York Historical Society, New York City.

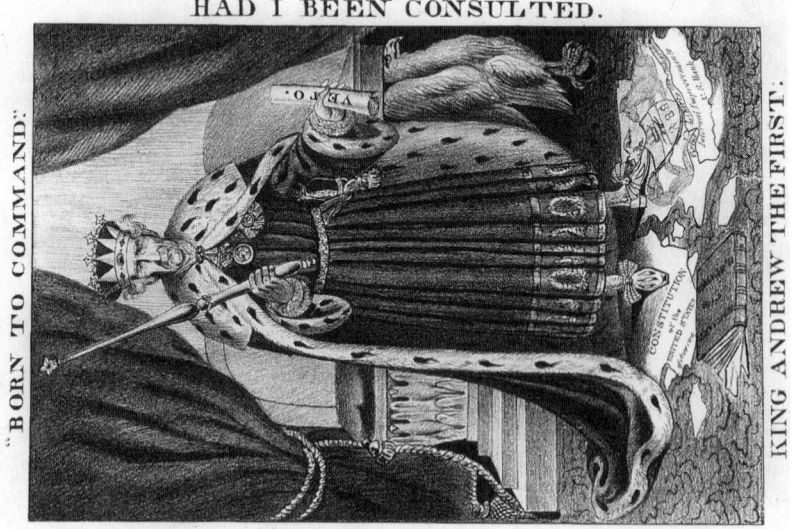

"WHAT? YOU YOUNG YANKEE-NOODLE, STRIKE YOUR OWN FATHER?"

London Punch, 1846

See editorial of September 8, 1842.

THE AMERICAN ROVER-GENERAL WOT TRIED TO STEAL A CUBA

London Punch, 1850

See editorial of November 7, 1856.

The Mexican eagle before the war

The Mexican eagle after the war

PLUCKED

Yankee Doodle, 1847

See editorial of December 31, 1847.

SOUTHERN CHIVALRY — ARGUMENT VERSUS CLUB'S.

Drawing by J. Magee of the attack on Senator Charles Sumner. See editorials of May 23 and 24 and July 24, 1856. Print Collection, Miriam and Ira D. Wallach Division of Art, Prints and Photographs, The New York Public Library, Astor, Lenox, and Tilden Foundations.

Henry Clay. Drawing by David Johnson, *The New York Times*.

Bryant (left) with Daniel Webster at the funeral of James Fenimore Cooper (detail) by Daniel Huntington. See editorial of March 8, 1850.

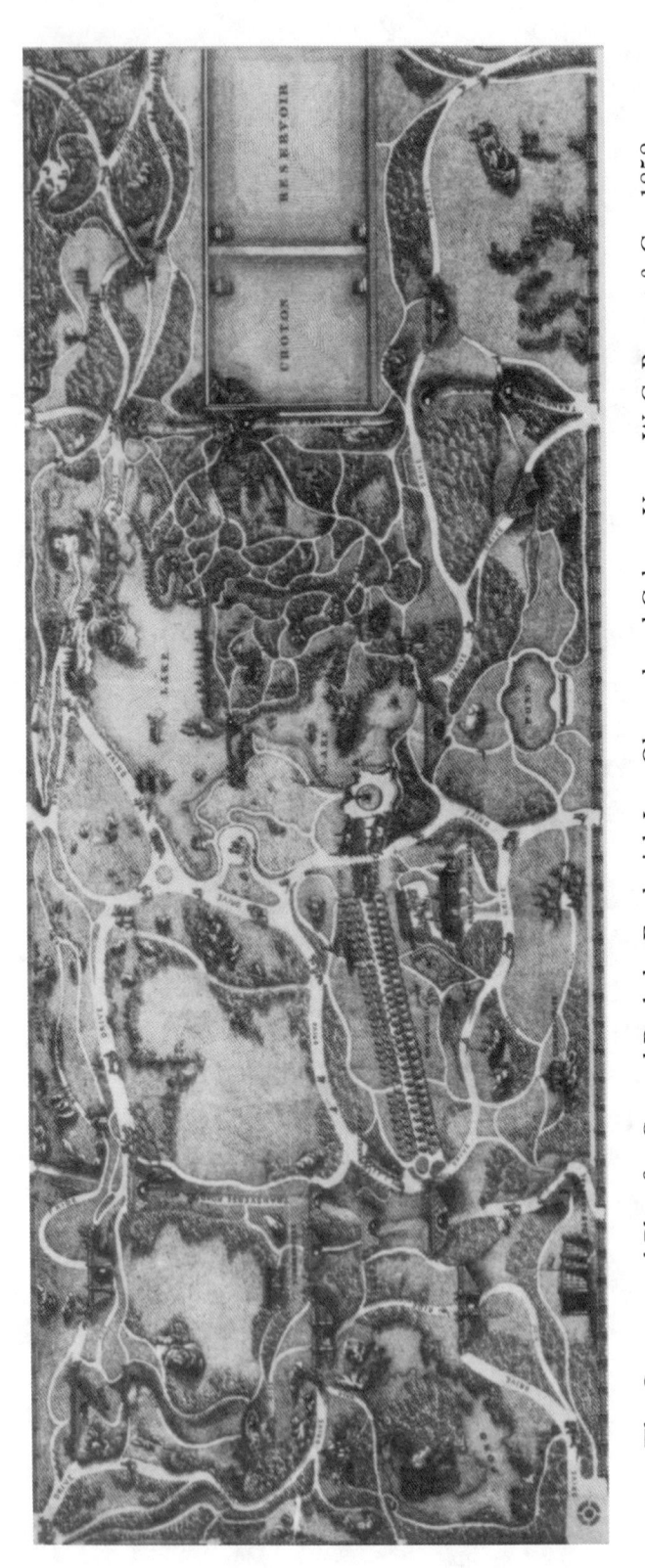

The Greensward Plan for Central Park, by Frederick Law Olmsted and Calvert Vaux. W. C. Bryant & Co., 1858. See editorials for July 3, 1844 and July 2, 1853.

"Harper's Ferry Insurrection—Bringing the Prisoners out of the Engine House." *Frank Leslie's Illustrated Newspaper*, November 5, 1859. See editorial of October 18, 1859.

"Tell W. C. Bryant in my dying hour I freed the slaves of America," scrawled on a scrap of paper found among Bryant's papers. Is the signature that of John Brown? See editorial of December 5, 1859.

"Kiting" in Wall Street
August 19, 1841

"Greek"—i.e., "unintelligible." William Cowper, in Table Talk *(1782): "Nor would the nine [muses] consent the sacred tide / Should purl amidst the traffic of Cheapside, / Or tinkle in 'Change Alley, to amuse / The leathern ears of stock-jobbers and Jews." For Ulysses' winds, see Bryant's translation of Homer's* Odyssey, *X, 1–33. Emanuel Swedenborg (1688–1772), a Swedish philosopher and religious mystic, influenced such American idealists as Emerson and Henry James the Elder.*

A correspondent in the country desires to know the meaning of a strange expression which he found in our paper of Tuesday—the word *kiting*. We will explain its signification as well as we are able.

Our correspondent must know that Wall street and its purlieus are inhabited by a peculiar tribe of men, ingenious and sensitive in a high degree, and endowed with most lively and poetic imaginations. They are supposed to be descended from the ancient Greeks, a theory which is confirmed, not only by their poetic temperament, but by the fact that there are still a great many *Greeks* among them. Cowper, in speaking of a division of the same tribe of men inhabiting Change Alley in London, talks of

"The leathern ears of stockjobbers and Jews"

but Cowper is guilty of a slander. Nothing can be of a more silken and delicate texture than the auditory organs of this race of men; their susceptible ears will not endure plain prose. They express themselves only in metaphors and similitudes. Like the Frenchman who alarmed Mrs. Trott, by informing her that he was come to stab her to the heart, they "do speak figuratively." They deal as liberally in figures of speech as they do in figures of arithmetic.

Wall street, for example, in the imaginations of this poetic race, is one of the most picturesque places in the known world. Gloomy bulls and shaggy bears glare at the passer-by from their stalls and dens, or bellow and growl as they roam the streets. Full grown men amuse themselves with blowing bubbles, and other full grown men admire and buy them,—some with the desire of possessing such beautiful objects, and others in the hope of selling them at a profit before they burst. Nor are aquatic animals wanting to give variety to the spectacle; sharks move about with as much facility as in the ocean, and lame ducks waddle in and out with the most engaging familiarity. The powers of the air are also under the dominion of the dwellers in that region; there the wind bloweth not where it listeth, but men raise the wind with certain magical ceremonies, and give it the direction which pleases them. There the wind is bought and sold, an early practice of the Greeks; for we read that Ulysses, when setting out on one of his voyages, purchased a couple of bags filled with winds, and put them on board his vessel. Men from the various commercial quarters of our city rush into Wall street, and having raised the wind in a given direction, send up huge kites, which mount mystically in the skies, and unrolling the long spools of packthread, pass out of sight to the great joy of the kiteflyers below.

Such is the picture of Wall street as it exists in the minds of that imaginative race whose pleasant heritage it is. From this our correspondent will gather that *kiting* or *kite flying* is a metaphorical expression, a similitude, a correspondence, as the followers of Emanuel Swedenborg would call it.—A kite is a domestic bill of exchange, and kiteflying is a method of obtaining accommodations from the banks under the form of negotiating bills of exchange. For example, a merchant wants money, but he does not care to make an application for an accommodation, he prefers to deal in what is called business paper. He therefore sits down and draws an inland bill of exchange upon his associate in New Orleans, payable in a certain number of days, presents it to the bank, and obtains the money, deducting the discount and the price of exchange. In other words he sends up a kite. When this bill falls due his correspondent at New Orleans sends up another kite; he draws a second bill of exchange upon the New York merchant, sells it to a bank at New Orleans, and pays the first. The merchant at New York in the fulness of time sends up a third kite—or draws a third bill of exchange and pays the second. Thus the game goes on; kite is sent up after kite; the original debt to the bank is kept like a shuttlecock constantly in the air; and the trader has the appearance of doing a great business, when in fact he is only borrowing money.

It is manifest that the nearer our exchanges can be kept to a uniform state, the greater are the facilities for kite-flying, inasmuch as the sport costs less. A national bank dealing in exchange, with branches in the several states, would be an admirable contrivance to raise the wind for the kite-flyers. One who desired an accommodation would then only have to make his note payable in a neighboring city, in other words, draw a domestic bill of exchange, and pay the small rate of exchange in addition to the discount, and his business is done. Just before the late suspension of specie payments in 1837, the game of kite-flying was carried on to a prodigious extent; the banks themselves entered deeply into it, and huge kites to the amount of a hundred thousand dollars and more, were sent backwards and forwards. The suspension of specie payments, by deranging and arresting the exchanges, spoiled and broke up the sport, both among banks and individuals.

It turns out that of the prodigious and ruinous loans made by the late United States Bank, the greater part were made not on local paper, but on bills of exchange. It was by means of bills of exchange also, that Mr. Biddle's bank attempted to break the banks of New York. A national bank, with general powers to deal in exchange, and exchange only, having branches in the principal cities in the Union, would be a most dangerous engine of speculation, worse by ten times than a bank confined to the safer and more certain business of local discounts. No man who knows to what an enormous extent the kite-flying of 1836 was carried will deny this position.

We hope that we have explained the meaning of kite and kite-flying to our correspondent's satisfaction. We shall enclose one copy of this number of the EVENING POST to his address, and another to the address of John Tyler, acting President of the United States.

VAN BUREN IN RETIREMENT
August 24, 1841

Ex-President Van Buren was living in retirement at his estate, Lindenwald, on the Hudson River. The quotations, freely rendered by Alexander Pope from the Latin of Horace, allude to the Roman general Cincinnatus who retired voluntarily to his farm. Jackson's home, the Hermitage, was near Nashville, Tennessee. Whig Senate leader Henry Clay was trying to force replacement of the subtreasury by a recharter of the United States Bank.

FROM KINDERHOOK.—People are almost weary of hearing from Washington; its debates, its broils, its intrigues, and even the failures by which these intrigues are punished, no longer interest them as they did a little while since. The members of Congress are tired of a summer session; the whigs are tired of proposing schemes which come to nothing; the democrats are tired of being gagged on the floor of Congress; —Mr. Clay is tired, the Cabinet is tired.—Mr. Tyler is very tired, and so are the people. Those who are the most sick of the special session are probably those by whose procurement it was called.

Meantime our readers might, perhaps, like to hear what is doing in a more peaceful quarter. —We learn from Kinderhook that Mr. Van Buren is cultivating his private grounds with much better success than the whigs are administering the government. He raises finer cabbages than Mr. Clay raises banks. The Kentuckian's crop of "fiscal corporations" is likely to be what would be called in the market a "total failure"; the ex-president, on the contrary, has astonished his brother Dutchmen by producing the best and earliest cabbages in the neighborhood.

When Mr. Van Buren was coming on from Washington, after the

inauguration of his successor, and had left Philadelphia in the rail road cars, —just before they were put in rapid motion, a little lad, very neatly dressed, was seen running to keep up with them, and looking hard at Mr. Van Buren, as if he had something to say. With his usual kindness of manner, Mr. Van Buren spoke to him in an encouraging tone, on which the boy, the blood rushing into his face, called out, "So, Matty, you are going to Kinderhook to plant cabbages, eh!"

The style of the lad's address was not very respectful to be sure, but they who put it into his mouth were probably not aware of the compliment it implied. He who can leave the cares of government, and apply himself, as Mr. Van Buren is doing with cheerfulness and interest to the task of tilling the earth, is a true philosopher. Poet scarcely ever paid a finer compliment than when alluding to the illustrious companions,

> Chiefs out of war and statesmen out of place,

who graced his retreat in the country, he introduces a great commander in these lines:

> There he, whose lightnings pierced the Iberian mines,
> Now forms my quincunx and now ranks my vines,
> Or tames the genius of the stubborn plain,
> Almost as quickly as he conquered Spain.

Cincinnatus, as we all learned at school, was a famous ploughman in his day, and no doubt raised excellent wheat and lupines, and if the ancient inhabitants of Italy resembled the present in their husbandry and modes of living, excellent cabbages also. Washington was not only a great president, but a most intelligent agriculturist, and Andrew Jackson keeps his Hermitage in admirable order and cultivation. The greatest talents for civil government have been possessed by men who loved the tillage of the soil.

No doubt Mr. Clay wishes he were back at Ashland, breeding mules and short horned cattle, instead of toiling in the sterile field of which he has taken charge. He begins to see that he would have done better to leave it fallow until the time for the regular session of parliamentary labour had arrived, —that his special session is seen by every body to be a special humbug, and that he has called together his workmen to tug and sweat in the heat of dog days, to no purpose. No bank will be raised this session—one has been blasted already, and the second crop is pretty certain to be nipped in its flower by a killing frost. The land bill is in danger of a blight, and the revenue bill is sure to come to nothing. Harvest-time will be a melancholy time with the whigs; a time to sing dirges and penitential psalms. We would not give one of Mr. Van Buren's fine early cabbages for all that Mr. Clay will glean during this session in the field of politics.

BANK OF THE UNITED STATES: FINAL DEMISE
September 8, 1841

It is uncertain which if any verses Bryant parodies in the epigraph, or whether the lines may be of his own coinage: nor has the verse couplet within the text been identified.

> Thy pomp is in the dust, thy power is laid
> Low in the pit thine AVARICE hath made.

The wits of Wall Street are cracking their jokes over the deceased Bank of the United States—Mr. Biddle's bank we mean—which has just given up the ghost at Philadelphia.

"Do you own any United States Bank stock?" says one of them to another. "No" is the answer. "Then you are not so poor as I thought you were." And thereupon the questioner relates a story of a man seen by a traveller leaning with his arms on a fence by the road side, in that worn out and sterile tract which lies between Baltimore and Washington. "You need not look so hard at me, stranger," said the man observing that the traveller eyed him rather sharply, "I am not so poor as you think; I do not own this land."

Another astonishes hearers with declaring that the purchase of United States Bank stock is the safest speculation in which any man can engage, and on being called upon for the proof of his assertion, demonstrates that the purchaser can lose but seven and half per cent, the price he pays for the shares, and asks what other speculation there is in the market in which one cannot by any possibility lose more than seven and a half per cent.

Thus do men amuse themselves at the expense of the fallen. Time was, and not long since, when the United States Bank inspired the profoundest awe in Wall Street; but their late idol is now become their laughing stock. The claws of the monster are sheathed forever, the flame of its breath is extinct, its fangs and its sting are motionless, and now the most timid jester insults its carcase with impunity. The most helpless of its debtors lifts up the heel against it; the very dogs of the street do it indignity. Its day of mischief is over. It can bribe no more members of Congress. It can buy no more newspapers. It can hire no more pamphleteers and travelling agents to influence our elections. It can never again speculate in cotton. It can borrow no more money. It can no longer regulate the currency by making money scarce or abundant at its pleasure. It can form no more plots to break the New York banks. It can purchase no more majorities in the Pennsylvania legislature. It is as harmless as the petrified rattlesnake found the other day at Dubuque, or a millennial cockatrice in that happy period when

> "The smiling infant in its hand shall take
> The crested basilisk and speckled snake."

It is gathered to dead cheats and swindlers and quacks of every age,—to coiners and counterfeiters who were hanged when coining and counterfeiting was a hanging matter—to extinct humbugs of all past time. Bel the Dragon, and John Law's Mississippi Scheme, and Andrew Dexter's Exchange Bank, Redheiffer's Perpetual Motion, rise from their seats and welcome it to its place in the pit.

For our part we are in no mood for jesting when we think of the mischiefs the bank has wrought, partly, it is true, on account of the obstinate credulity of its victims, but partly because they followed the advice of men who should have known better. We have in our mind at this moment the case of a Philadelphia merchant, who died about three years since in the possession of a plentiful fortune, which he left by his will to a family of young children, directing his executors to invest it until they should become of age, in stock of the United States Bank. The direction was followed and the children are now destitute. Thousands of persons have paid for their confidence in that bank with the loss of every thing they possessed. An instance of escape occurs to us, in which a lady directed her agent, a democrat, and therefore sure of the unsoundness of the bank, to invest a considerable amount of property in stock of the bank. He disobeyed her instructions and saved her money; but these cases are rare, and a large proportion of the loss will fall upon persons unacquainted with business, helpless, and at the mercy of advisers who ought to have cautioned them of their danger.

The best friend of these unfortunate persons was an old man whose hairs are now whitening with a late old age on his farm in Tennesse[e]. If they had withdrawn their confidence from the bank when Andrew Jackson withdrew his, and counselled them to do the like—or even if the stockholders had insisted that the bank should close its affairs with the close of its charter from Congress, much of what is now lost might have been saved.

Mean time, if the National Bank has been a source of evil it will be henceforth a source of good. Its example is a warning to the republic—all its mischiefs, and corrupt practices,—its briberies, speculations, frauds, and robberies, enormous and many, are so many lessons to the nation—so many admonitions against ever allowing the existence of a like institution, against entrusting the same power to any hands whatever. The monster now that it is dead, is not merely a harmless but a valuable monster,—as the live asp is dangerous and deadly, but the dead asp, preserved in spirits, is a useful specimen of natural history. We cannot afford to lose a single claw or scale of the monster, for a moral belongs to each—it should be carefully embalmed entire for the instruction of succeeding generations.

Much of the iniquity of the bank will probably, after all, never meet the public eye. The assignment which is now made of its assets, with a view to the liquidation of its affairs, does not include fifteen millions of its suspended debt, which it has been thought proper to reserve and keep out of sight. To this suspended debt probably belong those corrupt transactions in which every body knows that the bank has been engaged, the particulars of which are withheld by a sense of shame, covered up for the present, and perhaps forever.

Daniel Defoe
November 15, 1841

Defoe's Robinson Crusoe *was first published in 1719. When the Duke of Monmouth tried in 1685 to claim the English crown as Protestant leader, he was defeated by the Catholic king James II, tried by Lord Chief Justice George Jeffreys, and executed in the Tower of London. After the Revolution of 1688 deposed James II, William, grandson of Charles II, was crowned, together with his wife, Mary. Anne, daughter of James II, was queen of England from 1704 to 1714. Confined in 1703–1704 to Newgate Prison for political libel, Defoe started his* Review *while there, and composed his mock-Pindaric ode* Hymn to the Pillory *(1704). During a famine, the prophet Elijah was fed at God's directions by ravens (1 Kings 17:2–7).*

"Robinson Crusoe"—The publication, by D. Appleton & Co., No. 200 Broadway, of an illustrated edition of this narrative, of which Sir Walter Scott says, "few have yielded such incessant amusement, and, at the same time, developed so many lessons of practical instruction," recalls the eventful history and estimable character of its author, Daniel De Foe. We do not place De Foe in the first class of English writers, but we assign him a high place in the second. In many qualities, he is even superior to those who have been elevated, by common consent, to the highest rank, although his general merit does not entitle him, to adopt the language of Addison's allegory, to be set at the head of the table. No mean place, however, is occupied by the writer of the "Account of the Plague in London," and the delightful work before us, "Robinson Crusoe."

No less, as a man and a politician, does De Foe deserve high admiration. Born in 1661, he lived during one of the stormiest periods of English history. When a mere boy, he joined the ill-fated expedition of Monmouth, and barely escaped punishment in that series of savage executions, under the immortally infamous Jeffreys, which James was accustomed, with heartless levity, to call Jeffreys' Campaign. He was still young when the revolution of 1688 terminated so auspiciously for the liberties of England. With a boldness and ardor that ever afterwards characterized his conduct, he espoused what was then considered the side of freedom. He spoke, wrote and acted against the iniquitous designs of the king, strengthening the purposes and enlightening the judgment of many, older than himself in years, but not older or more determined in their hatred of tyranny.

But, unlike some who shared the glory of that contest, he did not lay down his arms with the triumph of his party. His had been a struggle, not for party, but for principle; and subsequently, when the Protestants, under the reign of Anne, resorted to the same methods of persecution which had before been condemned in the Catholics, he warred against them with equal fearlessness and spirit. The cause of the suffering dissenters became his cause; priestly bigotry and injustice was still as offensive, under the Episcopal domination, as it had been under the Roman; and the arrogant invasion, by the High-Churchmen, of the religious rights of the people, seemed to him no less criminal than the Catholic audacity of the house of Stuart. He resisted the encroachments of spiritual despotism with every weapon that the possession of commanding talents and a rigid will put into his power. His writings, in defence of the nonconformists, were numerous, pointed and effective. By argument, by appeal, by declamation, and by ridicule, he sought to expose the pretensions of the bigots, and thwart their schemes. Keen, sarcastic, unrelenting, he had too much power not to become troublesome to the government. The menials of office, and the hirelings of the church, maligned and persecuted him; a reward was set upon his person; he was prosecuted for a political libel; he was condemned to the pillory and to Newgate. But penalties of this kind could not arrest his pen. A mass of the people were with him. His pillory was hung with garlands, and in the noble ode to the Pillory, written while exposed to the public gaze, "he pilloried," as some writer has said, "his persecutors." Imprisonment only gave him more leisure, and more cause for strenuous exertion. Paper after paper, full of burning invective against the tyrants, was issued from the dungeon, illuminated by his genius.

In allusion to his vicissitudes, he says, in the preface to the last volume of his Review,

"I have gone through a life of wonders, and have been subject to a vast variety of providences; I have been fed more by miracle than Elijah, 'when the ravens were his purveyors. Sometime ago I summed up my life in this distich—

'No man has tasted differing fortunes more,
'And thirteen times I have been rich and poor.

"In the school of affliction I have learnt more than at the academy, and more divinity than from the pulpit; in prison I have learnt to know that liberty does not consist in open doors and the free egress and regress of locomotion. I have seen the rough side of the world as well as the smooth; and have, in less than half a year, tasted the difference between the closet of a king and the dungeon of Newgate."

De Foe's intellectual labours, however, were not confined to politics. He wrote voluminously on trade, manners, domestic economy, and literature. His "Review," a periodical that led the way for the more celebrated "Tattlers," "Guardians," and "Spectators," continued, three times a week for more than nine years, without intermission and without assistance, is one of the most remarkable instances of fertility on record. When we add to this, his many fictions, his Dickory Crooke, his Captain Singleton, his Cavalier, his Duncan Campbell, his Colonel Jacque, his Moll Flanders, his Plague, his Robinson Crusoe, &c. &c., the activity and power of his mind appear prodigious. As a writer, De Foe excels in the minuteness and accuracy of his descriptions, the simplicity of his style, and the readiness of his invention; as a man, he was distinguished for a strong love of truth, liberality of sentiment, and an indomitable independence of thought and action. He was, in relation to most subjects, much in advance of his day, and his works abound in passages that may be read, not only with delight, but instruction even at this time. A disciple of the school which teaches the great doctrine of human progress, if not pre-eminently a great man, he was still of the number of those described by Burke, "the silence of whose closets is more beneficial to mankind, than all the noise and bustle of courts, senates and camps."

International Copyright
February 11, 1842

The paper-makers who belong to the Home League in this city are hostile to an international copy-right law, from the apprehension that it will make some difference in the quantity of paper which they manufacture. The Home League, at its meeting last evening, according to the report of its proceedings in a morning paper, entered into the views of the paper-makers, and directed a memorial to be drawn up, addressed to Congress, requesting our government not to adopt the measure which secures to Americans their literary property in other countries, and to foreign authors their literary property in this country.

If there is any justice at all in the copy-right law, as it seems to us there is—if the composition which an author produces by the exercise of his talents and industry, be as much his own as his purse,—which it is, or else our copy-right law is a gross absurdity—he ought to be equally secure in its possession—secure every where; the people of foreign countries ought not to be allowed to plunder the American, nor the people of this country to plunder the foreigner.—If our own laws were such, that the moment a stranger presented himself on our shores, his baggage, and the very change in his pocket, ceased to be his own; if our courts were not as much open to him as to our own citizens in a claim of property, or a demand of reparation for injustice, for pillage, or swindling, we should be condemned by the general voice of the civilized wor[l]d, not merely as a churlish and inhospitable nation, but as a nation of robbers. When we deny a stranger the same right to the profits of his own writings as we give to our citizens, we commit this very injustice; the only difference is, that we limit the robbery to one kind of property.

We will not, at present, engage in the controversy respecting the propriety of having any copy-right law whatever. It is enough for our purposes, that the constitution of the United States recognizes the right of literary property, and gives Congress the power of securing to authors the exclusive right to their own productions; it is enough that the subject has, from time to time, been brought before the nation, and that our legislators, in obedience to the general voice, have, from time to time, strengthened and enlarged the provisions which protect authors in the disposal of their own writings. Thus the right of literary property has been acknowledged and established in the most solemn manner, by the constitution, by Congress, and by public opinion. This being done, why should we protect one set of persons in that right, and abandon another set to general pillage? The reason given for making this unjust distinction is, that it is for the benefit of the paper-makers.

It might be for the benefit of the wreckers on the Long Island coast, and that of New Jersey, if they were allowed to possess themselves of the effects of all whom the storms cast upon their shores. It would be very convenient for a certain class, who hang about our wharves, if they were allowed to pick the pockets of those who arrive from abroad, or run off with their baggage, without fear of punishment; but this benefit and this convenience, we think, would hardly be a sufficient ground for depriving strangers of the protection which the law grants to our own citizens.

After all, however, the paper-makers, it seems to us, may dismiss their fears, and the Home League may suppress its contemplated remonstrance, without any apprehension that our papermills will be obliged to stop if an international copy-right law should be passed by Congress. The late increase of cheap reading, the multiplication of literary and other papers and periodicals, does not arise from the absence of an international copy-right law. If that were the case, we ought to have had this inundation of cheap reading years ago, inasmuch, since there was as little obstruction from any copy-right law as there now is. On the contrary, it arises from the improvements which have been made in printing, and the manufacture of paper—the invention of presses which throw off impressions almost with the rapidity of light, and the discovery of methods which turn out vast sheets of paper by an almost instantaneous process. This is the secret of the cheap books and cheap periodicals with which the market is filled, and these causes will continue to operate in spite of an international copy-right. Books are cheap in consequence of perfecting the mechanical processes by which they are produced and will continue to be so. Whatever course Congress may adopt in relation to this matter, the paper-makers need not fear that the world will cease to read, or that they will be thrown out of business.

INTERNATIONAL COPY RIGHT
May 9, 1842

Other signers of the "Address" sent Bryant about May 1 from Niagara Falls by Charles Dickens were Thomas Hood and Alfred, Lord Tennyson. From 1842 to 1846 Washington Irving was the American minister to Spain.

We publish in this sheet several papers received this morning from Mr. Dickens, relating to the subject of an international copy-right. The "Address to the American People," with so many illustrious names among its signatures—Campbell and Hallam, and Rogers and Bulwer and others, worthy to be placed by their side—will be read with a strong and respectful interest. The letter of Mr. Carlyle to Mr. Dickens is highly characteristic of the writer.

It is a mistake to suppose that, if we refuse to make an arrangement for securing to the authors of America and Britain a copyright in both countries, the advantage of the injustice will be on our side; that, if wrong be committed for want of such an arrangement, the profits of the wrong will go into the pockets of American publishers. American authors are every year producing more and more work, for the republication of which there is a demand in England. Within the last year, the number of books written by American authors, which have been successful in Britain, is greater than that of foreign works which have been successful in this country. Robertson's work on Palestine, Stephen's Travels in Central America, Catlin's book on the North American Indians, Cooper's Deerslayer, the last volume of Bancroft's American History, several works prepared by Anthon for the schools—here is a list of American works republished in England within the year, which we might easily enlarge, and for which we should be puzzled to find an equivalent in works written in England within the same time, and republished here. Our eminent authors are still engaged in their literary labors. Cooper, within a fortnight past, has published a work stamped with all the vigor of his faculties, Prescott is occupied in writing the History of Peru, Bancroft is engaged in continuing the annals of his native country, Sparks is still employed in his valuable historical labors, and Stephens is pushing his researches in Central America, with a view of giving their result to the world. We were told, the other day, of a work prepared for the press by Washington Irving, which would have appeared ere this, but for the difficulties in the way of securing a copy-right for it in England, as well as here. He has done this, however, we presume, on his way to Spain.

The success of so many of our authors will have the effect of raising up a host of literary adventurers among us. In no part of the world are hope and emulation so easily awakened as here; there is no part of the world where a few brilliant examples have so powerful an influence in calling up rivals and competitors in the same path to fortune or to fame, as in this republic. We shall have men preparing themselves by intense study, and exerting their faculties to the utmost, to reach the same eminence which has been attained by other authors, their countrymen, and, if possible, to go beyond it. In a conversation which we had the other day with an eminent American author, now abroad, he remarked, that if American literature continued to make the same progress as it had done for twenty years past, the day was not very far distant, when the greater number of books designed for readers of the English language, would be produced in America. If we look back to the year 1820, and compare the state of authorship in our country at that time, with what it is now; if we consider how barren our literature was then, and how prolific it has now become; if we look at the quality of the works produced at the two different periods, and the rewards received by their authors, we shall find ourselves obliged to admit that the prediction is a very probable one.

The plea against an international copy-right, that it gives our publishers an advantage over those of Great Britain, is not true, or if true, is true for the present moment only. If our publishers enrich themselves at the expense of British authors, British publishers enrich themselves at the expense of ours, and will continue to do so, from year to year, until the advantage will be shifted from our side to theirs. The policy of our country is to secure for its authors the benefit of an international copy-right before that time arrives.

Mother and Daughter
September 8, 1842

In 1842 Alexander Baring, First Baron Ashburton, came to Washington to negotiate a settlement of the boundary dispute which had led to the "Aroostook County War" referred to above (January 27, 1841). In a rare oversight, Bryant here gives the clown in A Winter's Tale *lines belonging to his counterpart in* All's Well That Ends Well.

"So long as there is a tie to link a child to its parent, America will not forget that England is her mother."

These are words addressed by the Mayor of Boston to Lord Ashburton, at his late public reception in that city. If America be the child and England the parent, if our people be the daughter and England the mother, and if, as the poetical mayor of Boston says, we are to keep this relation always in remembrance, it follows that we should act accordingly. The child must reverence its parent; we must look up to England as a superior; we must acknowledge the right of this venerable mother to exercise a parental interference in our affairs; when she snubs us, we must endeavor to bear it with good humor; we must pay her a filial deference on all occasions, and dutifully strive to behave ourselves to her satisfaction.

The Mayor of Boston has not, however, stated the relation rightly. The people apprehend the matter much better. With them, England is John Bull, and America is Brother Jonathan—not Son Jonathan—not the offspring of England, but one who derives his blood from the same parents, and stands by his side on a footing of equality, as tenacious of his rights as John himself, acknowledging no filial reverence or duty towards him—nothing but fraternal good will and the obligation of justice. This talk of parent and child, mother and daughter, implies a dependence on the one side, and an authority on the other which do not exist. It should be laid aside.

It may be said that it is a mere metaphor, well enough for a holiday occasion, and that we must not criticise the metaphors of Mayors too severely. But there is mischief in a false metaphor. We say, with the clown, in Shakespeare's Winter's Tale—we hope the phrase is not too coarse for quotation in this fastidious age—

"If a metaphor stink, I will stop my nose against any man's metaphor."

The constant use of a phrase which implies what is not true, leads to false notions in those who use it. He who is always talking of a person as his mother, is a hypocrite if he do not treat her with the deference and submission due to that character. There was a time, it is true, when England was called the mother country, and when we were her colonies; but a hard mother she proved towards us; she behaved like a step-mother in the old tragedies, *dura noverca;* and we were obliged to shake off her authority, although we had to spill blood for it. Since that time, the parental relation of England to us exists no longer, even metaphorically. The England of that day is gone; the generation with whom we waged a successful war, are all in their graves, and the new race that has sprung up—the England of the present day—this modern fine old lady, is our cousin, or our sister if you please, but no mother of ours.

How to Destroy a Commercial Town
October 11, 1842

Henry Clay's protective tariff of 1842 was called by Southern planters the "Black Tariff," because it forced the price of their cotton to fall below that of any previous figure. As Bryant's title suggests, the law was also anathema to New York merchants, who, as the chief exporters of raw cotton and importers of cotton goods, held a common interest with their Southern customers.

There are several methods of bringing ruin upon a city which owes its prosperity to its flourishing commerce with foreign nations.

One is to fill up its harbors, or obstruct their channels, so as to make it impossible or highly dangerous for vessels to arrive and depart.

When this cannot be done, the same end may be attained by a non-intercourse law, forbidding the entrance and departure of vessels, enforced by revenue cutters and ships of war.

In case either of these methods should be odious to the people, the object in view may be accomplished, in a more indirect but quite as sure a manner, by a law laying, upon merchandize imported from abroad, duties so enormously high that they cannot be paid, amounting to a prohibition of foreign commerce.

Under the effect of such a law, a great commercial city, seated on a noble harbour, the mouth of a mighty river, with long canals and railroads stretching far into the interior, crowded with an active and enterprising population, full ship yards, and long rows of warehouses, her wharves and docks thronged with ships, —such a city, with the passages to her haven unobstructed and no warlike fleet keeping blockade, may see her growth arrested at once, the activity of her citizens checked, and her commerce taken out of the hands of the regular merchants and dispersed along the land frontier and the solitary places of the coast, to be carried on by smugglers.

At its last session Congress passed the very law of which we are speaking. Its effects are already felt; a backward movement has already begun in this city. Lines of packets go to and fro across the Atlantic without freight. Cargoes of mer[c]handise are every day arriving, upon which the importers find the duties recently laid heavier than they can pay, and they are sent immediately back. No circumstance can more fully illustrate the prohibitory nature of the new tariff than the fleets of ships deeply loaded with the products of foreign countries, turned away from our port by this virtual nonintercourse act.

We do not see what is to prevent the decline and decay of our city, unless this law should be early repealed. New York owes her existence, and her prosperity to the convenience of her situation for foreign commerce. But for the trade with Europe and other countries of the world, this island would have even yet been covered with farms, inhabited like Bergen Point, by the descendants of the settlers of Holland, with perhaps a little station near the Battery for the coasting trade. It is our foreign commerce which has made New York what she is, rich, populous, and the centre of enterprises which extend to the ends of the earth; it is this which has enabled her to overtake and leave behind all the other cities of the United States, Boston, Philadelphia, Baltimore, Charleston, and assume her place as the Queen of Commerce of the new world. Take away her foreign commerce and you take away the basis of her existence; whether you bar up the access to her port at the Narrows or put the harbor under perpetual blockade, or turn away vessels by prohibitory duties, like those just imposed by Congress, the effect is the same; the cause which has given our city its high rank, its vast activity, its growing population, is removed and its decline must begin. This is not a matter which interests importers merely, nor those classes whose occupations are immediately connected with the business of importing and exporting commodities. It concerns every individual who subsists by administering in any way to the wants or the convenience of the great population which our foreign commerce has concentrated at this spot, or of the multitides of purchasers whom it attracts hither; it concerns, in short, every inhabitant of the city who possesses property, or is engaged in any department of industry. If the general prosperity is destroyed, the individual prosperity must suffer. If our ships are without freight, our dwellings, warehouses and shops must become tenantless.

We perceive that some of the whig prints are attempting to make some apology for the new tariff by saying that it was passed in haste. We care not how it was passed; it was certainly framed with great deliberation—the most prolonged, the most cold-blooded deliberation. It was a measure which the whig party, among whom it originated, and who gave it its present shape, had for months upon the anvil, hammering upon it from day to day until the country was weary with the noise they made. The democratic members of Congress again and again attempted to amend it by the insertion of more liberal and moderate provisions, but without success. In process of time after a delay sufficient to frame the wisest, most considerate, and most politic law that ever was adopted in a legislative body, it was sent to Mr. Tyler, who refused it his sanction on account of the clause which provided for the distribution of the proceeds of the public lands. The House of Representatives then again took up the bill—this fruit of long consultation—and resisting all the attempts of the democratic party to amend it, struck out the clause respecting the distribution law, and passed it. In the Senate, its provisions were softened a little by a few amendments, which were afterwards adopted by the House, and the bill became a law.

The excuse of haste, therefore, cannot be admitted. The odious parts of the bill were agreed upon among the whig party, after a deliberation which was protracted till the country grew impatient of delay. There never was a public measure which had more the character of premediation than this blow given to our foreign commerce. It was aimed for months before it was given; its force was carefully calculated, and the place where it should fall was marked with the utmost precision. Now that the blow has fallen in all its violence, the whig journals in this city, alarmed at the symptoms of public indignation, endeavor to palliate the wrong by the apology of want of time. In a session of nine months, the whigs had not time to frame a reasonable revenue law!

The Raccoon: Symbol of the Whigs
October 22, 1842

The Whig Party had adopted the coonskin cap, along with the wigwam and log cabin, during the Harrison campaign of 1840, to promote the belief, though unjustified, that their candidate was an unlettered frontiersman. They embroidered these symbols by adding hard cider and spirits to their enticements of voters. In hoc signo vinces—*"under this sign shalt thou conquer" (Eusebius,* Life of Constantine *1.28):* Te Duce—*"Thou, Leader."*

The Egyptians were the first people who took the ox out of the common herd and made a god of him. They then had choice places for the living animal to move in, and at death preserved his hide. They made pictures and drawings of him, and in their public assemblies and on great moments, he was brought forth and installed as the guardian genius of the occasion.—Flags and banners were raised on high, and waved back and forth with his image engraved thereon, and emblazoned with words from which the Latin poet derived his idea, which is thus expressed—"In hoc signo vinces!" Triumphal odes and songs were made by the poets and sung to this deity on public occasions, and the people were taught to regard him as possessing a mysterious influence that would lead them to a glorious success.

The Greeks and Romans had more refinement in their ideas of the god who led them to victory.—The believed that he was a mortal who had been raised to the skies and endowed with superior attributes, and had the charge of all human battles. They considered him as stern, blood-thirsty and cruel. They called him Mars, or the God of War. And whenever his favor was desired they sung songs and poured out libations to him. They erected special places over which he presided, and adorned him with all such trappings as they thought peculiar to him. And when about to engage in any conflict, they shouted "Te duce," "In hoc signo," &c, and sung songs.

The civilized Indians of Mexico and Central America, selected several of the larger quadrupeds and made gods of them. And we find their profiles drawn on the decayed walls of their temples.

The old Jews always had an itching fancy to take up the calf and make a god of him. But generally, instead of taking the live animal, they would form some image of him from gold. And they would set it up even when the splendor of the deity of Heaven was shining with full blaze on their tents.

In various parts of the world, the people make a god of fire, or of the sun and moon, or of alligators, or other animals, and invoke their influence in their enterprises. But it remained for the whigs of this Christian nation to bring the raccoon first from his native woods, and set him up in the public places, and make a god of him. They adopted him as the presiding genius of their great occasion. They brought him to all their public gatherings. They erected log cabins as temples to him, where especially he might be found, and when these were wanting, they introduced him before the altars of Heaven, and profaned them with the polluting beast. In their processions, they carried banners emblazoned with his image, and with words like these in glaring letters, "In hoc signo vinces!" or "That same old coon." They set him on high at all their public meetings, and as he gazed about he was hailed with shouts. Their speakers, after they had come forth and been welcomed by the audience, would turn to the coon, and in effect make obeisance, exclaiming, "Te duce," and the shouts of the multitude would rend the air with clapping and stamping; and the god would frisk himself and rattle his chain, and the multitude would shout longer and louder. Then they would sing odes and songs, which had been composed by their poets, and made sacred to him. Then pour out libations of hard cider to him, and in the riotous excess of their joy intoxicate themselves. Thus they deified him as the presiding genius of their political campaign, and he was as kind and faithful a Deity to them as the ox to the Egyptians, Mars to the Greeks, or the quadrupeds to the Indians.

But the parallel, degrading as it is, does not stop here. Where are the Egyptians with all their greatness and glory? Where are the proud nations of Central America? Where are the veteran warriors of Greece, the fire worshippers of Northern India, or the devotees to the sun and moon, or the coon worshippers of America? They committed themselves to the guidance of low and detestable principles, and they are sharing one fate. In Egypt we find tombs, and sepulchres, and mummies. In Greece we see heaps upon heaps, and read only tales of their former splendor; and the remnant of the calf worshippers of Judea, is scattered as stragglers in every land. The worshippers of the coon shot up with a plenitude of power, that had been unequalled in this nation; yet all their might we have seen turned into weakness.—They possessed as they thought, wise and prudent men, yet their counsels have been filled with confusion and brought to naught. All their pride and success has been turned to folly. They were becoming a taunt and reproach with their opponents. In their dismay they brought out "that same old coon," and when they trusted that he should deliver them, he could not save them. In this day of their adversity, their god has proved himself to be trickish.

The Tariff with Country People
March 2, 1843

A great many very intelligent persons who are members of the democratic party and who live in small villages in the neighborhood of some large town form their opinion of the correctness of the

Tariff policy from the operations of trade among themselves. Many of the inhabitants of the villages, they say, pass by the stores of their merchants and the shops of their mechanics and go to the large town to trade. Now it would be better for the village, say they, if such persons would trade at home, and buy of their own merchants and mechanics; and in this respect the large town injures the village by drawing away so much of its trade. From these circumstances operating on a small scale, they infer that it would be better for a nation to trade altogether, if possible, within herself; and therefore any legislative policy that would secure such a result must be good and beneficial to a whole nation.

This argument appears very plausible and is the reason on which these persons oppose free trade. But why is it that so many in the village go to the town to trade? Or why do so many in the town go to the city to trade? Because they think it is better for themselves. Certainly, if they did not think so, they would not choose such a course. In what respects then do they think it is better?—Not because the articles for sale in the town are dearer than the same in the village. Nor because they are of a poorer quality. Nor because there is a smaller supply from which to select.—For if either, or all, these circumstances were true, they would not trade at the town. Neither do they think it better to trade in the town rather than the village, because the articles in the town are of the same price, and of the same quality, and there is the same supply in both places. In this case there would not be any complaint of their going abroad to trade. For the villagers would not travel a distance to gain nothing, if they were aware of the facts. There is no complaint of this kind in relation to the trade of two adjoining villages where markets are similar in these respects.—Therefore it must be that the villagers choose to trade in a town because the goods are cheaper, or of as good or better quality, and there is a larger stock from which to select, or all these things may be combined. This is not the case with every article of the trade; with some it is, and with others the contrary is true. When the farmer finds the latter to occur, he instantly replies; "I would rather buy it in our village! I can get it there at the same price and shall not be obliged to carry it so far home." What does all this amount to? Why that the inhabitant of the village can turn his dollar to a greater advantage to himself, by spending it for a certain article in the town than in the village. A dollar spent in the one place yields him more than if spent in the other. Now is it better for him to have perfect freedom in trading where he pleases, or to restrict him to the village altogether? The very conduct of the villagers, which is the ground of complaint, is the answer to this question. It needs no argument to show that what is best for the inhabitants of a village as individuals, is best for them as a community; for a community is but a collection of individuals, and the interest of the community is only the united interests of the several individuals. Does it follow from this that a restrictive policy is best for a nation?

Suppose now that we look at the other side of the case, and consider what is called, and falsely too we apprehend, the "good of the village."—The inhabitant of the village, trades in the town, because he apprehends each dollar there spent will turn to some greater advantage than if spent in the village. Here then is a certain amount, trifling perhaps, that is a gain to himself between a trade in the two places. Find the amount of the gain on each dollar thus spent by each villager, and we shall have a part of the advantage. There is yet an additional sum of gain that arises from the better market afforded to the farmer in the town, than in the village. If now the trade is cut off from the town and restricted to the village, here is a certain gain on each dollar or number of dollars, that was spent by the inhabitant of a village in the town, which he does not receive. It is so much taken from his advantage or property, by trading for those articles in the village. But this trade is a benefit, it is said, to the village merchant and mechanic. What then is this advantage lost by the purchaser, but so far a direct tax upon him for the benefit of the village merchant? And what is the restrictive policy of a nation, but a tax upon the community for the support and prosperity of certain classes. What, now, does the village merchant or mechanic perform, that he should deserve to be assisted by a tax on the other inhabitants?—He does not pay a similar tax for their benefit. He has chosen to locate himself in a village that is already better supplied from a neighboring town, than he can do it and flourish—therefore, the villagers must be taxed to make up the deficiency.—If a new lawyer or doctor, settles in the village, no one thinks of laying a restriction for his benefit. The restriction continues, and a certain number of merchants and mechanics flourish. Land rises to a certain degree, this is the land owner's gain—rents rise, this is likewise his gain. But it does not come from an additional wealth that has been imparted to them. A few are reaping the benefit of an imperceptible tax paid by a great number.—See the few landlords in England, and the millions of tenants.

If, instead of confining all the trade of the village to itself, but free trade had been allowed, the merchant and mechanic would have applied himself to another pursuit, and by his own exertions added his portion to the actual wealth of the village, and not taxed or crippled his neighbors to support him in a pursuit that would not pay.—Each one would freely use his means as he supposed to be most advantageous to himself. This makes sound prosperity. And so it would be when the gates of a nation are thrown open to all the earth.

JOHN QUINCY ADAMS
August 4, 1843

Having served a term as President from 1825 to 1829, Adams, son of the second President, John Adams of Massachusetts, entered the Congress, where he was a representative from Massachusetts from 1831 until his death in 1848.

Learned, eloquent; always acute, though often wrong; ambitious, disputatious, pragmatical, unforgiving; conscientious, except when some strong prejudice or personal grudge, as is too often the case, opposes itself to his moral sense; aged, yet preserving in a late old age his intellectual faculties as vigorous as ever, perhaps even sharpened during the last ten years of his life by constant and intense exercise in quarrels and controversies of every kind—John Quincy Adams is one of the most extraordinary men of his country and his time. He is now enjoying, what it was never his lot to enjoy before, voluntary demonstrations of respect from his fellow-citizens of every party. He has been making a kind of tour through this State, and wherever he goes he is welcomed with a formal reception; speeches of compliment are made to him, and he makes speeches in return. At Auburn, at Utica, at Herkimer, at Little Falls, at Schenectady, and at Albany this ceremonious reception was had; at the latter place it seemed as if the whole city rose up to welcome him. We are glad of this, for Mr. Adams, when we consider his long public life, has had few of those honors fall to his share. While he was President of the United States he used to come and go with as little notice as almost any other passenger on the steamboats and stagecoaches. Yet is he a better and an honester man than some who have snuffed more of this popular incense, owing, no doubt, to their possessing certain attractive qualities of character which do not belong to Mr. Adams? People are shy of approaching one who bristles with sharp points and controversies like a porcupine. For the present there seems a disposition to forego that shyness and do honor to one who, fifteen years ago, held the place of Chief Magistrate of our nation, who was probably the most learned man that ever administered the government, and who, in his old age, has become one of the most dreaded debaters of our national Legislature. The veteran politician wears gracefully the honors which have been so long in coming, and evidently enjoys with a high zest the demonstrations of respect which are paid him.

NAMES OF SECTS
August 14, 1843

The Churchman was an organ of the American Episcopal Church. The Oxford Movement, familiarly called "Puseyism" after one of its leaders, Edward Pusey, dean of Christ Church Cathedral at Oxford University, was an attempt begun in 1833 to restore early Christian doctrines to the Anglican church. Its most famous participant was the vicar of Saint Mary's Church, Oxford, John Henry Newman, who later became a Roman Catholic cardinal. The Italian exponent of an anti-Trinitarian doctrine, Faustus Socinius (1539–1604), had lent his name to that doctrine. John Gottlieb Ernestur Heckewelder, an English Moravian missionary, worked with frontier Indians. The Campbellites got their popular name from their founder, Alexander Campbell (1788–1866), a dissident Baptist minister from Ireland whose sect, the Disciples of Christ, became widespread in the American Middle West. George Fox (1624–1691), English founder of the Society of Friends, or Quakers, gave impetus to the spread of that faith when he visited North America in 1671–1672.

We had thought ourselves wholly safe from the charge of wounding the feelings of the members of any religious denomination, but a few circumstances have lately occurred which have very much abated our self-complacency on this score. The other day the *Churchman*, a paper which holds with the authors of the Oxford Tracts, complained that there was not a sing[le?] secular paper in the city which did not, at times, wantonly and gratuitously give offence to the friends of the church—we believe that was the phrase used. We were puzzled at first to understand what we, who had taken no part in the Oxford Tract controversy, or any other theological controversy, had done to offend the friends of the church, when we recollected that we had sometimes used the term Puseyism, which the *Churchman* disclaims as a nickname. We have now a correspondent who is displeased at finding in our columns the words "Roman Clergy," as applied to the priesthood of the Roman Catholic church. He insists that we should simply call them Catholic, or at least Roman Catholic.

The members of the different religious denominations are exceedingly sensitive in regard to the appelations by which they are called. If you call the Presbyterian of this country a Calvinist, he will, if he does not happen to be a very good Christian, take fire, and if he is, he will gently point out your mistake. Address a Unitarian by the title of Socinian, and he will let you know that you do him wrong, and will show you in what particulars, some of them very important ones, his church disagrees with Socinius. Yet those who hold with Dr. Pusey, we perceive, make no scruple of calling the Unitarian believer a Socinian. The Quakers have borne their common appelation so long that the world has almost forgotten that they do not acknowledge it, that it is a term of ridicule, and that among themselves they bear the title of Friends. Yet the term is so generally applied that nobody thinks of giving them any other; even the Pennsylvania Indians, who respected them very much, called them, as we are told by Heckewelder, Quaeckels. The Shakers are another denomination, who wear a burlesque name. The people who are called Christians, pronounced with the long dipthongal sound of the vowel I, do not recognize the name so pronounced, but simply call themselves Christians, drowning any sectarian appelation. The Campbellites, that numerous denomination of the west, who have laid a broad and comprehensive plat-form for their sect, except that they are a little strict on the point of baptism by immersion, and who confidently believe that ere long the whole Christian world will be ranged under the two great divisions of Campbellites and Roman Catholics, do yet object to the term Campbellite, as a very inadequate and idle appelation for their church, that true Church of Christ, which is neither of Paul, nor of Apollos, nor of Cephas.

Yet while the different denominations are so thin-skinned upon this point that a simple layman can hardly speak of any one of them by what appears to him the most convenient designation, without giving offence; they are by no means very particular in speaking of each other. Their scrupulousness has respect rather to what others say of them than what they say of others. We never knew any of them hesitate at calling a Unitarian a Socinian, or a Friend a Quaker.

For our part, we should be sorry to wound the feelings of any person in so small a matter, yet we fear that we shall never be able to call the followers of George Fox any thing but Quakers, and certainly, until we find a better designation, we shall call the new western sect Campbellites. In so doing, we beg our broad-brimmed friends, if the recent changes of costume will still allow us to call them so, and such of our readers as belong to the new church of the west, for we happen to know that some of them receive our sheet, to understand that we mean not the slightest disrespect, but simply use the most convenient and popular designation. The name will not make their doctrine or their practice any worse.

So, if we should happen to use the terms Puseyism and Puseyite, or speak of the Romish clergy or the Romanists, we hope our readers will do us the justice to believe that we do not use them in derision, but in compliance with popular usage, and as names which simply mean certain men holding certain doctrines. We shall endeavor to be at least as careful not to give offence as those who are so ready to complain.

Those who hold with Dr. Pusey, claim to be Catholics, but they deny strenuously that they are Roman Catholics. If we were to restrict the term Catholic to the latter, we might displease the followers of the Oxford school. Episcopalians believe in "the holy Catholic Church universal," of which they claim to be members. We are not acquainted with the formulas of the [G]reek Church, which embraces the great empire of Russia, and whose churches are scattered all over the east, but we presume she makes the same claim to Catholicity. The word Catholic means universal, and we who see in the Roman Catholic church only a part of the Christian world, may be forgiven if we hesitate in giving it so comprehensive an epithet, however fond it may be of wearing it. As to the terms Roman Church and clergy, we use them as we use the terms Greek Church and clergy. They refer to a denomination the head of whose church resides at Rome, and the language of whose devotions is that of ancient Rome, just as the Greek church has its patriarch at Constantinople and employs a Greek liturgy. In this point of view the appelation is not false, notwithstanding our correspondent calls it so.

THE CORN LAW CONTROVERSY
August 24, 1843

In 1815 a Corn Law had made the importing of grain into England expensive. An Anti-Corn Law League formed in 1839, especially led by members of Parliament Richard Cobden and John Bright, managed eventually, in 1846, to effect its repeal. Cf. Psalm 91; "Thou shalt not be afraid.... For the pestilence that walketh in darkness; nor for the sickness that destroyeth at noon-day."

A friend has placed in our hands numbers of the tracts which the corn law reformers of England circulate among the people. They are about the size and length of the religious tracts of this country, and are put up in an envelope, which is stamped with neat and appropriate devices. These little publications comprise essays on all the topics involved in the corn law controversy, sometimes in the form of dialogues, sometimes of tales, and sometimes of extracts from famous books and speeches. The arguments are arranged so as to be easily comprehended by the meanest capacities.

The friend to whom we are indebted for these, is well informed on the subject, and says that a more advanced state of opinion prevails among the people of England, in relation to the operations of tariffs, than in this nation generally so much more enlightened. It is a singular spectacle which is thus presented to the eyes of the civilized world. While the tendency of opinion, under an aristocratic monarchy, is towards the loosening of the restraints under which the labor of the people has long suffered, a large and powerful party in a nation, whose theory of government is nearly a century in advance of the world, is clamoring for their continuance and confirmation. Monarchical England is struggling to break the chains that an unwise legislation has forged for the limbs of its trade; but democratic America is urged to put on the fetters which older but less liberal nations are throwing off. The nations of Europe are seeking to extend their commercial relations, to expand the sphere of their mutual intercourse, to rivet the market for the products of their soil and skill, while the "model-republic" of the new world is urged to stick to the silly and odious policy of a semi-barbarous age.

We look upon the attempt which is making in Great Britain, to procure a revision of the tariff laws, as one of the most important political movements of the age. It is a reform that contemplates benefits, whose effects would not be confined to any single nation, or any period of time. Should it be successful, it would be the beginning of a grand and universal scheme of commercial emancipation. Let England—that nation so extensive in her relations, and so powerful in her influences—let England adopt a more liberal policy, and it would remove the only obstacles now in the way of a complete freedom of industry throughout the globe. It is the apparent unwillingness of nations to reciprocate the advantages of mutual trade, that has kept back this desirable reform so long. The standing argument of the friends of exclusiveness—their defence under all assaults, their shelter in every emergency—has been that one nation cannot pursue a free system until all others do, or, in other words, that restriction is to be met by restriction. It is a flimsy pretence, but such as it is, has answered the purposes of those who have used it, for many centuries.

The practice of confining trade by the invisible, but potent chains of law, has been a curse wherever it has prevailed. In England, more dependent than other nations on the extent of its commercial intercourse, it may be said to have operated as a scourge. The most terrible inflictions of natural evil, storms, famine, and pestilence, have not produced an equal amount of suffering. Indeed, it has combined the characteristics of the worst of those evils. It has devastated, like the storm, the busy hives of industry; it has exhausted, like famine, the life and vital principle of trade; and, like the pestilence, it has "walked in the darkness and wasted at noon-day." When we read of thousands of miserable wretches, in all the cities and towns of a great nation, huddled together like so many swine in a pen; in rags, squalor, and want; without work, bread, or hope; dragging out from day to day, by begging, or the petty artifices of theft, an existence which is worthless and a burden; and when, at the same time, we see a system of laws, that has carefully drawn a band of iron around every mode of human exertion, which with lynx-eyed and omniscient vigilance, has dragged every product of industry from its retreat, to become the subject of a tax, can we fail in ascribing the effect to its cause, or suppress the utterance of our indignation at a policy so heartless and destructive?

Yet, this is the very policy that a certain class of politicians in this country would have us imitate. Misled by the selfish and paltry arguments of British statesmen, but unawed by the terrible experience of the British people, they would fasten upon us a system whose only recommendation, in its best form, is that it enriches a few, at the cost of the lives and happiness of many. They would assist a constrictor in wrapping his folds around us, until our industry shall be completely crushed.

Cheap Postage and No Discontinuance of Post-Roads
December 18, 1843

Post roads were established in the American colonies as early as 1672 with the opening of one between Boston and New York City which anticipated the course of modern highway Route 1. In 1840 a uniform penny postage was substituted in the United Kingdom for previously exorbitant rates and a system of greatly varying charges for letters of different sizes and shapes.

It has been said by those who oppose a reduction of postage, that if we strike off a part of the present rate of postage, we must strike off also several of the post-roads and post-offices. Against this conclusion we protest, in the name of the friends of cheap postage. It is no part of their plan to lessen the accommodations enjoyed by any part of the country, but rather to increase them; they would not cut off a single post-road or discontinue a single post-office in the most distant and least inhabited part of the country; but they would send to the people of these remote districts their letters for a lower charge than they now receive them. That is their plan; the discontinuance of post-roads forms no part of it, but is an incumbrance which the adversaries of cheap postage are attempting to fasten upon it. We disclaim the odious appendage, and throw it back upon those who bring it forward.

The friends of cheap postage contend, in the first place, that the government ought to pay its own postage, instead of making it a special tax upon those who send their letters by mail. They say, abolish the franking privilege; or, if it must be preserved, make an honest appropriation for meeting it, for which the whole community shall be taxed, and do not charge it upon the dif[f]usion of knowledge and the communications between distant friends. Let the government pay for sending its own despatches, as men of business pay for theirs; and if members of Congress must distribute their speeches at the public expense, let the cost be defrayed out of the common fund of the nation. This tax upon epistolary intercourse, beyond the bare expense of carrying letters by mail, is a tax of the most onerous and odious kind—it is a stamp tax upon private communication, worse than a stamp tax upon printed documents.

Make this deduction from the expenses of the post office; relieve its revenue from a tax which is as unjust as it is hateful, and it is agreed upon all hands that a very considerable reduction might be made in the rates of postage. The postmaster general, himself, admits that there is no difficulty in the way, provided this prodigious weight of the franking privilege be removed from the mails. It is the load of franked documents which make the wheels of our post waggons run so heavily. It is not post-roads which are to be discontinued, but the drain which the franking privilege makes upon the post-office revenue. Here is the true place for amputation; here is the diseased member which requires the surgeon's knife. Leave to the remote districts their post-roads and post-offices, to which, so long as we have a post-office department in the government, they are justly entitled, and strike boldly at the crying injustice of a special tax, a stamp duty upon the diffusion of knowledge, the correspondence of business, and the intercourse of friends.

Again, say the friends of cheap postage, the number of letters which the present exorbitant rates keep out of the mails, and which a reasonable reduction would recall to them, is immense, almost beyond calculation. It has become a regular practice in some of our business streets, that men carry on a daily correspondence with other cities, and yet pay no postage. "I am in constant communication with Boston," said a gentleman in Wall street to us the other day. "I send or receive letters daily. Yet for the whole year past, I have only paid postage on ten letters. I send neither by mail nor by any private express, but by individuals going to Boston. We have a regular system among us, by which we give each other notice of all private opportunities of sending letters to Boston, and these occur daily." Thus it is that a voluntary and gratuitous system of mails is established, which takes from the government mails two thirds perhaps of the letters which pass between this city and Boston. If the rates of postage had not been exorbitant this would never have been done. Reduce the rates to a low, a *very* low charge, and you will call back gradually most of these letters to the mails, to increase the revenue of the post-office. In England the reduction of the postage has greatly increased the number of letters. But in England all letters, formerly as now, passed through the post-office, and the carrying of a sealed letter from place to place was punished by severe penalties. The increase in the number of letters would, therefore, be greater here than in England, since here we shall have two causes of increase, while in England there has been but one.

The very same cause which prevents individuals from sending by mail while the present high rates continue, namely, a regard to the expense, causes the franking privilege to be used freely. Every year the mails carry fewer letters charged with postage; every year the mails carry more franked letters and documents. Last year there was a small falling off in the revenue of the post-office; this year there is a falling off which amounts to a quarter of a million; next year the falling off will doubtless be still greater. The population of the country increases rapidly, yet the communication by mail grows less and less; business revives, yet business men do not communicate with each other by mail. This shows something wrong in the system. It cannot be amended by restrictions and penalties; the restrictions will be evaded and the penalties will be braved; for public opinion in those parts of the country, where the attempt to enforce them could be made, is vehemently and universally against them. The sole remedy is cheap postage.

The Presidency: "Neither To Be Sought Nor Declined"
December 29, 1843

James Buchanan, later President of the Untied States, from 1857 to 1861, was in 1844 an unsuccessful aspirant for the Democratic nomination won by James K. Polk. In light of Bryant's opinion stated in this article, it should be remarked here that on two later occasions he refused to consider running for the Presidency himself.

We were compelled yesterday, for want of time and space, to leave unsaid part of what we had to remark concerning the maxim which the Washington *Spectator* applies to Mr. Buchanan's letter to the democrats of Pennsylvania, namely: that the Presidency of the United States is not an office either to be sought or declined. The necessity of getting the journal ready for the press at a certain moment, no doubt often spares our readers much tediousness. In this case, however, we do not mean they shall escape us.

Of all the offices in the g[ift] of the people, it seems to us that those which are the most gratifying to personal ambition, those which are most el[e]vated in their nature, which imply the fullest confidence of the people, and carry with them the highest testimonial of public favor, are the offices which a man may decline with the most satisfaction to his own conscience. Of this class, and the highest of this class is the Presidency. To put aside such honors requires self-denial, the root of all virtue; it requires modesty, the grace and ornament of all virtue. It is hard, we admit, to impose silence upon those who choose such agreeable topics as our own merits; it requires some firmness to receive the flattering notoriety which arises from being talked of for the first office in the nation; but so much the more honor is due to him who voluntarily forgoes this notoriety.

If there are any offices which are not to be declined by the citizens of a free country, it is those which are obscure and laborious, which no man covets, which bring with them no reward of power, of pat[r]onage, or public deference. To undertake the humble but useful services of such offices, bringing to them talents, industry and probity, is an act of great public virtue. For services like these, it is harder to find competent men than it is for the Presidency.

We do not say that there may not be great emergencies, and which a citizen of peculiar fitness for the place may not find himself urged by the strongest motives of public duty to accept the presidency and in which it would not be a sort of treason by the country to decline it. Such times and such men are rare. In ordinary times the candidate who assents to the opinion that the office is not on any account to be declined, must act under the notion that nobody but himself is able to discharge its duties properly, which would be a prodigious mistake.

De Mort[ui]s Nil Nisi *Verum*
February 28, 1844

Langdon Cheves (1776–1857), a Charleston, South Carolina lawyer, had been the effective president of the United States Bank from 1819 to 1822. Boston-born Joseph Dennie (1768–1812), a Harvard graduate, edited the Port Folio *at Philadelphia from 1801 until 1811.*

The news of the death of Nicholas Biddle is announced in the Philadelphia *Gazette,* of yesterday afternoon.

This man whose conduct as president and sole manager of the Bank of the United States, for many years, has been the subject of so much comment, was born in Philadelphia, in the year 1786. He was educated at Princeton, New Jersey, where he was graduated at the age of fifteen. In 1804, he went to France as Secretary to General Armstrong, the American Minister. At the age of twenty-two he returned to Philadelphia, where he engaged in the practice of law. In 1810 he was elected to the Pennsylvania House of Representatives, and in 1814 to the Senate. In 1819, President Monroe made him government director of the Bank of the United States, and four years afterwards, on the resignation of Lan[g]don Cheves, he was elected its President. From that time, he may be said to have had the sole control of the bank. He wielded the powers of that great institution in its protracted battle with General Jackson and the people, and when defeated at last, and compelled to give up all hope of a second charter from Congress, he had the address to secure for it a charter from the State of Pennsylvania, by which its existence was prolonged until even the prejudice and credulity of the strong political party by which it was supported, could no longer resist the evidence of the vices and blunders of its management, it exploded in one of the most prodigious bankruptcies ever known. After this, as in fact there was no alternative, he returned to private life.

We would willingly have remained silent concerning his character, had we not seen it extravagantly eulogized in some of the journals. The praise of goodness bestowed upon bad men, is an offence to morals, and should not be allowed to pass unquestioned.

Mr. Biddle was a pretty scholar, and wrote drawing room verses with considerable facility and grace. He is said to have been a frequent contributor to Dennie's Port Folio, then almost the only literary magazine in the country. He was a man of courteous and showy manners, although in these as in every thing else about him, the show predominated. He was at one time, highly admired by a certain class, for the supposed possession of great financial talent, but as a financier, he was incapable, blundering and dishonest, with no foresight beyond the petty expedients and shifts of the day. He had however, the talent which is so useful in keeping alive a willing credulity in other men—the talent of making plausible statements, with much apparent clearness, and a quiet self-possession. After bringing thousands to utter poverty, by the frauds and extravagances of his bank, he passed the close of his life in an elegant leisure at his country seat on the Delaware. If he had met with his deserts, he would have passed it in the penitentiary.

A Friendly Word to the Manufacturers
March 12, 1844

Certain newspapers, we perceive, are violent in their opposition to the tariff bill lately brought into the House of Representatives by the Committe of Ways and Means. Those who do this are not, whatever they may pretend, the friends of the manufacturers. Will they listen to a word of honest advice? We address them thus:

"It is a long battle, gentlemen, that you have been fighting with the consumers, or if you do not like that term, with the adversaries of the restrictive system. What have you gained by it? What is the fruit of this, your unceasing warfare of thirty years? Perpetual change, perpetual uncertainty, perpetual anxiety; great occasional advantages and great occasional losses, enriching you at one time, and ruining you at another. The tariff of 1816 produced an excessive competition, by which many of you lost every thing. When, by your clamors, you had extorted from Congress the tariff of 1824, laying still higher taxes on foreign goods for your benefit, the same effect was produced in a still higher degree; and in two or three years you began to demand another tariff. You obtained one in 1828, but you quarrelled among yourselves in regard to its provisions.

"Mr. Webster supported it, but Mr. Clay, your great champion, not then in Congress, tells you it was an unprincipled and mischievous measure. In 1832, after a struggle between the friends and the enemies of the restrictive system, which very nearly severed the Union, the compromise act was passed, by which the entire system of restrictive duties was gradually abolished, and a plan of duties for revenue substituted. You reluctantly submitted to this for ten years, but in 1842 you allied yourselves with the whig party, and obtained from them the black tariff, a system of duties more exorbitant than any of its predecessors. The first effect was what has been always observed in the history of the tariff; manufactures were excessively stimulated, there was too much activity and too many competitors in the same business. Many of you thus became bankrupt, among whom Mr. Simmons of Rhode Island, a member of Congress and a manufacturer of printed calicoes, who had assisted in laying the heavy duty on imported prints, was a remarkable example. You are now prosperous again; but your prosperity is principally owing to the fear that the black tariff, now becoming unpopular among the farmers, will be repealed. But for this alarm, which keeps new competitors from engaging in manufactures, and allows you to divide the exorbitant taxes laid for your benefit among a moderate number, we should have seen nearly twice the number of cotton and woollen mills erected, and Congress by this time would have been besieged with applications for still higher duties.

"Such is the history of the past; your prospect for the future is even less encouraging. A great change in public opinion is taking place among the agricultural population. The doctrine of free trade is supplanting the doctrine of protection with astonishing rapidity. The farmers of this country, which should be the granary of the world, are not content with a home market; they claim the market of all countries washed by the ocean. They begin to say to the manufacturers, 'You do us a double wrong; you tax us on what we buy, and you contract the market for what we sell.'

"You cannot keep the present tariff long; and, if you succe[e]d in protracting its existence a year or two, it must be at great cost and by great exertion. The warfare against the restrictive system will never cease as long as the system exists, and you must be wilfully blind to the state of opinion among your countrymen, if you do not see the gathering and swelling of that wave which is sure to overwhelm you. You will act prudently to meet it and take its force now. You cannot do better than accept the bill rendered by the Committee of Ways and Means, as the best compromise you can make with your adversaries. If you wait till another Congress, you will get worse terms. It is wise to make an early peace with an enemy who is strengthening his force every day."

The Convenience of an Average
March 20, 1844

Nathan Appleton of Boston, in partnership with Francis Lowell, established at Waltham in 1814 the first power mill in the country to spin cotton cloth, and later founded mills at Lowell and Lawrence, Massachusetts, and Manchester, New Hampshire. For a dozen years after 1830 he was a United States Congressman. Appleton was the father-in-law of Henry Wadsworth Longfellow; Lowell was an uncle of the poet James Russell Lowell. Matteawan later became a part of the city of Beacon, New York.

A lodger once complained to his landlord that in cold weather, although he kept up a good fire, the outer air came in so freely through the broken windows and chinky walls, that while his shins were roasting and his face scorched, his back was freezing. "You must make an average, my good sir," answered the landlord, "and your objection to the lodgings will vanish. By balancing the heat on one side of your body against the cold on the other, you will find you are perfectly comfortable."

A letter is going the rounds of the whig prints, which they attribute to Mr. Nathan Appleton, of Boston, making an equally successful application of the doctrine of averages to the defence of the present tariff. Mr. Appleton says:

> "Why call it [the tariff] black? Do you mean by that, it is too high? It averages from 34 to 35 percent on the dutiable articles imported, according to the custom house returns."

So our readers will see that the tariff is a reasonable tariff, and by no means high, if we will only follow the advice of the ingenious landlord, and the equally ingenious advice of Mr. Appleton, and make an average. For example:

The owner of a woolen manufactory pays five per cent duty upon the dirty wool, not coarse wool, for it is often of fair quality, but cheap because clogged with dirt, imported from South America. A mechanic of a humbler class, a blacksmith, pays a hundred and twelve percent upon the bar iron, out of which he hammers horse shoes for his customers. This has a bad appearance to be sure, but make an average of the two rates of duty according to Mr. Appleton's prescription, and they become much more reasonable.

On gold watch chains the rich man pays seven per cent. On log chains the farmer pays one hundred and sixty per cent. Here is another opportunity for applying Mr. Appleton's doctrine of averages.

On the poor man's coarse flannel shirt a duty is levied amounting to at least fifty per cent. On the rich lady's Cashmere or Thibet shawl only twenty per cent. This makes, according to the doctrine of averages, a very reasonable duty of thirty-five per cent.

The cheapest ingrain carpet pays one hundred and three per cent duty. The Brussels carpets, which cover the floors of the more opulent, pay but sixty per cent; and Wilton carpets, the finest of all, and destined to be trodden only by the feet of the most luxurious class, pay a duty of only thirty-one per cent. All this inequality, however, is beautifully reconciled by the doctrine of averages.

We might go through the whole of the tariff, which is full of these atrocious distinctions to the oppression of the poorer classes, but let those examples suffice. There is however another matter to which the doctrine of averages applies equally well. Mr. Appleton and those who with him own shares in manufacturing companies are now making it is said thirty per cent on the capital invested. The farmers are not making three per cent. But apply Mr.. Appleton's convenient rule of making an average, and we are all clearing a profit of fifteen per cent, at least.

It is asked why we should call this the "black tariff." That is all we get for our money. That is all the laborer gets for paying fifty per cent duty on his fustian pantaloons, for the benefit of Mr. Schenck of Matteawan, while Mr. Schenck pays no duty at all upon his logwood and madder. That is all the equivalent the laundress is allowed for the duty of one hundred and forty per cent on her smoothing irons. That is all we have in return for the salt tax, the sugar tax, and the molasses tax. Is it not enough that our hands are tied while our pockets are rifled, but must we [be] restrained from giving the deed its true name?

Mr. Appleton says of the tariff: "I am ready to defend it as a very good, an excellent one."

It is a very good tariff, no doubt, for those who like Mr. Appleton, own manufacturing stock. It is an excellent tariff for merchants like him, through whose hands the goods fabricated at Lowell and Waltham pass, and whose large commissions on their sale are said to amount to fifty or sixty thousand dollars [y]early. So large a revenue from an unjust law may go a great way in making a man blind to its injustice. "They talk of distress," said a rich miser, in a hard winter; "I feel no distress." The same happy frame of mind must have led Mr. Appleton to indite the closing words of his letter, which we here quote:

"It is, I repeat, an excellent tariff for revenue, falling chiefly upon luxuries, protecting all the great interest, and operating with apparent equality upon all portions of the country."

"By the help of an average," Mr. Appleton should have added.

Nathan Appleton's Letter of March 23 (Printed)
March 25, 1844

A moderate tariff bill, introduced into the House of Representatives in 1844 by Democratic Chairman of the Ways and Means Committee James McKay (1792–1853) of North Carolina, was not adopted into law until two years later. Mr. McKay served in the Congress from 1831 to 1849.

To the Editors of the Evening Post:

Gentlemen—I find in your paper of the 20th instant, an editorial article in which my name is used very freely, and in a manner to which I feel bound to take exception.

I am not particularly sensitive, and in many papers the remarks would pass without my notice; but I have always understood that the Evening Post was conducted by men claiming the character of gentlemen, and of course professing to conduct the paper in a gentlemanly manner.

Now, I appeal to you whether the personal application of those remarks is not inconsistent with that assumption?

I published an article in the *Journal of Commerce* with my initials, contradicting some statements made in that paper in relation to the manner in which the tariff of 1842 was made and passed through Congress. As a member of that Congress, I felt myself called on to correct these misstatements, and the more especially as being the only practical merchant connected with its passage.

I have no objection to any comments which you may think proper to make upon that communication. It is open to your criticism, and I make no objection to the use of my name in connection with it.

But you go further, and attribute to me motives in my approval of the tariff which I utterly disclaim. You attribute my approval to the circumstance that I am "interested in manufacturing companies now making, *it is said,* thirty per cent on the capital invested."

This, I think, would be highly indelicate, on the supposition that the assumed rate of profit was true; and being destitute of foundation, [a harsher?] name might be applied to it. In voting for the tariff I was acting in a public capacity. I sincerely believed its passage would restore the credit of the government and the general prosperity of the country, in which I have not been disappointed.

I claim for my opinions as high a sanction as you can challenge for yours. I have no objection, if it will be any gratification to you, to furnish you the rate of profit which I have derived from manufacturing stock up to the present time. I have made up an account of all the cotton establishments in Lowell for the last two years ending 1st February, which I forwarded to Mr. Bates, giving a gain for the first of these two years of $220,000, for the second $875,000, being an *average* on the capital of $9,500,000, of 5/76-100 per annum. My own income from this source must *average* about the same result.

It is true Mr. McDuffie stated that, by a calculation which he had made, founded on the census of 1840, he had ascertained that the profits of the cotton manufacture were 35 per cent per annum. I know of no one else who has said any such thing.

I think there i[s] a want of ingenuousness in the manner in which you give a coloring to a single paragraph in my communication, which could not be applied to it in connection with what follows. I applied the *average* of this tariff in comparison with previous ones, which had never been called black.

But let that pass. I see in the *Journal of Commerce,* of Thursday, my second communication, sent there more than ten days ago. Should it be thought worthy your notice, I trust you will do me the justice to publish my remarks without mutilation.

I am glad to perceive, by the article which I have be[e]n noticing, that you will, at any rate, oppose Mr. McKay's tariff, which proposing free trade and equality, imposes duties of ninety-three percent upon both iron and sugar, the greatest necessaries of life.

I am, gentlemen, very respectfully,

Your very obedient servant,
N. APPLETON.

Boston, 23d March, 1844.

Mr. Appleton's Letter
March 25, 1844

Some remarks which we made the other day on the "Convenience of Averages," have induced Mr. Appleton, of Boston, to write us a letter which, believing it to be intended for publication, we lay before our readers in this sheet.

As to using the name of Mr. Appleton in connexion with the communication which called forth our remarks, if we were wrong, it was because we followed the example of the tariff papers which republished the communication from the *Journal of Commerce* with Mr. Appleton's name, ostentatiously displayed, quoting him as an eminent and experienced merchant, whose opinion of the excellence of the present tariff was decisive of the question. To show that this merchant, with all his eminence and experience, might be misled by his own interest in the matter, we mentioned the well known fact that he was a large owner of manufacturing stock, and largely and profitably engaged in making sales of the fabrics of the eastern woollen and cotton mills. This is not denied, but Mr. Appleton denies that the stock produces thirty per cent profit, and denies also that his own interest has either influenced his judgment in the question, or affected his public course.

In regard to the profits of manufacturing stock, our readers have before them Mr. Appleton's statement, making the profits of all the Lowell Manufacturing capital, well or ill invested, for the last ten years, about five and three quarters per cent, "on an average." Opposed to this we quote from the money article of the *Boston Morning Post* of March 12th, the following passage:

> "There have been some statements made in reference to the profits of manufacturers at Lowell, which are to say the least disingenuous, as they in reality include only the two years 1842 and 1843, when the stopping of dividends was occasioned by bad debts and high salaries. We have already stated the fact—and no one has yet dared to deny it—that from the first start of the Lowell factories to the present time, they have averaged ten per cent per annum dividend. During the past year the dividends have been much larger, and would probably average fourteen per cent, besides large reserves. One of the companies has, it is well known, been making of late more than they dare divide, as some of its managers have frankly avowed."

What shall we say to this? If the explanation given in this passage be not grossly and outrageously at variance with facts, it excuses us from making any comment.

But, whether the actual profits derived from manufacturing capital be, as has been said, thirty per cent or not, it is not to be denied, and never has been denied that they have been increased by the tariff, and that manufacturing stock has risen in the market. Mr. Appleton claims that it is not "gentlemanly" to allude to the fact that the tariff has this favorable effect upon his personal interests. If it be not "gentlemanly," we are sorry for it. In penning the article we only thought of what was right, and what was due to the public. A member of Congress first votes for the tariff; he afterwards defends it in the newspapers, and his opinion is quoted by the friends of the tariff as decisive of the question. We come forward and tell the public, that this author and champion of the tariff makes money by the measure. It does not appear to us that the question is whether this is gentlemanly or not, but whether it be true. We must deal plainly in this matter. No man whose personal interests are involved in a question before Congress should permit [him]self to be concerned in legislating upon it. If he be an owner, for example, of a cotton mill, he should not allow himself to act as an arbiter in the question of laying on a duty, the effect of which is to raise its value and give it occupation, by shutting out the cargoes of cotton goods imported by our shipping merchants. In all our tribunals of justice we follow a similar rule. A judge is not allowed to try a case in which he is interested. The suitor in such a case demands, as he has a right, an impartial tribunal. Is that ungentlemanly? A juror is found to be interested in the event of a trial; the party against whom he is interested demands that he leave the jury box; is that ungentlemanly? The party who loses the cause, discovers it was tried before men who had a direct interest in the verdict; he demands a new trial; is that ungentlemanly? We hope, for our part, to see the time—perhaps we hope against all probability, and perhaps it is not gentlemanly even to express the hope—when a similar principle will prevail in legislation, when any member of a legislative body whose private interests are involved in any question before it, will be compelled either by his own sense of justice, or by the force of public opinion to resign his seat rather than give a vote which promotes his private interests.

Meantime, we do not charge Mr. Appleton with insincerity in approving of the tariff. He undoubtedly supposes it a beneficial measure; the misfortune is that he is not in a situation to make up an impartial opinion.

We shall publish his second communication to the *Journal of Commerce* as soon as we have room, and we reserve until that time what we have further to say on the subject of the average duties imposed by the present tariff.

Mr. McKay's tariff we certainly shall not oppose. We object, it is true, that it does not go far enough in some of its reductions, but it is a much better rate of duties than the present one.

Mr. Franklin's Letter
April 6, 1844

Morris Franklin, the Whig candidate for mayor of New York, lost the support of his party's journals to the candidate of the "Nativist," or American Republican Party, formed in 1843, the publisher James Harper, who was elected on April 9, 1844. The street disorders to which Bryant refers were apparently those in Brooklyn against foreigners, reported in this issue of the Evening Post. *Since its founding in 1841 Horace Greeley and Thomas McElrath had been the publishers of the New York* Tribune.

Formerly in Turkey whenever a new prince was to ascend the throne, a summary method was adopted of ensuring the public tranquility by getting rid of all troublesome competitors. The brethren of the royal family were all strangled like dogs, and thrown into the Bosphorus. We perceive the whig party are for applying the Turkish method to Mr. Franklin, their own candidate for Mayor. Mr. Harper, who has been nominated by the Nativists, is as much a whig as Mr. Franklin; he is a younger brother of the same family, and a large proportion of that party have made up their minds to give him their votes. To prevent confusion, therefore, an attempt is made to apply the strangling process to Mr. Franklin, the elder born. Mr. Franklin, naturally enough, resists the bowstring, and makes an outcry. He appeals to the public in a letter which several of the whig journals, cruelly smothering the dying cries of the legitimate prince, do not publish. As his letter is a sensible and firm one, we shall do it that justice which his whig friends refuse, and give it a conspicuous place in our columns. The bowstring, however, will do its work, and next Tuesday we shall see Morris Franklin floating in the political Bosphorus.

If we needed any evidence of foul play in this matter, the treatment of Mr. Franklin by the whig journals is sufficient. Two of them place his letter in an obscure corner of their sheet, without a single word of theirs to bespeak the reader's attention, or a single expression of approbation and sympathy. In the other papers, except that in which it first appeared, it is not published at all; one of them, however, mentions its existence, and gives a short extract from it. He is as completely abandoned by the press of his own party as if they had substituted another name in his stead. One of their journals said the other day that the whig party had nothing to do with the candidate of the Nativists. It is evident now that they have nothing to do with Mr. Franklin. The ticket of the Nativists is virtually dropped; the anonymous communications with which Mr. Franklin has been pestered, and the importunities of "professing friends" as he calls them, having failed of the desired effect, it remains to be seen whether he cannot be effectually shouldered aside by the coldness and silence of the press.

We come then to this, that we are merely fighting the old battle. The Nativists are but a division of the whig party, and the larger division, comprehending the greater part of its swaggerers and bullies, as the disgraceful disorders in the public streets which they have lately committed bear ample witness. We are only contending with the old enemy under a new name; it is democrat against whig; it is the spirit of political equality warring against the spirit of exclusiveness and proscription. If the Nativists succeed it will be a whig success; we shall simply have a rush of whigs into office and a division of the spoils of victory among the party who have so successfully applied the bowstring to their own regular candidate.

New York, April 4, 1844

Messrs. Greel[e]y and McElrath.

GENTLEMEN:—Unwearied efforts are being made by professing friends and others, to induce me to withdraw my name as a candidate for the Mayoralty at the approaching Charter Election, and numerous anonymous comunications are daily received urging me to such a course, and many entertain the belief that it is my intention to do so.

The nomination was tendered to me by my whig friends without solicitation or request on my part, and having been accepted and sanctioned in the usual manner, I have now no control over the matter, and could not, if I would, with any degree of propriety, withdraw from the situation in which they have placed me; and for the purpose of putting at rest the many rumors which are afloat, and allaying the apprehensions of some of my whig friends who entertain a fear that I may be induced to yield, I now unhesitatingly declare that, under no circumstances whatever, will I consent to withdraw from the contest, unless I become satisfied, through the action of the regularly constituted organs of the whig party, to wit, its General Committee, that it is their wish that I should do so; in which case I shall not hesitate for one moment to comply; but until then, I shall not shrink from maintaining my position, unawed by the threats and promises with which I am assailed. And, notwithstanding many who have heretofore acted with the party to which I am and always have been associated may be determined to withdraw their support in the present emergency. I feel myself imperiously called upon to show my faith by my works in the principles of that party, by fearlessly maintaining my integrity and keeping covenant with those by whom I have heretofore been zealously and successfully supported. For myself, personally, I care not what the result may be; but in reference to the great National contest, and the important bearing which this election may have upon that issue, I feel a deep and abiding conviction that it would prove the death-knell of our proudest hopes, if we should at this time desert our own standard and unite with a party whose object is to proscribe all those who have left the oppressions of their native land, and sought a refuge and a home in this country of equal liberty and equal laws; for there are thousands and tens of thousands thus situated who are the firm and steadfast friends of Henry Clay, scattered throughout this State and Union, who would at once desert a party professing such narrow and contracted views; I cannot consent to become the instrument of such a result.

If the principles of the party in favor of whose candidate I am solicited to resign, were confined only to reforms in our city government, and opposition to the present school law, I could most heartily co-operate with them, because I believe that in reference to the former there is but one sentiment throughout this community, and should be but one as to the latter; but there are other vital and important issues to which I cannot subscribe or yield an assent by pursuing a course different from that to which I have referred, and therefore I repeat, that under no circumstances, except the one to which I have alluded, will I consent to withdraw my name as the candidate of the whig party, let the result terminate as it may.

With sentiments of respect,
I remain your friend and ob't serv't,
MORRIS FRANKLIN

Mr. Appleton's Second Letter
April 11, 1844

The Englishman David Ricardo and the Frenchman Jean Baptiste Say were early nineteenth-century economists. For Appleton's verse quotation, cf. Macbeth III, iv, 78–80. In Shakespeare's A Midsummer Night's Dream (I, iii, 32), as the artisans are preparing to entertain the Duke and Duchess of Athens in a play on their wedding night, the weaver Bottom boasts, "I could play Ercles [Hercules] rarely, or a part to tear a cat in, to make all split."

To the Editors of the EVENING POST:

I presume you would consider me wanting in respect, or perhaps entirely silenced by your eloquence, should I permit your lucubrations on my defence of the tariff of 1842 to pass without notice. However irksome the task, I have no alternative.

In the first place, I am obliged to you for the publication of my letter, which was, I confess, written with no such expectation. That, at least, I consider "gentlemanly." I propose then to follow such of your remarks as seem to call for notice in the order in which you present them.

In your communication of Monday, the 25th ult., you quote a paragraph from the *Boston Morning Post*, in reference to my statement of the profits of the Lowell companies, as disingenuous, as it includes only the two years 1842 and 1843, (not ten years, as in your text.) How disingenuous? Will you or the *Morning Post* tell me? I send you the original article in the *Daily Advertiser* of 9th February, which I will thank you to publish, and point out its disingenuousness.

It was an answer to Mr. McDuffie's statement, that the cotton manufacturers were making 35 per cent per annum. As to what it says of "high salaries" and *making more than they dare divide*, it is such stuff as dreams are made of. Because such crudities are thought unworthy of notice or contradiction, they furnish a miserable ground work on which to found assertions of fact. There has been no reduction of salaries.

On a critical examination during the period of greatest depression, it was found in all cases, I believe, that these concerns were managed with the greatest possible economy. As to dividends, the tendency always is to divide too much, and I know of no case in which a dividend has been withheld through fear.—In general, the reserves are barely sufficient to cover the wear and tear of machinery. In taking all the Lowell cotton mills, I take the highest possible standard. There are no bad investments there as you suggest.—The stock of every company is something over par—and is there any other fair mode of estimating the profits of the business, but by an average of such concerns?

The nearest approach to truth in the paragraph of your oracle of the *Morning Post*, is the average profit of well conducted manufacturing establishments, which he states at about ten per cent, which is not far from the truth in some few cases. I find the average of all the cotton mills in Lowell, for the last seven years, between 8 1–2 and 9 per cent per annum. But how does this support your allegation that they are pocketing thirty per cent? Would any man go into any trade or business, involving so much risk and care, without a reasonable prospect of a return of nine or ten per cent per annum? In England, the business of manufacturing is thought bad, when it will not give a return of 10 per cent net profit.

You next come to a more serious matter. You say, "no man, whose personal interests are involved in a question before Congress, should permit himself to be concerned in legislating upon it." Indeed!— Then no farmer should vote on a question that he thinks will benefit agriculture; no merchant for the benefit of commerce. Legislation is to be performed by those who know least, and care least, upon the subject on which they are acting. To be consistent with this theory, no vote should be permitted, tending to the elevation of a party, from which the voter hoped or expected office, or emolument, or personal advantage of any kind. The established rule is better, which excludes a man from voting on a question in which he has an interest separate and distinct from the community.

In voting for the tariff of 1842, I thought then, and I think now, that I was promoting the interest of every individual in the United States, yourselves among the number; and with your permission, I venture the opinion, that I was then, and am now, in as good a "situation to form an impartial opinion" as yourselves.

Your second article is a touching Jeremiad upon the sufferings of the poor, inflicted by the Lords of Lowell, in the enormous price of their goods—"The dreadful aggregate of twelve millions of dollars wrung from them by the tariff on the coarser cotton fabrics." "From the children of toil, the poor widow with her children, the wretched inmates of garrets and cellars." "Is that no grievance? then no exortion, no pillage, no secret larceny, nor violent robbery is a grievance."

Heaven bless us! what are we coming to? If this is not poetry run mad, the genuine Ercles vein, I should be glad to know what is. Mark, how a plain tale shall put all this down. The grievance complained of, is the advance on printed calicoes and coarse cottons, under the tariff of 1842. Why, gentlemen, it seems to me, you blow hot and cold in less time than the rustic in the fable, who thereby so disgusted the poor satyr. If I am not much mistaken, it is but a very short time since you said that this tariff had ruined the manufacturers as well as the rest of the world. It had so stimulated the production of goods, especially of printed calicoes, that in consequence of the excessive production, the prices had fallen so ruinously low, as to cause several failures. In connection with which, you referred, (not very delicat[e]ly) to the misfortunes of a distinguished Rhode Island Senator. Was it not the EVENING POST which said this? Now forsooth, these goods have advanced four cents the yard, levying six millions upon miserable shivering wretches.

There is about as much truth in one statement as the other. Printed calicoes were sold very low in the spring of 1843, and there has been a considerable advance, but not one half what you state it to be. I have the best authority for saying, that the advance on Merrimack prints, does not average over one cent upon the yard, upon the lowest sales of 1842 or 1843. The best criterion is the standard and uniform article of dark blues, constituting one fourth of their manufacture, none of which have been sold at a greater advance than a cent a yard, and a very small quantity at that.

Your quotation of the advance of Appleton sheetings is correct, being two cents the yard, from 6 1–2 to 8 1–2 cents. But at the former price, it was a losing business, and this company made no dividend for three successive semi-annual periods, their whole dividend for the last two years, having been but six per cent.

These heavy goods follow the price of cotton, the advance on which, from 6 to 9 1–2 cents, has been equal to about 1 1–4 cents on the yard of cloth. They are now drooping with the decline of cotton.

But have not cotton manufactures advanced in England? for there lies the gist of your argument, if there is any gist in it. You seem very familiar with Manchester price currents. I refer you to that of Du Fay & Co., of 1st March, which, no doubt, some of your Manchester friends can furnish you. It contains a table of comparative prices for every month in the year for eight years. You will find it there set down that the leading printing power loom cloth, 72 Reed, in May and June, 1842, sold at 4s.9d., in February, 1844, at 7s., an advance of two cents on the grey cloth for a yard of calico, or upwards of 45 per cent on an article of which the raw material constitutes one-third of the value, against one tenth per cent advance on a similar article, or thirty-one per cent on an article of which the raw material constitutes two-thirds of the value. Thus this raw head and bloody bones vanishes into thin air. What shall we think of the writer? He either wrote upon a subject which he did not understand, or was guilty of a wilful misrepresentation—he may take either horn of the dilemma from which to dangle.

We next come to an annunciation which develops a new principle on political economy. It is stated that the farmers "lose a market abroad for such of their produce as would be exchanged for the goods imported under a moderate tariff." Spirit of [S]ay and Ricardo! What next? The full feeding work people of Lowell, do not consume as much of our beef, flour and potatoes, as the starving operatives of Manchester would do if we would buy our calicoes of them. How do you break through the corn laws? But that does not matter—it would not be true, were no corn laws in existence.

Does not every mechanic or manufacturer eat and drink as much of farmers' produce, if he does his work in America, as if he does it three thousand miles off? Then, you say, our ships lose the freight. But, i[s] that a disadvantage? Is it not better for the respective consumers to make the exchange on the spot, rather than compel each to carry his product across the Atlantic? There lies the whole question, in an economical point of view. It is an exchange of labor against labor—and the free competition among the farmers on one side, and the manufacturers and mechanics on the other, will be sure to cause the exchange to be made on equal terms, dividing the peculiar advantages of their position, in this country of cheap land, between them.

The Bostonians, however, are of opinion, that the protective system has increased our commerce immensely, whilst it has changed its direction. The trade between Boston and New Orleans employs a greater amount of tonnage than that between New York and Liverpool ever did. Upwards of fifty square rigged vessels, mostly ships of the larger class, have arrived at this port during the sixty-days of February and March—one-half of their cargoes, at least, consisting of the produce of the valley of the Ohio. This trade is the result of the protective system. How could we take their beef, pork, flour, lard and wool, if they did not take our calicoes, cottons, cabinet wares, shoes, and other notion[s]?

Your last article is a violent phillippic, written certainly in your very best style—but it is an attack upon an obsolete idea, the oppression of the tariff on the consumers of our coarse cottons. This idea has been dead and buried for more than ten years. Its ghost occasionally makes its appearance, as in the present case, but not amongst men of business. Its aspect is always political. Its best quietus is a visit to your annual exhibition of American manufactures at Niblo's.

> "The times have been.
> That when the brains were out, the man would die,
> And then the end."

I shall content myself at present with referring you to the enclosed price current from the British port of Calcutta, received by the last steamer, the publication of which I commend to your commercial department. You will find under the head of American domestics, the ennumeration of upwards of twenty different cotton fabrics, known in that market, with the quality of each wanted for consumption monthly, amounting to upwards of three thousand packages per annum, with the remark that the quantity will doubtless increase materially. These goods pay an extra duty over British products, and still find a regular market amongst the labouring population. Can there be a stronger proof that the same class of men with us are not suffering under our lower prices?

I cannot agree with you that the cotton manufacture brings no revenue to the government. On the contrary, it enables the farmer, who feeds it, and all whose industry it sustains, to consume foreign products. Why are our most intelligent importers in favor of the system, but because they find in our manufacturing towns and villages, the best market for silks and other luxuries? You quarrel with my use of this term, and show an acquaintance with the nomenclature of Manchester goods, in which, I am unable to follow you. "Are cambrics, jaconets and printed lawns" you ask, luxuries. Certainly. I think so. Why not? "Are fustians luxuries"? This is a generic term, including velvets, of which according to Mr. McKay's table, seven eighths of the quantity imported cost over 35 cents the square yard, and are not affected by the minimum at all! As for the lower priced goods, passing under this general name in England, we have made substitutes of our own, better suited to our climate, both better and cheaper. The term fustians is not used in this country. You cannot have learned it from an American—it smacks of Lancashire—"imported for the use of farmers." It is all humbug.

You mention an article called "Orleans"—I know of nothing which passes by that name. I enclose you however, a sample of an article, of which large quantities are made for the New Orleans market, which is very probably the same thing which is stouter, and about half the pri[c]e of a very similar French manufacture.

You refer to the enormous profits of the Waltham and Merrimack Companies. The Waltham Company was the pioneer in the introduction of the power loom, and has been eminently successful. You are correct in your statement of its dividends for the first seven years, but it does not give the whole story. Its dividends for the last seven years have been only 250 dollars per share, or less than [8?] 60-[1?]00 per cent per annum.

I find the aggregate dividends for the entire twenty seven years since it first made one, amount to 3,050 dollars, or 11 28–100 per cent per annum for the whole term. Nor is this all. On a valuation of the property some years ago, it was found that they had divided 25 per cent of the capital—so that the share of 1000 dollars was only worth 750—which is rather above the present market price. Taking this into consideration, the average dividends fall to ten 37–100 per cent per annum—and no dividends were made until about three years after the capital had been advanced. I send you a statement from the Treasurer's books, with the dividends made, which you are at liberty to publish. Their sheetings sold in 1816, at 30 cents, and were the identical article which sold in 1843 at 6 1-3¢[,] and the advance of which to 8 1-2, has called forth your eloquent burst of indignation. Such has been the effect of competition upon profits and prices under the system which you so deprecate.

In 1819, we imported cargoes of these goods from Calcutta. In

1843, we shipped three thousand packages to that port, and upwards of twenty thousand to China—the last accounts of which are most encouraging to a further increase of this trade. Has the world ever before seen such a revolution in commerce in the course of a quarter of a century?

I could furnish some facts and reminiscences connected with these two companies, which would probably be interesting to your readers, but this communication has been sufficiently extended. Should a continuance of my correspondence be agreeable to you I may perhaps find leisure to furnish it. N. A.

Boston, April 6, 1844

An Apology for the Tariff
April 11, 1844

And a lame one too, will be found in our paper of to-day bearing the signature of N. A. which our readers will understand to mean Mr. Nathaniel Appleton, the Massachusetts manufacturer, who was in Congress when we were all taxed to increase the value of his cotton mills, and gave his voice for the measure. As his letter is long, and our remarks upon it will not be very brief, we have been obliged to delay its publication until after the election. Look at it, kind and patient reader, and then extend your forbearance so far as to run your eye over these remarks, and see how completely even the framers of the tariff fail to make out a plausible defence for it. The letter is a tissue of the most unhappy misstatements and sophi[s]tries.

In the beginning of his letter the writer attempts to defend himself against the alleged immorality of voting for the direct promotion [of] his private interest and that of the few hundred more who belong to his class. The bare mention of such an act carries its condemnation with it. At present we notice the subject no further than to refer our readers to an article copied into our columns from the Washington *Spectator*, which will show that others speak of it in much harsher language than we chose to employ.

Mr. Appleton sends us his remarks in the *Daily Advertiser* in answer to Mr. McDuffie, and asks us to publish them and point out their disingenuousness. We shall gratify him in both respects. The remarks in question, our readers will find subjoined to his letter, and their disingenuousness consists in this. They purport to be a reply to Mr. McDuffie's statements [in] regard to the profits of the manufacturers and the price of the raw material of cotton fabrics in 1840. Mr. McDuffie calculates the raw material of cotton fabrics at one-fourth of the cost, and estimates the profits of the manufacturers, who came as he says to Washington in 1842, "begging for more bounties," at thirty-five per cent annually. Mr. Appleton meets this, by alleging that the dividends of the Lowell companies, were in the years 1842 and 1843, something less than six per cent. This is disingenuous because it takes the two very worst years of these companies, the years in which they made the least profits. It is disingenuous because it does not include the dividends of the prosperous years of 1840 and 1841, before as Mr. McDuffie says, the manufacturers come to Washington begging for bounties. It is disingenuous, because, while it admits that during the last six months, "the cotton manufacture has been highly prosperous," it does not tell us what profits it is NOW making. Mr. Appleton asks us how the statement of the Lowell dividends for the last seven years supports the allegation that the owners of the mills are pocketing thirty per cent?— Aye, sure enough, how does it? It neither supports nor refutes it. Let Mr. Appleton tell us what his mills are now making, let him give the profits for the last three months and he will then speak to the purpose, which he has not yet done. He is seeking to hide the real profits of this prosperous season, when his mills are so many mints, amidst a jumble of ancient dividends which have nothing to do with the question. We should like to see a statement of the profits of the Middlesex Mills, at Lowell, which have recently made large dividends for surplus profits. The owners of the York Mills, at Saco, have lately done the same thing. Yet we are allowed to hear only about the average dividends of past years.

Again, in regard to the raw material of cotton fabrics, which Mr. McDuffie calculates at only one fourth the cost, Mr. Appleton, in order to show that the manufacturers are making very little money, estimates it at three fourths, and proceeds to exult that the basis of Mr. McDuffie's argument being overthrown, his conclusion concerning the exorbitant profits of the manufacturers falls to the ground. We shall show that Mr. McDuffie is right and Mr. Appleton wrong, and leave the reader to apply the blame of disingenuousness where he pleases.

We have not the cost of the raw material in 1840 before us, but we have its present cost in Boston.—Last week, says the Boston *Courier*, of the 8th instant, the sales in that city were 1,732 bales, on six months' credit, at prices from eight cents and a quarter to eight cents and three quarters a pound. Now, by the published statistics of the Lowell Manufactures for 1844, it appears that a pound of cotton averages in cloth 3 1–5 yards, a little less than three yards and a quarter to a pound of cotton. We have taken an aggregate of forty-eight of the principal articles made at the new mills in Lowell, the only ones engaged in manufacturing cotton, with the prices as furnished by the largest buyers here from the lists of the selling agents, and we find the average price to be a little more than 10 cents a yard, which being multiplied by 3 1–5, the number of yards to a pound of cotton, gives the product of 32 cents as the price of a pound of cotton made into cloth. Here then is a demonstration that Mr. McDuffie's estimate is true, and that the estimate of Mr. Appleton is destitute of the least foundation.

The average dividends of all the Lowell mills are admirably selected for the purpose of mystifying the question. Those years commence with the disastrous year of 1837, and include the period of the suspension of specie payments throughout the country. They include also the second suspension of payments by the United States Bank, and most other banks south of New York. They include year after year of enormous failures among merchants and bankers, and all that class who adventure in business or give extensive credits. In the midst of this calamitous time, when every body else was losing money, when the most solid credit was shaken, and the most prosperous in other branches of enterprise suffered loss, the Lowell mills were dividing among their stockholders an annual profit of nearly nine per cent on their capital. Yet this according to Mr. Appleton, is not to be accounted a very fortunate dividend. "In England" he tells us "manufacturing business is thought bad when it will not give a return of ten per cent net profit."

Now we aver that this is not true with regard to incorporated manufactories, like those of Lowell. They are content with dividends of six per cent; they are satisfied with two thirds of what the Lowell mills were making in the worst times the commercial world of America ever saw. The manufacturer in England who looks for ten per cent annually buys his own raw material, superintends the mills through some member of his family and sells his own merchandize. He does not dissipate his profits in salaries to buying agents, selling agents and treasurers. Cotton mills in England, with two or three exceptions, are not parcelled out in shares but are managed personally by the parties interested. That is the way they make ten per cent upon their capital. This profit is partly the wages of their labor and their attention.

Do our readers know how the Lowell and other mills are conducted? They are incorporated; they have large salaries to pay to persons who are employed to buy their cotton, and liberal commissions to those who are employed to sell their goods, and handsome compensations to their treasurers. Some rich and large stockholder has sons who are to be provided for, and he makes them selling agents, or buying agents, or treasurers. We have heard of one person of this class who was treasurer to three companies at once, receiving some ten or fifteen thousand dollars yearly. Thus these institutions, which we are supporting by high duties, are, among their other excellent uses, contrivances to form a provision for the families of the nobility of the cotton mills. These employments are like the English places in the army and the church. Formerly these young men studied Blackstone, and put up a lawyer's sign in Boston, but they are now more profitably employed. When the younger scions of the cotton mill aristocracy are liberally paid, the remainder of the profits are distributed among the stockholders. The dividends, therefore, by no means, show the actual emoluments of the manufacturers, which are in reality vastly greater than appears on the books of these companies.

We have shown the fallacy of all Mr. Appleton's positions thus far. We have no more space to-day, but to-morrow we shall make quite as summary work with the rest of his letter.

The Remainder of the Apology for the Tariff
April 12, 1844

Our readers, we hope, will not be repelled from this article by seeing that it is a continuation of the subject of yesterday. All continuations are not necessarily tedious and uninteresting. The Eastern storytellers, the most skilful of their tribe, prolong their tales from evening to evening, and splice one wonder upon another. Let the reader resume the subject with us, and we promise to set before him out of the rest of Mr. Appleton's letter, wonders almost equal to those of the Arabian Nights.

Mr. Appleton denies that the late increase in the price of printed cottons is half what we have stated it to be. Let us see how this is. We, who are no manufacturers, may easily make a mistake in these matters, but Mr. Appleton ought to be precise. We supposed that printed American calicoes had risen four cents per yard, which might be a trifle too high. Mr. Appleton says they have not risen over two cents. To prove this, he says that the dark blue Merrimack prints, which he thinks afford the best criterion, have not advanced in price more than a cent a yard from the lowest sales of the two last years.

Now, our answer to this is, that Merrimac prints and Merrimac dark blues are an exception to the general case of American printed calicoes, and are no criterion of the increase of prices. Of dark blues, not one yard is consumed to thirty of other kinds. The Merrimac prints are those which have suffered the least fluctuation in value. The reason is, that the company which is prosperous and in no haste to sell, always withhold[s] its goods when the market is low. Still they have gained considerably in price. On what is termed the two-and-three-colored machine work, and on the French plates of the Merrimac company, the present prices are from twenty to twenty-five per cent higher than in April and May, 1843.

But let us take other companies than the Merrimac, so dexterously selected by Mr. Appleton. Take the Blackstone, the Great Falls, the Perkins, the Lawrence, the Boot, and other companies, and we find that the printing cloths of these manufactories which send out immense supplies for the market, have gained on an average an increase of 2 41–100 cents a yard above the lowest prices of last year, which is nearly two cents and a half. This is the rise on the cloths before they are printed, but we have the best mercantile authority, the authority of those very persons who deal in American prints here, that Sprague's prints, Robertson's fancy prints, with those of Philip Allen, Brown & Adams, and all other manufactories, with the exception of the Merrimac co[m]pany, were at the time we write, from three to four cents higher than they were last year. Strike one of those averages which Mr. Appleton is so fond of when they answer his purpose, and so willing to avoid when they do not, and you have a rise of three cents and a half. This, on one hundred and fifty millions of yards of printed calicoes, which is the annual product of the American mills, as estimated by Mr. Appleton in another letter, make an aggregate of between five and six millions of dollars, levied principally upon the poorer classes to enrich a set of men who were prosperous already. This is too heavy a tax to pay for the pleasure of saying that the sprigs and flowers on the calicoes worn by the laborer's children are stamped in Rhode Island.

But, says Mr. Appleton, the prices of cotton manufactures have also risen in England, and this, and not the high duties, accounts for their rise here. To prove this, he refers us to the price current of Du Fay & Co., which, he thinks we can get from our "Manchester friends." Alas! we have no Manchester friends, and we cannot get the circular of Du Fay & Co. That is a German house, and does not purchase for the United States market, so that it is of no consequence. But we have the circular of Gibson, Ord & Co., American commission merchants at Manchester, dated January 1, 1844. They quote the price of 72 reed, power loom printing cloth, weighing five pounds, at from six shillings to six shillings and three pence sterling; or 150 cents the piece; or 30 cents a pound for the cloth manufactured. Deduct from this 12 cents for the price of raw cotton at Liverpool, and you leave 18 cents for the cost of making and the profit.

Contrast this with the prices here. The present price of the corresponding article made in this country is 2,03 cents the piece, or 40 cents a pound. Deduct from this 10 cents, the price of raw cotton at New York, and you leave 30 cents for the cost of making and profit, which is sixty-six per cent more than in England. The difference between the wages paid in this country and those paid in England will account for but a small part of this difference, and the greater part of this sixty-six per cent is an additional profit to the American manufacturer, who, by the help of the tariff, extorts it from the consumer. If there be any truth in price currents, cotton goods could be imported and sold at lower prices under a moderate tariff, than we now get them in the market.

Mr. Appleton ridicules the idea that a moderate tariff would increase our exports, affirming that a Lowell operative consumes as much beef and flour as an Englishman. The answer to this is, that if we had a moderate tariff, a great many additional articles would be imported and consumed in this country, the payment of which would be made by additional shipments from our exporting states. Mr. Appleton talks as if the Lowell operatives were the great devourers of the harvests of the states. Why, the operatives of all the cotton mills in the Union do not consume a third of the products of the single state of Illinois. Our country opens every day a wider market for manufactures. All that are now produced here are wanted for the south; the west and other regions of the Union could take off as many more from abroad, and the employment given to our shipping by bringing in these importations would enable them to carry our produce for a lower freight to foreign countries, and thus increase the profit of the farmer. The south and west have certai[n]ly a right to seek the best marts in which to exchange the products of their industry.— Mr. Appleton's plan of restricting them to what he calls necessaries, and obliging them to buy at Lowell, appears to us a little arbitrary. He tells us, however, that it would be a pity "to compel them to carry their produce across the Atlantic." No doubt it would be—both a pity and a shame—but it is well to give them the right to do as they please in this matter. If they can obtain the goods they want on a fair exchange at Lowell, they will do so—but if by sending their produce abroad they can obtain a better price and larger returns, after paying the expenses of the voyage, who can rightfully restrain them? The fears of the manufacturers, lest freedom of trade should drive their fabrics out of the market, are idle. In 1825, when Mr. Huskisson brought into the English parliament a bill reducing the duties on imported silks, the silk manufacturers became alarmed, and prophesied the extinction of their trade if it passed. It did pass—a large amount of silks is now annually brought over from France, and yet the silk manufacture in

England extends itself every year. The result would unquestionably be the same in this country; a moderate tariff, in enlarging our commerce with foreign countries, would not diminish the commerce along our coast.

We hear from the printing office that there is no further space for our remarks, and we are compelled to break off here for the present.

The Late "Whig" Victory
April 12, 1844

We copy from the *Albany Evening Journal,* the following rebuke administered to its delirious friends, the whigs. Never was there a political party so utterly devoid of common sense or sagacity. Their recent conduct in this city, over which they rejoice so senselessly, is suicidal. It has inflicted a stronger blow upon their friends throughout the United States than the most overwhelming defeat could have done. But we shall permit one of themselves to read them the lesson of the day.

> "We have the satisfaction of announcing the overwhelming defeat of the Tammany ticket at the election yesterday, by the united votes of the Native Americans and Whigs.— For the whigs in most of the wards, aware that adherence to their own ticket would ensure the success of the Tammany candidates, dropped them and voted for Native Americans.
> Out of the seventeen wards the Tammany party have carried but five. Last year they had thirteen. Their majority of nearly six thousand has fallen into a minority of eight or ten thousand.
> In the result of this election, the whigs of New York have great cause for congratulation. The Tammany rule, which has disgraced our city so long, is at an end. Better men, with better measures, will take the place of those the people have so signally rebuked for the profligacy and misrule["].— *Express.*

We copy this shameless avowal of the New-York *Express* with pain and mortification. It is painful to know that so many Whigs have, in a crisis like the present, deserted their standard; and it is mortifying to hear a Whig newspaper avow that *"Whigs in most of the Wards, aware that adherence to their own ticket would ensure the success of the Tammany Candidates, dropped them and voted for the Native Americans."* There is cause for anything but "congratulation" for Whigs in the result of the New-York Election. In deserting their own candidates and banding themselves with demagogues who have fanned the embers of political fanaticism, into a blaze, they have inflicted an incurable wound upon the whig cause. Long and bitterly will the honest men who have been beguiled into this unholy crusade, lament their infatuation.

Before whigs "congratulate" themselves upon the result of the Charter election in New York, let them inquire into the character and objects of the successful party. In the nomination of Aldermen an equal number of whigs and locofocos were taken, who stand pledged to appoint an equal number of whigs and locofocos, excluding all persons not born in America, to office. Now we pronounce this Coalition more atrocious in design, and more diabolical in spirit, than any that has ever disgraced our state.— And whatever may be thought and said in the delirium of success, not six months will elapse before this proscriptive, persecuting, unrighteous amalgamation will be as deeply deplored by thousands who are misguided by it, as it is now execrated by those who foresee the end of its brief but inglorious career.

The only cause of "congratulation" that we discover in this result is, that there are no Whigs in the Common Council. Let these Modern Reformers, who, after excluding Adopted Citizens from Office, may, perhaps, attempt to drive them from the country, or burn them at the stake, go into power with all its responsibilities. To the five thousand Whigs who have been true to their principles, be all honor and praise. Let the Whig candidates in the several wards who, refusing to traffic with the Ishmaelites, have gone down with their "colors torn but flying," be remembered and cherished as men to be relied on at all times.

> The Tammany folks bore their defeat, last night, remarkably well. They remained in the hall till a late hour, and even had some singing on the occasion before they separated.— *Express.*

The "Tammany folks" had abundant reason for bearing their "defeat remarkably well." Through such defeats they look forward to many triumphs. Tammany Hall had become so odious that, had the Whig party maintained its integrity, they would have carried the city triumphantly. But now all is gone. The Native Americans will fall to pieces. The Whig party has fallen into disgrace. Tammany Hall will "purge and live cleanly," for a year, and then be restored to popular favor again. And all this to benefit some office-seeking gentry and to gratify a persecuting spirit against Irishmen, who, though often misled, are better and truer and more disinterested friends and supporters of Free Institutions and Republican Government, than most of those who are to be turned out or those who will go into office.

A Case of Delicacy
April 13, 1844

In his Discourses Upon Trade *(1691) the British merchant and economist Sir Dudley North (1641–1691) anticipated by nearly a century arguments in favor of free trade made by Adam Smith in* The Wealth of Nations *(1776). Senator George McDuffie of South Carolina strongly opposed the protective tariff as unjust to the cotton planters. Cf. Macbeth, III, iv, 78–79: "the times have been, / That, when the brains were out, the man would die."*

Before proceeding to examine the remaining statements in Mr. Appleton's letter which we published on Thursday, we are stopped by a case of delicacy.

Mr. Simmons, of Rhode Island, a calico printer, was a member of the United States Senate when the tariff was passed, and procured a heavy duty to be laid on cheap printed calicoes. That duty has since caused them to rise in price; as he no doubt expected, three or four cents a yard, but before he could take the benefit of this result, Mr. Simmons' boat was swamped in the conflicting currents of the old and new commerce. He failed in the time of low prices and glutted markets which immediately followed the passage of the tariff, and we recorded his instructive story. Mr. Appleton says that this was indelicate.

Our readers will understand that there are things which it is delicate to do, yet not delicate to speak of. It is a very delicate proceeding, in a person who holds a public trust, to pervert it to his own private interest, but it is shockingly indelicate in any person to call him to account for it.

Tried by this rule, we confess our conduct to have been grossly indelicate. The person who behaved with delicacy in this matter was Mr. Simmons. It was exquisitely delicate in him to aid in making and passing a tariff which was to raise the price of his calicoes three or four cents a yard. It was equally delicate in Mr. Appleton to vote for a tariff which raised the price of the Appleton sheetings two cents a yard, and lifted him out of what he calls a losing business in which he received but six per cent upon his capital. These are high refinements of delicacy; there is nothing finer woven in the looms of Lowell or strapped under the cylinders of the Rhode Island printing mills.

Mr. Appleton labors to create the belief that we are supplied with cotton fabrics as cheaply as they are sold abroad. It is true, that formerly, certain kinds of the cheaper cotton cloths were sold here about as low as in Europe, but this is no longer the case. In Manchester and Glasgow, brown or unbleached shirtings, are from fifteen to twenty per cent cheaper than here. This will surprise [our] readers;

but such is the fact.— There is no doubt that at the present low rate of wages, with the recent improvements in machinery an economically conducted cotton mill—the profits of which were not intercepted by an array of agents and treasurers fattening on high salaries and commissions, can make and afford to sell the various leading articles of cotton manufacture as cheap as the English. We shall be glad to see our manufacturers do this, and content themselves with reasonable returns on their capital. The home consumer who submits to taxation, ought at least to have the opportunity of purchasing goods made in American mills at prices as low as the foreign consumer buys them from our manufacturers. We shall show, however, that this is not the case.

Mr. Appleton and his associates sell their goods cheaper at Calcutta than at New York. The consumer abroad has the advantage of the extravagant bounties paid by the consumer at home. Mr. Appleton sends us a Calcutta price current, which he says will show upwards of twenty different kinds of American cotton fabrics known in the Calcutta market. We have looked over the list and find that many of them are marked not wanted, and the letter of advice annexed to the price current recommends only the shipment of twilled cottons. It says:

"The drills and jeans will doubtless increase materially. But shirtings, sheeting and satin jeans, we are as yet unable to allow will answer in this market. Bleached goods certainly will not, nor can we obtain the prime cost of sheetings."

These drills which met with so good a sale at Calcutta, and of which the letter in question recommends that four-fifths of the shipment should consist, figure in the price current as follows:

"Suffolk drills" are quoted at 3 anas,	2 piece. the yard.
Deduct *ten* per cent for freight, insurance and commissions,	4
	2.10
Duty at Calcutta,	6 piece.
	2.4 or

at 48 cents the rupee, equal to seven cents, our money, the yard.

The lowest price asked to-day, by the resident agents of manufacturers *here*, to the jobbers for *home* sale, is 8 3–4 cents per yard, or 25 per cent more than the Calcutta merchant sells them for deliverable at Calcutta.

These goods are admitted into the British dominions on very liberal conditions. While our citizens are compelled to purchase their cottons at Lowell, Britain allows her subjects to buy where they can get them cheapest. American cottons pay on entering her ports what we should call a mere nominal duty; they are subject only to a duty of ten per cent on going into England; from five to ten per cent on entering the British East Indies, and seven per cent on entering Nova Scotia and Canada. On similar goods introduced from abroad into this country, the duty ranges from 30 to 120 per cent.

But we take higher ground with Mr. Appleton. If it be true, as he labors to show, that the American manufacturer can undersell his British rival in the British provinces, there is no occasion for protective duties even on his own principle. The American manufacturer has as wide a market before him as the British, and enters it, according to Mr. Appleton, with greater advantages. What more is wanted? But if, on the other hand, the profits of the manufactories are so beggarly as he would make the world believe, why should this enormous tax be levied to keep them in existence? Let them go to ruin, if the few hundred men who are engaged in making cotton cloths, are to be supported by an annual drain upon our resources as great as the expense of the Florida war. The truth is, that Mr. Appleton's arguments refute each other. If we can, as he says, undersell the British in Calcutta, our manufacturers are making money at a prodigious rate. If they have been doing "a losing business," how can they afford to undersell the British in Calcutta?

Mr. Appleton asks:

"Why are our most intelligent importers in favor of the system, but because they find in our manufacturing towns and villages, the best market for silks and other luxuries?"

Our most intelligent importers are by no means in favor of the protective system. Those who live near "the manufacturing towns and villages," which afford "the best market for silks and other luxuries," and who supply them with expensive tissues from the European looms, are doubtless in favor of the system. The farmers, poor fellows, the immense population, who live by cultivating the fields, are starved by the tariff into an abstinence from luxuries. But the importer of larger views, and there are such, is perfectly willing that the farmer should be released from that ceaseless tribute to the manufacturer, which keeps him poor and prevents him from being a good customer. He is willing that the planting and farming districts should have the opportunity of becoming as "good markets for silks and other luxuries" as "the manufacturing towns and villages." An enlightened American importer is a statist, a political economist of the school of Adam Smith; he concurs with old Sir Dudley North, who in 1691, in his discourses on trade remarked:

"That the world *as to trade is but as one nation or people, and therein nations are as persons.*

"That to force men to deal in any *prescribed manner may profit such as may happen to serve them*; but the public gains not, because it is taken from one subject to give to another."

We spoke the other day of fustians—a most cheap, durable, and useful material of clothing worn by laborers, which pays the enormous duty of ten cents and a half per square yard. Mr. Appleton says:

"This [fustians] is a generic term, including velvets, of which, according to Mr. McKay's table, seven-eighths of the quantity imported cost over 35 cents the square yard, are not affected by the minimum at all! As for the low priced goods, passing under this general name in England, we have made substitutes of our own, better suited to our climate, both better and cheaper. The term fustians is not used in this country. You cannot have learned it from an American—it smacks of Lancashire—'imported for the use of farmers.' It's all humbug."

No, Mr. Appleton, we find the word in your own tariff of 1842, where you distinguish it from velvets. It is a low priced cloth, a cotton twill of a dark brown color, with a nap somewhat like Canton flannel, and it is well known in this country by the name we gave. Mr. Schenck manufactures it in vast quantities at Matteawan, and it has been manufactured at Paterson; it is bought and sold under that name, and worn by the laboring classes under that name.— The fustian which is fabricated of cotton is as well known here as the fustian which is woven of words in the neighborhood of Boston. In England fustians form the working dress of the manufacturing and agricultural population; we have in this country no adequate substitutes for the low qualities of this class of cloth, and so thought Mr. McDuffie when he walked through the streets of Manchester during his late visit to England. We are surprised at the ignorance manifested by Mr. Appleton, a manufacturer and merchant, in a matter with which no man of either class could reputably be unacquainted.

We may, hereafter, take occasion to say something about the fabric which is called Orleans, and to give the instructive history of the Waltham Company, but this article is perhaps already too long.

Good reader, for good thou must be, a miracle of forbearance and perseverance, who hast attended us thus far in the discussion; thou hast here—we mean this as an answer to the quotation made by Mr. Appleton from Macbeth, about the "brains being out"—thou hast here the brains of the advocates of the tariff, carefully extracted and served up in a tureen, with salt and pepper. Thou seest what a miserable garnish it is to thy daily repast. We have gone over the best defence that can be made for the tariff, a defence by one of its framers, a man well acquainted with its operation, and we have shown that not a single one of the statements and arguments used in its favor can stand the test of fact and reason. We might retort upon Mr. Appleton the dilemma which he politely offered to our acceptance, of confessing either to profound ignorance or wilful misrepresentation. This is the only notice we take of the arrogant style of his letter, which breathes a certain consciousness of mighty revenues. We should have thought the language of some passages a sufficient reason for excluding it from our columns, had we not desired to show our readers how little even the framers of the tariff could urge in its excuse.

Political Ventriloquism
April 24, 1844

The Frenchman Nicolas Marie Alexandre Vattemare (1786–1864) had performed in New York in 1839. At the Democratic convention at Baltimore the month following Bryant's remarks, James K. Polk defeated former President Martin Van Buren for the nomination.

"I'll read you the riot act and bid you disperse," was the closing line of Walter Scott's poetical address to Mons. Alexandre Vattemare. M. Vattemare, the author of a plan of literary exchanges, our readers may perhaps recollect, is a famous ventriloquist, and has performed in public in this city, personating a dozen or more characters at once. There were voices from the ceiling, and voices from below, and voices from the next room; voices from the window, and voices from the key-hole, and voices from behind the screen; voices harsh and voices smooth; voices burly and deep, and voices sharp and squeaking; yet the voices were all the single voice of the amiable and ingenious Alexandre Vattemare, whose versatile talent induced Sir Walter to address him as a mob of personages in one, and to threaten him, in his capacity of Sheriff, with reading the riot act.

Just upon the eve of a nomination of the democratic candidate for the presidency, the comedy of politics is enlivened by the appearance of a few ventriloquists of another sort. They are not quite so expert performers in their way as Mons. Vattemare, and are less ingenious in diversifying their entertainments.—The burden of what they have to say is, that it is impossible to elect Mr. Van Buren President of the United States, and therefore he ought not to be nominated. As the day appointed for holding the Baltimore Convention approaches, the activity of these performers increases. We have voices from the east and the west, from the north and the south, from town and country; sometimes speaking through the penny papers and sometimes through the mammoth sheets, sometimes in the Tyler papers, sometimes in the neutral journals, sometimes in the whig prints, and now and then we think we have detected a stray whisper of the same origin in a democratic paper, all agreeing with wonderful unanimity in the opinion that if the Baltimore Convention nominate Mr. Van Buren, their party is sure to be hopelessly defeated at the next election. All these voices, we have reason to believe, are uttered by a very few performers, with a design to influence the members of the Convention by an ingenious show of what they would have pass for public opinion.

It is remarkable how very friendly to Mr. Van Buren are the people who express these apprehensions. The political ventriloquist who personates a farmer in Ohio, for example, and muffles his voice so as to make it appear as if coming from a distance, is one who greatly admires Mr. Van Buren and highly values his services, but who sees with regret and sorrow that he cannot be elected. He is, therefore—reluctantly to be sure—in favor of some other candidate whom the whole party will support with cordiality.—It is a hard necessity, but he submits to it for the good of his party and for the good of the country.

Sometimes, however, the performer is awkward in his part, and makes different personages utter the same words in the same tone of voice. The letters, for example, written from different parts of the Union, written in the name of zealous but desponding friends of Van Buren, who find it necessary to abandon him for another candidate, are often surprisingly identical in their language, and contain whole paragraphs precisely alike. This destroys in some measure the charm of the illusion. These ventriloquists should carefully keep up the distinction of the characters they personate or the effect will be lost.

We hope, however, that no man, be he a member of the Baltimore Convention or not, will allow himself to take the entertainment set before him for serious reality. Let him not believe that he hears the cries of an army of doubters and croakers because a single juggler has the art of making his voice appear to come sometimes from the ceiling and sometimes from the cellar. Any sincere indications of public opinion are entitled to respect and consideration, but these are tricks of the press, which two or three industrious writers, with proper instructions from Washington, can keep up for as long a time as is thought necessary.

Friar Tuck Legislation
April 26, 1844

Robert Macgregor (or Campbell), 1671-1734—"Rob Roy"—was a Scottish cattle rustler and extortionist, the subject of Walter Scott's novel Rob Roy *(1817). Thomas Gisborne (1794–1852) was a Whig member of the British Parliament.*

> A famous thief was Robin Hood;
> But Scotland had a thief as good,
> It was—it was the great Rob Roy.
>
> Old Ballad.

A speaker, Mr. Thomas Gisborne, at one of the recent meetings of the Anti-Corn Law League, made a happy allusion to what he called Friar Tuck legislation. He had in his mind the story which is told in some of the old chronicles of Robin Hood and his merry foresters, when they were once assembled in Congress to deliberate upon the proper distribution of a pretty large amount of spoils. These legislators, persuaded by the soft and honied words of Friar Tuck, left it to him to frame a law for the proper adjustment of their claims. When the law was reported, by the able committee which had it in charge, it became instantly evident that Friar Tuck himself would get much the largest share. Public opinion, continues the history, thereupon went against the holy man, and a league was formed to resist the inequity of his decision.

Now, what did the good Friar in the emergency? Why, he met the people boldly and openly, and said, "For whose benefit are laws made, I should like to know?" And then immediately answering his own question, lest some silly objector might give it another turn, he went on, "first, for the benefit of those who make them, and afterward as it may happen." Nor did the disinterested judge stop there, but he proceeded, "Am I not the lawmaker, and shall I not profit by my own law?" The story runs, we believe, that the good man next quietly pocketed his share of the booty, and left his unreasonable companions to make the best of what remained.

Friar Tuck represents a class; he is a type and pattern of a large circle of imitators; his peculiar method of legislation is not obsolete. There are many persons at this day whose morality seems to be framed according to the same standard. Members of the United States Congress, for instance, who pass tariff laws to put money into their own pockets, are the legitimate descendants of Friar Tuck.

It is quite remarkable how many are the points of resemblance between this legislation of Sherwood Forest and that of the manufacturers at Washington. In the first place, the plunder to be distributed is raised from the people, in either case, without their being formally consulted; in the one by high duties, and in the other by the strong arm. Then the persons who take upon themselves to decide how this plunder is to be divided, like Friar Tuck, have a deep interest in the result, and generally manage to appropriate to themselves the largest share. They are the owners of manufacturing capital, and they contrive to make this capital return an enormous interest. "For whose benefit," they gravely ask, "are laws made?" and then answer, "First for the benefit of those who make them, and afterward as it may happen." Let us impose high duties; let us fill our pockets; let us who make the laws take all that we can get—and as to the people, the mass of laborers and consumers, why that's as it may happen! This is virtually the reasoning of one sort of our just and disinterested legislators.

But there is one point in which the resemblance does not hold. Friar Tuck was a bold, straight-forward, open-mouthed statesman, willing to proclaim his principles and justify the consequences to which they led. His followers in Congress act upon precisely the same principles, but assign another reason. He avowed that he wished to cram his pocket; they hold up some mock pretence of public good. "Shall I not benefit by my own law?" he said, and gathered up his gains; but they gather the gain and leave the reason unsaid, or rather hypocritically resort to some more palatable reason. The advantage of consistency is on the side of Robin Hood's priest. There is a frankness in his philosophy which throws the sneaking duplicity of the legislators of the cotton mills quite into the shade.

Disturbance of Public Meetings
May 27, 1844

Between May 3 and 9, 1844, Nativists rioted against foreigners and Catholics in Philadelphia. On April 24 Bryant had been one of several presiding officers at a meeting in the Broadway Tabernacle called to protest the proposed annexation of Texas, when a small gang of rowdies led by the notorious demagogue Mike Walsh tried to break up the proceedings. On April 12, 1844, Secretary of State John Calhoun had submitted to the Senate a secret treaty providing for the annexation of the Republic of Texas to the United States. Learning of this, Bryant had exposed in his newspaper correspondence relating to the proposal, and had joined opponents of the plan in organizing a mass meeting. As a result, the treaty failed to pass the Senate in June.

An observer of the course of events in this country for the last ten years, must have been struck, not only with the frequency of riots, but with the connection of many of them with the disturbance of public meetings. The late Philadelphia outrages, we are told, grew out of the disturbance of a meeting of Native Americans held in an

Irish district. Some desperate characters among us seem determined to give the lie to all our professions of freedom of speech and of the press, and of the right of the people peaceably to assemble and petition for a redress of grievances. So common have these outrages become, that what was at first viewed by everybody as a gross breach of law, has come some way or other to be looked on in some quarters as a sort of right, or at most as a very trivial offence. We have seen, indeed, that when at the late meeting at the Tabernacle the police officers were requested to put the handful of disturbers out of the house or prevent their interfering with the meeting, they refused, declaring, as it was understood, that so long as the disturbers committed no violence to person or property, they had a right to remain, and to make as much noise as they pleased.

Now inasmuch as these interruptions have become too frequent to be longer endured, and as there will always be in a large city desperate men, who are restrained by no consideration but fear of the law, it is worth while, before other meetings are held, to settle in our minds what are our rights, and what the duties of the police, to the end, that those who assemble peaceably hereafter, may feel no hesitation about righting themselves on the spot, and that those who are entrusted with the duty of preserving the peace and are paid for it, may not neglect that duty with impunity.

1. *When a meeting is held in a private building*, no person has a right to come but those who are invited, and no person has a right to remain any longer than the owner or hirer of the building chooses to permit him. The Tabernacle, for instance, is private property. The owner may open it or close it when and to whom he pleases. If he lets it for an evening, the hirer may open it to whom he pleases. He may call a meeting of such persons as he likes, and none but those whom he includes in his call have any *right* to enter. And if those who are included come and deport themselves in a manner disagreeable to him, he may request them to depart, and if they refuse, he may put them out by force. He may use as much force as is necessary for the purpose, and if he is resisted, he may proceed to extremities. The case is just like that of a private citizen inviting a party to his house. If any of them is rude to him, he orders him out; and if the order is not obeyed, he puts him out. In the particular instance of the meeting at the Tabernacle, the intruders were not included in the call. They had no right to enter the building. And if it were otherwise, being there, they might be ordered out at the pleasure of those who had hired the room. Upon their refusal to go, they might be put out by the occupants, or any persons authorized by them. If they had resisted in a manner dangerous to life, the law would have justified extremities even to the taking of their lives.

2. *If the place of meeting be not private property*—the Park, for instance, which is common to the city—any person who goes beyond a fair expression of his voice in the proceedings of the meeting, who interrupts it by noise or violence, or makes any other disturbance, intended to break it up or prevent its orderly proceeding, is guilty of a breach of the peace; and in such case, every private citizen is authorized to interfere to prevent a continued breach of the peace, or to remove the offender from the ground. For this purpose he may use as much force as is necessary, which, of course, must be proportioned to the kind and degree of resistance made.

3. The peace officers are under a legal obligation to assist every citizen in removing an intruder from his premises, in preventing a breach of the peace, and in putting an end to a disturbance at a meeting. If they refuse or wilfully neglect to do so, they are liable to indictment and to a private suit by the party injured. We all recollect the indictment of the Mayor of Bristol, for not doing his duty in suppressing the riots of 1830. The same law which obliged him to preserve the peace, obliges, also, every inferior officer in his own sphere.

4. *The disturbers themselves may be indicted and punished by fine and imprisonment.* Any two or more persons conspiring to commit a breach of the peace, (which the disturbance of a meeting is) may be punished for a conspiracy; and any three or more persons committing a breach of the peace, or guilty of a riot, may be punished by fine and imprisonment. Perhaps some of our readers may recollect the case of the disturbers of the Covent Garden Theatre. The law laid down on this occasion by the Chief Justice, in his charge to the jury, was this—(2 Camp. 350.):

> "I cannot conceive upon what grounds many people conceive they have a right, at a theatre, to make such prodigious noise as to prevent others hearing what is going forward on the stage. Theatres are not absolute necessaries of life, and any person may stay away who does not approve of the manner in which they are managed. The audience have certainly a right to express, by applause or hisses, the sensations which naturally present themselves at the moment, and no body has ever hindered, or would ever question, the exercise of that right. But if any body of men were to go to the theatre with the settled intention of hissing an actor, or even of damning a piece, there can be no doubt that such a deliberate and preconcerted scheme would amount to a conspiracy, and that the persons concerned in it might be brought to punishment. If people endeavor to effect an object by tumult or disorder, they are guilty of a riot. It is not necessary to constitute this crime, that personal violence should have been committed, or that a house should have been pulled in pieces."

This, be it remembered, was the case of a disturbance in a place of public amusement, where the rioters had purchased, with their tickets a right to enter and remain, so long as they conducted themselves peaceably. With much more force does this language apply to the case of disturbance in a place where the rioters were not invited, and had no right to come; or the case of a meeting of citizens assembled to discuss subjects of the greatest public concernment, and where order is of the first necessity.

These are the doctrines of our law, as derived from the common law. But they have received a higher sanction from our own peculiar institutions. The right of meeting to discuss all questions, lies at the foundation of our civil polity. The Constitution of the United States, for example, has declared that no law shall ever be passed abridging the right of the people peaceably to assemble and petition for a redress of grievances.

If the two houses of Congress were to pass and the President were to approve a bill directing the military to break up any meeting assembled to protest against the Texan treaty for instance, the law would be a nullity. Then surely, what the government could not authorize any body of men to do, these men cannot do of themselves, whether they be the military or custom house officers, or any of the hangers on of the executive. If it were otherwise, the framers of our constitution took a great deal of trouble to no purpose. There would be no need of a law to break up a meeting, if any half dozen desperate and abandoned persons (and any President can always command hundreds of such) can do the same thing. Fortunately the law gives no countenance to any such doctrines, and we trust that the next time a disturbance occurs, the offenders will be made to suffer.

As the time is approaching when the political agitation of the country will lead to a great many popular gatherings, we have thought it important to prepare this full statement of the requirements of the laws relating to the subject.

A New Public Park
July 3, 1844

This editorial is generally credited by historians of Central Park with initiating a continuing effort, led by Bryant and Andrew Jackson Downing, which culminated fifteen years later with the establishment of that pleasure ground in New York City. The Massachusetts Loyalist Benjamin Thompson, Count Rumford, knighted after the American Revolution by the British sovereign, later performed many services for the Bavarian Elector, among them the organization of an Academy of Arts and

Sciences as well as the English Garden which Bryant had greatly admired during his residence in Munich in 1835.

The heats of summer are upon us, and while some are leaving the town for shady retreats in the country, others refresh themselves with short excursions to Hoboken or New Brighton, or other places among the beautiful environs of our city. If the public authorities who expend so much of our money in laying out the city, would do what is in their power, they might give our vast population an extensive pleasure ground for shade and recreation in these sultry afternoons, which we might reach without going out of town.

On the road to Harlem, between Sixty-eighth street on the south, and Seventy-seventh street on the north, and extending from Third Avenue to the East River, is a tract of beautiful woodland, comprising sixty or seventy acres, thickly covered with old trees, intermingled with a variety of shrubs. The surface is varied in a very striking and picturesque manner, with craggy eminences, and hollows, and a little stream runs through the midst. The swift tides of the East river sweep its rocky shores, and the fresh breeze of the bay comes in, on every warm summer afternoon, over the restless waters. The trees are of almost every species that grows in our woods:—the different varieties of oak, the birch, the beech, the linden, the mulberry, the tulip tree, and others: the azalea, the kalmia, and other flowering shrubs are in bloom here at their season, and the ground in spring is gay with flowers. There never was a finer situation for the public garden of a great city. Nothing is wanted but to cut winding paths through it, leaving the woods as they now are, and introducing here and there a jet from the Croton aqueduct, the streams from which would make their own waterfalls over the rocks, and keep the brook running through the place always fresh and full. In the English Garden at Munich, a pleasure ground of immense extent, laid out by our countryman Count Rumford, into which half the population pours itself on summer evenings, the designer of the ground was obliged to content himself with artificial rocks, brought from a distance and cemented together, and eminences painfully heaped up from the sand of the plain. In the tract of which we speak, nature has done almost every thing to our hands, excepting the construction of paths.

As we are now going on, we are making a belt of muddy docks all around the island. We should be glad to see one small part of the shore without them, one place at least where the tides may be allowed to flow pure, and the ancient brim of rocks which borders the waters left in its original picturesqueness and beauty. Commerce is devouring inch by inch the coast of the island, and if we would rescue any part of it for health and recreation it must be done now.

All large cities have their extensive public grounds and gardens, Madrid and Mexico their Alamedas, London its Regent's Park, Paris its Champs Elysées, and Vienna its Prater. There are none of them, we believe, which have the same natural advantages of the picturesque and beautiful which belong to this spot. It would be of easy access to the citizens, and the public carriages whic[h] now rattle in almost every street in this city, would take them to its gates. The only objection which we can see to the place would be the difficulty of persuading the owners of the soil to part with it.

If any of our brethren of the public press should see fit to support this project, we are ready to resign in their favor any claim to the credit of originally suggesting it.

Blue Law Legislation
July 3, 1844

Two years earlier water from the new Croton Aqueduct had been drawn into a receiving reservoir at Fifth Avenue and Forty-Second Street—later the site of the New York Public Library and Bryant Park—from which fountains in Union Square and other public spaces were supplied.

The spirit which in ancient Connecticut forbade making of beer on Saturday, lest it should work on the Sabbath, seems to be fast reviving in this city. Our new municipal authorities, if we are rightly informed, not satisfied with their invasions of the apple women and the overturning of pea-nut stands, are carrying the war into the fountains. They have, in some way, discovered that it is wicked to allow water to run on Sundays, and will soon be seized with scruples as to the propriety of sunshine.

In other words, we are told that the fountain in Union Park has been stopped on Sunday, and the old woman who used to make a penny or two by letting chairs to visitors, has been ordered into the streets. We do not know how much truth there may be in this report, but we suppose it altogether true, because the two movements are quite in character with a great deal of our late city legislation. Both acts must be regarded as outrages to common sense, no less than upon the comforts of our citizens.

What pretense is put forth to justify expulsion of the chairwoman, we have not inquired, knowing that the hot zeal of these apple-pie reformers will always have ingenuity enough to frame a plausible excuse for its excesses. We only know that these chairs were a public convenience, and hoped to see the practice of letting them allowed on all our public grounds, such as the Battery Park, Washington Parade Ground, &c. When a person has been seething for several hours under the hot roofs of the city, and wishes to enjoy an hour or two of fresh air in more open places, it would be a great comfort to find an easy chair at his command, instead of being obliged to sit on a hard, unshaded bench, often dirty, and always without a back. It seems, however, that a chair would be too great a luxury for our good authorities and that it has been forbidden.

As to the stopping of the Union fountain on Sundays, we think that the people should remonstrate against it instantly and with vehemence. The city is not so cool, that it should be deprived of any mode of freshening its atmosphere. It is true, as it has been said, that the fountain usually attracts a large number of people to the Park on Sunday afternoons, yet we see no great harm in that fact. Those who visit the Park, so far as our observation extends, are respectable and orderly, and are no doubt much better, both physically and morally, for a sight of the sparkling waters and a whiff of moist air. It is a most miserable policy, which would diminish the means of recreation furnished to the people. What we particularly want in this country is a greater variety of innocent modes of relaxation. A great deal of the intemperance and rowdyism that prevails is to be ascribed to the absence of those popular festivals and methods of enjoyment, through which the love of excitement would be harmlessly dissipated. Among the people of Europe, who are in the habit of assembling in public gardens and other places of light and agreeable entertainment, there are few or no manifestations of the coarseness and violence which is often seen in this country.

Industrial Feudalism
July 3, 1844

Orestes Brownson, a Unitarian clergyman who became a Catholic convert, voiced radical political opinions in Brownson's Quarterly Review *(1844–1865).*

We perceive that the *Commercial Advertiser* of last evening, remarking upon an extract from Mr. Brownson's writings which appeared in this paper, observes:

> "And then he goes on to define what he means by Whiggism—a definition not easy to understand, being plentifully interspersed with terms that have no specific and generally recognized meaning, such as 'industrial feudalism,' &c., but the amount of it seems to be that Whiggism does too much for general prosperity—enables people to grow rich—enhances the value of property—and brings into existence too many cities and villages; all which are hurtful to the primi-

tive simplicity, innocence, intelligence and unsophisticated integrity of the Democracy."

We have no disposition to defend such an extremely uncertain writer as Mr. Brownson; but as it happens in this case that he utters the truth, we will enlighten the *Commercial*, in its ignorance as to what is meant by the term "industrial feudalism." We suppose that it is aware, there once existed a state of society called Feudalism, which was chiefly characterized by the fact that a few persons were in the possession of the political power, whilst the masses were held in complete and slavish subjection. We say that we suppose the *Commerical* has heard of this peculiar state of society; but lest it should not have done so, we take leave to refer it to any of the histories of the Middle Ages, where some account of it will no doubt be given.

Now, there are a great many thinkers who have come to the conclusion that modern society is tending to the establishment of distinctions similar to those which prevailed under the feudal system. They say that the course of legislation, in nearly all civilized nations, unless counteracted by some peculiar circumstances, i[s] building up a rich class at the expense of the poorer classes. They say that banks confer enormous advantages upon capitalists, which are subtracted from the substance of labor; that monopolies put into the coffers of a few men what they secretly pick from the pockets of others; that tariffs, impose grievous taxes on the many in order to foster huge overgrown manufactories that divide their thirty per cent yearly; and in short, that all government which does not recognize the equal rights before the state, of every individual man, only widens the breach in society, and hastens the general prevalence of a "feudalism," in which working men would become the mere instruments of capitalists.

The whig party is the avowed advocate of this mode of legislation. It sustains banks, monopolies, tariffs, and injustices of all kinds; and when, therefore, Mr. Brownson charges it with bringing about "industrial feudalism," he may use terms not "generally recognized," but which certainly have an important meaning. The "prosperity" for which whig[g]ism labours is not general but particular;—it enables men "to grow rich," but at the expense of the people; it "enhances the value of property," which is in the hands of an inconsiderable number of citizens and it "brings into existence cities and villages," but mostly in the form of lithographic maps, by which speculators profit, but the poor are robbed.

Texas
July 25, 1844

Throughout 1844 articles in the Evening Post *by Bryant and Theodore Sedgwick repeatedly attacked proposals in Congress that the Texas republic be admitted to the Union as a slave state. In April Bryant helped organize an anti-annexation mass meeting in New York, and the same month he published details of a secret plan of Secretary of State John Calhoun and other pro-slavery leaders to effect annexation by stealth. Both of these actions were instrumental in the defeat of an annexation bill by the Senate in June. In July Bryant joined several prominent New Yorkers in appealing to electors to oppose an annexation resolution adopted by the Democratic convention in May which had nominated James K. Polk for the Presidency. The "gallant man" to whom Bryant refers in the final paragraph was his former associate William Leggett.*

The Texas Junto, which desires to get the Democratic party into its keeping, apply sundry phrases to those who oppose this previous project, the truth of which it may not be useless to examine. They are termed abstractionists, federalists, abolitionists, and British emissaries. Now we propose to see who the gentlemen thus complimented are, and how far they deserve it.

In the first place, it is worth while to notice, that the whole movement on this subject is in the strictest sense a party juggle—and a very poor one. It would disgrace a thimble-rigger of the most ordinary pretensions.

We were informed by the Baltimore Convention "that the annexation of Texas at the *earliest practicable* period," was a cardinal feature in modern democracy. Now, we should be glad to know what the "*earliest practicable period*" means. Who objects to annexing Texas "at *the earliest practicable period*"? We see no reason why the moon should not be annexed "at the earliest practicable period"—that is to say, as soon as it can. As soon as the just claims of Mexico can be disposed of—as soon as the question of slavery can be got out of the way, we abandon our opposition to the annexation of Texas.

Such may be the interpretation of this phrase; and such may be the sense in which thousands of democrats will take it; but such is not the sense in which the Texas hocus-pocusers mean it.

The annexation of Texas with them means nothing more than the *extension and perpetuation of slavery at the risk of war and with war if it cannot be got without.* It is the pure southern Upshur–Tyler scheme—it is the pill without the gilding—the dose without the sugar.

It is plain enough to see, that if this question had been committed at the outset to men of mind large enough to take in all the interests of this great nation, Mexico would have been satisfied, the question of slavery avoided, and Texas annexed with honor and satisfaction to the entire people. But for our shame and misfortune the matter fell into the hands of a few fanatics as crazy on the subject of the "domestic institutions," as the maddest abolitionists in the Union—men who believe or affect to believe, that the *summum bonum* of Republican freedom lies in the possessing of a few hundred slaves; and by these slave-holding fanatics was the question of Texas, a great question of extension of empire, dwarfed into one of enlarging the influence of that pernicious institution which defaces and disgraces our otherwise glorious country.

This abortion, rejected with contempt and disgust by the whole country, a few northern democrats are swaddling and nursing and trying to coax into life. Now we say it with mere reference to the interests of the party, interests which no wise person can overlook, that any northern democrat who seeks to identify the party with the extension of slavery, and to make that the rallying question, is only fit for bedlam; no greater political insanity can be imagined.

Slavery is an old, decrepit, worn-out feudal institution. Shall the young democracy, in its heroic youth, stifle its ardent nature by so unnatural an alliance? Where slavery and slave representation exist under the constitution, let them exist. It is the bargain—it is the bond. But to extend these evils to another portion of the western hemisphere, and, above all, to make this the rallying cry of the party, is evidently suicidal.

Those sagacious gentlemen, therefore, who undertake to denounce such democrats as are content with the old issues as abstractionists, &c. are acting with perhaps less sense than they may imagine.

With some people names have weight. Mr. Van Buren, Mr. Wright, Mr. Benton, to say nothing of the many prominent democrats in this state, have declared their irreconcileable hostility to the Texas scheme, urged on the new ground of slavery and for the benefit of slavery.

Is it to be supposed that these gentlemen are all to come to the right-about-face, because a few men in Baltimore see fit to pass a resolution in regard to which they received no mandate from the people?—If the democratic party has such ability to "jump about and turn about," as they would imply, not Mr. Polk but Jim Crow should have been our candidate.

We are very tranquil as to the result of all this flurry. The EVENING POST knows by experience the impotence of a few selfish men to denounce an honest press. Men familiar with the course of this paper will well recollect the effort made to bear it down some years ago. They will well recollect the triumphant resistance of that gallant man, now no more, who combined in his noble nature the heroism of a warrior and the reflection of a student. They will well recollect how effectually trust was vindicated and a selfish cabal annihilated. So will it be now. The vipers bite a file.

A DISCOVERY
July 27, 1844

Feeble was an ineffective comic soldier, the butt of Sir John Falstaff's sarcasm in Shakespeare's Henry IV, Part Two, *III, ii, 179. The "Confidential Circular" was an appeal signed by Bryant and six other anti-slavery Democrats, published in the* Evening Post *on July 24, inviting a number of local Democratic politicians throughout New York State to sign a joint letter, the text of which would appear in the* Post *on August 20; it expressed support for Democratic Presidential nominee James K. Polk, but strongly opposed a resolution which had been hastily adopted at the Baltimore nominating convention calling for the "re-annexation of Texas at the earliest possible period."*

One—nay, we are told, two—of the morning journals have been so sagacious as to discover that the EVENING POST is secretly working to secure the triumph of the whig party at the next Presidential election. It is in these words that the remarkable discovery is announced by one of the Sir Forcible Feebles to which we are indebted for the important information:

> "In reviewing this matter in our minds—in casting about for reasons explanatory of the strange procedure of the Abolition clique which surrounds the EVENING POST—we can arrive at no other conclusion than that the 'confidential circular' we discovered, was but one of a course of movements designed to cast this state in the hands of the Federalists, and, if possible, defeat the nominees of the Baltimore Convention. We will qualify so far as to say, that we believe some one or two whose signatures are affixed to that 'circular,' have been misled as to the real intent and design of the wire-workers. But we say, and we religiously believe what we say, and the great, democratic masses of this city, with an unanimity which rejoices us exceedingly, are coincident with us in opinion, that the exposed 'confidential circular' was but one idea, a single 'fixed fact' of the plot to distract, embarrass, and if possible, defeat the democratic party in this state. The reader may ask us for our reason. We will tell him. We have long thought that the EVENING POST, if we except a few points which have characterized that journal, among which we instance its abstract views of Tariffs and Banking, has had no idea, no sympathy in common with the democratic party."

When we consider the course of the EVENING POST, it must be confessed there is some reason for supposing that it wants sympathy with the democratic party. It is about twenty four years—nearly a quarter of a century—since that paper, for the most of the time under its present management, unfurled the flag of democratic principles. During all the stormy contests of that period, that flag has remained unfurled, and neither the hostility of open enemies, nor the treachery of pretended friends, have been successful in inducing those who placed it there, to swerve for one day from the frank and earnest vindication of the creed which it was raised to represent. In good report, and in evil report, assailed or supported, by friends or by enemies, the EVENING POST has stood as fixed as a rock in the midst of the tempest that howled around it.

While other journals have been seduced by prospects of temporary advantage into corrupt alliance with the foul spirits of "conservatism," or been terrified by the menaces of federalism into a timid and shrinking policy, there has been one democratic journal, at least, in the United States, that has retained its fidelity. You may search its columns, for twenty years, and not find a line in which devotion to the cause of impartial government, the equal rights of the people, sparing legislation, unfettered trade, universal suffrage, and all the other cardinal principles of the democratic faith, has not been the pervading spirit. For the course of this journal has been adopted, not through impulse, nor a sinister and selfish love of gain, but on the strongest convictions of duty, as clearly formed, as they have been and will be, resolutely maintained.

It is true, that the very inflexibility with which the EVENING POST has discharged its duty, has sometimes brought it in conflict with those who professed attachment to the same creed. There have been occasions, when the democratic party has been misled for a brief moment, to listen to the suggestions of selfish schemers and unprincipled men, and when we have withstood its departures from the right track, and exposed its deceivers. It is a significant fact, that this whole class of politicians have been, and are now, the enemies of the EVENING POST. It has sometimes happened, too, that men of superior art and cunning, but quite destitute of even the suspicion that such things as truth and honesty, were in the world, have acquired undue influence in that party, and met the chief obstacle to the execution of their nefarious designs in this journal.

From such men it has never had, and never wanted sympathy. It has been, on the other hand, a peculiar source of offence, and they would willingly have dispensed with its existence; and are active now, by falsehood and clamour, in seeking to impair its influence. But in the midst of all the opposition of these powerful men, the issue of events has proved the correctness of our course, by showing that the safest, as well as the honestest policy for the democratic party, at all times, is rigid faithfulness to its high and benevolent principles.

In all the controversies, however, which the EVENING POST has had with either friend or foe, it has never found it necessary to sacrifice any one of its principles, or to abandon a solitary position. Whenever a sense of duty has caused it to rebuke what was honestly considered the mistaken policy of its friends, it has done so, modestly but firmly, and as the result has proved generally, much to the benefit of the democratic cause.

It is not likely, then, at this day, that we shall either play into the hands of our opponents, or be frightened into an inconsistent and dishonest course by the shallow declamation of a few officious democrats.

THE NEW TEXAS TEST
July 27, 1844

Late in 1843 the administration of President John Tyler drafted a treaty with the Republic of Texas providing for its admission to statehood in the United States. This was introduced into the Senate, but defeated in June 1844 after the exposure in the Evening Post *of Secretary of State John Calhoun's reply to a letter from the British minister at Washington in which Calhoun made a detailed defense of slavery.*

The advocates of the immediate annexation of Texas, not content with having obtained the nomination of candidates who consent to make this a question, wish to thrust out of the democratic ranks all those who do not happen to agree with them on the propriety or expediency of incorporating Texas into the Union at the present time.—Their course in this matter has not, it seems, wrought mischief enough: they would go still further, and, with a ferocious zeal, destroy all who will not yield implicit obedience to them on this point. It is not, therefore, surprising that they lose sight of common prudence, and in violation of all the courtesies of political discussion, go so far as to denounce men of at least equal weight with themselves, as traitors and enemies to the democratic faith. One would think that such intemperate bigotry was hardly consistent with the freedom of speech and action, which is the birthright of an American, and would not find very general approval in a country, where each member of the community is entitled to an equal voice in public affairs, and an equal right of opinion on all questions of public policy. It savours too much of that fanaticism, which, like Native Americanism, would exterminate a man because he happens to have been born in Europe, or to entertain a religious creed different from that of his neighbors.

The attempt, however, to try men's faith by such a narrow standard, is as impotent as it is unfair. The mass of voters cannot be brought to the polls on any one question of minor importance, upon which there always has been and always will be difference of opinion among men of all prejudices, of all occupations, and of all creeds, political and religious. To call the immediate annexation of Texas an American question is mere declamation; for of any ten Americans taken at hazard in any assemblage, no two will be found to entertain the same view of a subject so new to all, and about which so much is yet unknown. The opinion of every citizen on all questions of importance, which have been before the country since the formation of the government, may be predicated upon his habits and associations, his natural turn of mind, and his general bearing in political controversies; whether he is for [or] against a strict construction of the Constitution; in favor of or opposed to all governmental interference with the currency, with the industry of the citizens; approves or condemns a protective policy, a national bank, a wholesale system of bribery in the assumption of the state debts or the distribution of the public lands; an extension or limitation of the right of suffrage; all this may be ascertained without inquiry; but we must ask our best friends, and give them time to think, before we can learn whether they would like to remove the seat of government to New Orleans or annex Texas to the Union, when it can be done honestly and in good faith. This is no American question; to say there are but two sides to it—an American and a British side—is an idle piece of rhetoric. No mass meeting can be led to raise a shout by such a flourish.

Thus far the reasons which have been assigned for objecting to the present Texas scheme are certainly worthy of some consideration. It was a Tyler project; an abortion conceived of whiggery on a spurious democracy; an office holder's stratagem; the ruse of a wily ambitious but disappointed politician; a measure calculated, and intended to throw discord into the ranks; and a mercenary stock-jobbing speculation. The people of the United States are not asked whether they think it desirable to extend their territory by fair and honorable negociation; it has no resemblance to the acquisition of Louisiana; they are roughly summoned to endorse the cabal of a weak administration and corrupt cabinet, and that too without delay, or time for reflection. No imperial mandate, nor ukase ever asked for a more blind submission from a serf.

It is not wise, therefore, for the friends of such a project to threaten others with excommunication, even if they do constitute the true church. Even "seven" good votes are not to be thrown away; and it may happen that there are more than seven democrats who do not approve of Tyler and Texas, and do not acknowledge such watchwords as true ones. It is perhaps more than probable that there is a common ground upon which all can stand united in a firm and durable opposition to the error and corruption of all mercenary schemes, and in unyielding support of all the cardinal doctrines of universal democracy.

THE RHODE ISLAND AND PHILADELPHIA CASES
July 27, 1844

In May Bryant had repeatedly deplored anti-Catholic riots in Philadelphia during which churches had been burned and many persons killed or maimed. Under a constitution based on a charter granted Rhode Island in 1663 by King Charles II, more than half its adult males were denied the ballot. After a commission of those disenfranchised had framed a "People's Constitution" in 1841 and installed Thomas W. Dorr as governor at Providence in 1842, his administration came in conflict with that of Charter Party Governor Samuel W. King at Newport, which declared the Dorr faction as insurrectionist. The "Dorr Rebellion" was put down by Newport militia aided by federal troops sent in by President Tyler. Dorr fled, then returned and surrendered, and on June 25, 1844, was sentenced to life imprisonment.

A correspondent sends us the following observations: "The *Journal of Commerce* speaking of the Rhode Island suffrage party, attempts to identify the principles of it with those of the Philadelphia rioters. No greater encouragement could be offered to the further exertions of the mobites in Philadelphia, than such a comparison furnishes; nor could two things more completely dissimilar be compared together. The rioters in Philadelphia were opposing laws of their own enacting, resisting officers of their own appointment, and attempting the overthrow of a constitution of their own adoption. The Rhode Islanders lived under a royal charter which, of course, contained no provision for amendment or alteration; it denied the right of suffrage to all but freeholders and their oldest sons; and the legislature, if they acted in conformity with such a charter, could take no step toward adopting a new one. What did the suffrage party do? For more than forty years they petitioned for relief; but their legislature refused action, while the conservative members declared they had no right at all, under the charter, to act in the premises. The great mass of the citizens looked around upon those of the neighboring states, and found no equality in their respective conditions.— Compared with others, the Rhode Island men were little better off than Russian serfs. What was to be done? This they did: They convened the people in primary assemblies; established a correspondence throughout the state; held town meetings and elected delegates to a convention, where they adopted the plan of a constitution for the state, and submitted the same to the people, who met in every town, and by a large majority of votes, approved and adopted the new constitution. An election under the new law was held for members of the legislature and for Governor; it was peaceably conducted and all the officers duly qualified, commenced the discharge of their official duties; when the malcontents rose up against the newly appointed officers and resorted to, or threatened violence. In this fearful crisis a few hundred men assembled and took a position to defend the legislature against rebellion, and fortified themselves to preserve order and uphold law; but the demagogues who had so long trampled rough shod upon the rights of their fellow citizens, backed by the *Journal of Commerce* and aided by United States troops, drove off the friends of equal rights, and adopted a more aristocratic form of government.— And to call things by their right names, 'might has overcome right.' Thus ends the chapter."

THE REPUBLIC NEWSPAPER
July 27, 1844

The New York Republic *was a daily paper briefly published in 1844–1845.*

This journal declares, in its leading editorial of this morning, that it will hereafter support the cause of Mr. Clay and his party. In making the declaration, it proceeds to state the reasons which have induced it to abandon its neutral position, and adopt the principles of the whigs. But it seems to us that it is hardly just towards the two parties, respectively, in its attempts to contrast their claims and prospects. Of the democratic party, it says:

> "The Democratic party, strange to say, has arrived within four months of a Presidential contest without any clear, harmonious declaration of the principles upon which it purposes to carry on the administration of the government. It limits itself to a feeble expression of its dissent to all the proposed measures of its opponents without the will or the ability to gainsay, or disparage them. Torn by dissention, abandoned by many of its most prominent members, divided by disputes, and split up into fragments as endless as they are various, the Democratic party, once so powerful, influential, and prosperous, has dwindled into insignificance and almost sunk into abeyance."

This is almost the first time in its history, that the democratic party has been charged with a want of positive principles. We have all along supposed that the feature which distinguished it from other parties, and which gave it its general ascendancy with the people was the possession of a clear and decided faith. It has contended, at any rate, since the time of Jefferson with more or less fidelity, for equal and exact justice in legislation—a princip[le] which has made it a stubborn and resolute opponent of partial schemes of action under whatever guise they have been presented. It is now, as it ever has been, the advocate of a separation of the government from the banking system, which places it in irreconcilable hostility to the wicked project of a national bank—it is in favor of a revenue tariff, and of course opposed to a tariff for mere protection; it cannot consent to see the money of one class of the people filched from their pockets by iniquitous imposts, in order to be distributed to another class, through corrupt measures of the federal Congress; and it condemns that wholesale system of plunder and corruption, which would convert the public lands to the use of gambling and bankrupt states, which having ruined themselves, would retrieve their losses by the ruin of their neighbors.

It is true, as the *Republic* intimates, there is now some division in the ranks of the democratic party; but it is a division which will only be temporary in its effects. It will neither diminish the zeal nor the votes of its members. It is the fate of all parties to be troubled with men whose zeal outstrips their discretion, and who for transient success, readily leave the high ground of permanent principle. But such men can not, for any length of time distract a body which has really any vitality. They are absorbed or thrown off in the natural process of growth, and "the places that once knew them, know them no more forever."

Manufacturing in a Pigstye
September 19, 1844

Within the last two years a method has been discovered of manufacturing cotton goods twice as cheap as they are made, or at least sold, at Lowell or Matteawan. The principle of the invention it is true has been long known, but it is only within a short time that its practical application has been rightly apprehended in this country. One great advantage which it has over the methods of Mr. Schenck and the Merrimac Company is that it requires little capital, and may be set up any where, on a Long Island farm, or on a western prairie, in a dairy room or in a stall where cattle are fattened. All that is wanted is a little legislation "for the encouragement of domestic industry," a removal of the severe restrictions imposed by what the whig handbills posted up in this city call "the whig tariff of 1842."

A conversation which took place a few days since will illustrate the principle of the discovery to which we refer. We mentioned not long ago that samples of cotton-goods, manufactured in England and sold there for seven cents and a half a yard, were to be seen at the office of the *Journal of Commerce,* and that they were of equal quality with the American fabrics which are sold here for fourteen cents a yard. The samples have been inspected by hundreds of people and nine out of ten, we are informed, declare the British goods to be better than the American. On one occasion a gentleman who was present dropped the remark that such goods could not be manufactured in this country for seven cents and a half a yard. A friend of ours, who was present, replied:

"I will engage to make precisely the same goods in this country for the same price."

"How will you do that?" asked the other.

"I will do it in a pig-stye," was the answer.

"You are trifling," said the gentleman; "it is impossible to produce such goods in this country at so low a price; and as to what you say about making them in a pig-stye, I am sure I do not understand you."

"I will make the goods," said our friend, "and they shall be made in a pig-stye. I ask for but one condition; remove the high duties on imports which prevent the free exchange of goods between nations. I will then engage in making pork for the market.—The money obtained in this way will represent whatever I choose to buy. If I want a piece of cotton goods, I have it in my till; two dollars will then purchase the same piece of shirting or printed calico for which I am now obliged to pay nearly four. The same goods which are now sold at fourteen cents a yard, I shall then produce for seven and a half."

This view of domestic industry is the true one, yet it somewhat surprises us that it has not been generally taken by our country population until now. Those who are employed in raising pork, or in making butter and cheese, or in any other occupation which adds to the great total of the necessaries and comforts of life, are merely making salt, and sugar, and cotton and woollen clothing for their families. They manufacture these things in pigstyes, in dairy rooms, in fields of wheat and maize. The more of these articles they can obtain for the same labor, the better for them; they then manufacture by a cheaper process; they have a larger surplus to lay by, and are all the richer. The tariff of 1842 steps in and obliges the farmer to work twice as hard to procure the same amount of necessaries; it makes his dollar represent but half the quantity of cotton cloth which it would represent, under a system of free trade, and when he looks into his till he finds his piece of Appleton shirting shrunk into half a piece.

For our part, we do not see why those industrious and useful people, who are manufacturing in the fields, in dairies and in stalls, should not be allowed to make the greatest amount of cotton and woolen cloth, salt, sugar, and other articles of daily consumption for their families which the nature of their occupation will allow. Why a law should be made to restrain them from making by their labor more than half the quantity of cotton cloths and other goods which they otherwise could. Laws are passed to enable Mr. Schenck and Mr. Simmons, and the Merrimac Company, to manufacture more goods and sell them at a higher profit, but the very effect of these laws has been to compel the farmer, and in fact every other consumer, to give more of his labor to produce them for his family.

THE NATIVE AMERICAN PARTY
November 12, 1844

At a recent mass meeting in Faneuil Hall, Boston, Webster had charged that illegally naturalized immigrants in New York had been voting for the Democratic ticket, and urged that the period of residence in this country then required for the franchise should be greatly lengthened.

If the friends of Mr. Webster, who has lately declared himself in favor of a change in our naturalization laws, should join in the procession of the Native American party, which takes place to-morrow, they will augment its numbers very considerably.

We have been assured by some of the leading members of the Native American party that they do not mean to enter into any alliance or coalition with the whigs of any kind. If the whigs vote for their candidates, say they, it is what cannot be helped, nor is it a thing which they should desire to prevent, but beyond this they do not acknowledge nor submit to any union or concert of the two parties.

All this we doubt not is very sincere. The Nativists do not mean to coalesce with the whigs, but the whigs mean to coalesce with the Nativists, nor do we see how the Nativists can hinder it. They are as much at the mercy of the whigs as a small and feeble state is at the mercy of a large, powerful and warlike one at its side; they will be overrun and subjugated without their leave being asked. Suppose the whigs to adopt, as Mr. Webster proclaims himself to have done, the principles of the Native American party; of course they will attend their assemblies, and as they greatly outnumber the Nativists, they will give to their public proceedings such a direction as best suits their purpose. A meeting of the Nativists is called—three hundred of the party attend; six hundred of the whigs holding the same doctrines, and desirous to promote the same objects attend also; the whigs will appoint the chairman, organize the meeting, raise the committees and pass the resolutions to which, of course, they will give a strong whig seasoning, in the outset, and at last, when the Nativist force is submerged in their own they will make them whig in spirit and in language altogether.

In other words the majority of the Native American party will have the direction of its proceeding, as is the case in every other party.

Suppose, again, that Mr. Webster, who has just declared his adherence to the creed of the Native Americans, should be taken up by that party as a candidate for one of their highest offices. His talents, his standing as the great northern leader of his party, and the almost idolatrous admiration with which he is regarded by many, point him out as a leader in the Native American party the moment he joins its ranks. Mr. Webster of course in being a Nativist does not cease to be a whig. He takes into the Native American party his whig principles and whig friends, and uses the influence which his new position gives him for the promulgation of whig doctrines and the advancement of whig measures.

Every party formed, like that of the Nativists, for the support of a single political measure, is always in danger of being swallowed up by one or the other of the two great political parties. It naturally falls into the ranks of the party with which it has the greatest affinity. There is nothing, that we can see, in the way of a union between the Whigs and the Nativists. The principle of excluding a part of the inhabitants of our country—those who are of foreign birth—from political rights and from public offices, is, as we have often urged, perfectly in accordance with the doctrines of the Whig party, inasmuch as it is a principle of proscription and exclusion; it places a class of our people under political disabilities, it creates a class inferior to the native-born; a class who are denied all participation in political power; a class who are merely governed, and who are shut out from all share in the government. This is in perfect harmony with the views of the Whig party, which seeks to create inequality between different classes, delights in imposing disabilities and strives to confine political power to as few hands as possible.

On the other hand, there can be no sympathy between the democratic party and the nativists. The moment an attempt is made so to order our future legislation as to give rise to a peculiar caste in our midst, excluded from the rights which others enjoy, the democratic party would be false to all its principles and faithless to all its professions, if it did not come forward in direct opposition to such a proceeding. There can therefore be no concert of action between the nativists and the democratic party; between the nativists and the whigs, on the other hand, the tendency to coalesce is almost inevitable.

Meantime, the title of whig has been borne long enough by the aristocratic party to become odious.— They have been soundly beaten under it, and it recalls unpleasant recollections. They appear about to give it up in disgust, and adopt the name of Native Americans. In an Italian comedy, one of Alberto Nota's, we believe, or it might be from some obscurer hand, a fellow is introduced who had been flogged in a mask and domino, during the carnival, and could never bear the sight of a mask and domino afterward.

The Charge of Fraud
November 13, 1844

James G. Birney, a Southern anti-slavery leader, was the unsuccessful Liberty Party candidate for the Presidency in 1840 and 1844. The quotations cited by the Evening Post's *correspondent are from* Paradise Lost, *I, 105–109. Birney had charged in a letter to the* Evening Post *that a forged letter had resulted in a Whig victory in an Ohio election. Rowland Hill (1744–1833), a Cambridge graduate, had been refused priestly orders because of his itinerant preaching. He established himself as pastor of the Surrey Chapel in London, where he held Sunday schools and wrote hymns and a tract advocating innoculation for smallpox.*

We hope our readers looked at the statement of Mr. Birney, published by us yesterday, in relation to the forged letter, by the help of which the state of Ohio was carried for the whigs. The forged letter was circulated with the utmost industry in that state just before the election, and the proof that it was spurious only reached Cleveland on the day of the election—a period too late to allow the effect of the fraud to be counteracted. Mr. Birney, it will be seen, states that the whigs in Detroit were privy to the existence of the letter some time before it reached Detroit in the public papers. They were waiting, it appears, to see the effect of the fraud which had been concocted. It answered its purpose but too well in Ohio.

It is amazing with what face the whigs can complain of the frauds of their adversaries with the proof of this enormous crime on their part spread before the world. Their journals are silent on the subject, and seek to evade its effect by idle stories unsupported by proof, of acts of individual misconduct on the part of the democrats. This is no such case; it is a palpable, certain fraud—a confessed forgery— a cheat put upon a whole state, and brought home to the whig party by the clearest evidence.

Mr. Webster, we perceive, in his late speech at Faneuil Hall, is shameless enough to complain of fraud, in terms which show his inability to state the most accessible facts with accuracy. He tells us that the entire vote given at the last election in this city was sixty thousand, and this in a population of three hundred thousand, making one vote to every five persons. He therefore infers that many false votes were given, and strangely takes for granted that if such was the case, they were all given for James K. Polk. Now the vote was but fifty-five thousand, and the population of the city is, according to a moderate computation, three hundred and seventy-five thousand, allowing that it has increased twenty per cent in the last four years and a half, which is a modest estimate. This would give one vote to every seven persons in the city. Mr. Webster overstates the vote eleven percent, and understates the population more than twenty per cent, and then expresses his astonishment that such a population should furnish so large a vote. This is a cheap way of getting up an affectation of astonishment.

But Mr. Webster is not content with this misstatement. He goes on to say:

> "It is notorious that immense numbers of naturalization papers are obtained by perjury, and many foreigners have been made citizens and voters, by the same *set* of papers. Masters of vessels, who have brought over foreign paupers to this country, in thirty days after their arrival, have seen the same persons sworn in as citizens, and giving their votes, without knowing, in the slightest degree, the questions at issue, or even the names of the candidates—thus counteracting and overwhelming the will of legal voters."

If the fact be as notorious as Mr. Webster pretends, it can be substantiated. These masters of vessels are responsible men. If Mr. Webster means that they have been guilty of subornation of perjury in this matter, they can be prosecuted and punished; if he merely means to say that they are witnesses of the fact—let their affidavits be procured, or their testimony against the delinquents. The courts of this city, in which certificates of naturalization are given, were carefully watched, previous to the late election, by the whig party, and the names of all the persons naturalized were taken down and published in the whig newspapers. How happens it, if Mr. Webster's assertion contains one particle of truth, that no instance of illegal naturalization has been detected? A whole party is on the watch, agents and informers innumerable surround the courts, and none of those perjuries of which Mr. Webster talks have been discovered. The polls were surrounded by challengers, and men who took down the names of the voters—and none of these instances of voting twice in the same name, with the same set of papers, have been detected.

The truth is, that Mr. Webster is as accurate in this statement as he is in the other. He affirms, at a venture, whatever suits his purpose. Round assertions, bold declarations, without the slightest regard to their truth or falsehood, seem to compose the staple of his speeches at public meetings.

This attempt to direct the attention of the public from the conspiracy to carry the election of Mr. Clay by a forgery will not answer Mr. Webster's purpose. The fact can neither be denied nor extenuated.— There it remains, adhering fast to the skirts of the whig party. They see it is not to be shaken off, and the next expedient is that adopted by Mr. Webster, to get up a clamor about something else, by charges against their adversaries unsupported either by proof or probability. This is a trick which Mr. Webster learned at the bar, but he is pleading before a jury too well instructed in the truth of the case to be managed in this manner.

A friend of ours who heard the eccentric Rowland Hill preach in Dublin once heard him relate the following anecdote from the pulpit. An old lady had resolved to partake of the communion, and with that view began on Monday morning diligently to con her "Week's Preparation." She continued in this manner through every day in the week, until Sunday, when she presented herself at the church. When the morning service was over she saw, to her surprise, that all the congregation left the church, and on inquiry learned that it was not communion day. "Not communion day!" exclaimed the old lady. "Bless my soul! then I have had all this trouble for nothing."

The whigs it must be owned have not lost the election of Clay for want of any of those expedients to which the unprincipled agents they employed could be tempted by the liberal distribution of money. The devil's own preparation has been going on for months but our comfort is that the whigs have had the trouble and incurred the disgrace for nothing.

AN APT QUOTATION

A correspondent furnishes the following note on Mr. Webster's speech:

The arch-angel of whiggery, Daniel Webster, at a rally of his routed and discomfited partizans in Faneuil Hall, on Friday, made a speech full of dogged resolution, which he commenced with the following quotation from the first book of Milton's Paradise Lost:

> "What though the field be lost,
> All is not lost, the unconquerable will."

This is part of Satan's speech after his rebellion against the majesty of Heaven had been defeated; and himself and his host whelmed in the sulphureous pool of Tartarus. The orator did not like to quote any more of the original, so dropping the quotation, he goes on in plain prose, weaving into his speech, as if original, the ideas and many of the words of his Satanic model:

> "And study of revenge, immortal hate,
> And courage never to submit or yield,"

says the Devil.

"The courage to resist, the firm purpose, the devoted adherence to our principles," says Black Dan.

Now we call this plagiarism. With excellent judgment the god-like man compared the coalition of the fallen whigs to that of the Satanic crew. With equally excellent taste he likened himself unto the Devil, and adopted the speech which Milton had prepared for him. But he should have given the Devil his due, and continued the quotations. Would not an action lie for violation of copyright? We wish some printer or lawyer would advise us.

IRISHMEN AND CATHOLICS
November 20, 1844

During the preceding May, petitions before the Senate to extend to twenty-one years the period of residence in this country required of foreign immigrants before they might be granted the franchise had been laid on the table until December.

There are two or three sober words which we wish to say to those who are in favor of refusing political rights to individuals living among us, on account of their birth or their religion.

The reason given by the whig journals for demanding an alteration of our naturalization laws which will oblige all persons born abroad to reside in this country twenty one years before they are admitted to the rights of citizens is, that they sometimes enter into combinations to exercise political influence; that Irishmen, and Irishmen are generally Catholics, associate to carry a particular measure of legislation, or to procure offices for some of their own number, and that they have sometimes succeeded.

We will allow, for the sake of argument, that all this is true—we admit, indeed, that so far as the politics of this city are concerned, there has been something in these respects of which we might justly complain. But we maintain that this is no reason for excluding men of foreign birth from political rights.

The same thing happens with other classes of men. The class of firemen, at one time, when they had some difficulty with the Common Council, played an important part in our city politics. They held the balance between the two political parties, and made it incline to one side or the other, according as they chose. They sent their representatives to the Senate and the House of Assembly; they put their Aldermen and their Assistant Aldermen into the Common Council; they directed, in some measure, the bestowal of offices.

Both parties feared the firemen, and the whigs who courted them and coalesced with them carried the election in this city by their help. What would have been thought of a proposition to take from every fireman the power of voting, because they are inclined to be clannish, and to vote in a body? The reign of the firemen is now over; their quarrel with the corporation is at an end, and a fireman is now as harmless as any other citizen.

It is impossible to prevent combinations of this sort in a free country. Any class of men, whether it be a religious or professional class, when they suppose, whether truly or not, that their interests and rights are not properly regarded, will resolve themselves into a political party, carry on the controversy by public meetings and votes, and elect their officers, and influence legislatures if they can. Suppose that numerous and powerful religious denomination, the Presbyterians, in some way or other, to come into collision with the Common Council.— Does any body suppose that they would be at all scrupulous of using the ordinary means of political influence to effect their object and secure what they believe to be their rights? Would no public meetings be called, no eminent men of their persuasion, little seen in political life, clergymen perhaps, declaim on the wrong done, and appeal to the people for redress? Would not a new party rise up in our midst which both the other parties would regard with anxiety, and which would be very apt to give the victory for the time to that party which favored it the most?

The effect of that victory would be Presbyterian representatives in the House of Assembly, Presbyterian members in the Common Council, Presbyterians in office everywhere. What would our readers think of a proposition to disenfranchise for that reason all who belong to the Presbyterian denomination? How would the question sound at the polls, put by a challenger or inspector, "Are you a Presbyterian?"?

The proper remedy when any class of men obtain an excessive predominance in this way is not to cut off the individuals who compose it from the right of suffrage, but to put them down by a majority. As soon as the grievance reaches any magnitude, or as soon as the people imagine it to have done so, it is at an end. A year ago there was much complaint that there were too many Irishmen in the city offices. If that were the truth then, it is no longer so; the Native American party is in power, and not an Irishmen is left in office in all the city. It was said in certain quarters that the Irish elected our members of Congress and our members of Assembly. If that was the case then, it is not the case now; the Nativists have the choosing of our members of Assembly and our members of Congress. What more do these people want?

They have the power, the patronage, the offices, the salaries, the control of public affairs in every place where the complaint a few months ago was made that the Irish interest predominated. All beyond this is sheer persecution; the fanaticism of intolerance, which sooner or later will recoil on the heads of those who are guilty of it.

The Police Magistrates
February 14, 1845

In another part of this paper will be found a continuation of the examination of Justice Haskell, one of the magistrates who administer the city police at the Tombs. The first part appeared in our paper of Wednesday.

Job Haskell was appointed to the post by the Native American party, when they came into office about a year since, as a reward for the services he had rendered them. Job, we are willing to believe, is not dishonest, but he is ignorant and silly, and if you were to give the commission of police magistrate to the first man you might pick up in a walk along the wharves, the chance is that you would light upon a person better qualified. We believe that Job has had some difference with the Nativists since he took office, but that does not relieve his party from the disgrace of appointing him. The selection of such a man for such a place, shows an utter want of discretion, if not a sad lack of principle, in the body who conferred it. This is the particular inference; but there is a lesson of more extensive utility to be learned from it, and that is the folly of allowing such offices ever to be given as a recompense for party services. Once admit the practice, and you will have the bench of justice, from its highest to its lowest tribunals, invaded and occupied by a swarm of adventurers the worst fitted for the exercise of its high duties.

The examination to which we refer, shows what manner of proceedings are had at the Tombs under our present administration. Justice Haskell, it appears, had been told or suspected that something was in the wind; he thought there was a "conspiracy," as he called it, against him in Captain Hopper's Watch; a conspiracy the source of which was in a political committee, and he was curious to know the particulars. Determined to get at the bottom of the matter, he issued a process to bring before him Mr. Hufty, a person who he suspected must know something of the conspiracy, and subjected him to an examination in regard to the secrets and designs of the executive committee of his patrons, the Nativists.

We have no doubt for our part, that Job Haskell transgressed through mere ignorance and lack of sense. He had no idea that he was going out of his province as a magistrate, until the suggestion was made to him by a friend. "Do you think so?" was the question which he put in his astonishment to the person who intimated to him that he was doing what the law gave him no right to do. The men who appointed him are the most to blame. It is not to be expected of Job Haskell, that he should know exactly what he is fit for; that he should be able to take the gauge and dimensions of his own capacity; but the Common Council ought to be able to do it.— If the Common Council give it as their deliberate opinion, that Job is the fittest man in our whole population of three hundred and fifty thousand to perform the duties of police magistrate, Job is not the man to gainsay them; he accepts the office of course.

We hear of other charges of gross malpractice against another of the Justices appointed by the Nativists, the investigation of which will follow this examination into Haskell's case. It is surprising how many bad appointments that party has made. It is to be hoped that their errors in this respect will serve as a beacon to the party which is likely to supplant them at the approaching municipal election.

THE MUNICIPAL ELECTION
March 13, 1845

Dudley Selden, the Whig candidate for mayor of New York in 1845, was deserted by many of his party's voters in the election on April 8 in favor of the incumbent Nativist mayor James Harper, who was in turn defeated by the Democratic candidate, William F. Havemeyer. Saul Alley, a longtime acquaintance of Bryant's and a leading Democrat with a reputation for integrity, was a New York City dealer in wholesale textiles.

The evidences of the success of the democratic party at the ensuing election for charter officers, are too plain to be mistaken. It may be assumed as one of the events inevitably about to take place, and is already so conceded by many of the most intelligent among the mechanics who have hitherto ranked with the whig party. Native Americanism is now more odious with them than it perhaps is with a portion of the democrats; and as whigs, a greater affront could not have been given than the desertion of a staunch and able candidate for Mayor last spring, by the greater portion of the whig ranks, and the nomination of an unpopular conservative this year. Mr. Selden, they say, was once a democrat, then a neutral, then a conservative, but never a whig; and, although they yield to the policy, sometimes followed by their party, of gaining over some democrat of acknowledged ability as a politician, and then uniting under his lead, they do not admit that this nomination of Mr. Selden is a case in point. Mr. Selden is a lawyer of some cleverness, and very adroit in some of the intricacies of his profession; but no master mind, no party leader, and no manager of men.

The success of the democracy being therefore almost certain, it is very incumbent upon the nominating committees to be careful in their selection of candidates. We happened to be present the other evening at a primary meeting, in one of the strongest democratic wards, and found this subject discussed and dwelt upon with great interest by the large body of voters there assembled. A nomination for committeemen made in secret caucus was set aside by an overwhelming vote, and a ticket, formed upon true democratic grounds, was selected with great cordiality. The name of SAUL ALLEY as the best and strongest man for the Mayoralty was suggested in our hearing and met with a hearty approval from all present, not excepting the caucus, which had merely for local reasons, confined to their own district, desired a set of nominees to be elected other than those chosen for nomination by the spontaneous voice of the whole room. It is only necessary to mention this fact for that portion of the hangers on at Tammany Hall, who are accustomed to doubt the availability of any candidate, whose credit is good among business men, and who happens to live in a three story house. A better man for this high office could not be found, and a more popular name than that of Saul Alley could not be selected: and the great mass of the citizens of New York could not be called out with more zeal and more unanimity than by such a nomination, which we cordially recommend to the consideration of the nominating committee when it shall have met and been organized.

THE NATIVISTS AND OUR CITY FINANCES
March 13, 1845

There may be great want of capacity where there is no want of cunning. The men who represent the Native American party in the Common Council are an example of this. They have shown a lamentable want of talent in administering the affairs of the city; but, at the same time, they have shown great readiness in expedients to cover up and keep from sight their delinquencies.

These pledged reformers, who have boasted so loudly of their retrenchments in expense, particularly in relation to the tea-table; these economisers in Souchong and Bohea, had their eyes opened not long since to the fact, that through their incompetency and prodigality, the expenditures of the city had been made to exceed the amount of the tax levied, by at least a quarter of a million dollars. They discovered, also, that the expenditures of the present year were likely to exceed those of the last by about the same sum. They are now attempting to make the public believe, by a cunning and confused arrangement of their accounts, that instead of wasting the public money, they have actually lessened the expenses for the support of the city government by $229,679.00, during a period of seven months and a half.

This statement, the result of a calculation made upon a false basis, inserted in the annual report of the city comptroller, and appearing under his sanction, was well calculated to deceive the public. Many of the public journals adopted the statement, supposing it entitled to confidence; it was promulgated with great pomp by the press of the party, and immense numbers of the comptroller's report containing it were circulated by means of the watchmen and other officials, at the public expense.

The statement was but a trick however, and it was performed in this way. The comptroller's report for the year 1844, embraces four months and a half during which the city affairs were administered by a democratic Common Council; during the remaining seven months and a half they have been administered by the present nativist Common Council. To swell the expenses of the four months and a half, the statement has included the expenses incurred in the last three weeks of the preceding month. At the same time a much larger portion of the expenses of the last seven months and a half of the year 1844 are thrown over into the present year. The whole process was pointed out very clearly in a communication signed E. which we published a day or two since. By this method the nativists have enlarged the expenses of the four months and a half under the rule of their predecessors, by about $50,000, and made the expenses of the subsequent seven months and a half about $150,000 less than they really are.

For example, in salaries alone the amount of $16,715.66 has been improperly added to the expenditures of the first four months and a half of 1844, and the amount of $32,888.60 has been withdrawn from the expenses of the rest of the year, and thrown over into the present year for payment. This makes a difference of $49,104.26 in salaries merely. In the expenses of the alms house, the loan of $1,494 has also been thrown over into the present year for payment.

After all this legerdemain, after all this adroitness in parrying expenses, and making the year 1845 pay the expenses of 1844, the expenditures within the year, under the excellent and economical management of the present Common Council, have exceeded the amount of the tax levied by $171,000. Thus the retrenchments of the Common Council, putting the best face possible upon the matter, and taking their own statement for true, lead to a lamentable and unexpected deficiency.

We hope that every man who has a copy of the Comptroller's Report will examine it by the aid of the communication to which we have referred, published in our paper of Tuesday. It reviews the report by the help of information furnished by its pages. It exposes the fallacy of the claim which the present Common Council make to the praise of economy, and convicts them of actual and inexcusable prodigality. The two documents together—the Report and the Review—will convince our readers of the fraud attempted to be practiced upon the public.

THE DAY AFTER THE ELECTION
April 9, 1845

On April 8 the Democrats ousted from office the Nativist mayor James Harper, electing their candidate William F. Havemeyer and winning a majority on the Common Council.

The victory obtained by the democratic party in the municipal elections of yesterday is even more signal than we had anticipated. Not only are the Nativists beaten, but almost beaten out of existence. Every trace of them is completely obliterated from the Common Council, where they were lately supreme. The only office of which we can hear which they yet retain is a constableship in one of the lower wards and even that, we are told, is disputed.

It is not simply because the offices of the city are to be filled by new men that we rejoice at this result. Those whom we have elected may disappoint our expectations of good conduct, and may engage in acts or be guilty of neglects for which it may be difficult to find an apology; for good as our cause is, the men whom it employs as its instruments are necessarily imperfect, and not always the best that ought be chosen. But we rejoice because the result of the election is the assertion of a great principle, that of the political equality of man wherever be his birth place. The odious principle of exclusion from political rights on account of the accident of birth in a foreign land is solemnly disowned, rejected, flung to the ground and trampled on with scorn by the vast population of our city.

We saw the other day in an evening paper claiming to be neutral in politics, an attempt to show that the principle which forms the basis of the Nativist party was essentially popular, and must prevail, because it is identified with the love of country. But it is possible, we would remind those who reason in [t]his way—it is possible to love our country in too narrow and selfish a spirit. Those who maintain with us, the right of all men who adopt our land as their home, to enjoy the same political rights as if born among us, love their country for what she is, a land of refuge, and not for what the illiberal and inhospitable spirit of some would make her, a land where he to whom the world allows no other home must always remain an alien and a stranger.

We love her as the adopted land of our ancestors, that glorious company of emigrants from the old world who brought with them the spirit of liberty, ou[t] of which grew our free governments, as the plant from the seed. We love her as the mother, by adoption, of the kindly and honest burghers of New Amsterdam, of the gallant founders of Virginia, the venerated pilgrims of New England, the tolerant and generous-minded men who planted Maryland, the brave, courteous and devout Huguenot fathers of Carolina, and many other bands of adventurers from Europe, to whom we can refer with no less pride as the progenitors of our mingled race. We love our country for the large and comprehensive humanity of her institutions, and we would not change either them or her. We would not wish to see her different from what she was to our fathers, and what she has remained hitherto—an asylum from the severities of arbitrary governments, and the wretchedness they produce, and as such, we would keep open her gates to all time.

These are the principles which were involved in the issue of the election which has j[u]st been held, and we cannot but feel proud of our city, which has decided this great question so justly, humanly and worthily.

Pius IX—A Public Meeting
November 12, 1847

Elected to the papacy in 1846, Pius IX (1792–1878) granted a constitution to the Papal States, beginning a program of wide reforms.

Arrangements are making to arrange a public meeting to express the satisfaction with which the citizens and residents of New York regard the steps taken by Pius IX to give liberty to his subjects of the ecclesiastical states. It seems to us that it should be a subject of fervent and general congratulation among all the friends of the human race, that the political influence of the pontifical office, strengthened as it is by the religious veneration of so large a proportion of Christendom, is no longer employed in favor of despotic and arbitrary rule.

From no quarter could an example of liberality in government, of friendly and well-placed reliance on the people, come with more effect than from the papal chair. Its influence has been seen in all the Italian principalities except such as are under the immediate government of Austria. Tuscany is following, though with tardy and reluctant steps, the example of the ecclesiastical states; the kingdom of Sardinia, a little while since one of the most arbitrary monarchies of Europe, begins to introduce enlightened reforms; and some symptoms of regard for the popular welfare have manifested themselves, though feebly, in the monarchy of the two Sicilies.

Hitherto the Italians, who lamented the abject condition of their beautiful peninsula, under a league of governments fantastically attached to the maxims of despotism, have looked to the north for deliverance. The liberties of Italy cannot rise, they said, from the grave, until Germany is regenerated. Those who thus spoke have been suddenly surprised with the dawn in an opposite quarter of the horizon—the very quarter where they least expected to behold it—and by one of those events which deride all political foresight, it may happen that Germany herself will be liberalized by the example and influence of Italy.

Those who most passionately desired to see Italy raised up and placed under free institutions scarcely ventured to hope for a peaceful fulfilment of their wishes; they anticipated a great struggle of force with force before the work could be accomplished; in their vision of the future they saw the star of liberty through clouds of blood. In this respect also it is their good fortune to be disappointed. The birth of Italian liberty, thus far, is without throes. The work of reform goes on with the most perfect sympathy between the governing and the governed parties, amidst the peaceful rejoicings of the people. If any disturbance of the public tranquility should arise, it will be the work of absolute governments of Europe, or their instruments. The only apprehension now entertained is of guilty violence from that quarter; the only cause which can prevent the great change now going on in the ecclesiastical states from being carried onwards to that happy consummation which recognizes the people as the source of political sovereignty, will be the armed interference of Austria and her confederates. Even Austria, it appears, shrinks, either from the responsibility or the danger of the attempt, and it may be reserved for this century to see popular liberty recovered by a race long trodden in the dust, without bloodshed; to see a nation reaching the Promised Land of freedom with their feet unwet by the waters of the Red Sea.

The Year 1847
December 31, 1847

On September 14, 1847, victorious American forces captured Mexico City, all but concluding a war which had been declared by the United States fourteen months earlier. By 1847 Eastern cities from Boston to Baltimore were linked by telegraph, as they were also with Cincinnati and Chicago. In 1846 the technique of printing by wire had been patented.

This day closes the year 1847, a remarkable year in our annals, and in some respects in the annals of the world.

Within the year we have seen a more general recognition of the beneficent doctrines of free trade than the world ever knew before since the exchange of products between nations began. The famine with which Europe was visited had, no doubt, much to do with bringing its governments to a right view of this subject. It pleased Providence, as it often does, when the devices of human selfishness have acquired an apparent permanency by long duration, and the acquiescence of mankind, to inculcate great truths by great suffering. The governments of the civilized world are now revising their commercial codes with a view to liberalizing them under the new light which has broken in upon their statesmen, and the apostles of free trade are receiving [these?] with an enthusiastic welcome, in nations whose commercial policy has hitherto been of the most narrow and jealous character. In all this we see a surer pledge of the continued peace of the world, than we could find in almost any other circumstance.— We do not overlook the spread of a feeling of humanity, which in this age of mankind, awakens a stronger aversion to the mode of deciding the disputes of nations by the bloody arbitrament of war, than ever before existed, but we feel much more certain that this aversion will have its full effect when we find it reinforced by new considerations of interest. We rejoice, therefore, at anything which strengthens the mutual dependence of nations, and makes it indispensable for them to remain friends. If Mexico had been, in a moderate degree, a commercial country, and in that constant, frequent and free intercourse with the United States, to which the different occupations followed by the inhabitants of the two countries, and the diversity of their products, would seem naturally to lead; if the wants of the Mexican population had been those of a civilized nation, and the policy of its government, enlightened and liberal, there would long ago have been formed, between that republic and ours, ties which it would have been hard to break, and when broken easy to unite. We should without question at this moment have been at peace with Mexico.

The election of a Pope of liberal opinions, who begins his reign by recognizing the people as entitled to a share in the government, is one of the most remarkable events of the present century. History has but just begun to record its consequences, which reach doubtless infinitely beyond what the Pope himself now foresees, deeper into the institutions of his own states and the Italian principalities, and wider among the absolute kingdoms of Europe. If this beginning of reform should not be early checked by some sinister event, it will form an era in the annals of Europe separating the latter half of the nineteenth century from the years which immediately followed the dethronement of Bonaparte.

In our own country the year has been marked by the sudden and extraordinary growth of our commerce under the mitigated tariff; by the successful working of the independent treasury scheme, which has preserved a remarkable steadiness in the money market amidst the causes that, under a different policy, gave rise to the most violent and pernicious fluctuations; by the progress of our arms in Mexico, encountered at every step, by vastly superior numbers, yet always victorious till our army entered the most magnificent capital of the new world; and finally, by the extension of telegraphic lines all over the United States, conveying intelligence between the most remote parts with such rapidity, that the moment a despatch arrives at New Orleans from our armies in Mexico, its contents are known on the borders of the northern lakes.

We hope a more glorious distinction for the year to come—that it will be signalized [by] the conclusion of a peace with Mexico, on conditions so just and mutually satisfactory as to secure its duration. With this wish, which ought to be most fervently cherished in the heart of every friend of this country and of humanity, we might conclude this article, did not our relations with our readers seem to require a word or two of a less general nature. To them our acknowledgments are particularly due for the tokens of good will which our sheet has received during the past year. Within the twelvemonth our circulation in the country has increased to twice the extent which it had at the beginning of the year, and is at this moment enlarging itself more rapidly than ever. We accept this as a mark of the public approbation, both of the doctrines we have maintained, and the temper in which we have maintained them. It convinces us that it is not requisite to the success of a newspaper that it should pander to prejudices in which its conductors do not share, or suppress convictions which they truly feel, and that a fearless, just and magnanimous course towards friend and foe is not fatal to the prospects of a political journal.

Mr. Webster's Speech
March 30, 1848

On March 10, 1848, the treaty of Guadaloupe Hidalgo ending the victorious war with Mexico passed the United States Senate over the objection of Daniel Webster, who tried later to justify his vote by a blustering speech in which he characterized the overwhelming portion of the territory gained as a "barren waste," peopled by "coarse landholders and miserable peons." The otherwise obscure travel writer George Fredrick Augustus Ruxton (1820–1848) had recently published From Vera Cruz to Chihuahua, *which was reprinted in New York in 1915.*

The speech lately delivered by Mr. Webster in the Senate on the Ten Regiment bill is mainly, as it appears to us, a defence of his vote for rejecting the Mexican treaty. Mr. Webster, it appears, is an enemy to all further acquisitions of territory in the Southwestern quarter. His objection is two-fold. In the first place, he urges that the States which will be formed out of this territory will possess but a small population, and will therefore be represented in the Senate by two members, while they will not send any more, or perhaps not so many, members to the House of Representatives, which, he says, "will inevitably break up the relation existing between the two branches of the legislature and destroy its balance." In the second place, he objects that the character of the inhabitants, whom the annexation of New Mexico and California will introduce into the Union, is so degraded, that their morals are so depraved, and their ignorance so gross, that we shall debase our national character by admitting them as citizens.

The first of these objections certainly has very little force. If what Mr. Webster calls a balance between the two branches of the national legislature be what is wanted, it is what we never have had. There has never been a time, since the adoption of the Constitution, when there was anything like an equality of representation in the Senate. In 1790 Virginia had eight times as many inhabitants as Georgia, and Pennsylvania seven times as many as Rhode Island, yet the Constitution which gave each of these States two members, and two only, in the Senate, was adopted in spite of these differences. . . .

We do not get rid of the inequality concerning which he declaims so loudly by refusing to receive New Mexico and California into the Union. It is an inequality which was born with us as a nation; a congenital distemper, which was with us at first, has been with us till now, and which will not be done away with till the Constitution is essentially changed. Mr. Webster's argument is therefore, if it be worth anything, an argument against the Constitution, and not an argument against the acquisition of new territory. It is as good a reason for a dissolution of the present Union as it is against extending that Union to new States.

To alarm us by the prospect of the future, Mr. Webster affirms that California and New Mexico can never sustain a considerable population. New Mexico, he says, contains sixty thousand inhabitants—an exaggerated estimate doubtless—and cannot contain any more. Let us see how this is. New Mexico, it is admitted, abounds in mines; it is known also that Mexican agriculture is the most slovenly and superficial in the world. When emigrants from the North work the mines will there be no essential addition to the population? If there be not, the result will be contrary to all former experience. When our modes of agriculture are introduced, under the direction of our industry, will the soil be able to support no more inhabitants than now? Mr. Webster, we think, would be obliged to answer this question in the affirmative. New Mexico, says Mr. Webster, is an old settlement, and therefore must have nearly all the inhabitants it can well contain. We remind him that Florida is as old a settlement as that, and has just begun to be peopled.

Mr. Webster takes it for granted that the soil of California is barren and incapable of affording sustenance to a large population. He is mistaken in this, so far at least as relates to a tract of land one hundred and fifty or two hundred miles in width, running the whole length of the coast. Here a population as large, if not larger, than that of all New England, might be supported in comfort from the produce of a fertile soil which only requires occasional irrigation to make it as fertile as the valley of the Mississippi. We speak from the information of intelligent persons who have seen the country.

The morals of the people who are to be taken into the Union, if the treaty with Mexico goes into effect, occasion Mr. Webster much anxiety. The Boston Cato certainly does well to be vigilant in this matter, and we applaud the zealous severity with which he exercises his censorship. We do not think much of the authority he has quoted, the book of the traveller Ruxton, but we are willing to admit that the morals of the people of that country are not what they ought to be. Under better institutions they will doubtless improve—those of the whites at least—while for the Indian portion of the population, we see nothing to prevent the gradual waste and early extinction of their race, a fate which has fallen upon the Northern tribes. Both New Mexico and California will shortly be as fully Americanized as Florida has been.

Thus it will appear that two objections raised by the great Eastern champion of the Whig party against the treaty, even if we admit that they have any present application, are but objections which the lapse of a few years will remove. They are not of sufficient permanence to form the elements from which the statesmen of large views, "looking before and after," estimates the unfolding of that destiny which lies wrapped up in the present as the leaf lies sheathed in the bud. We recollect that when Mr. Webster made his treaty with Great Britain concerning the Maine boundary, he endured many attacks on account of his concessions to that Power. The time for retaliation has arrived; his political adversary of that day has made a treaty, and he is paying off the old debt. We cannot congratulate him upon having added anything to his reputation as a statesman by the choice he has made of the grounds for his attack.

The Result of the Election
November 8, 1848

On November 7, 1848, the hero of the Mexican War, General Zachary Taylor—"Old Rough and Ready," as he was popularly known—Whig candidate for the Presidency, defeated his Democratic opponent Lewis Cass, a Michigan Senator, as well as former President Martin Van Buren, who ran on a Free Soil ticket supported by the Evening Post. *John Alsop King, a Jamaica, New York lawyer, was later Republican governor of New York from 1857 to 1859.*

The electoral ticket nominated by the friends of General Taylor has carried the city of New York by a large majority over all the other candidates. The preference for this ticket has secured the success of the other Whig candidates in the city; members of Congress, members of the Assembly, and county officers, including the recorders, though by smaller majorities. The returns from different parts of the State show also that the Taylor electoral ticket has been chosen, and the vote of this State is certain for Taylor by a huge majority.

The causes of this result lie upon the surface; everybody who attended yesterday at the polls, whether in the city or in the country, saw and felt that Taylor had carried the State, not on account of any high personal popularity, not on account of any strong confidence which the people have in the ability or wisdom with which his Administration will be conducted, but because they believe the contest to be between Cass and Taylor, and they preferred the latter. Cass had declared himself against the prohibition of slavery in the territories. Taylor had said nothing on the subject, with the exception of some general declarations concerning his veto power, from which, however, numbers, with little ground in our opinion, drew the inference that he would not apply the veto power to any future edition of the Wilmot Proviso.

With those who regarded the matter in this light, the desire to express their disapprobation of the nomination of General Cass overbalanced every other motive. Hundreds of Whigs, known to be free soil men, appeared yesterday at the polls with votes for Taylor in their hands. "We know that your principles are right," said they in answer to the remonstrances of other Whigs who had heartily espoused the Free Soil party. "We esteem your cause to be just, and we prefer your candidate for the Presidency. We should be glad to vote for Van Buren, but we do not believe that he can possibly be elected. We regard this as a struggle between Cass and Taylor; the choice lies between these two, and we cannot afford to take a course which will in any way increase the chance that Cass will be elected."

To secure the votes of the two parties for Taylor and [Cass], the friends of these candidates found it necessary to make the most profuse expressions of their zeal for the cause of free soil. We believe it will be found that not a single member of Congress has been elected in this State who has not probably pledged himself to resist the extension of slavery. John A. King, who is elected as the Taylor candidate to Congress from Queens County by a thousand majority, came out in the papers with a declaration of his devotion to the cause of free soil just before the election. Such declarations made by the Whig candidates no doubt had the effect of confirming the vague idea which numbers of both parties entertained that Taylor was not personally hostile to the Wilmot Proviso.

In spite of all these influences, in spite of the newness of our party, a party yet in its cradle, in spite of the difficulty of creating a large vote for any party at the very first election after it makes its appearance, we have, according to all indications, polled a large vote in the State, unprecedentedly large, considering the short time allowed us to organize and to employ the means of influencing public opinion. We have laid the foundation of a mighty party, with a great principle for its basis. The establishment of this party has already effected great results.

It has determined, indirectly but most effectually, the Presidential election between the two candidates of the Baltimore and the Philadelphia conventions.

It has compelled both parties to do homage to the principle of freedom in the Territories, and to acknowledge it as an established maxim of political conduct.

It has emancipated the Democratic party from the control of the slave power.

It has so disturbed the torn position of the Democratic party of the North, that it will compel it to reorganize with the principle of free soil in its creed as a settled doctrine.

It has taught an emphatic lesson to all politicians who are disposed to sell themselves to the South. That trade is broken up and Mr. Cass is the last adventurer in it.

Lastly, it has in all probability decided the question of freedom or slavery in the Territories. The agitation of that question by the Free Soil party, has, we believe, made the success of the slaveholders in this controversy impossible.

Mr. Webster's Speech
March 8, 1850

In his celebrated Seventh of March Speech, Webster urged passage of a compromise allowing the organization of territory ceded by Mexico without restriction on slavery, except in California. This brought down on him the opprobrium of many prominent people opposed to slavery. Notable among these was John Greenleaf Whittier, whose poem "Ichabod" expressed disappointment and disillusionment with a man who had once been their idol. It closed with the verses,

> *Of all we loved and honored, naught*
> *Save power remains;*
> *A fallen angel's pride of thought,*
> *Still strong in chains.*
>
> *All else is gone; from those great eyes*
> *The soul has fled:*
> *When faith is lost, when honor dies,*
> *The man is dead!*
>
> *Then, pay the reverence of old days*
> *To his dead fame;*
> *Walk backward, with averted gaze,*
> *And hide the shame!*

Submitted to the House of Representatives by David Wilmot of Pennsylvania in 1846, and passed by that body but defeated in the Senate, the Wilmot Proviso would have forbidden slavery in any part of such territory as might be ceded by Mexico as the result of the war.

Over the course of a decade two of Webster's sons had repeatedly enjoyed sinecures under succeeding Whig Administrations; at one time, while acting as his father's clerk in the State Department, Daniel Fletcher Webster, the elder of these, had actually served briefly in his father's place as Secretary of State during Webster's absence from Washington. (The balance of this editorial is unretrieved, but see the editorial of March 9.)

The *Journal of Commerce* exults at Mr. Webster's declaration that he will not support any measure to prohibit slavery in the territories.

We did not suppose that he would. We knew that the Administration had been generous to the family of the Massachusetts Senator, and that he is, by temperament, grateful, and sensible of the obligations which those who receive benefits are under to those by whom they are bestowed. It was for that, among other reasons, that we so confidently assured our readers, the other day, that he would not fail to support the Administration in its recommendation not to apply the proviso of 1787 to the new territories. It was as natural to suppose that he would do this, as that he could abandon, in the manner he has done, the doctrines of free trade, once maintained by him in their fullest extent, and taking the money of the eastern mill-owners, enroll himself as the champion of protection for the rest of his life.

We take no pleasure in making these animadversions, but they are forced upon us. Mr. Webster stands before the public as a man who has deserted the cause which he lately defended, deserted it under circumstances which force upon him the imputation of a sordid motive, deserted it when his apostasy was desired by the Administration, and immediately after an office had been conferred upon his son, to say nothing of what has been done by the Administration for his other relatives. It is but a little more than two years since that he declared himself the firmest of friends to the Wilmot Proviso, professing himself its original and unvarying champion, and claiming its principles as a Whig doctrine. In a speech which he made at a Whig convention held at Springfield in Massachusetts, in the year 1847, he said:

> There is not a man in this hall who holds to the principles of the Wilmot Proviso more firmly than I do, no one who adheres to it more than another. I feel some little interest in this matter, sir. Did I not commit myself in 1838 to the whole docrine, fully, entirely? And I must be permitted to say that I cannot quite consent that more recent discoverers should claim the merit and take out a patent. I deny the priority of their invention. Allow me to say, sir, that it is not their thunder.

But now, in the speech delivered yesterday on the floor of the Senate, in reply to Mr. Calhoun, of which our readers will find the telegraphic report in our columns, he ridicules the Wilmot Proviso as the invention of Northern Democracy, and declares that he "will not vote for the insertion, into any bill giving territorial government to the new Territory, of any provision prohibiting slavery."

Of course there is a pretext for this shameful renunciation of a principle once so zealously professed; no apostasy is ever without its pretext. Mr. Webster now pretends that it is impossible that slavery should exist in the new Territories, and says that the adoption of the Wilmot Proviso would be "a re-enactment of the law of God."

What would he have? Would he have an enactment contrary to the law of God? But what are his reasons for supposing that slavery cannot be transplanted to New Mexico and the portions of California not included in the new State? He states none. . . .

A Recipe for the Extension of Slavery
March 9, 1850

On March 4, a speech of the ailing John Calhoun of South Carolina had been read to the Senate by Senator James M. Mason of Virginia. In this Calhoun, who would in fact die within the month, urged that the Union could be preserved only by giving the South equal rights in the territory acquired from Mexico as the result of the war of 1846–1848, which comprised California, New Mexico, and Texas, with parts of what would become the states of Utah, Nevada, Arizona, and Colorado.

In comparing the speech of Mr. Webster, of which we gave, yesterday, the substance as reported by telegraph, with that of Mr. Calhoun on the same question, it seems to us that no man can fail to see how much the South Carolina senator has the advantage, not only in depth of conviction and earnestness of purpose, but in that important quality of the character of a statesman, a clear perception of the result of public measures. Mr. Calhoun sees clearly what Mr. Webster does not see, the causes which prevented the emigration of slave owners, with their work-people, to California, and which still operates as a constant discouragement to the introduction of slavery into the territory eastward of the new state of California. In the rejoinder which Mr. Calhoun made, on Thursday, to Mr. Webster's speech, after complimenting him on his declaration that he would not vote for the prohibition of slavery in the territories, he proceeded to say:

> "I am willing to leave it to Nature to settle and organize these territories. Organize them upon the principle of the gentleman, and give us free scope, and a sufficient time to get in—we ask nothing but that, and we never will ask it. When the gentleman says he is willing to leave it to Nature, I understand that he is willing also to remove all impediments now put in our way, deterring our people from going there—I mean the consummate folly of citing the Mexican law prohibiting Slavery in New Mexico and California."

These are the words of one who has considered this subject carefully, and who speaks in sincerity, of one whose great anxiety is that the slave states should never be left in a minority in Congress, and who will consent to no policy on the part of the federal government which does not look to the maintenance of their political power. Mr. Calhoun has the sagacity to see that it is not nature, it is not climate, it is not any peculiarity of productions or of soil, which, during the short period in which we have held the new territories, has prevented the introduction of slavery, or will prevent it hereafter. It is, as he acknowledges in the passage we have quoted, the danger that Congress may organize these territories with a prohibition of slavery; and the opinion, which is very common in the United States, and to which Mr. Clay has given a place in his plan of a compromise, that the Mexican law forbidding to hold men and women in slavery, is still in force within the territories.

Let these boundaries be removed, and Mr. Calhoun is satisfied, so far as regards the territories. Organize the territories without laying any restriction on the introduction of slaves, and give time for the institution to be fairly planted within their limits, and the slave owners will take care of the rest. Mr. Webster must agree, also, that he and his friends will not alarm the slave owners by foolishly talking about the Mexican law against slavery being still in force. That obstruction, however, the planters will take care to remove, by bringing the question before the Supreme bench of the United States, on which is a majority of southern jurists. With a decision that the Mexican law is superseded by the constitution, the gates of the new territory would be thrown wide open to slavery, which would make a triumphant entry upon its new conquests.

The possessors of capital, whatever be its nature, shrink from exposing it to risk. The most solid capitalists in this commercial metropolis are its most circumspect men in regard to the modes in which capital is invested and employed. They whose capital is invested in slaves, feel the same concern for their wealth, and having no commercial habits, are still less likely to embark in enterprises which may involve the loss of their property. This is one of the circumstances which sagacious men in all parts of the country rely upon to hold in check the plotters of disunion. A large slave owner cannot afford to be a disunionist; he incurs too certain and too great a risk by it, and has too little to gain. The same caution prevents him from emigrating with his slaves to a country in which his claim to hold them in servitude may not be allowed. Organize the territories, however, on what Mr. Calhoun calls Mr. Webster's principle, and the first great obstruction to the introduction of slavery is removed. If the territorial government cannot be persuaded to repeal the Mexican laws, the territorial courts may be induced to declare it void, and their decision may be affirmed by the Supreme Court of the United States, which fully removes the remaining obstruction.

Mr. Calhoun, therefore, very properly recognizes the plan of Mr.

Webster as meeting the wishes of those who desire the extension of slavery, and as removing the principal barrier to its introduction into our new possessions.

THE FUGITIVE SLAVE RIOTS
October 4, 1851

The Fugitive Slave Act, a provision of the Compromise which had become federal law in September 1850 (the Compromise itself was explained in the headnote to the March 8, 1850, editorial on Webster's 7th of March speech), mandated the arrest by United States marshals of runaways wherever found, and, after examination by commissioners whose compensation was weighted in favor of a decision against the fugitive, their return to their supposed owners. The law was furiously resented in many Northern communities, and rescues of fugitives were made or attempted, such as those of Shadrach and Thomas Sims at Boston, one "Jerry" at Syracuse, and another runaway at Christiana, all in 1851. For the quotation beginning "If we do these things in the green," cf. Luke 23:31. Earlier, Bryant had assured the Ohio anti-slavery Senator Salmon P. Chase, "The controversy concerning slavery will be kept open, and nothing of the zeal of an opposition to the fugitive slave law and the kindred enormities will be abated."

If we were asked to name the place in all this Union where crimes against the person and against property, were most rare; where a respect for order and subordination to the moral as well as penal sanctions of the law were most universal, and where deeds of violence of every kind received the least countenance from the people, we might well have hesitated in our decisions, between the village of Christiana in Pennsylvania and the city of Syracuse. Both are secluded places, exposed to few or none of the irritating excitements of large cities, inhabited by a homogeneous population, of rural and quiet habits, contented with their employments, prosperous and happy. We might well have doubted in which of these two places it would have been most difficult to provoke any act of violence against a public officer. And yet the journals of the whole country are now occupied with long accounts of fearful and bloody riots which have recently occurred in each of these places, in both instances resulting in a temporary defeat of the officers of justice, and in one case, the death of a citizen.

A stranger might naturally ask, if scenes like these occur in our most orderly and law-observing communities, what is to be expected from those of inferior pretensions, "If we do these things in the green, what will we do in the dry?" How does it happen, for example, that in the little city of Syracuse, usually so quiet, the blood-stained hand of rebellion is raised successfully against the officers of the law, and under its protection the imprisoned are set free, while the armed soldier and the citizen, clothed with the power of the country, stand by, the unresisting witnesses of the scene?

The answer is an obvious one, and yet it is one which the press and politicians of the country are determined not to apprehend. The people of the United States do not habitually obey the law, that is, they are not frequently conscious of the restraints of law or of doing any duty because the law prescribes it. They rather obey the dictates of their own consciences, and conform to the standards of right and justice which prevail in their respective communities. These usually correspond with the laws which are administered among them, but which, in ninety-nine cases out of every hundred, they have never read or heard of. Paradoxical as it may appear, it is nevertheless a fact that while there is no country in the world where the law is more rarely resisted, there is none where it is so rarely obeyed, in the active sense of that word; that is where the conduct of men are so little influenced or controlled by its provisions. Most people in this country govern themselves. The laws are made for and operate upon those chiefly who do not know how so to enjoy their own natural rights as not to trespass upon the natural rights of their fellows. These obey the laws, when they do not violate them, but the mass of our citizens habitually obey, their own sense of duty, of justice, and of propriety.

The consequence is, that in no country in the world does any law which violates the moral instincts of the people receive, comparatively, so little respect. The Austrian or the Russian serf is accustomed to obey unjust and unreasonable laws, and is accustomed to the most terrible penalties if he disregards them. The American has no such discipline; and it is only as a political student that he learns that he lives under a vast network of legal restrictions.— When a law conflicts with any of his sentiments, his first impulse is to resist it; and if he finds his sentiments correspond with those of his neighbors, it generally is resisted whenever an attempt is made to enforce it.

Such laws, commonly, are permitted to grow obsolete upon the statute book, with the silent acquiescence of the public authorities. In some cases, however, circumstances conspire to prevent the repose of such as are peculiarly unpopular and offensive. Its ministers, perhaps, are pursued by an influence from abroad stronger than the domestic sentiment which surrounds them, and they are compelled to enforce it. Then collisions, like those which recently occurred at Christiana and Syracuse, are almost inevitable, and nothing but a long subjection to the discipline of an oppressive and tyrannical government can prevent their occasional recurrence.

The Fugitive Slave Law is one of these offensive laws. In the free states its operation is revolting. The people feel it to be an impeachment of their manhood, to be asked to assist in manacling, for the purpose of reducing to slavery, one who has lived among them the life of an industrious and honest citizen; whom for years they have been accustomed to meet in their daily walks, and with whom, perhaps, they have broken bread. Every manly instinct of their nature is aroused at the very proposal, and it is not until they are advised by reflection, that it is better for one or a dozen men to suffer, than that the moral supremacy of the law should be shaken, that the most conservative and orderly of our people can be induced to remain quiet spectators of such barbarism.

It is the curse of this law that the people of the free states can never get reconciled to it. They will obey it after a fashion—that is, they will permit the officers of justice to do their duty unmolested, but every new warrant will open anew the fountains of bitterness, and extend farther and farther the dangerous habit of questioning the wisdom and the justice of our lawgivers.

There is one element which enters into all slave property, that is not sufficiently considered by those who discuss the rights and wrongs of the slave states; we refer to its constitutional and inseparable propensity to run away—to be other than it is—property. The slave will as surely seek to be a freeman as he will breathe, and it is [as] much a part of what every man buys when he buys a slave, as it is a part of the seedling to struggle upward from the soil towards the light, of ice to melt in summer, of all created things to perish without nourishment. The impulse towards freedom is one which no legislature can extinguish or control, and in legislating about slaves, it would be as great a folly to attempt it as it would be to require by law that fruit should not decay after it was ripe. When a man buys an orange, he buys it and pays a price regulated by the common understanding that unless speedily consumed, it will decay. The slaver also buys a slave with the full knowledge of the innate propensity of that kind of property to change its character. The price he pays for it is proportionately less than it would be, if, like his plough, or his cart, it had no capacity or desire to run away and be something other than a slave, and, its labor were voluntary and cheerful.

How far these considerations have been overlooked by the authors of the fugitive slave bill, and how far they are entitled to attention in selecting the most appropriate means for carrying out the constitutional provision for the surrender of fugitives from labor, we must, for the present at least, leave to the determination of our readers.

Public Parks
July 2, 1853

In 1844 the city of Philadelphia had acquired the former estate of Revolutionary War financier Robert Morris, and in 1855 set it aside as a public park. Jones Wood, a wooded tract of land on the east side of Manhattan Island between Sixty-Sixth and Seventy-Fifth Streets, had been the area Bryant proposed for a city park in his pioneering editorial of July 3, 1844. After early approval of this tract, it was finally rejected in 1853 in favor of the larger location along the center of the island which Central Park now occupies.

They are discussing in Philadelphia the question of opening a large park for the accommodation and refreshment of the people. In Philadelphia, where the summer heats are stronger than even here, the necessity of public pleasure grounds, shady and fresh, and carefully irrigated, is said to be almost universally acknowledged. If the necessity be clear at present, what, say the advocates of the project, will it be fifty years hence, when the grounds which might now be appropriated to the purpose will be all built on and covered with a dense population. The Philadelphia *North American* has the following speculations on the subject:

"The population of the city and county of Philadelphia in 1850 was four hundred and eight thousand eight hundred and seventy-three. The increase in the ten preceding years was over one hundred and twenty thousand—at the rate of 58.45. The mean average decennial increase from 1790 has been 40.40. Now, estimating the growth of our population at the last named rate, the city and county will have, in 1900, two million, two hundred and thirty thousand six hundred and seven inhabitants; or, if calculated at the rate of progress observable during the last ten years, the census will reach a figure exceeding four million. So much, then, for population: which, assuming only the rate of increase that has obtained for the last sixty years, must amount, in less than half a century, to more than two million people. In view of this fact, it becomes a grave question whether they shall have room to breathe in.

"Turning now to the probable results of building extension in the next fifty years, we shall find them to be no less startling. The total number of dwellings in 1850, as reported by the census takers, whose estimates are usually under the real figure, was sixty-one thousand two hundred and two, in the city proper, nine districts, seven boroughs, and twelve townships. This is exclusive of certain parts of Philadelphia Co., each of which contains several hundred buildings. The average number of houses erected annually during the last three years, is stated to have been three thousand five hundred. Allowing for such elements of progressive growth as railways, ocean and river steam lines, and whatever augments trade, population, and the accommodations for both at any given point, we may safely assume that the above measure of increase will continue up to the year 1900. If this shall be so, of which there can be no reasonable doubt, Philadelphia, with its districts and boroughs, will contain at the period named, two hundred and thirty six thousand two hundred and two buildings, or very nearly three times as many more as the number stated in the census returns of 1850.

"Let us next see what probable amount of space the city will cover forty-seven years hence, according to the above reliable estimate of building extension. The sixty-one thousand two hundred and two buildings, ennumerated in 1850, occupied fifteen square miles, or nine thousand six hundred acres. This number of buildings multiplied by four, which, has been shown, will be about the increase in the fifty years, dating from the current half century, the superficial area of ground which Philadelphia will stretch over, in compact form, in 1900, will embrace sixty square miles, or thirty-eight thousand four hundred acres."

If these considerations form, as they do, without question, a strong argument for the immediate purchase of land for a spacious public park in Philadelphia, what shall we say of New York? The limits of our island are narrow and while we are debating the question our population is covering the vacant spaces to the water's edge. The journal from which we have already quoted says, that there are tracks of land, bordering the Schuykill on the northwest, and admirably adapted for a park, and readily accessible to the population of Philadelphia. Here in New York we have scarcely a choice to make, and the lands which might answer the purpose are already distant from a considerable part of our population. What we do we must do quickly.

We entirely agree with those who, considering the quarrel between the friends of the Jones Park and the Central Park to be far of less consequence than the adoption of some plan for the immediate purchase and opening of public grounds somewhat answerable in extent to the greatness of our population, would end the controversy by a decision in favor of both. With a population increasing like ours, both will be wanted before the end of this century, and if the decision is in favor of one only, we are confident that twenty years hence every body will regret that the other was not included in the project.

A Word for the *Evening Post*
July 14, 1853

The Richmond Enquirer, *established in 1804 with the support of President Jefferson, had been ever since a leading voice of the Democratic party in the nation. On*

March 3, 1851, Bryant had charged in the Evening Post *that excessive subsidies had been given by the government to New York shipowner Edward Knight Collins to carry transatlantic mail. On March 4, 1853, Democratic President Franklin Pierce of New Hampshire had taken office. Edmund Burke (1809–1887), a New Hampshire Democratic leader, had been a United States Congressman from that state from 1839 to 1845.*

We have received from the *Richmond Enquirer* a polite invitation to withdraw from the democratic party. We have every disposition to oblige the conductors of that journal—whoever they may be—to any reasonable extent, but this is a request with which we cannot comply. We should as soon think of being turned out of the house we occupy as out of our party. If our neighbor or the *Commercial Advertiser* were to walk into the office of the EVENING POST and order us to quit the premises, we should hardly consider the summons more impudent—the Richmond print will pardon us if we speak plainly—than the one now given by the *Richmond Enquirer.* It strikes that this is one of the cases in which no writ of ejectment will lie.

Speaking of the EVENING POST, the *Richmond Enquirer* says:

"It is time that such newspapers should learn that they cannot fasten themselves on the democratic party. It is time that they should be spurned with indignation and scorn as the instruments and ehoes of the worst factions of the day."

These are honeyed words, to be sure, though we think we have seen them before; but we shall not allow ourselves to be coaxed from our purpose by any flatteries, however dexterously applied. Out of respect, however, to those who put the proposition to us so sweetly and delicately, we have concluded to state the reasons which weigh with us to remain where we are.

In the first place we shall abide by the democratic party, because it is our party, becuase it is the party with whose principles, as laid down by Jefferson and as expounded by many enlightened men both of his time and ours, we fully agree. We recognize the great basis of the democratic party, simplicity in government—as little government, as little patronage, as little expenditure as the structure of civil polity can subsist with, and a strict construction of the constitution. We are of the party which applies this test to public measures generally. We belong to no party established for carrying a single measure, for experience has proved that such parties rarely effect their object, and their fate is either perpetual impotence or early dissolution; besides that, so narrow a basis of association does not meet our ideas of the true value, dignity, and proper design of a political party.

In the second place, we adhere to the democratic party, because in its present state, it is a party which, in our humble measure, we helped to form. For a quarter of a century or more we have been occupied with the work of diffusing the information and stating the arguments on which the principles of this party rest, and contending for the measures in which its principles were put in practice. During the whole of that period we have been in the front rank of the combattants for every important reform which the party has effected—freedom of trade and the independent treasury, for example. It is not our intention to abandon what is in part our own work.

In the third place, we mean to remain in the democratic party, because knowing it to be, as the party of the people, sincere and powerful, and believing that it is intended by Providence to shape the destinies of our great country, we mean to lend such aid as we are able in keeping it true to the work to which it is called. Our task is to prevent, if we can, false doctrines from being incorporated into its creed, and corrupt measures from being favored by its members, and to engage it in all salutary forms. The politician who connects himself with a small and feeble or despised party, gives up an important opportunity of being useful. If his conscience dictates such a course, there is no help for it, but nothing short of a clear vocation of conscience can excuse him for thus parting with the means of resisting corruption, and influencing the councils of his country for good.

We shall remain in the democratic party, in the fourth place, for the sake of the honest men who are in it. There are knaves in all parties—at least in all which have any strength and any means of operating upon legislation or on the elections. The moment a party, no matter how pure its origins, or how seemingly disinterested its first members, begins to find itself so numerous as to be able to impose conditions on other parties, knaves will rush into it, and make it, so far as they are able, the engine of their corrupt designs. Let no man deceive himself with the belief that he will ever find a party in which there are no unprincipled men. We shall not leave the democratic party on account of the rogues who may be in it—we shall remain in it for the sake of the honest men who form the large majority. With the sincere, the disinterested, the enlightened, the fearless minds who are the honor of our party we shall keep up, as we have ever done, a good understanding, and with them we shall always zealously cooperate.

In the fifth place, we shall adhere to the democratic party for the sake of resisting and disappointing the knaves of that party. As we have already said, there are dishonest men in all parties. When a plan to rob the treasury is on foot, as for example, when a project is started for giving a few hundred thousands to the owners of an ocean steamer, the rogues on both sides have a perfect understanding of each other. The democratic knaves take to manage the democratic members, the whig knaves engage to bring the members of their party into its support, and in this manner the well-meaning men on both sides are cajoled, and the scheme of plunder slips through both Houses without the least obstruction. The EVENING POST has been of some service in checking these robberies, and it may be of some service hereafter. The attempts which have recently been made to destroy its influence with the democratic party, by the *Washington Union,* the *Albany Argus,* the *Richmond Enquirer* and other papers in the interest of the steamship party, have all this origin. They all act with the unanimity and with the promptness of a preconcerted plan. It is feared by the steamship party that they may have some trouble with General Pierce, and accordingly, while with one hand they strike at the EVENING POST, they are digging a mine under the feet of the President with the other. The letter of Maurice, which we gave yesterday, was published by the *Albany Argus,* with expressions of approval, to convince him that he must not look for support from that quarter unless he would lend himself to the designs of the steamship party. Meantime the *Union* does its part of the work with so little energy, that Edmund Burke, as we hear, is about to go to Washington to establish a journal in the interest of that party which is to apply a stronger coercion to the President than the *Union* has the courage to do, and which if he should manifest himself finally intractable, will be restrained by no scruples on the part of its conductor, already strongly disaffected, from throwing off the mask, and coming out in direct opposition to his administration. There is likely to be, our readers will perceive, ample occupation for the EVENING POST for the next four years in withstanding the designs of that insatiable crew with whom we have been in a constant strife for several years past. We do not mean, for our part, to relax the zeal of our opposition in the least, and we shall keep up the cannonade upon them from our old station in the democratic fortress.

These are really some of the reasons which determined the EVENING POST to keep its place in the democratic ranks, and having made up our minds to do this we should like to know who or what is to prevent it.

BACKBONES WANTED—A NORTH
February 27, 1854

While Secretary of State in the administration of President Millard Fillmore, Daniel Webster had died on October 24, 1852, having courted favor in the South in a vain effort to secure the Whig nomination for the Presidency. On January 23, 1854,

Democratic Senator Stephen A. Douglas of Illinois proposed a Kansas–Nebraska Act which, in providing for the organization of the territory of Nebraska, would permit its admission to the Union as a state or states with or without slavery as determined by popular vote, in effect repealing the Missouri Compromise of 1820. Whig Senator from Massachusetts Edward Everett had abstained from voting on this bill. Massachusetts Free-Soil Congressman Charles Allen had publicly charged Webster with granting favors to a banking syndicate to which he was indebted for monetary gifts. Senators Charles Sumner of Massachusetts and Salmon P. Chase of Ohio were leading signers of an "Appeal of the Independent Democrats" which called the Kansas–Nebraska bill a "gross violation of a sacred pledge." Senator Preston King of New York was another opponent of the bill. The popular "Prince" John Van Buren of New York, son of the former President and an early Free-Soiler, had gradually modified his views. Democratic Senator Jeremiah Clemens of Alabama was a strong Unionist who opposed the bill, as did New York Whig Senator William H. Seward. Former Democratic Senator John A. Dix, a veteran of the War of 1812, was a prominent Free-Soiler who had been prevented by Southern opposition from becoming Secretary of State in President Pierce's cabinet.

"There is no North," said Daniel Webster. Mr. Webster was mistaken, and in the little time that intervened before his death, after he had given himself up entirely to the South, he found out his mistake. There is a North; but the instinctive, strong, conscientious love of liberty, felt by the North, finds but feeble and imperfect expression through the politicians or public men—statesmen, so called. Now and then an exceptional voice speaks out in clear and loud tones; but it is mortifying to witness the general feebleness which has characterized the opposition in Congress to Senator Douglas's bill of abomination. Our public men want stiffer backbones. A weakening of the spine is epidemic amongst them. Not one in a hundred stands straight.

Look at that polished icicle, Edward Everett—the man who, when in the pulpit, was said to have offered up the most eloquent prayer ever addressed to a Boston congregation—look at that finished statute, hear him express his high "admiration" (that is the word he uses) for the compromise measures of 1850—the damnable Fugitive Slave law not excepted—and if you doubt any longer that his lips are made of marble, because you see them move, you will not doubt that his heart is made of stone. Educated, learned, accomplished, elegant, what a pity that, while God gave him ten talents, the Devil—who always puts in weak ones—should have supplied his backbone. The freedom of a great territory, the highest right—the right to liberty—of millions yet to be—the cause committed to his hands is no less than this. And yet with what an effeminate, and soft, flattering voice he pleads a case worthy of a giant's struggle! How carefully he treads among the toes of the southern senators, by the very gentleness of his opposition tenderly wooing future southern support for the Presidency! How, while he argues this great case, does he at the same time concede the main point to his opponents, by falsely admitting that the great question is of no practical importance! Ah yes! how blandly he smiles away the liberties of the unborn generations of men and women, who shall toil and bleed under the lash while he shall be sleeping—if their groans will let him sleep—in his grave! And yet this is the same man who, a few years ago, when a candidate for Governor of Massachusetts, wrote a letter to William Lloyd Garrison, avowing himself in favor of immediate emancipation. No backbone has he.

But this humiliating spectacle—the more humiliating sight of the northern men who, prostrating themselves at the feet of the administration, and meekly taking on their dishonored shoulders the heavy burden of this wicked measure—all this does not prove that there is no North. It does, indeed, prove that there are white slaves—pitiable and despicable too—in Congress—whether or not there may hereafter be black slaves in Kansas and Nebraska—but it does not prove that the masses, who want no office and ask no favors, are not earnestly and strongly in favor of glorious liberty; and opposed, bitterly and forever opposed, to the further extension of slavery. Does anyone doubt, that our own strongheaded and lion-hearted Charles Allen would have more truly expressed the real sentiments of Massachusetts had he been where he ought to be, in the United States Senate? Does anyone doubt, that the recent masterly speech of Mr. Everett's colleague Mr. Sumner who, though perhaps too formal and measured, nevertheless has still a stiff backbone—does anyone doubt that his great speech, and Chase's, are heartily concurred in by almost the entire population of the free states?

There is a North, but it wants more voices. And we wish, more particularly, to inquire if there has been any weakening of the spine among the democratic leaders—not in Congress, but out of Congress—or if they are troubled by bronchitis, or loss of voice, that more of them are not heard from.

Preston King—always true as steel, and wise—has written a letter which will tell for freedom wherever it is read. But where is the people's favorite, John Van Buren? He has called out a letter, it is true, from ex-senator Jere. Clemens, on the right side; but the popular ear listens expectant for his voice. Will he let the mighty occasion pass by in silence? It is idle for him to say he is not in public life. Whether holding office or not, such men are, in one sense always in public life. In critical times the people look to them for words of counsel and encouragement, and for a strong and faithful expression of the public sentiment. If Mr. Van Buren does not stir himself, he will find his rival, Gov. Seward, who, loaded with political heresies on other questions, is buoyed up and borne aloft by his fidelity on this, ahead of him in the general estimation.

A correspondent makes the inquiry—Where is General Dix, whose physical courage would not quail at the cannon's mouth—has he no bold word for freedom now?

Stiffer backbones are wanted; not amongst the people, but amongst the politicians.

It is not a few ranting abolitionists—it is not a few noisy brawlers who constitute the opposition to Judge Douglas's unholy, treacherous and monstrous proposition. It is the masses—the laboring masses—the honest masses—the masses, all lovers of liberty, with backbones stiff and straight—it is the masses, almost without exception, who are opposed to it. If there are for these any more orators, with clear voices and stiff backbones, let them speak soon.

Touching It Off Softly
March 2, 1854

George Wallace Jones, Democratic Senator from Iowa, supported the Kansas–Nebraska bill, as did one of its zealous authors, Kentuckian Democrat Archibald Dixon, Henry Clay's successor in the Senate. Senator George E. Badger of North Carolina was another proponent of the bill.

Two Irishmen were going to fire off a cannon just for fun; but, being of an economical turn of mind, they did not wish to lose the ball. So one of them took an iron kettle in his hands to catch it in; and stationing himself in front of the loaded piece, he exclaimed to the other, who stood behind it holding a torch, "Touch it off softly, Jemmy."

We were never very forcibly impressed with the wisdom displayed by the Irishman; but he has imitators in high quarters. Senator Everett, of Massachusetts, would really prefer that this Nebraska cannon should not be fired at all; he has not so much relish for the fun of the thing as the Irishmen had; but he fully credits the assurance given by the honorable Mr. Douglas, and perhaps the honorable Mr. Jones, and his friend, (if he may be permitted to call himself so), the Honorable Mr. Dixon, of Kentucky, that it shall be touched off softly; and he seems to entertain no further doubt that the ball can be safely caught in a cast iron kettle.

Mr. Everett has not the slightest idea that slavery can exist in Kansas and Nebraska. To be sure, household slaves will be taken there. That his honorable southern friends admit; but then he, Mr. Everett—benevolent, innocent gentleman that he is—really cannot believe that slavery will exist there long. He has been told that there is no great practical question at issue, and he believes it. He is credulously holding the cast iron kettle, and when the cannon shall have been fired off, he shall be very much surprised if he does not catch the ball.

Senator Badger is quite positive that the question is of no practical importance. But he becomes as plaintive as a mourning dove while discussing the subject, and asks, if, in God's name, he should be debarred from taking his servants, next to his immediate kindred, he loves as well as he does anybody on earth—should he be debarred from taking them with him to this new territory? And should a gentleman be deprived of carrying with him the old colored woman at whose breast he was nursed, and whom he called "mammy" until he left home for college, and, perhaps, after his return? All this the pathetic gentleman regards as extremely cruel.

But we should like to have the distinguished gentleman from North Carolina—the pathetic senator—we should like to have either of them inform us what is to become of one of these dear old "mammies" or of these precious household servants, in case their owner should happen, from any cause, to become insolvent, and an execution should be levied on his human chattels by the sherrif? These dear creatures in that case, are stripped and inspected by heartless speculators, and knocked off to the highest bidder. Such things are of common, if not of every-day, occurrence at Richmond. Where is the slave auction block that a "mammy's" foot never mounted?

Not many years have elapsed since a gentleman, who has had the honor to fill a much higher office than has ever been held by the North Carolina senator—a gentleman, too, distinguished for his amiability—was constrained, by pecuniary embarrassments voluntarily to dispose of a mulatto "household servant" on whose features his own image was stamped as plainly and indelibly as the Eagle and the "*E pluribus unum*" were ever stamped upon an American coin. Will slaves be held only, and never sold, in Kansas and Nebraska?

Again the blacks are a most prolific race. What is to become of the offspring and descendents of these household servants and dear mammies?

No; such propositions are almost too weak to require serious refutation. Wherever slavery goes, the whole brood of evils which naturally appertain to the accursed institution, will follow in its train.

JAPAN AND JAPANESE EXPEDITIONS
March 7, 1854

Having visited Japan in July 1853 with a naval squadron at the behest of President Fillmore in an insuccessful attempt to secure a treaty with that country, which at that time refused intercourse with the West, Commodore Matthew Galbraith Perry returned there in February 1854 and concluded a treaty at Yokohama opening Japan to occidental nations. The verse quotation is from Thomas Gray, The Bard, *I, ii. Bayard Taylor, one of the "supernumeraries" to whom Bryant refers, was a prolific writer of travel books and a journalist with the New York* Tribune. *In 1846 Commodore James Biddle had visited Tokyo Bay, but the Japanese had rejected American trade. Commodore George Henry Preble was later distinguished in the Civil War. In 1851 a filibustering expedition led by General Narciso Lopez, a Spanish refugee, and supported by Southern annexationists, failed for a second time to arouse a Cuban revolution. Lopez was captured and executed in Havana.*

What will Commodore Perry do? His well-provided squadron, with its invincible tars, its complement of scientific travellers and supernumeraries, its supply of cannons and other firearms, its presents for his Japanese Majesty, and under the patronage of an administration whose prodigality was, to say the least, bounded by nothing short of its constitutional restrictions, set forth in gallant trim,

"Youth at the prow and pleasure at the helm."

as if the main purpose of those enthusiastic adventurers had been, whatever reverses they might encounter, to have a good time.

This object, at least, has been attained. The national treasury has been bled in their behalf, to we do not know what amount. Our jolly midshipmen have had the full benefit of their excursion to foreign parts, free of expense. They have even secured a landing, an exploit which Bayard Taylor thus jubilantly recounts:

"On the 14th of July, 1853, the shores of Japan witnessed for the first time in two hundred and fifty years, the landing of an armed foreign force. It was a most brilliant and imposing spectacle. Long lines of Japanese soldiers, with their splendid banners and gay devices, and the American armed force, with the determined look of the gallant tars, combined to form a picture which none who shared in it can ever forget. The very stars on our ensign seemed to brighten as the flagstaff which held them was planted in Japanese soil; and when, after the interview, the band played 'Hail Columbia' and 'Yankee Doodle' the glow of the weather-beaten faces of the American force told, that whatever might happen, the honor of the flag would be maintained."

But there are certain other objects, apart from that of furnishing our naval officers with an experience of foreign travel, in which they have not been, and from all appearances are not likely to be, so successful. These objects—the ostensible grounds of the enterprise—were, the securing of good treatment for our shipwrecked sailors, supplies of wood and coal for our destitute ships that may touch the coast of Japan, and the opening of commercial relations between that country and our own. To be sure, the President's letter, embracing these demands, was presented to the Emperor, together with the announcement, that after a short cruise along the shores of the neighboring empire, the commodore could return to await the reply, in the following spring; but before that delightful season has the occasion to smile on the transaction, information is received, that nothing can be done; that the potentate of Jeddo has expired, and that according to the rule in such cases made and provided, no diplomatic negotiations can be attended to for three years! Whether this be one of the ancient, established regulations of the kingdom, or a mere invention to stave off the consequences of Perry's second visit, is not certain. Or whether the Emperor be actually frightened to death by the terrible visages of our Yankee marines, or, to use the backwoodsmen's phraseology, be only "playing possum," is equally left to conjecture. The former supposition is, doubtless, more consonant with the views of the commodore, while the Emperor's known dislike of the expedition, and the duplicity of the Japanese nature, afford color to the latter. At any rate, without some further enlightenment on the matter, the American squadron will be obliged to return home, while our merchants would have been much better satisfied had the money expended on it been devoted to a scientific exploration of the shoals which endanger the navigation of the seas over which it has been cruising.

We cannot but regret the failure of the attempt of our squadron to accomplish the purposes for which it was equipped; but the national mortification may find some relief in remembering the similar and even more disastrous mishaps of previous trials, on the part of foreign governments. The Portuguese, Dutch and English nations have each zealously entered into the contest for the trade of Japan, and each, after gaining a transient foothold, has repeatedly been obliged to retire. On one occasion, indeed, the English were allowed the very same concessions, ratified by the Emperor, which the United States have, so far, sought in vain. At last, however, in 1640, the Dutch obtained the monopoly of the Japanese commerce on nearly the same humiliating terms on which it still exists. They were then permitted to retain a factory on the island of Nagasaki, and to import such articles as the Emperor might require. An arrangement which, notwithstanding the disagreeable restrictions connected with it, yields them an immense revenue. The cautious and ceremonious way in which their business is conducted is thus described: About the time the Dutch ships are expected, several outposts are stationed on the highest hills by the government, fully provided with telescopes. When seen at a distance, notice is given to the governor of Nagasaki. As soon as they anchor in the harbor, officers go on board with interpreters, to whom is delivered a chest, in which all the sailors' books, the muster roll of the whole crew, six small barrels of powder, six barrels of balls, six muskets, six bayonets, six pistols, and six swords are deposited, this being the whole remaining ammunition allowed after the imperial garrison has been saluted. These articles are conveyed on shore and housed, but restored on the day when the ship quits harbor. The wares, the kinds of which are strictly defined in advance, are then taken out exclusively by Japanese officials, who also reload the ship, while all intercourse with the inhabitants is prohibited to the crew.

In the efforts, however, to establish intercourse with Japan, our own nation, even at an early period, in its history, has not failed by default. As there were great men before Agamemnon, so there have been Japanese expeditions before that of Perry. Long before our whalers floated in the Pacific, American vessels had visited Japan; and during the war of 1812 the intercourse between Batavia and Nagasaki, was carried on by American vessels. In 1807, also, an American shipmaster, Captain King, on the arrival in China of a number of Japanese sailors, fitted out a vessel with merchandise and sailed for Japan with the Japanese sailors; but he committed the mistake of going unarmed, and had no sooner anchored in the bay of Jeddo, than he was driven off and returned to China. In 1846, Commodore Biddle was dispatched with the ships Columbus and Vincennes, by our government, to open a communication with the island. He allowed himself to be surrounded by a cordon of boats, who watched him during his whole stay. Indeed, so little did he impress the Japanese with sentiments of respect, that on visiting a junk, he had no sooner stepped upon her deck, than he was tumbled back into his boat.

Com. Preble, on visiting the islands to recover two American sailors who were in the hands of the Japanese, pursued a different course. He demanded their release within two days, and although the Japanese brought their guns to bear on his decks, and thousands of hostile people lined the coasts, boldly sailed up the bay to a suitable anchorage. At the expiration of two days, the men were safely under the American flag. An equally dignified and commanding style of negotiation was adopted by Commodore Perry, whose expedition succeeded that of Preble. We should certainly rejoice to witness the accomplishment of the purposes of these expeditions, especially in view of the rich opening it promises to our commercial enterprise. Here are probably fifty millions of people who, under proper influences, might be converted into our most desirable customers; not like the stolid average of the Asiatic races, but a set of oriental Yankees, of a decidedly down-east pattern, fore-handed, inventive, courageous, skilled in manufactures, arts and sciences, and careful to provide for themselves not merely the necessaries of life, but also some of the luxuries of cultivated nations. And we cannot doubt that a further acquaintance with their brethren of another hemisphere, will induce them to dispense with the law by which any of the natives, who has ventured to enjoy the hospitality of other nations, must submit to the inconvenience of losing his head.

These people occupy a numerous group of islands, extending from the 80th to the 41st degree of latitude, and from the 130th to the 147th degree of east longitude, with a climate and soil favorable to the growth of all the varied productions of the tropics, having an abundance of the precious and useful metals, and opening for the use of our future steamers, coal-beds of inexhaustible fertility. Travelers from Marco Polo, who have described this country, from the accounts of the Chinese down to Bayard Taylor, unite in its praise. "The island of Loo Choo," says the latter adventurer, "is one of the most beautiful in the world, and contains a greater variety of scenery than I had ever seen within the same extent of territory. It is remarkably well cultivated. Its villages are embowered with arching lines of bamboo, and a tree resembling the magnolia in its foliage. In the valleys the sego, palm, and banana trees give the landscape the characteristics of the tropics, while on the hills the pines recall the temperate zone. The southern part of the island is a vast garden."

Alas! that such golden chances for American commerce should be lost! that a Canaan so rich and so enticing to our fillibustering propensities should, on account of the stolid, impracticable depotism that lies like a nightmare on its resources be closed against us! Is not the earth the common heritage of humanity? and is not some compliment due to human nature? Is not the maxim, that we should so use our own as not to incommode another, applicable to communities and nations as well as to individuals? And is not the present state of things in Japan a serious inconvenience to the universal Yankee nation—a grievance, in fact, demanding our prompt interference? Who can deny it? So reasoned Filmore's administration. So, or nearly so, also, though in another case, reasoned the followers of Lopez.

Unfortunately, this philosophy, like many others, has its obstacles to encounter. It often leads to the gallows, to decapitation, and to the garotte, and is, consequently, not so popular as it otherwise might be. Our own country can only afford to make a partial application of the theory to those nations whose feebleness and unprotected condition, or, in other words, whose "manifest destiny" indicates a fitness for its operation.

All we can do for the present then, is to lie on our oars, and await further developments. Commodore Perry must come home. But we will not surrender the hope that something may yet be done. We have some outstanding grievances that are not yet rectified. If we cannot establish commercial intercourse with the Japanese, we can, at least, insist that they shall not imprison or murder our shipwrecked sailors, and that our vessels entering their ports in distress shall have such relief as common humanity requires. Until these points are gained, his Japanese Majesty may as well resign himself to the troublesome visits of his barbarous contemporaries.

THE KNOW-NOTHING MOVEMENT
August 16, 1854

The American—popularly known as the "Know-Nothing"—Party, the anti-foreign and anti-Catholic Nativism of the 1840s, was briefly revived after the national election of 1852. By 1854 it was a powerful political force, but within two years more it began to decline with the growth of the new Republican Party. The Alien and Sedition acts of 1798, passed during the Presidency of John Adams, were chiefly aimed at foreign-born opponents of his administration. The acts were repealed after Thomas Jefferson took office in 1801. In the 1854 St. Louis elections a riot resulted in the death of ten men, and in New Orleans four died in clashes between native and foreign groups.

In less than a year a new party has suddenly risen into notice, with no public meetings, no loud boasting of its strength, apparently with none of the ordinary instruments of electioneering, and without the countenence of any of the leading politicians, who are generally not slow in observing which way the cat is about to jump. Already it exercises an important, and in some cases, a controlling influence in most if not all the cities and large towns in the country. Boston, Philadelphia, Baltimore, St. Louis, New Orleans and Mobile, in their municipal elections, have all told a story of the triumphs, more or less complete, of the Know-Nothings, and even in our own city, last fall, their influence was felt without any previous suspicion on the part of outsiders, to an almost decisive extent. It is not easy on account of the secrecy of their operations, to form a very close estimate of their exact aggregate strength; but an intelligent Boston correspondent of this paper, upon a careful reckoning, lays their numbers for Massachusetts alone at not less than forty thousand—sufficient to control the election.

What is to be the end of these things? What will these formidable Know-Nothings do? are questions that are naturally suggested.

The Know-Nothings may flourish for their brief hour. By coalescing with parties and sections of parties, they make demonstrations that will utterly confound the shrewdest political calculations. They may possibly, by rebuking the unwise assumptions and clannishness of a few of the leaders of our foreign-born population, do some good. But the party is necessarily short-lived, and will speedily disappear, as all parties must which are founded on a platform so narrow and so in conflict with the principles of democracy.

The inexpediency of adopting, as a cardinal article of political faith, a principle like that of the Know-Nothings, which makes a discrimination unfavorable to our foreign population, was strikingly illustrated in the fate of the federal party, as well as in the more recent instance of Native Americanism. The two most objectionable features of the federal alien and sedition acts were the extension of the period of naturalization from five years to fourteen, and giving to the President the power, in case of war or invasion, to apprehend, secure, or remove at his discretion, all resident aliens who were natives or citizens of the hostile nation. This prerogative we know was never exercised, but, from the time of the passage of the act conferring it, an outcry of opposition was raised, which resulted in the defeat of John Adams, and sealed the downfall of the federal party.

There is, moreover, not a little danger in widening the space between our native and adopted citizens, and in giving the latter a distinct and isolated character under the denominations of Irishmen, Germans, Catholics. No such distinction should be recognized. They are all, in the regard of our laws and the Constitution, Americans, and any attempt to aggravate the natural jealousy and enmity of race should be frowned down, from whatever quarter it may come. Especially should the sectarian element in our politics be discountenanced. The vindictiveness of bigotry, when fairly roused, as all history teaches, is not scrupulous in sanctioning the most inhuman and detestable instruments for accomplishing its purpose, and will carry its subjects to greater excesses than any other motive, however selfish and unworthy. We need only revert to the late elections in St. Louis and New Orleans, which were marked to an unprecedented degree by tumult and bloodshed, to obtain a premonition of the probable results of a combined political and religious agitation in our own vicinity.

We do not believe that any organization, however adroitly managed, could subjugate this government to the control of a foreign power. The influences which bear upon our emigrant population are, almost without exception, such as tend to identify them with the interests of their adopted country, and would effectually stand in the way of any combination hostile to its welfare.

In the course of one or two generations these different races will become inseparably fused together with those whose ancestors emigrated at an earlier period. The children of the "aliens" of this generation will be native Americans in the next.

In the meantime we must not overlook the immeasurable benefits which this new country is reaping from its large foreign-born population. If turbulence sometimes grows out of their inexperience and their crude notions of liberty, it can easily be checked. But let us not be deluded or frightened into a needless crusade against the venerable and harmless hobgoblins, "Popery" and "Foreign Influence."

A Short Method with Disunionists
September 26, 1855

When in 1832 a state convention in South Carolina had passed an ordinance declaring United States tariff laws null and void, President Jackson secured from the Congress a bill authorizing him to enforce these laws by the use of troops, if necessary. This caused South Carolina to rescind its ordinance. David R. Atchison and B. F. Stringfellow were Democratic pro-slavery leaders and agitators in the Kansas Territory.

The Richmond *Enquirer* calls the attention of its readers to an article in the Greenville *Patriot*, a South Carolina journal, the views of which, it observes, it "seconds most heartily," beginning thus:

> "Northern Disunion.—We call the attention of southern disunionists to the article from the New Haven *Register*, headed 'The Disunionists Backing Out.' That the state of Massachusetts will back out from her abolition nullification whenever the issue comes, we have no doubt. But we do not wish those northern nullifiers and disunionists to back out. We wish to have the gratification of seeing them whipped out. The general government must give some signal instance of its ability to maintain itself. Old Massachusetts, 'the cradle of liberty,' is as fit place for this bloody contest as any other, and there is no blood more worthy of being shed to moisten the tree of liberty than that of the abolitionists."

This is the language they use at the South when disunion shows its northern face; they defy it to do its worst, and give themselves no further trouble about it. The defiance is well enough, though the style of the Greenville print, we must acknowledge, is a little ruffianly. When any party or any state talks of disunion, the true method of dealing with them is not to yield to their complaints or their threats anything which is not called for by a simple regard to justice; but, on the contrary, to keep on in a firm and even course till the unreasonable clamorers become weary. A good nurse understands this in the treatment of children; when they cry for what they ought not to have, and refuse to be pacified without it, she lets them cry themselves to sleep. If they are permitted to learn that their most unreasonable desires will be gratified if they only cry loudly and perseveringly, they will keep the nursery in a perpetual uproar. The way to keep the place quiet, she knows well, is to let them see they gain nothing by making a noise.

In our dealings with the South, we have for the most part taken a different method. The child has been allowed to have whatever it took a fancy to cry for. Missouri was received into our confederacy as a slave state under the threat of disunion. The compromise acts of 1850 were passed under the same threat. The Nebraska act was got through Congress partly by bribery, it is true, but partly, also, by bluster. Now we are told that if Stringfellow and his associates succeed in their plan of getting up the show of an application to Congress from Kansas for admission into our confederacy, with a constitution drawn up to their own liking, and Congress reject it, the Union will be broken into fragments. The trick of threatening a dissolution of the Union has been so successful that it is tried on every occasion.

We have had one memorable example of refusing the demands of the South, which ought to have convinced us of the benefit of a firm policy towards that quarter of the Union—a policy looking only to the right, leaving the event to Providence. Andrew Jackson was not the man to be moved by any threat of the dissolution of the Union, coming from any quarter. When the politicians of South Carolina sought to engage the other southern states in a conspiracy to withdraw from the confederacy, Andrew Jackson held South Carolina in its place with a firm hand, and disconcerted the whole plot, by the mere exhibition of a calm determination to keep the states together.

All that we of the North have to do when the questions raised by the late events in Kansas [come] before Congress for its decision, when the dispute respecting the authority of the legislature imposed upon Kansas by Atchison and Stringfellow shall be brought into the House of Representatives, is to imitate the coolness and unconcern for the event shown by General Jackson in dealing with nullification in South Carolina, and we shall come out of the controversy with the same success.

The Geography of Nativism
September 27, 1855

The New York branch of a recently formed Nativist society, the "Order of the Star-Spangled Banner," had hosted two national conventions of the society at New York in May and June of 1854. Governor Henry J. Gardener of Massachusetts, a former Whig elected as a Nativist in 1854, was one of a very few men of moderate distinction to attend a national convention of Know-Nothings at Philadelphia in 1855. Augustus Baldwin Longstreet, a Methodist minister and president of the University of Mississippi, had published the popular Georgia Scenes *at New York in 1840.*

It is worthy of notice that as the controversy between the Nativists and their adversaries in the northern states becomes obsolete and is dying out, in consequence of the growing weakness of that party, which arose so suddenly, achieved so many victories, and passed so soon into its decreptitude, the conflict at the South is carried on with greater heat and vehemence. We have amused ourselves this morning with looking over the newspapers brought by the mails from all parts of the Union, with a view of seeing what proportion of their attention is occupied by the question of repealing the naturalization laws. In the large majority of journals published in the free states the dispute is scarce once alluded to. It seems to be regarded as a subject which has been exhausted—on which the people have made up their minds, and there is no more to be said. It is true that there is a dispute in the newspapers of this state concerning the time when Curtiss Hawley withdrew his name from the list of Know-Nothings, and in some of the western states there is a disagreement as to the relations which a Mr. Johnson or a Judge Johnson bears to the order. There is a little effervescence among the friends of Governor Gardener at Boston, and we have the proceedings of the Know-Nothing convention in this state duly chronicled, but beyond this, there is scarce a sign of life in the Nativist party in all the northern states. The journals are occupied with the Kansas question, with the Maine law question, with the war in the East, the politics of Europe, the revolution in Mexico, and almost every other matter except the discussion of the question whether the citizens of foreign birth shall be denied political rights. In regard to that controversy, every circumstance conspires to strengthen the belief that the public mind at the North has become settled in a fixed aversion to any change.

The moment we step over Mason and Dixon's line we find a different state of things. There the dispute wages with a virulence which proves the combatants to be in earnest. We take up a Baltimore paper—it is occupied with arguments for or against the repeal of the laws allowing political rights to the emigrants. Here is the Richmond *Enquirer*; it devotes two elaborate columns to an attack on the Know-Nothing association, in which the whig party of Virginia is merged. Here is the *National American*, a daily print, published also at Richmond, which makes a counterattack of as many columns. Here is the Savannah *Republican*, defending the cause of what it calls the

American Party, and publishing a florid account of a mass meeting of that party at Macon, with reports of the eloquent and masterly things said in its defence by Judge Garnett Andrews and Mr. James E. Belser. Here is the Savannah *Georgian,* demolishing the same party in an equally eloquent and masterly speech of Mr. Wm. H. Stiles, delivered at a meeting of the other side, held last week in Savannah. The *Union,* published at Nashville, Tennessee, is filled from first to last with discussions of the propriety of secret oaths and mysteries as the bonds of the Know-Nothing organization; the Brandon *Platform,* a Mississippi paper, discharges a letter of six columns, not yet concluded, written by the Honorable J. D. Freeman, against the same organization; the Florida *Sentinel* ridicules its orators, and the Mississippi *Free Trader* labors to show that the Know-Nothing party is identical with that of the abolitionists. On the other hand, the Washington *Telegraph,* an Arkansas print, quotes passages from the writings of Thomas Jefferson to show that the Nativism of the present day is a much milder doctrine, and far more favorable to the rights of foreigners, than the Nativism of Jefferson himself. The New Orleans *Crescent* vindicates the right of a party association to lay its plans in secret and to secure them from disclosures by oaths; and on the other side the New Orleans *Courier,* publishes a letter of A. B. Longstreet—President Longstreet, it calls him—addressed to the Methodist Church South, the object of which is to dissuade the Methodist clergy from lending their influence to the cause of Nativism.

From day to day the southern journals keep up this war, which for the time leaves them little leisure to attend to their controversy with the North. The ardor and perseverance with which it is carried on by both the parties to it can scarcely be appreciated except by those who are in the practice of frequently looking over the southern journals. Whatever may be the cause, it is evident that Nativism has struck deeper root at the South than here, and is likely to maintain itself with more vigor and constancy against its adversaries.

The Republican Convention
September 29, 1855

The New York State Republican Party held its inaugural convention in September 1855. Abijah Mann, like Bryant, was a former leading New York Democrat who had switched his allegiance to the new Republican Party. The "Accident of an Accident" was probably Attorney General Caleb Cushing.

There is no doubt that in the resolutions adopted by the late Republican and Whig Conventions, in regard to slavery, the candidates in their joint nomination have an element of strength which no other ticket will possess. They express distinctly, unequivocally and earnestly the sentiment of at least three-fourths of the people of this state in regard to the administration policy in Kansas, and that has been done by no other convention. In the selection of candidates an equally distinct issue is made with the Kansas–Nebraska party. Not a man is named about whose views any doubt can be entertained; not a man (with a single exception, perhaps,) who is not prepared to make the nationality of freedom and the sectionality of slavery paramount to every other political question in the present canvass.

Among them will be recognized some whose names have been identified with the most memorable triumphs of the democratic party during the last quarter of a century—men who in various public capacities have served their country with distinguished ability and fidelity; men who have been exposed to such temptations as are rarely resisted, and who have come from them like gold from the refiner's fire, more pure and more deservedly valued. They have been constrained to form new, and, to some extent, perhaps uncongenial associations by the course pursued by their old friends, and to take upon themselves the responsibility of commencing the dissolution of an organization which has ceased to serve the cause of freedom and justice.

We cannot announce this result without emotion. We cannot look with indifference upon old personal and political friends, whose joys have been our joys—and whose sorrows have been our sorrows,—men whose honor and patriotism are above suspicion, arrayed against each other, with their swords crossed and ready, we had almost said, to spill fraternal blood.

And who is responsible for this painful spectacle? But one answer can be given. The delegates who composed the Syracuse Convention of the 29th of August, who, instead of reflecting the sentiments of their constituents, chose to take their law of action from Washington; who, instead of letting New York be ruled by New Yorkers, have taken counsel from the Washington *Union,* the Richmond *Enquirer* and Caleb Cushing; they are responsible. Rather than break their relations with such creatures as direct the slavery policy of President Pierce, they have consented to alienate from their organization democrats like Preston King and Abijah Mann, either of whom is more valuable to whatever party they connect themselves than a wilderness of such men as the Accident of an Accident, who now dispenses the patronage of this government at Washington.

One by one the leading democrats of the nation, who have given to the party its fame and to democratic principles their popularity, have been driven from public life by the proscriptive influence of slavery.

Messrs. Mann and King have concluded that this course has been pursued about long enough, and that the party which bears the name of democracy should feed upon something beside its traditionary merits; that all its value should not be like that of the potato, under the ground, and that living principles are better worth fighting for than dead heroes. They have yielded, therefore, like the Israelites of old, to the necessity of going out of Egypt to wander for a while in the wilderness, until they shall find the men who are fit to enter with them and enjoy the Land of Promise, where the true democracy shall have no enemies to fear.

Charity Made Easy
February 18, 1856

Mrs. Lincoln, Presidentrix of the American Ladies' Association for the Benefit of American Orphan Girls, who was arrested recently for getting money under the pretence of conducting an institution of charity, handed us for publication, the other day, what purports to be a statement of the financial management of the institution under her charge from its commencement. It professes to give the sum total of the receipts and expenditures up to the 1st January, 1856.

It did not quite come up to our notions of an official report from a lady who bears such a formidable title, and, as she was at the time in bonds for swindling, we concluded, before giving publicity to so much bad ciphering and worse grammar, to send a reporter to see what sort of an institution Mrs. Presidentrix Lincoln conducted. His report will be found in another column. It contains about all the information the public requires, except the verdict which the jury will surrender at her trial.

Her books, it appears, do not give the items of her cash receipts, and in stating her expenses she leaves out of her first statement what she paid for provisions and fuel for her recipients, which she says, at the time of her arrest, were eighteen in number, besides her brother and herself, though our reporter says there were but six beds in the whole house.

There were two or three of the fair beneficiaries visible when he first called, though Mrs. Lincoln assured him that fourteen were now in the plenary fruition of her bounty. He asked where they were, and was told that part of the other ten had gone to the theatre, and the rest on a pleasure trip to Brooklyn. He was promised a sight of them, however, the next evening, if he would call, but it did not appear that the rest of the party had got back from the theatre and the other pleasure excursion.

We recommend our citizens to give Mrs. Presidentrix Lincoln and her "travellers" a wide berth. They have done all the good to American orphans they are likely to do this season, we fancy.

The Outrage on Mr. Sumner
May 23, 1856

On May 20 Senator Charles Sumner of Massachusetts had attacked the Kansas–Nebraska Act in an uncompromising speech, "The crime Against Kansas," intemperately criticizing Senators Andrew P. Butler of South Carolina and Stephen A. Douglas of Illinois for supporting it. Two days later while seated at his Senate desk Sumner was violently clubbed by a relative of Butler's, Representative Preston S. Brooks of South Carolina, abetted by another South Carolina Congressman, Lawrence M. Keitt. Although Sumner managed to return very briefly to the Senate a year later, he was incapacitated for three and one-half years, and suffered lingering effects until his death eighteen years after the beating.

The friends of slavery at Washington are attempting to silence the members of Congress from the free States by the same modes of discipline which make the slaves unite on their plantations. Two ruffians from the House of Representatives, named Brooks and Keit[t], both from South Carolina, yesterday made the Senate Chamber the scene of their cowardly brutality. They had armed themselves will heavy canes, and approaching Mr. Summer, while sitting in his chair engaged in writing, Brooks struck him with his cane a violent blow on the head, which brought him stunned to the floor, and Keit[t] with his weapon kept off the by-standers, while the other ruffian repeated the blows upon the head of the apparently lifeless victim till his cane was shattered to fragments. Mr. Sumner was conveyed from the Senate chamber bleeding and senseless, so severely wounded that the physician attending did not think it prudent to allow his friends to have access to him.

The excuse for this base assault is, that Mr. Sumner, on the Senate floor, in the course of a debate had spoken disrespectfully of Mr. Butler, a relative of Preston S. Brooks, one of the authors of this outrage. No possible indecorum of language on the part of Mr. Sumner could excuse, much less justify an attack like this; but we have carefully examined his speech to see if it contains any matter which could even extenuate such an act of violence, and find none. He had ridiculed Mr. Butler's devotion to slavery, it is true, but the weapon of ridicule in debate is by common consent as fair and allowable a weapon as argument. The *Journal of Commerce* of this morning apologizes for the brutality of Brooks and his confederate, by saying that Mr. Sumner was guilty of "wholesale denunciation and bitter personalities;" and quotes what the Washington *Star* says of the character of Mr. Sumner's speech. What the Washington *Star* may say is nothing to the purpose; the question is what Mr. Sumner said, and as this has been published, the *Journal* should have placed it before its readers, that they might judge for themselves. It prudently, however, keeps the provocation, whatever it might be, out of sight. Our readers have already had the speech, and we leave it to them to say whether there is any wholesale denunciation or bitter personality in it; whether it contains anything which goes beyond the fair decorum of debate. There is surely, no wholesale denunciation—for Mr. Butler is assailed on one point only, his insane devotion to slavery; there is no bitter personality in it, for his character as a man in the ordinary relations of life is left unquestioned. We agree fully with Mr. Sumner that Mr. Butler is a monomaniac in the respect of which we speak; we certainly should place no confidence in any representation he might make which concerned the subject of slavery, and we say this without any expectation of an attempt being made upon our lives, or even of having our heads broken, for our boldness.

Has it come to this that we must speak with bated breath in the presence of our Southern masters; that even their follies are too sacred a subject for ridicule; that we must not deny the consistency of their principles or the accuracy of their statements? If we venture to laugh at them or question their logic, or dispute their facts, are we to be chastised as they chastise their slaves? Are we too, slaves, slaves for life, a target for their brutal blows, when we do not comport ourselves to please them? If this be so, it is time that the people of the free States knew it, and prepared themselves to acquiesce in their fate. They have labored under the delusion hitherto that they were their own masters.

Even if it were true, as it is not, that there were "wholesale denunciation and bitter personalities" against Mr. Butler in Mr. Sumner's speech, the denunciation should have been repelled and personalities rebuked by some of the fluent speakers of the powerful majority to which Mr. Butler belongs, and the matter should have ended there. The sudden attack made with deadly weapons upon an unarmed man in the Senate Chamber, where he could not expect it or have been prepared for it, was the act of men who must be poltroons as well as ruffians. It was as indecent, also, as it was cowardly; the Senate floor should be sacred from such outrages; or if they are common, if at all, it should only be by Senatorial blackguards. It is true that the Senate had just adjourned, but the members were still there, many of them in their places; it was their chamber, and this violence committed in their presence was an insult to their body. Yet we have no expectation that the Senate will do anything to vindicate the sacredness and peace of their chamber, or the right of their members not to be called to account for words spoken in debate. There will be a little discussion; some will denounce and some will defend the assault, and then the matter will end.

The truth is, that the pro-slavery party, which rules in the Senate, looks upon violence as the proper instrument of its designs. Violence reigns in the streets of Washington; violence has now found its may into the Senate chamber. Violence lies in wait on all the navigable rivers and all the railways of Missouri, to obstruct those who pass from the free States into Kansas. Violence overhangs the frontiers of that territory like a storm-cloud charged with hail and lightning. Violence has carried election after election in that territory. In short, violence is the order of the day; the North is to be pushed to the wall by it, and this plot will succeed if the people of the free States are as apathetic as the slaveholders are insolent.

CONGRESSIONAL PRIVILEGE
May 24, 1856

Aethelbert, King of Kent (560–616?), promulgated the earliest surviving Anglo-Saxon code of laws. The Plantagenet sovereigns ruled England from 1154 to 1485; the Stuarts from 1603 to 1714; Roman Catholic rulers were Mary Tudor (1553–1558), James II (1685–1688), and Charles II (1660–1685), who professed his faith secretly in 1670 and openly on his deathbed. Sir Fortunatus Dwarris was the author of A General Treatise on Statutes *(1830–1831); John Hatsel, of* A Collection of Cases of Privilege of Parliament *(1776) and* Precedents of Proceedings in the House of Commons *(1781).*

Both houses of Congress have ordered committees to examine and report to them the circumstances attending the late assault upon Senator Sumner. So far well. It is important that they should have official evidence that one of their number had been assaulted, or in the words of the constitution, had been "questioned for words spoken in debate." Beyond that, so far as Congressional penalties are concerned, the facts are of trifling importance; and outside of the wide circle of Senator Sumner's personal friends, the question is not as to the depth or length of his wounds—not the amount of brutality necessary to the creature who could have inflicted them—nor yet the nature or extent of the provocation, if any, which Mr. Sumner had given in his speech—it is simply this: Has the freedom of speech of the United States Senate been put in peril? has a senator been questioned by a person not a member of that body and put in bodily peril for words uttered in debate? If he has, then the constitution has been violated; the law of Congress, the *lex parlimentaria* which Blackstone calls "the most essential part of the common law, as it directs, guides and ought to protect the very formation of all laws," has been violated, the dignity and supremacy of a co-ordinate branch of the government has been invaded; a wrong has been perpetuated which if not properly punished, exposes every department of the government to the intimidating influence of brutality and violence, and must soon compel even the President himself to surround his person and fortify his residence with a military guard.

There never was a time when England was barbarous enough to excuse any violence to a member of their Parliament, or to permit the author of such an offence to go unpunished. The right to "freedom of speech," is coëval with the existence of Parliaments and legislative assemblies; and is protected against every encroachment, whether under color of laws, or by open and ruffian violence. In England, it is protected by statute, as one of the liberties of the people; and with us, the constitution of the United States declares that senators and representatives, "for any speech in debate in either house, shall not be questioned in any other place."

"If the King," (says the old Saxon law of Ethelbert,) "does an injury to one of them, let him be fined." This was the Anglo-Saxon spirit in the earliest antiquity.

Under the Plantagenets, a period not remarkable for its political liberty, the Commons demanded a rigorous punishment of one who had assaulted a member. In the times of Roman Catholic rule, and under Protestant Elizabeth, two offenders were imprisoned by the Commons for striking members. Under the Stuarts, a fellow who, like one of our southern bullies, was seen around the House "with a pistol charged with three bullets," threatening the members, was committed a close prisoner.

Here English precedents end, for strange as it may appear to the chivalrous members of the South, we can find no reported cases of violence in either House of Parliament for the last two hundred years. The American case, which is to form a weighty precedent, is yet to be reported.

Even to this day, the Speaker of the House of Commons, following a custom as old as the British constitution, immediately after his election, waits upon his monarch and prays for a pledge that the members of the House, over which he presides, shall enjoy entire freedom of debate, without risk of being called to account elsewhere, for anything they may say, and he gets it.

We trust the American Parliament does not place a lower estimate upon its liberties than the English, and that there will be a disposition among a majority of both houses to establish a precedent in this case, which will not compare discreditably with those reported by Dwarris and Hatsel, in the days of the Plantagenets and the Stuarts.

The responsibility for fixing the parliamentary penalties which belongs to Mr. Brooks's assault rests with the House of Representatives. We presume there is no authority in the Senate to punish any offence committed even upon its own members by a member of the other House. The Senate exhausts its power when it reports the offence to the other body, or to the civil tribunals, and asks that the offender be tried and punished. That the Senate ought to do at once. Only a few hours can be needed to ascertain the facts necessary to give the Senate an occasion for the exercise of its utmost power in the premises, and the sooner that power is exercised, the longer it will be before Congress will be the theatre of another such disgraceful scene.

The Representatives have scarcely a broader issue to investigate than the Upper House. The severest penalty they can impose is expulsion, and Mr. Brooks admitted yesterday, in his place, all that is necessary to convict him of having assaulted a member of the Senate for words spoken in debate, for which the heaviest penalty is the mildest that the House can possibly think of imposing. Anything short of that must cover them with infamy, and fill the whole country with shame.

Brooks's Canada Song
July 24, 1856

These verses, which Bryant did not reprint in his collected poetry, are in the vein of other doggerel he had directed against editorial opponents in his early years with the Evening Post. *A few days after Brooks's attack on Sumner, Bryant took prominent part in a mass meeting in the Broadway Tabernacle in New York City protesting against "violence as a means . . . of affecting or restraining personal freedom." In the Congress Representative Anson Burlingame of Massachusetts challenged Brooks to a duel in Canada, but Brooks avoided it, drawing the charge of cowardice. William Lloyd Garrison was the most prominent Abolitionist of the day.*

> To Canada, Brooks was asked to go,
> To waste of powder a pound or so,
> He sighed as he answered, No, no, no,
> They might take my life on the way you know.
>   For, I am afraid, afraid, afraid.
>   Bully Brooks is afraid.

Those Jersey railroads I can't abide,
'Tis a dangerous thing in the trains to ride.
Each brakeman carries a knife by his side,
They'd cut my throat, and they'd cut it wide;
              And I am afraid, afraid, afraid.
              Bully Brooks is afraid.

There are savages haunting New York Bay
To murder strangers that pass that way;
The Quaker Garrison keeps them in pay,
And they kill at least a score a day.
              And I am afraid, afraid, afraid.
              Bully Brooks is afraid.

Beyond New York, in every car,
They keep a supply of feathers and tar;
They daub it on with an iron bar,
And I should be smothered ere I got far.
              And I am afraid, afraid, afraid.
              Bully Brooks is afraid.

Those dreadful Yankees talk through the nose;
The sound is terrible, goodness knows;
And, when I hear it, a shiver goes
From the crown of my head to the tips of my toes.
              For I am afraid, afraid, afraid.
              Bully Brooks is afraid.

So, dearest Mr. Burlingame,
I'll stay at home, if 'tis all the same,
And I'll tell the world 'twas a burning shame
That we did not fight, and you're to blame.
              For I am afraid, afraid, afraid.
              Bully Brooks is afraid.

Threats of Disunion from Head Quarters
October 6, 1856

John Charles Frémont, controversial soldier and explorer of the far West, was in 1856 the first Presidential candidate of the new Republican Party; his victorious Democratic opponent was James Buchanan of Philadelphia. "Both in a tale": that is, in agreement. Much Ado About Nothing, *IV, ii, 34. John Buchanan Floyd had been governor of Virginia from 1849 to 1852; he became Secretary of War in Buchanan's cabinet in 1857. John Minor Botts, former Whig Congressman from Virginia, was a strong advocate of an indissoluble Union, for which he was threated with lynching by the* Virginia Enquirer. *Governor Henry Alexander Wise of Virginia warned voters against supporting Frémont, whose election, he charged, would* hoist the "Black Republican flag in the hands of an adventurer." Nathaniel P. Banks of Massachusetts, elected Speaker of the House in 1856, was an anti-slavery man. The Washington Union was a Democratic administration organ.

The organ of the administration at Washington has made the discovery that abolitionism and confidence in the duration of the Union are the same thing. "This glorious Union," says the *National Intelligencer*, "has stood firm during sixty years, and, with the blessing of Heaven, it will stand for sixty years longer." "Such remarks," says the Washington *Union*, in reply, "are of genuine abolition coinage." Nobody who does not join in the threat, that if Colonel Freemont [*sic*] is chosen President they will have the Union dissolved can be a friend of slavery. The friends of Buchanan are for a dissolution of the Union, if that event should happen, and Mr. Filmore, for his part, has declared that the Union cannot survive Colonel Freemont's election. "They are both in a tale," as Dogberry says; both are striving to work on the fears of foolish people at the South, in the hope of preventing them from voting for the man of their choice; and if the *National Intelligencer* will not enter into the conspiracy and commit itself against the continuance of the Union if the republican ticket should succeed, it is guilty of downright abolitionism.

While the mouthpiece of the administration is thus intimating the threat of disunion, we have it more plainly expressed by one of the creatures of the administration who has just come from its hands. Representatives newly elected, are said to be fresh from the people, but here is Mr. John Forsyth, of Mobile, our newly-appointed minister to Mexico, fresh from the administration, who says, that if Colonel Freemont is elected, "the South ought not to submit to it," and what is more, *will* not submit to it. "The government of the United States," he says, "will be at an end; there must be a new political organization;" the South will not endure "an abolitionized federal government;" will not "bow down to the yoke of a fanatical Yankee administration." This is Mr. Forsyth's warning to the North, promulgated just after he had received his instructions from the President how to comport himself as our minister to Mexico. It is the last article he writes for the Mobile *Register*, and he probably writes it by dictation.

It will make the North tremble to be told that if the republican candidate should be elected President, and Mr. Forsyth's commission as minister to Mexico should be revoked, he will dissolve the Union. Mr. Forsyth has formed his plan, and it is a most satisfactory one. The fleets of merchant ships which now make the harbor of New York bristle with masts, are to be "moved South." The cotton and woolen mills, the great establishments of the carriage makers, the hatters, the shoemakers and the sadlers are to be "moved South." Capital, enterprise, capitalists and traders are all to be "moved South." In this way it is clear that the South may be expeditiously built up in population and in wealth, and Mr. John Forsyth is doubtless the man to see that it is done. One thing, however, Mr. Forsyth omits to make provision for. What is to be done with James Buchanan if he shall be defeated? Must not he also be "moved South?" They will want a President, as well as owners of merchant ships and cotton mills, as well as carriage makers and hatters.

Mr. Forsyth, fresh from the administration, admits that if there are any chances for Mr. Fillmore, he would be glad to vote for him. In this he agrees with Governor Floyd, that for the sake of securing the extension of slavery in the territories he would consent to put the Know-Nothings in power, with all their plans for altering the naturalization laws, and would give up the advantage of what Governor Floyd called the "foreign vote." But there is no chance for Fillmore, and therefore the South should rally on Buchanan. Meantime that hint is thrown out to let the friends of Mr. Fillmore know that the Buchanan party is ready for a fusion.

It will be seen in looking over Mr. Botts's letter to the editor of the *National American*, which we give today, that he imputes the threats of disunion contained in the speech which Governor Wise delivered the other day at Richmond to a disordered mind. That Wise is not perfectly sane may be true enough—a more well-balanced mind than his might be overset by the excitement and want of sleep of which he complained so pathetically at Richmond, but all this blustering about disunion is simply a deliberately laid plot to frighten the North. If any votes for Buchanan can be obtained by it; if Freemont can be deprived by it of any votes, its object will be effected; if not, no harm will be done; and the politicians of the slave states will submit as quietly as they did when General Jackson enforced the laws of the Union in spite of the nullifiers, and as when Mr. Banks was elected speaker of the House of Representatives.

Our readers may rely upon it, therefore, that Mr. Botts is too charitable. They who make this threat of disunion are more knaves than madmen. Mr. Forsyth and Governor Wise, and the men who speak through the Washington *Union*, if they were absolutely mad, might make a serious attempt to carry their project into effect; but not one of them all at present, has any more thought of attempting a dissolution of the Union than of attempting a dissolution of the solar system. With the election of Colonel Freemont impending over them not the slightest preparation has been made on their part for the event which they so studiously with one voice represent as inevitable.

The Conspiracy Against the Working Class
October 29, 1856

Bryant had visited his brothers, who had homesteaded on the Illinois prairie, five times, most lately in 1854. Professor Benjamin S. Hedrick of the University of North Carolina, a native of that state but educated at Harvard, was forced to resign his position after having stated that, though not an Abolitionist, he thought the South for its own good should re-examine the slavery system, and that, furthermore, he would support Frémont's candidacy. Prince Aleksander Mikhailovich Gorchakov (1798–1883) was Russian Minister of Foreign Affairs, 1856–1882.

That those who are attached to the party of Mr. Buchanan by official ties should give him their support does not surprise us; it is the infirmity of human nature to cheat itself with the idea that what is for our present interest must be right. That those who own slaves at the South, and those at the North who are connected in any way with the slave-holding class by interest or other affinities, should support him is quite natural; he is the slave-holder's candidate. But that any man who depends on the labor of his own hands for sustenance, who wishes that honest labor should be honored, and that the great West should be open to him and the class to which he belongs, and to their children, as a region in which they may exercise their callings without social degradation—that any such man should stand ready to give his vote for Buchanan, is what we cannot account for.

There are, we believe, very few farmers and mechanics at the North who are not fully aware that if slavery goes into the territories, free labor must go out. When they look at the map of the United States they perceive that the slave states are one-fourth larger in their area than the free states. When they look at the census of the United States, they perceive that the number of white inhabitants in the free states, though their area is so much less, is more than twice the population of the slave states. They perceive that slavery is an engrossing, encroaching institution, a greedy devourer of land, requiring three or four times as much space as free labor. They perceive also another important fact, that the less wealthy part of the southern population are constantly migrating to free territory or to the western free states, where labor is held in honor, and where they can till the soil, or toil in other callings requiring bodily exertion, without being regarded as an inferior class. We published the other day a letter from Professor Hedrick of North Carolina, in which he spoke feelingly of this constant necessity of removal to free territory, a necessity which forces his old friends and neighbors to leave their homes, and keeps down the natural increase of population in his native state. The census shows that a large proportion of those who settle the free states of the west come from slave states. Go where you will in the new settlements, you meet the emigrant from Virginia, from Kentucky, from Tennessee, from North Carolina. We have ourselves frequently partaken of the hospitality of those sons of the South in their cabins on the prairies. Southern Ohio, Illinois, and Indiana are peopled by them and their descendants; they follow up the rivers to Iowa, to Wisconsin, to Minnesota, to Nebraska; they help to swell the population of Cinncinati, Chicago, Madison, and the other flourishing towns of the free West. Thus it is the South casts out her offspring; she keeps slavery, and parts with her children, who should make her strength and her honor. Free labor cannot live by the side of the oligarchy which tills the soil by the hands of its bondmen, and sells carpenters, blacksmiths and masons under the hammer. The free white laborer of the South finds that in a thin population public schools cannot be supported. The planter, with a domain of from three to ten thousand acres, can send his children to some private school or keep a tutor; but the poor man must see his children grow up in ignorance. No wonder that he should remove to a place where education is brought to his door, and where labor is no longer a badge of degradation.

If therefore, slavery is introduced into the territories, as the southern politicians, with the co-operation of all that party of the North now supporting Buchanan, are attempting to introduce it, we see what the effect must be. We of the free states, may enter those territories with the purpose of settling there, but if we do not become slaveholders, we must go out again. The farmers who go thither to work with their own hands, must consent to be looked down upon by the planters, with their domains of thousands of acres and their hundreds of work people whose muscles and bones are their property. The white farmer will take his place by the negro field-hand; the white carpenter be looked upon as a proper companion for the black carpenter who is sold at auction. In going to such a community, the farmer from the free states must renounce the advantage of schools; he must see his children brought up as the poorer population of Missouri are brought up, in utter ignorance, and with the propensity to debauchery which is nourished in those who have no intellectual resources. They cannot live in such a community. They will come thronging back to the new free states, as they now come from Virginia and North Carolina, driven out by the stinging sense of degradation which at the South is connected with poverty, and by the frightful dearth of the means of education, which makes this degradation more complete. They will come back to us with their families, all the worse in mind and morals, from their sojourn in a land which to them and their children will have been like the land of Egypt to the Israelites. These are some of the reasons which make the attempt to establish slavery in the territories a direct attack on the rights of the working class. It is a scheme for the benefit of a few, a scheme for the advantage of the three hundred and forty thousand slaveholders of the southern states who form about a twentieth part of the white population of those states. For the sake of that small class of capitalists the country is convulsed with the agitation of the slavery question; for their sake, frauds and violences, which are the scandal of the country are perpetuated with the connivance of the federal government and the direct cooperation of its agents. The class of slaveholders is to be installed in the territories, as the masters of that region, and the people are to be thrust out. This conspiracy against the rights of the working class is as atrocious as if the plan were to give Prince Gortschekoff of Russia the sole right of settling Kansas, with power to introduce the system of serfdom or white slavery which is in practice on his patrimonial estates.

Yet this is the scheme which the working people of the North are called upon to sanction. It is Mr. Pierce's plan; it is Mr. Buchanan's plan. The party under whose auspices it is now in process of execution, have all along supported Mr. Pierce, and have now nominated Mr. Buchanan. They have in solemn conviction passed a resolution approving of the entire policy of Mr. Pierce's administration, and Mr. Buchanan has declared his entire concurrence in that resolution. All the most zealous friends of the extension of slavery support Mr. Buchanan; they consider his success so important, that they threaten to dissolve the Union if a candidate hostile to the extension of slavery is elected. "Tell me who you live with and I will tell you who you are," is an old adage full of wisdom; and if Buchanan's declaration, had not already convicted him, his associations with the slaveholders would be enough. He is now the head of this great conspiracy against the rights of the working class, and not a man of them who votes intelligently can give him his support.

WHAT MAY HAPPEN IN THE NEXT FOUR YEARS
October 31, 1856

The veteran Mexican War soldier John White Geary, a Free-Soil advocate, was appointed governor of Kansas Territory by President Pierce in 1856. During his brief tenure of less than one year he brought calm to the troubled area, but pro-slavery agitators so harried him that in 1857 after Buchanan's inauguration he resigned in broken health. Kenneth Raynor was one of several Congressmen from western North Carolina who were uneasy with the domination of their pro-slavery associates. The verse quotation has not been identified.

The Washington *American Organ*—the central organ, as its name denotes, of the Fillmore party—says of the matter in dispute between the Buchanan party and the Republicans:

> "The Republicans were at first horror-stricken at the passage of the Kansas–Nebraska bill, in the fear that slavery would be extended into territory north of thirty-six and a half degrees of north latitude, and obtain permanent foothold there; but they have now been advised and understand that whilst it is possible that, by a forcing process, slavery may possibly be incorporated into the constitution of Kansas, it cannot remain there a dozen years; and, moreover, that the natural operation of the 'squatter sovereignty' doctrine will ultimately prevent the formation of another slave state out of territory now belonging to the United States, or out of any further territory likely ever to be acquired by this government. Hence, at the North, the excitement which was created by the enactment of the Kansas–Nebraska bill has rapidly subsided, and will ere long wholly cease to exist."

This is a sample of the manner in which some people delude themselves in regard to the question of excluding slavery. They try to represent it as of little consequence whether the empire of that institution be enlarged or not, since if enlarged it must shrink again to its original limits. The Fillmore organ is candid enough to admit that slavery may possibly be forced upon Kansas. The laws of Kansas, passed at the Shawnee Mission, legalize it there already, and the relentless enforcement of these laws, so hopefully inaugurated by Governor Geary, will make its establishment in the territory sure. Then will come the forcing process of which the *Organ* admits the possibility and the danger. A constitution, under Geary's auspices, will be framed, in which slavery will be made the fundamental law of the state. The Republicans being in a minority in both Houses, Kansas will be admitted into the Union as a slave state.

By what process of reasoning this organ of Mr. Fillmore has satisfied itself that if slavery be engrafted on the constitution of Kansas it "will not remain there a dozen years," we cannot imagine. Slavery once admitted into a new country grows rankly; it finds ample space for large plantations, and the virgin soil in its first fertility yields its fruits abundantly to the rude and superficial tillage of slaves. Missouri in 1830 had but twenty-five thousand slaves; she has now a hundred thousand; the slaveholding influence rules the state, blockades its roads, besets its rivers, and denies a safe passage through its limits to all who do not profess allegiance to slavery. What shall prevent the same thing from happening in Kansas? The counties of Missouri bordering on that territory, with the same latitude, climate and soil, are already the most fanatically attached to slavery, and are of themselves a standing admonition against allowing it to extend any further to the West. Once there, it is there for a period of time which our fears do not venture to measure.

In this example we see the fate of Kansas, if we once allow the curse of slavery to be fixed upon her. Once admitted as a slave state, she is wrested from freedom, with no more hope of recovery than we have of Missouri. Will the people of the free states endure this? The people of the South may—the people of the South, as distinguished from the oligarchy who rule them—are in part cheated by ignorant prejudices into the belief that the South is interested in the spread of slavery, and a part of them, and by no means an inconsiderable part, who think otherwise, are silenced by the ferocious and intolerant despotism of the master class. But the people of the North will not endure it.

In another part of this sheet we publish a letter from Kenneth Rayner, of North Carolina, in which he tells us what the South will do if Frémont should be elected. We, in our turn, have a right to say what the North will do if, to the misfortune of the country, Frémont should not be elected. Mr. Rayner assures us that there will be no attempt to dissolve the Union if Frémont should be chosen to the Presidency. We can affirm that if he should not be elected, the struggle for the possession of Kansas which we have hitherto witnessed will be but pastime and holiday sport in comparison to what will follow. The mighty population of the North, conscious of their rights and equally conscious of their strength, exasperated by these successive experiments on their endurance, will put forth their power as it has never been put forth yet. We have long been attentive spectators of political events, and not merely spectators but actors in the strife; we have often seen the public mind agitated by political controversies, but never have we seen the moral nature of the people moved as it is moved now. Never have we seen society so deeply agitated—agitated even in its most quiet and indifferent classes— agitated into even the inmost recesses of domestic life. The feeling which prevails is like a tempest of such fearful might that it disturbs the waters of the ocean even in their remotest and profoundest caverns.

This organization, which now seeks the election of Frémont, and through his election to compose and settle the agitation of the slavery question, will not be a vain or idle piece of machinery if it should fail of its immediate object. It will resolve itself into a great emigrant aid society. It will possess itself of the territories, and defy the power of the slaveholding class to exclude or expel those whom it sends to occupy the region west of the Mississippi.

> A multitude like which the populous North
> Poured never from her frozen loins to pass
> Rhene or the Danaw,

will move westward under the auspices of that organization of which we have spoken, and crossing the Father of Waters will establish itself on its right bank. It will use none but lawful and peaceful means; but wo[e] to those who resist them by violence. Kansas will be ours and a new state will be added to the Union, on the support of which we may confidently rely in another Presidential Election.

They who count upon the readiness of our people to relapse into indifference when a political question is once settled by legislation, and fancy that, if Buchanan should be made President, the question involved in his election will be forgotten and Kansas be left to its fate, are under a delusion. The people of the free states submitted sulkily to the annexation of Texas as a slave state, with a provision for dividing it hereafter into three or four more states of the same class. They bore, with suppressed discontent, the cost and bloodshed of the Mexican war, and worst of all, the baneful effects of that war on both public and private morals. They submitted, with some outbreaks of a fierce dissatisfaction, to the fugitive slave law. But the repeal of the Missouri Compromise crowded the people over the boundary of endurance, and the atrocities, the frauds, the violences, the usurpations practised under the Nebraska act, with the cooperation of the federal government, have deepened the public indignation into a feeling as permanent as that awakened by the events of our own Revolution. Let no man flatter himself that it will be quieted by anything short of the speedy restoration of the territories to the area of freedom. Storms which are long in gathering, rage long. The danger of a disquieted state of the public mind, if a candidate of the slaveholders should be advanced to the Executive chair—the danger of a fearful collision between the people and the oligarchy which rules the councils of the country—the danger that the peace of the country will be broken, are dangers which only the election of Frémont will dispel, and leave the political sky as serene and bright as Mr. Rayner has candidly and truly predicted. Let those who entertain the foolish fancy of voting for Buchanan in order to keep the South quiet, reflect on these things.

The Election of Yesterday
November 5, 1856

Nominated by the American, or "Know-Nothing," Party to oppose Buchanan and Frémont, ex-President Millard Fillmore got the electoral vote of only one state, against Buchanan's nineteen and Frémont's eleven. But the combined popular vote for Buchanan's opponents exceeded his own by a considerable margin, making him a minority President. John Wien Forney, a Pennsylvania journalist and strong Buchanan supporter, later broke with the President over Buchanan's leniency toward slavery in Kansas. After 1860 Forney took his influential Philadelphia Press *to the support of the Republican administration.*

The battle is over and we are all waiting for the smoke to clear away that we may see the exact position of the armies which have been engaged in the conflict. The present aspect of the field is disastrous for the cause which we have supported. We will not undertake to say at present that all hope is lost; we will not affirm that it is impossible that the reports we are yet to hear from Pennsylvania may change the apparent defeat into victory; we will not yet affirm that there is no chance that the election may be carried into the House of Representatives. The chances for Fillmore in Kentucky and Louisiana were thought a week since to be as good as in Maryland, which it is said has been carried for the Fillmore electoral ticket.

But taking it for granted that Buchanan has succeeded, we confess that there are some considerations which, with us, mitigate the pain of disappointment. If we have not carried the United States, we have obtained heavy majorities in a part of the Union which stands high in the confederacy for intelligence and prosperity, and which, through these characteristics, exercises a powerful influence on public opinion. We have at least laid the basis of a formidable and well-organized party, in opposition to the spread of slavery—that shame which is the scandal of the country and of the age. In those states of the Union which have now given such large majorities for Freemont, public opinion, which till lately has been undecided and whiffling in regard to the slavery question, is now clear, fixed and resolute. If we look back to 1848, when we conducted a Presidential election on this very ground of opposition to the extension of slavery, we shall see that we have made immense strides towards the ascendancy which, if there be any grounds to hope for the perpetuity of free institutions, is yet to be ours. We were then comparatively weak, we are now strong; we then counted our thousands, we now count our millions; we could then point to our respectable minorities in a few states, we now point to state after state—to powerful old states on the Atlantic, and flourishing young states in the West—which rally with us under the banner of resistance to the extension of slavery. The cause is not going back—it is rapidly going forward; the free-soil party of 1848 is the nucleus of the Republican party of 1856; but with what accessions of numbers, of strength, of illustrious names, of moral power, of influence, not merely in public assemblies, but at the domestic fireside!

If not strong enough to triumph now, it is growing up to win a glorious triumph hereafter. It is a youthful cause and with all the vigor and health of youth in its constitution, it is able to bear hardship. The present hardships will knit its frame more firmly and give it strength. It is triumphant already in those parts of our country in which knowledge is most generally diffused, and public opinion is most readily influenced by free discussion. It has fought a good fight, even in those parts of the free states in which the population are the most ignorant, and cling longest to the prejudices which they attach to party names. Even there it has made a progress which promises it the mastery hereafter.

Meantime if the victory be, as it now seems, with Buchanan, Mr. Fillmore will stand before the country in no enviable light. But for him and his friends, the opposition to the administration of Mr. Pierce and to the continuance of his policy under Buchanan, was strong enough to have beaten the party of Cushing and Forney—ignoble names both—and by that defeat to have settled the question of slavery, wrested from the slaveholders the monopoly of the territory which they have grasped, and give peace and prosperity to Kansas. Mr. Fillmore has merely played into Buchanan's hands, and having done all the mischief in his power, is dismissed to that obscurity and contempt which is the just lot of weak men who, by appeals to their personal ambition, are persuaded to interfere with the success of a good cause.

The Duty of the Republican Party
November 7, 1856

After a United States merchant vessel had been seized at Havana the previous February, Buchanan, John Y. Mason, and Pierre Soulé, ministers respectively to Great Britain, France, and Spain, wrote a dispatch from Ostend, Belgium, on October 18, 1854, to President Pierce urging that the United States either buy Cuba or seize that colony by "wresting it from Spain." This was taken by Republicans as an effort to extend slave territory. In July 1856 the Tennessee adventurer William Walker, who had seized Nicaragua in a filibustering expedition and set himself up as its president, issued a decree opening that country to slavery. William Shannon, a former governor of Ohio, who favored slavery, had preceded John Geary as territorial governor of Kansas. The Virginia Free-Soiler John Curtiss Underwood had been virtually forced from his home state for criticizing slavery during the 1856 campaign. The Reverend Orville Dewey was Bryant's intimate friend and Williams College classmate. Bryant's comment that Northern settlers must go to Kansas armed reflects the then widespread provision of weapons to emigrants by churches and other Eastern organizations, which earned them the euphemistic title of "Beecher's Bibles," from a remark of the prominent Brooklyn Congregational preacher Henry Ward

Beecher that such weapons were a "greater moral agency among ruffians than the Scriptures."

If Frémont had been elected President of the United States, the question which has so deeply agitated the country would have been settled. The territories, out of which new states are yet to be formed, would have been quietly colonized by laboring men of the white race, from both North and South, and divided into small farms for a thrifty and industrious agricultural population, living under free institutions, and sure of the protection of the federal government. The freedom of discussion at the South would have been restored; a party friendly to the new administration would have been spontaneously formed in that quarter, and that despotism in which its oligarchy hold the masses who surround them, would have been broken. In a few months the question would have disappeared from the political world as absolutely as the question of a national bank. No event so propitious to a good understanding between the North and South, and so much to be desired by all liberal minds in the South, could possibly have happened as the election of Frémont.

But reason and humanity were not to obtain so easy a victory. It is the condition of great achievements that they are slowly accomplished. If there be no error in the returns received this morning, Mr. Buchanan is elected President of the United States. We must now, we fear, make up our minds to see the policy of Mr. Pierce's administration, in regard to the territories, rigidly enforced. The South, flushed with victory, is in no mood to listen to moderate counsels, and so far is the controversy between the oligarchy and the people from being ended by this election, that it is just begun. We have, in fact, but just entered on the threshold of this war—a war waged in a wider field than hitherto, and on which depend more momentous consequences. We shall now have to face the question of reviving the slave-trade with all its brutalities—a question which has been reserved by the oligarchy only till they could have the assurance of another four years' term of power. The Ostend Manifesto will now occupy the Executive chair in person, and we shall have to consider whether we shall yield to the necessity, which Mr. Buchanan has proclaimed, of seizing upon Cuba for the advantage and aggrandizement of the slave power. We shall have to face the question of annexing to our confederacy the Central American state, Nicaragua, with the new slave constitution imposed upon it by its Dictator. We shall have to consider whether we will allow the right claimed for the southern master to own the persons of his attendants in the free states—to insult us with the abomination in our very streets—to call the roll of his slaves, as one of them threatened, on Bunker Hill. To these controversies the victory of the pro-slavery party, which has just been accomplished, conducts us. It opens a path into the midst of new dangers—a path in which we cannot refuse to walk, and which we must enter armed to the teeth.

And yet we will not prejudge Mr. Buchanan. We have already stated the reasons why we have no confidence in him, but we stand ready to support any judicious course which he may take, and any proper measure which he may propose. If he should discard those who have hitherto influenced him, and call wise and good men to his counsels, we should be very unreasonable if we did not admit that we have great hopes of him. We believe we have established such a character with our readers that it is not necessary for us to say that we shall not oppose Mr. Buchanan simply because he was not our candidate. If he should recall the men whom Pierce has sent to Kansas to act as confederates with the border-ruffians, we shall give him all the credit he deserves. But he must not follow the example of his predecessor, who recalled the wretched Shannon, and substituted for him the smooth-tongued and equally desperate rascal, Geary. If he should treat the usurpation of the border ruffians and their spurious code as they deserve to be treated, and as the House of Representatives has treated them, we shall cheerfully applaud his conduct. We shall gladly commend him if he pursues a just and pacific policy towards other nations; if he follows Jackson's maxim of asking nothing which is not clearly right, and submitting to nothing which is wrong; if he breaks up piratical expeditions against our neighbors, and will neither commit a robbery nor connive at it. We shall rejoice if he sees the folly of the extravagance to which he once gave his sanction, and sets himself firmly against squandering the accumulations of our territory, in purchasing, at exorbitant prices, new regions in which slavery may extend and perpetuate itself.

But we have no expectation that the new administration will be conducted on any such principles. The least symptom of a disposition on the part of Mr. Buchanan to revolt against the rule of the oligarchy will be treated with strong remedies, and speedily cured. There is no association of men, religious or political, which enforces uniformity of opinion so rigidly and remorselessly as the slaveholding class. They who drove out Mr. Underwood from Virginia, because he was hostile to the extension of slavery, will not tolerate a like heterodoxy on the part of the man whom they have made President. They who overwhelmed the Rev. Dr. Dewey, lately their favorite, with denunciation, because he ventured to say an honest word in favor of freedom in the territories, will not allow Buchanan to withdraw from Kansas the machinery under which they hope to plant it there. With regard to Nicaragua, they are already laying down the law for him. We have before us the Charleston *Mercury* of Tuesday, applauding Walker for reviving slavery and the slave trade in Central America, and the Cincinnati *Enquirer* of Wednesday, a Buchanan print, which gives a friendly view of the argument in favor of both these measures, and declines to express any opinion against them.

Meantime, there is one matter which requires the immediate attention of the friends of liberty throughout the Union. Kansas is in imminent danger of being made the monopoly of the slaveholders. One reason why the battle in which we have just been engaged was so desperately fought by the party supporting Buchanan, was to secure the advantage which slavery has already gained in that territory. The free state party in Kansas, having been prevented from tilling their fertile soil by the struggle they have been obliged to maintain against the ruffians of the border, are starving in their cabins, which afford them but a wretched shelter, and the tidings of the success of their enemies in this election will almost drive them to despair. They will be crushed by the news which the mails are now bringing them. They must be cared for; they must be supplied in some way or other with the necessaries of life; they must be comforted and encouraged; for on them we must depend as our vanguard in the strife for the occupation of the great central region of our republic. With the early spring the main body must follow; with the swearing in of Buchanan on the 4th of March, our myrmidons must be in readiness to take possession of the territory in the name of freedom.

No course is left to make head against the aggressions of the South but this. There is no longer any hope from Congress—the next Congress, according to present appearances, will have an administration majority in both houses—and there is no scheme of the slaveholders which it will not connive at, if not directly sanctioned. The means of peopling the territories with free laborers are in our hands, if we will but apply them. Moneyed men might invest their funds without disadvantage in loans to the settlers, secured by mortgage on their lands. But no efforts of individuals or societies will prove equal to the emergency. The state legislators should look to it that their citizens who migrate to the territories are neither obstructed in their entrance, nor expelled by an usurped authority, and that they find in their new abodes the free institutions which the fathers of our republic supposed they had provided for their descendants. We are in favor of the speediest action of the legislatures of all the free states on this question, the most liberal provision for the wants of the emigrant, and the largest supplies for sending out reinforcements to strengthen the colonies and to vindicate the land for freedom. They must go armed, in such numbers and array that to allow their entrance will be the part of discretion. All this is in our power; and if, with our large resources, and our vast and enterprising population, we neglect to use that power in the amplest manner, we shall deserve to wear the yoke of the southern oligarchs forever.

FATE OF SQUATTER SOVEREIGNTY
March 3, 1857

In 1847 Senator Lewis Cass of Michigan had made the first full exposition of Popular, or "Squatter" Sovereignty, in denying the constitutional power of Congress over slavery in the territories, arguing that they were entitled to self-government in all non-constitutional matters. In 1857 Cass became Buchanan's Secretary of State. The former Mississippi Congressman Jacob Thompson, Secretary of the Interior from 1857 to 1861, was later a Confederate soldier and a secret Southern agent. In 1856 Benjamin F. Stringfellow of Missouri, who had maintained that "the interests... of the slave and his master are identical," led a force of pro-slavery "Border Ruffians" into Kansas and set up a rump government over the opposition of free settlers, under a constitution which legalized slavery.

What will become of the doctrine of squatter sovereignty under the administration of Mr. Buchanan, is a question in regard to which there is considerable speculation. Mr. Cass is the reputed father of the doctrine, and to him is assigned a high place in the cabinet, but Mr. Cass has hitherto been most unfaithful to his creed, never recognising it in practice in his votes since the passage of the Kansas–Nebraska bill. With him, it has been merely a doctrine professed and paraded for effect—but whenever he has been called upon to interpose in favor of the people of Kansas against those who usurped by violence that sovereignty which the law professed to give them, he has invariably been found wanting. His whole course in Congress has been a persistent denial to the people of Kansas of the very rights he at one time pretended to claim for them.

In the new administration which will be inaugurated tomorrow, Mr. Jacob Thompson of Mississippi holds an important place, that of Secretary of the Interior. Mr. Thompson is the person who, in the convention held at Cinncinati by which Mr. Buchanan was nominated, introduced resolutions denying and condemning the doctrine of Squatter Sovereignty. Of course a cabinet so constituted will not recognize it now. Betwixt a vehement and decried enemy of the doctrine, like Thompson, and a timid, compromising, paltering friend like Cass, it may be already regarded as a doctrine utterly renounced.

The latest intelligence from Kansas shows that the pro-slavery party are proceeding in their attempt to govern the territory, in spite of the people, with as much confidence and assurance as if they had been duly elected by a popular vote. Betwixt Stringfellow and his associates, on the one hand, voted into their places by the armed invaders from Missouri, and Governor Geary, on the other, commissioned by the federal government, not the least fragment of power to regulate their own affairs is left to the people. Geary is on excellent terms, it seems, with Stringfellow's legislature. He has not been at all in their way. He refused his signature to the bill for taking a census and calling a convention to frame a state constitution—deeming, no doubt, its provisions so odious to the people of the territory that he would be unwilling to face them after having signed it—but they passed it afterwards in spite of his veto; and as he recognises their authority to pass laws, his business will be to see it executed. The bill which declares the resistance to the Stringfellow code is treason, and subjects the disobedient settler to the penalty of death, was duly approved by Geary, and signed without objection. It will be his part of the work to arrest and hang all whom he finds obstructing the execution of those laws which more than half the members of the Senate, so long ago as at its last session, including several of the zealous friends of slavery, declared to be a reproach to the country and to the age.

Under this state of things, with an administration in power which practically abjures the doctrine of popular sovereignty, so ostentatiously paraded at the North in the late autumnal elections, and with a Governor of the territory who, after coquetting a while with the free-state party, enters into a close confederacy with their enemies, and joins them in passing an edict of extermination against the free-state men, dooming them to the gallows for any act of resistance to one of the grossest and most shameless usurpations of power ever, practiced on this continent, the interest which all lately felt in the fate of Kansas is revived. The difficulties which surround the free-state settlers are again thickening. Congress has done nothing for them. The House of Representatives has passed a bill authorizing them to form a constitution, which has lain for some time on the table of the Senate, but the Senate has no disposition to help them out of the strait in which they find themselves. We are not without some fears that the days of anarchy and bloodshed, from which we had hoped that the territory was delivered, may return.

THE NEW FEDERAL CONSTITUTION
March 9, 1857

On March 6, 1857, Chief Justice Roger Taney of the United States Supreme Court read a decision adopted by a majority of seven justices to two in the case of Dred

Scott v. Sandford, ruling that since a Negro slave was not a citizen he had no right to sue for his freedom on the ground that he had been taken by his master into free territory; that, indeed, the Congress had no power to exclude slavery from federal territory, and that therefore the Missouri Compromise of 1820 was unconstitutional. The five slaveholding judges to whom Bryant refers were Chief Justice Roger Taney of Maryland, and Associate Justices John Campbell of Alabama, John Catron of Tennessee, Peter Daniel of Virginia, and James Wayne of Georgia.

Some of the journalists who support the cause of the administration are pleasing themselves with the fancy that the decision of the Supreme bench of the United States in the Dred Scott case will put an end to the agitation of the slavery question. They will soon find their mistake. The feeling in favor of liberty is not so easily smothered; discussion is not so readily silenced. One specific after another has been tried, with the same view and with the same success. The Fugitive Slave law, we were told, was to quiet all agitation, but it did not; the Nebraska bill was to stop all controversy on the slavery question, but it proved to be oil poured on the flames. The usurpation of the government of Kansas by the inroad from Missouri, was thought for a time to be a blow to the friends of liberty which they could not survive, but it only roused them to greater activity. The election of Mr. Buchanan as President in November was to put an end to the dispute, but since November the dispute has waxed warmer and warmer. It will never end till the cause of liberty has finally triumphed. Heap statute upon statute, follow up one act of Executive interference with another; add usurpation to usurpation, and judicial decision to judicial decision, the spirit against which they are leveled is indestructible. As long as the press and speech are free, the warfare will be continued, and every attempt to suppress it, by directing against it any part of the machinery of the government will only cause it to rage the more fiercely.

This has been the case hitherto. The more our Presidents have meddled with the matter—the more the majority in Congress have sought to stifle the discussion—the more force has been employed on the side of slavery, whether under the pretext of legal authority, as when Mr. Pierce called out the United States troops to enforce the pretended laws of Kansas, or, without that pretext, as when armed men crossed the border of that territory to make laws for the inhabitants, the more determined is the zeal by which the rights of freemen are asserted and upheld against the oligarchy. It will not cool the fiery temper of this zeal to know that slavery has enlisted the bench on its side; it will rather blow it into a stronger and more formidable flame.

Here are five slaveholding judges on the bench, disciples of this neologism of slavery—men who have espoused the doctrines lately invented by the southern politicians, and who seek to engraft them upon our code of constitutional law—men who alter our constitution for us, who find in it what no man of common sense, reading it for himself, could ever find, what its framers never thought of putting into it, what no man discerned in it till a very few years since it was seen, with the aid of optics sharpened by the eager desire to preserve the political ascendancy of the slave states. We feel, in reading the opinions of these men, that local political prejudices have gained the mastery of that bench and tainted the minds of the majority of the judges. The constitution which they now profess to administer, is not the constitution under which this country has lived for seventy years; it is not the constitution which Washington, Franklin and Jefferson, and the able jurists who filled the seat of justice in the calmer days of our republic, recognised; this is not the constitution to which we have so long looked up with reverence and admiration; it is a new constitution, of which we never heard till it was invented by Mr. Calhoun, and which we cannot see adopted by the judges of our federal courts without shame and indignation.

Hereafter, if this decision shall stand for law, slavery instead of being what the people of the slave states have hitherto called it, their peculiar institution, is a federal institution, the common patrimony and shame of all the states, those which flaunt with the title of free, as well as those which accept the stigma of being the Land of Bondage; hereafter, wherever our jurisdiction extends, it carries with it the chain and the scourge—wherever our flag floats, it is the flag of slavery. If so, that flag should have the light of the stars and the streaks of running red erased from it; it should be dyed black and its devices should be the whip and the fetter.

Are we to accept, without question, these new readings of the constitution—to sit down contentedly under this disgrace—to admit that the constitution was never before rightly understood, even by those who framed it—to consent that hereafter it shall be the slaveholders', instead of the freemen's constitution? Never! Never! We hold that the provisions of the constitution, so far as they regard slavery, are now just what they were when it was framed, and that no trick of interpretation can change them. The people of the free states will insist on the old impartial construction of the constitution, adopted in calmer times—the constitution given it by Washington and his contemporaries, instead of that invented by modern politicians on the bench.

What results will grow out of this decision—to what conflicts of legislation between the states and the federal government it may lead—with what difficulty these clashing views may be composed, or how this last attempt to sustain the cause of slavery, to spread it as widely and keep it in being as long as possible, may be overruled and rendered futile by causes now in operation, we do not undertake to conjecture.

Judge Taney's Opinion in the Dred Scott Case
March 10, 1857

Benjamin R. Curtis of Massachusetts and John McLean of Ohio were the justices who dissented from the majority opinions. McLean argued that Negroes were eligible for citizenship, that the Missouri Compromise remained valid, and that Scott had become free through residence in Illinois. From 1786 until 1815, when a United States naval force under Captain Stephen Decatur forced a renunciation of their piracy, the Barbary states of North Africa—Algiers, Morocco, Tripoli, and Tunis—had levied tribute on American merchant ships trading in the Mediterranean. The longtime outspoken champion of lost causes in the Congress, John Randolph of Roanoke, Virginia, though himself a slaveholder, denounced the inhumanity of domestic slave trading in the South. Redemptionists were immigrant indentured servants. The source of the "frizzled hair" quotation is undetermined.

Our Washington correspondent furnishes us with a brief but clear abstract of Judge Curtis's opinion in the Dred Scott case, and in another part of this sheet we publish Judge M'Lean's at length. It is very able and satisfactory, and cuts up by the roots the position assumed by Judge Taney in the opinion which we published yesterday. It will be read with profound attention by that immense class whom the late course of political events in this country has brought to regard with interest this great question—a question which has involved the slave-holding judges in an apparent collusion with the slave-holding politicians.

In saying that Judge Taney's opinion is creditable neither to his research nor to his reasoning powers, we but repeat what is the common remark. There are some who call it superficial and shallow, and really, if we were to speak of it as we think it deserves, we could not conscientiously dispute its title to these epithets.

In denying to colored men the claim to be citizens of the United States, Judge Taney imagines a state of public opinion throughout the civilized world, in regard to the African race at the time when our constitution was adopted, which, in fact, had no existence. He imagines the black race to have been considered and treated by all civilized men of the white race as inferior beings, neither politically nor socially the equals of whites, and as having no rights which the whites were bound to respect. There is a great mistake here. It was not as black men, it was not as Africans, it was not as individuals of a different species of the animal creation, that the civilized races exercised the power of stealing, selling and enslaving negroes; it was as persons of a lower degree of civilization than themselves, as heathens and barbarians, as ignorant and helpless creatures, reared up in pagan practices, from which it would be a mercy to deliver them. They captured and enslaved them as the corsairs of the Barbary states captured and enslaved the Christian dogs whom they met on the high seas. They enslaved them for the same reason that the Greeks enslaved the barbarians against whom they made war, or the Romans the inhabitants of the provinces they conquered. They made slaves in like manner of the Indians. Examples of Indian slaves occur in our own colonial history—slaves belonging to the race from which the eloquent Virginian, John Randolph, claimed to be descended. The Spaniards enslaved the original inhabitants of St. Domingo; the Spanish conquerors of Peru enslaved the inhabitants of that country. Our ancestors went farther than this; the French colonists of Acadia, a peaceful, simple, defenseless race, were carried by violence into captivity, and made house servants and field laborers among the people of New England. German Redemptioners, as they were called—poor people of the class of peasantry—who came as passengers to this country, were sold into temporary slavery.

But we deny that the origin of slavery is to be traced to the idea that the black man, on account of his race, was not, as a matter of strict justice, entitled to equal rights with the whites. There is not a particle of proof to support this position. This prejudice of race has grown up gradually in our country and it is of late origin; it hardly existed seventy years ago and does not even now exist to any extent in any other; it has grown out of the institution of slavery, and not the institution of slavery out of the prejudice. This prejudice is stronger now in our country than it ever was before; it has become greatly strengthened within our own remembrance. There were colored persons among the citizens of New England at the time the constitution was adopted, just as there are now colored persons among the citizens of Cuba, and as there were colored persons among the citizens of Florida and Louisiana when they were received into the Union. Judge McLean has referred to these two cases, as well as to that of our late treaty with Mexico, in which we acquired New Mexico and California. We made the citizens of these countries citizens of the United States without inquiring into their color; we took in Chinos and Zambos, men

"With frizzled hair implicit—"

brown men and yellow men, and they are citizens yet. The squeamishness in regard to the bestowal of political and civil rights was therefore not only later in its origin by many years than Judge Taney has placed it, but never existed to the extent that he pretends.

That the importation of slaves, under the phraseology, "the migration or importation of such persons as the states may think proper to admit"—for the framers of the constitution would not use the word slave—would not even indirectly recognize the detestable institution of slavery—was by the constitution not to be prohibited till the year 1808—is true enough, but it does not follow that the framers of the constitution thought that the black man had no rights. They yielded this concession to the cupidity of those who made a profit of bringing in slaves—they yielded it because they feared to hazard the acceptance of the constitution by all the states. As to the provision of the constitution for the delivering up of persons bound for service, which will include the case of the German redemptioners as well as that of the negro, it is not a recognition of the original right of slavery, but only an admission of a certain claim to service; it asserts no inequality between the African race and the white; it does not speak of the black race as property—as Judge Taney assumes that it does.

With the demolition of this position of Judge Taney, the whole structure he has reared upon it falls to the ground. There having been no such state of opinion in regard to the African race as he labors to make out, there is no reason for the conclusion to which he arrives that the framers of the constitution intended to exclude them from citizenship. They declared that "all men are created equal"; and they meant precisely what they said. They would not say in the constitution that any man was a slave; they jealously excluded that word from the instrument; they would not agree to refuse political and civil rights to any man.

The examples of federal legislation on which Judge Taney relies to show that negroes have never been regarded as citizens, show no such thing. They are not enrolled in the militia; neither are men over forty-five years of age, nor clergymen, nor Quakers, and yet these three classes are citizens. They do not serve on juries, neither do women, and yet women can sue in the United States courts.

We do not recollect, in all our lives, to have seen a judicial decision erected on so slender a basis as this. If the habitual, immemorial recognition of the possession of civil rights by colored men be necessary to complete the refutation of Judge Taney's argument, it may be found in the fact that colored seamen sue the owners or commanders of vessels every day in the courts of the United States which have admiralty jurisdiction. They do this as citizens of the United States, as men who have civil rights under our constitution, and nobody has ever thought of questioning their claim to the impartial attention of the tribunals. If Judge Taney's amendment of the constitution should be recognized, no man of this class, however wronged, can ever sue in those courts again. His decision sweeps away rights that have been acknowledged and held sacred from the very adoption of the constitution in its original form, before the southern jurists took a fancy to change it.

The other branch of Judge Taney's argument—that relating to the inhibition of slavery in the territories—is equally feeble, and we may perhaps give some attention to it hereafter.

One or Two Results of the Late Change in the Constitution
March 11, 1857

The constitution of Rhode Island limits the right of suffrage to citizens of the United States, and, under this provision colored persons have been allowed to vote in the elections held in that state. But this was under the old state of things—under the federal constitution which was in force till last week. It is, however, an indication of the manner in which that constitution has been all along interpreted. Nobody in Rhode Island has till now supposed that a colored man, born within the state, within the jurisdiction of a republic the founders of which declared that "all men are created equal," was not a citizen, was not entitled as such to vote in the elections and prosecute his civil rights in the courts of the United States, was no more a member of civil society, in the view of the federal constitution, than a horse or a dog, but was left precisely where Judge Taney in his late decision of the Dred Scott case affirms him to have been found by those who framed our constitution—that is to say, in the condition of one who has "no rights which the white man is bound to respect," no claim to protection, no power to demand justice from the federal tribunals in any possible case of wrong or oppression. Nobody in Rhode Island, until the new constitution was promulgated by Judge Taney and his associates, looked upon the colored man as literally an outcast, simply on account of his race, disowned by the government under which he was born, and without a country.

Something, of course, will be done in his favor, now that the federal constitution is amended according to the new reading of the slave-holding judges. The Providence *Journal* of yesterday says:

> "The subject should receive the immediate attention of the General Assembly, so that the amendment (of the state constitution securing the right of suffrage to colored men) if it is necessary, may be submitted to the people in the coming political year."

We shall have plenty of agitation of matters like these, in addition to a spirited discussion of the grounds of the conclusion assumed by Judge Taney and his fellows. In all the free states, the legislatures will be occupied with looking over their state constitutions, to see whether any amendment is necessary to meet the exigency which has so suddenly arisen, and supply, if the occasion should require it, the want of protection to the colored man so unexpectedly created. Plans of amendment to the state constitution will be prepared; plans of legislation to countervail the effect of the decision will be brought forward, and whether anything be done or not, we shall have plenty of agitation. Where we stand since this judicial innovation—what part of the opinions of the majority of the court will, according to the usages and principles of administering law, govern in future cases—what part of them may be explained away—the effect of what part may be avoided by the ingenuity of state legislation, will be fruitful sources of earnest and animated discussion.

More earnest than this, and more universally interesting, will be the discussion of the means by which we may defeat and break in pieces the political party formed to diffuse and propagate slavery—a party the doctrines and practices of which have so infected our judiciary as to make it the instrument of a local oligarchy in wresting the constitution to bear a meaning which nothing but a perverted ingenuity could find in it, and which contradicts the judgment of the wisest and purest men of the first half of the century of our republic. Now that this party has brought over the judiciary to be its accomplice in nationalizing slavery, the necessity of thrusting it out of power is more manifest than ever. The more wide-spread is the conspiracy the greater the necessity of an energetic concert of action among ourselves. These assaults, made one after another, from Congress, from the Executive, and now from the judiciary, on the rights of the free states, should drive the citizens of those states into a closer union, as a tempest drives a scattererd crowd under a common shelter.

There is one advantage arising from this conjunction of the judiciary with the executive in the work of forcing upon the people the slave-holder's gloss of the constitution. It puts an end to the hypocrisy of those who, while supporting Mr. Buchanan, pretend to oppose the spread of slavery. The cry of "Free Kansas and Buchanan," "Buchanan and Freedom to the Territories," is silenced forever. The politicians of Mr. Buchanan's side, and he among the rest, emboldened by the countenence they receive from the bench, no longer affect to claim for the territories the right to frame their own institutions, but expressly deny it. That neither the territory nor Congress have power over slavery is the doctrine of the day, professed by those who call themselves democrats, and who are, in fact, the tools of a provincial oligarchy. There is no longer any ground for a middle course; the slaveholders and their abettors stand on one side, the people and the friends of freedom on the other; the politician must choose to which he will ally himself; there is no longer any room for equivocation. All those who supported Mr. Buchanan under the pretence that he was in favor of freedom in the territories are swept over in a heap to the side of slavery, and it will be for them to say whether they will allow their place to be assigned with so little ceremony.

The Cure for Dirty Streets
March 26, 1857

If the old saying be true, that "a peck of March dust is worth a king's ransom," New York should be the richest city on which the sun shines. Estimated at this rate, there is more dust in the air over our streets on the present twenty-sixth of March than would purchase the liberty of all the captive monarchs that ever lived, whose release could be bought with gold. If you go into Broadway, you bring home scarcely less than a peck of it on your hat, on your shoulders and in your bosom—you enter your house a rich man. Ladies return from shopping with lace veils so heavy with dust that they are worth their weight in diamonds. They carry in their ears a deposit of greater price than the jewels that hang from them. If you are in an omnibus, you travel amid whirlwinds of dust, which strike against the window like a storm of rubies and sapphires. And yet Broadway is altogether the cleanest street in the city. What were lately piles of mud have become piles of dust since the dry weather has set in, and the dust is ten times more annoying than the mud has been.

Some scold and some laugh at this predicament of our proud city—the most prosperous and populous of the western hemisphere, and the filthiest is the world; but neither censure nor ridicule is likely to cure the evil. If the dirt could have been scolded or laughed out of the streets, that would have been done long ago; but the administration of our municipal affairs is, for the most part, in the hands of those who regard nothing but the machinery of party nominations and the votes given at the polls.

There is only one method of setting the matter right. That large class of our citizens who are so absorbed in their own concerns that they give little thought to the manner in which the city is governed, except to grumble now and then at the prodigious rapidity with which the taxes increase from year to year, must spare a little time from their business for our municipal politics. They must enter the lists against that class who regard the city treasury as their own proper plunder, and the taxes collected from the citizens as their own proper income. They must take the choice of our municipal authorities out of the hands of these men. They must keep themselves constantly informed of what our city authorities are doing, instead of waking up when the tax-gatherer comes round and wondering what so much money can have been spent for. They must provide in season for the nomination of honest men to all city offices; they must interest themselves in the elections. The public business of the city must be transacted by somebody, and if honest men will not attend to it, they may rest assured that the rogues will. It is with the affairs of the city as with those of an individual—if they are neglected, things will go wrong. Nobody who neglects his own business has a right to expect that it will prosper, and nobody who fails to take that part in the organization and working of our city government which the community has a right to claim of all its members, ought to blame [any]body but himself if the city is misgoverned.

If people do not mind paying high taxes, if they are willing to have a corrupt police; if they have no objection to see vice encouraged and crime bearding the laws, they may possibly have some regard to their own personal comfort. But as things are now managed, we shall never have a city fit to live in. We shall never get rid of this filth, which makes every street a nuisance to the dwellings built upon it; we shall never have done with wading in mud when the weather is wet, and walking in dense clouds of dust when it is windy; we shall never cease to breathe, in the warm season, an atmosphere compounded of all manner of noisome and unhealthy exhalations, and scented with all manner of horrid smells. Once in three or four months, perhaps, the authorities may be spurred up to make a feeble effort at clearing away the filth in a few of the principal streets, but they will be sure to relapse into their former neglect as soon as the public begin to talk of something else.

Better Late Than Never
October 5, 1858

Former governor of Mississippi Albert Gallatin Brown was a Senator from that state, ca. 1849–1861. "'A made a finer end" was Dame Quickly's tribute to John Falstaff upon his death, in Henry V, II, iii, 11. *Rufus Choate of Massachusetts had served out Daniel Webster's unfinished Senatorial term when Webster became Secretary of State in 1841; Joseph Ripley Chandler was a Whig Pensylvania Congressman, 1849–1855; William Bradford Reed, a prominent Pensylvania Whig,* had become a Democrat in 1856; William Preston, a Kentucky Whig Congressman, turned Democrat in 1854.

The old proverb, "better late than never," has perhaps done more good than any other four words of any language. What innumerable resolutions of amendment have been inspired or confirmed by this brief saying, and borne their proper fruit in consequence! The words "too late" are the utterance of despair; the words "better late than never" speak volumes of encouragement. In all instances of personal reformation, "too late" is the suggestion of man's evil genius, "better late than never" the suggestion of his good angel.

A correspondent suggests that, since Mr. Buchanan's chance of receiving a second nomination from his party is so very small, and seems to be lessening every day, he may possibly turn his attention to another object of ambition—that of going out of office with credit—a matter of which he seems hitherto to have taken no thought. It is really all that is now left him to strive for. Whoever may be the candidate of the Charleston Convention, when they meet to make their nomination, the friends of Mr. Douglas, who has been pursued with such rancor by the special partizans of the Administration, will not allow it to be Buchanan. In its attempt to expel Douglas from the democratic party, the Administration has proceeded as if it forgot that men have passions as well as interests. The friends of Mr. Douglas do not acquiesce in the sentence of expulsion, nor are the politicians of the South at all disposed to permit it to be carried into execution. Senator Brown has given the administration warning of this. The southern politicians will not disown the Douglas wing of their party on account of any difference of opinion which at present exists between them; they are ready to admit them into the convention; and if they go in, Mr. Buchanan goes out.

All that is left, therefore, to Mr. Buchanan, is to make what Mrs. Quickly calls a "finer end." Like Cæsar at the Capitol, what he has to do is to gather his robe about him and expire with decency. Two years earnestly devoted to undoing the mischief he has done, would cancel a part of the charges which history has already set down against him, and soften the sentence she is preparing to pronounce upon him for those mischiefs which cannot be retrieved. The acts of two years have, in some instances, sufficed to build up an illustrious name, or make the world forget a multitude of previous faults. If Mr. Buchanan were to act for the future with perfect independence of the slaveholders' party, which has hitherto employed him as its instrument, he would puzzle the world at first, but it would soon be acknowledged that it is "better late than never." If he would substitute a scrupulous frugality for the lavish policy which had emptied the public treasury, every body would at once say, "better late than never." If he would turn out certain blackguards whom he has placed in office, and fill their places with upright and able men, there are not nine men out of ten who would not say, "better late than never." We might go on with this list of opportunities for amendment, which are enough to keep him busy for the rest of his term, and to which the proverb we have so often quoted would be applied by four-fifths of the intelligent men who inhabit the United States.

But the misfortune in such cases is, that it is hard to make a man whose conscience has become callous with wrongdoing perceive that his interest and his duty coincide. Men who have often seen political elections carried by some delusion of the day, are very apt to believe in the permanency of such delusions; they think to deal with history as they dealt with the majority of the voters, and to deceive her as easily. By accustoming themselves not to regard the difference between the essentially right and the essentially wrong, but, on the contrary, to deem that right on which a fair face may be put for the moment, they lose their mor[al]-discrimination and come at last to grope about in utter blindness. Mr. Buchanan has grown old in a school which regards politics as a system of petty shifts and expedients, a certain dexterity in playing off one set of men against another, and the skilful use of the prejudices of the day for the purpose of personal advancement, as the boatman avails himself of the eddies of a river to go up the stream. Such is the confirmed habit of his mind, that we do not well see how he can now have any notion of any other principle of public life. Although there never was a case in which the maxim of "better late than never" was more properly applicable, we see no hope of its being made the rule of action by the present federal administration.

Nay, the true policy of the country is not to increase, but to diminish the taxes on goods brought from abroad. There is a multitude of articles the duties on which do not pay the cost of collecting them. The tariff has never been honestly revised with a view of cancelling these. The rule should be to put the duties on those articles only which are imported in large quantities, and this would allow the number of custom-house officers to be materially diminished, and prevent the revenue service from being the cumbrous and expensive machine that it is. If the tariff question comes up again at the next Congress, we hope there will be some men bold enough to bring forward a scheme of this sort—a scheme for putting the pruning knife into our revenue system and lopping off its costly superfluities without mercy.

The *Intelligencer*, however, thinks that a different course will be taken. "We are sure," says that print, "that in consideration of the pressing needs of the treasury, some slight relaxation from the rigor of the free-trade theory will be tolerated by the great majority of the democratic party."

That may be. We do not deny that the administration will be willing to get money under any pretext. The adhesion of so many of what are called Old Line Whigs to the democratic party must have brought with it some infusion of the ancient principles of the whig party, or at least will serve in some degree to counterbalance the zeal of the free-trade leaders. Mr. Choate and his associates in Massachusetts, Mr. Chandler and Mr. Reed and their associates in Pennsylvania, Mr. Preston and his friends in Kentucky, in allying themselves with the democratic party have not recanted their old opinions on the subject of protection, and they find themselves very comfortable in their new condition. The truth of the matter is, that the question of protection and free trade is remanded to the list of open questions which are no longer in dispute between the two political parties. The real controversy will be, whether the present administration is to be trusted with more money, or made to contend with some of the wholesome inconveniences of its loose administration of the finances, until the treasury, in the natural course of things, shall have recovered from the late depletion.

The Proposed Increase of Taxes
October 8, 1858

Thaddeus Stevens, like his opponent, an ironmaker, was a Lancaster, Pennsylvania, lawyer who served as a Whig Congressman from 1848 to 1853, and as a Republican anti-slavery leader in the Congress from 1858 until his death in 1868. He also supported a protective tariff.

The Washington *Intelligencer* has an elaborate article in favor of increasing the indirect taxes. High duties, providing a liberal income, have made our government extravagant in its expenses; the extravagance of the government has emptied the treasury, and here is a proposal to fill the treasury again by increasing the duties.

The *Intelligencer* may rest assured that the mischief will never be cured in this way. When an imprudent young man gets into debt, it is clear that the best thing to be done for him is to let him work himself out of it by a course of regular economy and daily thrift. To give him plenty of money, and bid him to expect more when that is spent, will never wean him from his extravagant habits. For intemperance the cure is abstinence, not the administration of new provocatives to excess. If the government has been wasteful, it must study to save; if it has foolishly or corruptly lavished its resources, it must learn to husband them. It has been in debt before now, but it has not been thought necessary to deplete the people by laying new taxes.

For our own part—and we are sure that we speak for a large number of the citizens of the United States—we hope that if the present tariff is to be modified by making it more protective, the change will not be made in such a manner as necessarily to increase the revenue; and for the reason which will be more fully stated in the course of our remarks, that duties which bring an adequate revenue now will produce an excessive income hereafter. We should regret to see anything done to restrain the freedom of trade, but we should regret still more to see the restraints take a form which would in the end produce a greater revenue than is wanted. If we are to revive the protective system, let us do it in all honesty and fairness; let it be proposed and urged on its own merits; let us not attempt to smuggle it into our legislation under the pretext that more money is wanted to carry on the government. We certainly, for our part, should be inclined to oppose a measure of mere protection with less energy than a measure framed with a double view to protection and the gorging of the Treasury. We should prefer the single evil to the twin mischief. If the tariff, therefore, is to be modified at the next meeting of Congress, let it by all means be done in an honorable singleness of purpose.

The *Intelligencer* remarks that in Pennsylvania and New Jersey the chief contest between the democrats and the opposition seems to be which shall show itself most zealous for a higher tariff. We do not dispute that there are parts of the Union in which the manufacturers have so much influence that the candidates of both parties vie with each other for their favor; nor do we question that in some cases they may do it in all sincerity. In one district of Pennsylvania the Republican candidate for a seat in Congress is Thaddeus Stevens, who was long ago the friend of a high tariff and the supporter of the doctrine of protection, and has not even yet seen his error. Opposed to him is the democratic candidate, Mr. Hopkins, an ironmaster, who, if he be elected to Congress, will go thither with the determination to aggravate, if possible, the duties on iron to such a degree that the ironmasters of his state may laugh at foreign competition, and make themselves the despots of the iron market. Mr. Hopkins has probably no doubt that what is profitable to him is beneficial to the country, a conceit which we might forgive, though it is a shameless request that he makes to be sent to Congress that he may vote money into his own pocket. We must remind the *Intelligencer*, however, that neither Pennsylvania nor New Jersey can be allowed to give law to the rest of the Union in regard to this question. In neither of these has the free-trade doctrine ever been fully accepted by either party; the democrats of both states have been more or less what are called tariff democrats; even Mr. Buchanan was at one time among the foremost in that class, and has never made his recantation.

The *Intelligencer* talks of the "harmony which begins to prevail among the leaders of opinion at the North" in regard to a revival of the heavy duty on imports. But let the question be put to the people of Indiana, Illinois, Wisconsin, Iowa, Missouri, and other states of the great West, and a different answer would be given from that which comes from Pennsylvania and New Jersey. What "leader of public opinion" in those western states would be followed a single inch if he attempted to coax his adherents into that path? What candidate for Congress in any of these states, unless stark mad, would venture to place the chances of his election on that ground? The avowal of such opinions and designs would bring upon him certain defeat.

It is said, however, that if we do not make the duties heavier, we shall be obliged to borrow. Let us borrow, then; it is the wiser course, provided we be able to repay, of which there is not the slightest doubt. A large debt before the eyes of the administration, of which it is a little ashamed, may possibly prove an incentive to frugality. There has never been a time within the last forty years in which under any of the different tariffs, the income, in an average of several years, has not steadily gained on the expenditure. Raise the tariff on imports, and you will soon have an excess of money in the treasury, and a swarm of greedy speculators and projectors will flock to Washington, eager to divide it among them. Leave the duties as they are, and keep our government within the limits of a reasonable economy, and if, within a few years, with the sure return of an active and prosperous commerce, the treasury be not soon replenished, then the lessons of experience are in no case to be trusted.

The Reaction in Pennsylvania
October 15, 1858

Several of the journals in the interest of the Administration strive to make light of the reverses which their party has suffered in the elections held on Tuesday; but Mr. Buchanan's principal organ, the Washington *Union*, admits that, so far as regards Pennsylvania, they are "heavy reverses, which would discourage any but the democratic party." It takes a melancholy satisfaction, however, in laying these disasters at the door of "Douglas and such instruments as Forney." "It is their work," exclaims the *Union*; "they and the Black Republicans have been faithful co-workers; let them rejoice together, and in common prepare for the final doom that awaits alike the original enemies and recent deserters of the democratic party."

We must disabuse the Washington *Union*. All that Douglas and Forney have done is to give a vigorous and decided expression to opinions and feelings which had already taken possession of the public mind. The political change in Pennsylvania is not their work; it is that of Mr. Buchanan himself. He disappointed the hopes of those who were indulgent enough to believe that he would administer our domestic affairs with that regard to justice and equity which even a selfish man, if moderately shrewd and sensible, takes care to observe both in public and private life. He disgusted many of his warmest supporters; out of this disgust a strong reaction arose, and into that both Douglas and Forney boldly threw themselves and took a leading part. The journal conducted by Colonel Forney, the *Press*, gained its large circulation only because there was a demand in Pennsylvania for just such unsparing exposures and vehement censures of Mr. Buchanan's policy as that sheet contained. If the *Press* had not been established, the demand would still have arisen, and would have been supplied from some other quarter. Douglas did not create the feeling in Illinois which has caused his phillippics against the federal administration to be eagerly heard by thousands of electors, interrupting him from time to time with tumults of applause. Douglas found the discontent already strong in his state, and only ministered to its gratification. If he had supported Mr. Buchanan in the Lecompton fraud, not the shadow of a chance would have remained for his hope of being sent again to the federal Senate. He simply took advantage of a popular feeling already awake and active. There is no greater absurdity than to attribute the weakness of a party to the defection of some individual politician. When a Chief Magistrate is essentially popular—when he has conducted himself to the general satisfaction of the country—he loses very little strength by losing such adherents as Douglas and Forney, able as they may be. General Jackson, while President, was abandoned by one distinguished man after another, who joined the ranks of the opposition, without causing the slightest diminution of the favor which the country bore him. So it would be now with Buchanan, if he had satisfied the people.

Who will say that Buchanan would not have retained his popularity in Pennsylvania, if he had taken the course which many of his friends who stood sponsors for him in the North—Ex-President Van Buren among the rest—engaged that he should? Suppose he had kept his own pledge to see that the people of Kansas should settle the question of slavery for themselves, without external interference, with what weapons could his old friend Forney have then attacked him? How could Douglas have appealed to the people against him? If they had desired to assail his administration, they must have resorted to other topics, and they could have found none in regard to which the minds of the people were already inflamed. All the weapons which Douglas and Forney are using were put into their hands by Mr. Buchanan and those who act with him; a whole armory was pitched at the heads of these two men, and can we wonder that they should be tempted to take them up? They are merely volunteers who joined a great army which was already on its march, and before which the last hold of the slave power on the free states has now been swept away.

Mr. Buchanan looked wholly to the South for his next election to the Presidency, without dreaming that the power would ever pass out of the hands of the slaveholders. He did not expect to satisfy the people of the free states by his measures, but seems to have imagined that the patronage which his official station put into his hands would be potent enough to gain him a majority in a sufficient number of the northern states, to incline the scale in his favor, and keep the country apparently with him. The experiment has been fully tried, and the result is utter defeat. All the resistance to public opinion which patronage could purchase has been like a barricade of straw before the flames of a conflagration.

It is an important lesson that is taught by this failure, and succeeding administrations will profit by it, even if that of Mr. Buchanan should not. It will be seen that a blind devotion to the interests of the slaveholders, by way of purchasing universal popularity at the South, and a skilful use of patronage with the view of securing the vote of two or three large states at the North, are by no means certain to have their intended effect. The country cannot be managed so. The opinion of the great mass of wise and thoughtful men throughout the republic must be consulted and respected; and due weight must be given to the wishes of the free states, or no administration can henceforward have even a show of popular support.

We do not mean to say that the battle is already ended, or that the army which has obtained the late successes can have leave to be disbanded on the battle-ground. It must still keep the field of which it has made itself master, and sustain skirmish after skirmish with an enemy unwilling to acknowledge itself worsted. But the great fact which the recent elections make manifest will still remain, that it will be impossible to carry on the government, as it has heretofore been administered, with a sole view to the aggrandizement of the slave interest. Whoever shall be President hereafter, will take office under a compulsion from the popular will to lean towards that large humanity professed by the great founders of our republic. Henceforward the inducement to incline to the side of freedom will be as strong as it has hitherto been to favor the cause of slavery. Even a President chosen under southern auspices—if such should be the case—a President chosen by the very party which now supports Mr. Buchanan—will feel the constraint of the national will urging him in a contrary direction from that which Mr. Buchanan has taken. The record of that man's course will remain as an acknowledged record of folly, and his fate will be a wholesome warning to those who may succeed him in the post he has filled with such deplorable loss of reputation.

The Bible in the Public Schools
November 24, 1858

A decision by the Maine State Supreme Court in 1854 which upheld the reading of the Protestant Bible in public schools over Catholic objections was influential throughout the other states for decades thereafter. In 1858 and 1859 students were expelled from Boston and New York schools for refusing to read the Protestant Bible.

The question of making the English translation of the Scriptures a book to be read in the common schools, is at present agitated with considerable warmth. Some are for excluding it; others insist on its being read, though we believe they do not desire to make it a book from which scholars are to learn to read, the effect of which might be to prevent it from being read reverently. The principal reason given for excluding the Sacred Writings, from our city schools especially, is that a large number of the population is Roman Catholic, and that their introduction would prevent the attendance of the children of Catholic families.

It has always appeared to us that this difficulty, were it the only one, might be obviated by having selections from the Scriptures made by a committee of both Protestants and Catholics, for the use of the public schools. We remember a little book of this kind called the "Beauties of the Bible," made by a retired clergyman, which some years ago was a favorite of the American firesides, and, if we mistake not, was often seen in the schools. It would not be difficult, we imagine, to take from the Bible portions—including many of its simple, touching, and instructive narratives, finer than anything in fiction, and passages from its wholesome teachings more impressive and of more comprehensive import than any pulpit address—which the Catholic himself would admit could not be read without edification. In those cases in which the schools contain children of Catholic families, we see no reason for objecting to these selections being made from the Douay Bible, as the Roman Catholic translation is called. It is not the Scriptures in either translation that make sects or divide society into different religious denominations; it is the different glosses which men put upon them; it is the comments with which they are accompanied. In those cases in which the Bible is directed, in general terms, to be read in schools, the teacher must make selections, and this task might as well be performed for him by a committee.

The importance of recognising in education the religious element, and of accustoming the pupil to the idea of strictly conforming his conduct to the will of the Supreme Being, has been much and earnestly dwelt upon by those who would have the Bible read in the public schools. They make out a strong case; but they are met by the Catholics with the remark, that all which is said of the importance of cultivating the religious instinct is very true, but for themselves they prefer to do it in their own way, in schools of their own, where their own peculiar tenets are taught and children are trained up to be Catholics. The *Freeman's Journal*, the organ of the Roman Catholics in this city, in an article of some length on this subject, expressly disclaims, for itself and for others of its religious denomination, all interest in the controversy about the Bible in the public schools. It says:

> "It is alleged that there are twelve of the public schools where there is no Bible reading. Some months ago the trustees of the Fourth ward met and agreed to discontinue the practice in the schools of their ward. We do not know the motive. It seemed to us a device to get Catholics to send their children to the public school—to increase the number of teachers needed, or to make larger jobs for stationery and books, or, perhaps, to crowd the present school-house for the time, and thus have a plea for a rich contract to build a new house in the ward. Some suggest that the trustees fancied the move would be popular with their Catholic constituents. If so, they have missed it, for the Catholics of that ward look on it as a miserable dodge. We simply refer to the card of the St. James Free School Society, in our 'Catholic Register' column this week, for evidence of what the Catholics of the Fourth ward think of state-schoolism, whether nominally Bible-reading, or professedly godless. We fear that an idea of Catholic interest in keeping the Bible out of the public schools, may draw off the attention of some from the outrageous failure of the state-school system in other respects. Outside of this, the dispute has for us no importance.
>
> "All the bigots, and all the fanatics, may reassure themselves. Schools whose religion is confined to Bible reading, and schools

whence all religion is banished, are alike institutions that no Catholic is at liberty to advocate as fit for the education of Catholic youth. Papal promulgations and Provincial Councils have settled that question for Catholics, both as a general principle, and as of local application. Let no one then be misled for a day by the Bible question. It is not a Catholic question. There may be contracts under it, there may be jobs, there may be salaries—but never an odor of 'Popery.'"

The same print refers to a report of the Free-School Society of the Catholic parish of St. James, as a proof of what its own religious communion is doing to educate its youth in the tenets of their church. That society, within the past year, has received in contributions between eight and nine thousand dollars, and has expended in the work of instruction a little more than eight thousand. More than a thousand children have been in attendance in the schools of the parish during the last year; their proficiency is commended and, as a further advantage of the new system, it is stated that six hundred and seventy-six children, within the year, have received confirmation in the church.

If we take the view of the matter expressed by the *Freeman's Journal* as that of our Roman Catholic population, the question is now brought within a very small compass. That denomination does not concern itself at all with the question whether the Bible be read in the public schools or not; it leaves that to be settled by the friends of the common schools among themselves. It is the heretical part of the population which sends its children to those schools; admit the Bible, or reject it, it is the same thing to the Roman Catholics, whose children are educated elsewhere.

This being so, we do not see, for our part, any further occasion for controversy. All must now see that the Bible ought not in any case to be excluded from the common schools. We suppose there are children of Roman Catholic families who attend these schools, notwithstanding they are forbidden by their clergy. Their parents, we may fairly infer, have no objection to portions of the English translation of the Scriptures being read in the hearing of their children; nor do the authorities of the church, if we understand the passages we have quoted, make that the ground of their opposition to the common school system.

A correspondent asks, In whom resides the power to direct what books shall be used in the common schools of this city? The matter is in the hands of the Board of Education. Some of the members of that board who have favored the exclusion of the Bible from certain wards, are rather harshly treated in the Catholic journal from which we have quoted.

Changes in Asia
November 29, 1858

In 1857–1858 the seizure of Canton by an Anglo-French force brought treaties which opened eleven more Chinese ports to Western trade. Rebellion in northern India in 1857–1858 against the British, with the massacre of more than two hundred British women and children, resulted in August 1858 in the Government of India Act, which transferred rule from the East India Company to the British crown.

There is scarce anything more worthy of note in the present aspect of the world than the breaking up of Oriental conservatism. Within a few years past changes have been introduced, and relations with the powers of Christendom established—either voluntary or compulsive—which look like the beginning of a new condition of society and polity in Asia.

In Persia—for a long time past a declining power—great reforms are taking place. Since the dismissal from office of Sadrazam Mirza Aga Chan, the Shah has been regulating the finances and reorganizing the army upon a European footing. Several efficient European officers have been engaged to teach the use of the different firearms to the Persian army. General Krisch, a former Austrian officer, is organizing the artillery; Colonel Barbara, a Neapolitan, is instructing the cavalry and guard of the Shah; while a number of French officers, who were engaged by Feruk Chan on his last visit to Europe, are likewise in the military service. The reforms of the present ruler of Persia extend not only to the military, but to the entire government of the country. European ideas are invading that ancient monarchy, which has remained for so many ages in the same imperfect stage of civilization.

The progress of Eastern Russia is one of the remarkable phenomena of the present time. Siberia has been civilized by the exiles sent thither, and by voluntary emigration from Russia, till nearly four out of the five million inhabitants of that region are Europeans or of European descent—more fortunate than their western kinsmen in this, that there is not a serf among them. On their southern frontier the Russians have been slowly but steadily encroaching on the Tartar provinces. They have gradually absorbed and changed the character of almost the entire province of Mantchooria. Russian cities, manufacturing towns and traders' posts are springing up on the banks of the Amoor as they spring up in our western country.

Whatever doubts may be entertained by some of the opening of a free intercourse between China and the civilized world, one thing is certain, that there never has been so strong a desire on the part of the nations of Christendom to break through the barriers she has set up against the intrusion of foreigners as there now is. All the rest of the world seems to be conspiring against China and her prohibitory system. Ravaged and weakened as that country is by civil wars, she must be fortunate indeed if she can long withstand the assaults of the power of the whole trading world, bringing their navies to open her ports at the cannon's mouth. Treaty after treaty is extorted from her, each treaty probably to be made the subject of new misunderstandings, which will be followed by a demand for larger concessions. We may presume that it will not be possible for China long to escape being dragged into the sphere of those influences which are rapidly changing the character of the East. Whether a freer intercourse with China would be of any benefit to our own country, except in a mercantile point of view, and whether the commercial advantage might not be more than counterbalanced by certain moral mischiefs, are points which we will not stop to discuss.

Japan, so long closed to all nations but the Dutch, and hitherto little known to the European world, is opened to the commerce of Christendom, and diplomatic intercourse is promised with the powers whose vessels she admits to her ports. If we may believe the favorable accounts lately given of the people of that country, they are more likely to be contaminated than made better by their intercourse with the people of Europe and America—else there is no truth in the maxim that evil communications corrupt good manners. We have already seen, in one of the journals, a philanthropic expression of sorrow for the virtuous Japanese, whose fate probably it is to be corrupted by the contagion of European vices.

Meanwhile the Arab race in Northern Africa sees the remains of Saracen civilization gradually becoming merged in the civilization of Europe. It is not probable that France will remain content with the provinces she now possesses in that region. Tunis and Morocco, if her system of Algerine civilization should prove in any degree successful, will fall next under her power. Egypt is becoming Europeanized—an Arab province governed by European influence—an arena on which the French and English enterprise are contending for the mastery. In Turkey, the discontents of the Mussulman population, and the outrages they have committed on the Christians, are caused by seeing the progress of Frank influence, and by a consciousness of the danger that the Christians may become their masters and lawgivers. All over Western Asia the useful and ornamental arts, in those forms in which they were practised by the Saracens, are passing into disuse. The Arab women of Jericho wear French and English calicoes—the looms of Manchester weave cotton stuffs for the Moslem of Damascus. French manufacturers go with their workmen into Syria, and set up mills on the streams that flow down from Lebanon.

The Indian peninsula, as soon as the rebellion of the natives is fully quelled, will become, under the new organization of its government, more unlike than ever to what it was under its Oriental rulers. The English have obtained a new station in the waters that part Persia from Arabia; they have seized the unoccupied island of Perim, commanding the mouth of the Euphrates, and will make it the resort of their fleets. Everywhere the power of the West is aggrandizing itself—everywhere the power of the East wanes and passes into decay.

THE DIRECT TRADE OF THE SOUTH WITH EUROPE
ca. January 1859

Howell Cobb, briefly a Unionist governor of Georgia, and a United States Congressman 1843–1851, and 1855–1857, served as Secretary of the Treasury from 1857 to 1860.

The Georgia planters have just been holding a convention for the purpose of promoting that time-honored craze, a direct southern trade with Europe. Howell Cobb, it is said, and one or two others, have been deputed to visit the old world for the purpose of beating up European supports, to enable the South to punish the North for its divers rascalities, by getting all goods sent to Norfolk and Savannah, and thus making New York pale its ineffectual fires.

We should be very glad, we need hardly say, to see every southern port doing a brisk business in anything but the slave trade, but there are, nevertheless, reasons for their not doing anything of the kind, and for their remaining, for the present, at least, dependent on New York, which we cannot, if we would, get over. New York owes its commercial pre-eminence mainly to its central position, its ready communication with the great northwest, and its admirable harbor, accessible at all seasons of the year; and, also, though in a less degree, to the abundance of labor with which the tide of emigration, which passes through it, has always kept it supplied. When once commerce falls into a certain channel it is, as we all know, extremely difficult to divert it, even to localities possessing precisely similar advantages. Nothing is more wedded to old places and old ways than trade, and the longer it cleaves to a place the more numerous do the reasons for its continuing to do so become. The most skilful and enterprising merchants congregate in it, capital concentrates itself in it in large quantities, banks are established in it, great facilities are created in it for loading and unloading cargoes, railroads converge upon it, and on the heels of these press social attractions without number, arts, literature, and science. It becomes the port best known to foreigners, often the only port in which they have trusty agents, or in which they think they can dispose of their goods with safety and ease, and perhaps no considerations affect a man in choosing a distant point of consignment so powerfully as these.

How easy it is for a place that has once got hold of all these advantages to keep them, is proved by Venice, and Genoa, and Amsterdam, and a score of other places in the Old World, which remained great commercial marts for centuries, in spite of the defects of their ports and the rival attractions of much better and much more carefully fostered harbors. Zeal, attention, industry, enterprise, and above all, good faith and integrity, will enable any thriving seaport to bid defiance to all the ranting conventions in the world.

In the case of Virginia, North and South Carolina and Georgia, there are reasons, however, for their never having any direct trade worth speaking of, which seem to us to be all but insurmountable. The first is the insecurity for life and property by which most southern cities are marked. Most of the men engaged in commercial pursuits, and trained to conduct them well, the only men, in short, who have the skill or experience necessary to build up trade in southern ports, are northerners or foreigners. Both these have strong prejudices against slavery. Possibly, as the South thinks, they are mistaken prejudices, nevertheless, they exist, and must be taken into account. They have moral or religious scruples about exacting forced labor from anybody, and, like all businessmen everywhere, they have strong economical objections to slave labor. Wherever they are, it is impossible to avoid letting their opinions leak out, and if, as they ought to be, in order to do the South any good, they are bent on making their fortunes rapidly, they must necessarily be eager for free men to hire, instead of men to buy. To such persons as these the South offers no inducements. In the present temper of the southern people, especially industrious strangers are not encouraged to cross the border, but are hunted away like mad dogs. Men will, however, bear the persecution of public opinion if they are only sure of protection from the law, but even this the South denies to any one who does not avow and prove his devotion to slavery. It is impossible to expect sane Englishmen, or Frenchmen, or northerners, to repair in great numbers to Savannah or Norfolk, for the purpose of converting them into great seats of commerce, when an indiscretion in speech, or the denunciation of a scavenger, may bring down upon them the visit of a mob, and an order to quit in twenty-four hours. No very large number of really useful men will ever be got to place a complicated business affair, a wife, family, house and furniture, at the mercy of a tribunal of this sort, and run the risk of being suddenly driven away from them, without a hearing, and without any longer warning than would be sufficient to wind up and close a thriving bar-room. If the leading southerners who are so rampant for commerce and manufactures could be got to look at the mob law, which is supreme in nearly every southern state, in the light in which foreigners and quiet commercial men everywhere look at it, they would never hold another commercial convention until they had discovered some substitute for tar and feathers and rides on rails. This and slavery, and this, perhaps, even more than slavery, is now the great obstacle to southern commercial progress. As long as she has a monopoly of the production of cotton, she will of course have a certain amount of exporting to do, but, to receive all her imports directly through her own ports, a much larger amount of security and liberty are necessary than her institutions at present afford. Security is the very breath of commerce, and this can only be had by certainty in the law and security in its own administration. The South can boast neither one nor the other. It has adopted the political code of pure despotism, but it has committed its execution not to trained judges acting under a recognised system of procedure but mobs casually raised, who act in a passion without taking evidence and without hearing the accused in his own defence. The censorship of the press, the sedition laws, and, in fact, every one of the safeguards for its political system which it has copied from the continental despots, are carried out by irresponsible "committees" without any attention to forms.

It may be said that if the North would leave slavery alone these anomalies would all disappear, and the laws in the South would, as in most other communities, be left for their execution to the normal action on the courts. But the trouble is that, as commercial men all over the world are well aware, the North will never do anything of the kind. Whatever course the majority here may be disposed to take on the question, there will always be a large number of enthusiasts who will agitate and conspire for its destruction. Into the midst of a community agitated by such constant alarms, shaken by such an abiding sense of insecurity, no large number of merchants or traders will ever be found to fling their capital and seek to build up their fortunes and make homes for their children. The tendency just now, even on the part of those who have been born and bred on the soil, is just the other way. Large numbers of wealthy Virginians are, we are assured, anxious to remove for ever from such scenes of disorder and trepidation.

Who Is the Intermeddler?
January 17, 1859

The Louisianan Congressman John Slidell had been President Polk's unsuccessful secret agent to Mexico in 1845 in an attempt to buy Upper California and New

Mexico. *As a Senator he served as James Buchanan's campaign manager in 1856. A pro-slavery advocate, he was, with Buchanan, a proponent of the acquisition of Cuba by the United States.*

Such of the members of the United States Senate as belong to the party of "National democrats," have just had a meeting to consult in regard to the support they shall give Mr. Slidell's bill for the purchase of Cuba. It is said that some of them expressed the sensible opinion that there was no probability of persuading Spain to cede the island, and that if we want it, we must take it by force.

Of all the brood of projects which have been littered at Washington within the last twenty years, there is none that we can recollect so childish, so senseless, so utterly impossible to be carried into effect, as this scheme of Buchanan and Slidell to buy Cuba from Spain. A bill appropriating thirty millions to buy the moon would not be a more brainless project. To do Mr. Slidell justice, however, we do not suppose that he, whatever be the case with his principal, means anything by this bill but to keep the public attention fixed on the acquisition of Cuba till a convenient pretext can be had for invading it and attempting to possess it by force.

It is said, in some of the discussions of this topic, that England and France are maneuvering to prevent our acquisition of Cuba, and much windy declamation is expended on their arrogance in presuming to interfere in the politics of this hemisphere. What ground there may be for imputing this intention to the two great powers we will not undertake to say, but most certainly, if the imputation were ever so true, they could not be accused of interfering in the politics of the American continent. They would simply interfere to sustain the rights of a neighboring European power, and protect it in its legitimate possessions.

At present Spain derives most of her importance from the possession of Cuba. From Cuba she receives a large revenue; to Cuba her children go to make their fortunes. Cuba is the market for her products; her commerce with Cuba is the school in which her seamen are trained; to her possession of Cuba she owes her navy. Cuba is to her what the western territories are to the United States—in Cuba are her new lands; in Cuba she finds an outlet for her surplus population, and a sphere for the enterprise which finds no room for its activity in the mother country. Take Cuba from Spain, and we deprive her of a country larger than the kingdom of Portugal, larger than any of the provinces of old Spain, with the exception of Old Castile, and richer than any three of them put together.

Suppose that the Western Powers of Europe should say to the United States: "You protest against our intermeddling in the affairs of your hemisphere; we must, then, hold you to the duty of abstaining from all interference in ours. You attempt to strip us of our possessions, because they lie in your neighborhood and are convenient to you. Spain, with the possession of Cuba, is a considerable power; by depriving her of Cuba you reduce her to insignificance. What right have you thus to take into your hands the task of adjusting the balance of power among the European governments, and making weak those whom we have agreed to leave strong? You talk of our arrogance, but what do you call this?" It would be difficult to answer such a remonstrance.

The truth is that by taking possession of Cuba we shall do precisely what we were warned against by the voice of Washington in his Farewell Address, and by the wisest of statesmen who have lived since; we shall entangle ourselves in the complications of European politics. The European powers will soon see that, if while one of them is plundered the others can be persuaded to stand aloof, it may be the turn of any one of them to be robbed next. France and England may be called on successively to surrender their West Indian possessions, and Russia to resign her dominion over the promontory of Alaska. It will be for them to consider whether they will consent to be robbed one by one, or whether they will at once make common cause against the plunderer.

Oysters and Letters
ca. April 1859

Joseph Holt, a Kentucky lawyer, was Postmaster General from 1859 to 1861, and briefly Secretary of War in 1861. His predecessor at the post office had been Aaron Venable Brown, former governor of Tennessee.

There are some who entertain favorable expectations from the administration of the Postoffice under our new Postmaster-General, Mr. Holt. We hope they will not be disappointed, but we have one question to ask. Will he take such measures that the government, hereafter, may be able to carry letters as cheap as individuals carry oysters? This is easy to do, but it is not done, and we fear never will be while the mail monopoly continues.

Wherever you go in the western country, whether you ascend rivers or follow the track of railways, you find that oysters have arrived before you. "Hand out the oysters," is the common cry at the stopping places. Oysters, as soon as they are drawn from their beds under the brine, are put in all haste on board of our steamers and our freight trains, and taken into the distant interior by the most speedy conveyance. A letter will keep; a newspaper with intelligence which has not been read before, is always fresh the moment it arrives; but oysters have not the quality of long-keeping; the process of spoiling waits for nobody; oysters must be sent to their destination with the speed of an express. All over our vast interior, at any village on the railways, oyster-stands are to be found so numerously, that one is astonished at the fecundity of those banks in the sea which supply them. But the most remarkable thing of all is the cheap rate at which we get all this despatch and all this punctuality. Like all those things for which there is a large demand, and of which there is a large supply, oysters are cheap even in the interior. It need not cost more to carry a letter a hundred miles than to carry an oyster, yet, for carrying a keg of oysters to an almost indefinite distance inland, only twenty-five cents are paid, while for the same weight of letters several hundred dollars would be demanded.

If the laws of trade were left to their own operation; if the government did not interfere with its prohibitions and penalties, the communication by letters between different parts of the country, which the wise ones at Washington are for burdening with an additional tribute to the government, should be among our cheap blessings. The demand for the speedy and regular conveyance of letters is large, the supply of letters is ample and constant, and the means of conveyance neither expensive nor difficult to be had. Postage, therefore, ought to be cheap, like Croton water, like bread, like oysters, instead of being made dear, as Secretary Cobb and the late Postmaster-General would have made it. If the bankruptcy at the Postoffice, now imminent, were to result in the breaking-up of that monopoly, the abandonment of the Postoffice Department as a separate branch of the government, the abolition of the office of Postmaster-General, and the substitution of private expresses all over the country instead of government mail routes, the loss of the Postoffice Appropriation bill in the last Congress would, within two years, be acknowledged as one of the most fortunate events in the history of the country. We have not the least doubt, for our part, that if a law were to be passed allowing private expresses to carry letters, but prohibiting them from taking more than a single penny for a single letter, the expresses would make it a gainful business.

We are to have, it is thought, an extraordinary session of Congress, to consult on the subject of appropriating money for the operations of the Postoffice. The question of the rate of postage will very probably come up again, as it came up in the last Congress. Some of the members will undoubtedly press the scheme of a five-cent postage. We have a right to ask of the majority in the House of Representatives that they resist this enormity to the utmost. We have a right, we think, to ask of them still more than this, namely, that if they touch the postage question at all, they do not forget the case of the oysters, but that they so shape their proceedings that at some future time, not too far distant, it shall not cost much more to carry a letter from New York to Buffalo than to carry an oyster.

At the present moment, what are the means of conveyance to which our banks and our bankers all over the country have recourse to carry money for them? Who are the confidential agents whom they employ in a matter which requires such absolute integrity and perfect promptitude? Not the government postoffice, not the mail contractors; the bankers and dealers in money will not, nay can not, trust the government. They have slender confidence in official fidelity, vigilance and exactness; they call for the integrity and activity of individuals, whose sole dependence for success is on the satisfactory manner in which they perform the service they undertake. Private enterprise carries their bank notes and drafts and certificates of deposite from place to place, just as it carries oysters. Millions on millions in this manner traverse the country in every direction, meeting and passing each other and intersecting each other's track, in perfect security, and reaching their destination with the greatest punctuality. When a note of hand, held in New York, is to be collected at Burlington in Vermont, the holder does not think of having anything to do with the mails; he knows of a far better method than that. He takes his note to the express office of Adams and Company; they give him a receipt for it, collect the money in Burlington, and have it ready for him in New York when he calls for it. At every important point in the interior, on the arrival of the railway trains, you see express-wagons harnessed, ready to start towards the four winds, the horses pawing the ground and impatient to be on their way. All the ways of communication between man and man, which the mail monopoly leaves open to individuals, are immediately occupied by a class of men who serve the public better than the agents of the government.

The letter trade is in the hands of the government, the oyster trade is in the hands of individuals. We shall never see the former in a satisfactory state till it is committed to the same hands which so ably conduct the latter.

The Impending War
May 6, 1859

The tidings from Europe, brought by the steamer *Niagara*, resemble those which have already reached us, in this respect, that events are rapidly bringing the great Powers of the Continent nearer and nearer to actual hostilities. Every time that we look at the war-cloud impending over Europe it is visibly darker, and perhaps, even while we write, it has begun to send down its lightnings to the earth.

If full reliance is to be placed on the intelligence just received, Austria had sent a message to the Sardinian government, threatening immediate war unless the Sardinian troops should be disarmed within three days. Of course so peremptory a summons would be unheeded. Sardinia will not acknowledge herself the vassal of Austria to obey such a mandate; and we cannot wonder that Britain, as is said, should protest immediately and with energy against such a proceeding. A requirement of that sort, accompanied with the menace of hostilities, is virtually a declaration of war. It cannot be obeyed without dishonor, and if it be not obeyed, Austria cannot draw back from her threatened purpose without confessing her fears and her impotence. What mediation might do we cannot say; but we have no faith in its efficacy; the British government is, without doubt, intensely anxious to prevent a war, but it is not at all likely that Austria would have taken such a step as we chronicle to-day, until all hope of successful mediation was at an end, and it only remained to frame a pretext for making an immediate attack upon Sardinia.

It appears that Sardinia is willing to disarm, on condition that she shall be represented in the Congress proposed by Russia. The obstacle to the maintenance of peace does not, therefore, lie in any objection to the plan of a general disarmament, which has been accepted by the five great Powers, but in the refusal of Austria to allow Sardinia a seat in the assembly which is to arbitrate on the destiny of Italy. Austria insists that Sardinia shall have neither voice nor influence in that question, but that it shall be referred simply to the governments which, nearly half a century since, parcelled out the great empire wrested from the first Napoleon, and which adjusted according to their own good pleasure the balance of Europe.

The policy of Austria in her recent message to Sardinia is, doubtless, to put an end to the delays of which the Emperor of the French is availing himself to prepare in the fullest manner for war. From the very first, the warlike preparations in France have not intermitted for a moment. Steadily, day by day, the French armies have been strengthened, munitions of war collected, and both troops and munitions moved towards the future seat of war. Austria is undoubtedly distrustful of the plan of a Congress, either as a device to give the French government time to collect a force so far superior to that of Austria as to throw all the chances of success against her, or by admitting Sardinia among the arbitrators, to strip Austria of the Italian possessions which she has held ever since 1815. To neither of these alternatives is she willing to submit, and we may fairly suppose that she regards herself as driven to make war in order to avoid a snare laid for the dismemberment of her empire. She prepares, therefore, to make the attack while Sardinia is the weaker power, and before she has her powerful ally at her side.

We have copied from an Albany journal an article giving a view of the dispute somewhat favorable to Austria, and expressing the opinion that before the strife shall be at an end the sympathies both of our own people and those of the British Isles will be with the Austrian government. What new aspect the controversy may yet put on we will not undertake to conjecture, but, as the case now stands, we do not see how the liberal-minded of our own countrymen can desire any other result than that the Italian race shall be delivered from a yoke which they abhor, even if the change be merely from one despotism to another.

We have no doubt that the despotism which Austria exercises over her Italian possessions would be far milder if the Italian people were more patient. The severities they endure are graduated according to the supposed necessity of the case. The Austrian government would be passably benign if its Italian subjects would allow it to be so. But the Italians hate the Austrians, and the knowledge of that hatred keeps the Austrian government in fear, and makes it austere and remorseless. The high-spirited steed rears and tries to shake off its detested rider, and the rider in turn plies the whip and plunges the rowels deep into the animal's side. In the name of justice, then, if the Italians must live under a despotism, let them choose what master they will obey; let them live under a despotism to which they will submit with some degree of content, and which they will not provoke to severity by impatience and unconcealed dissatisfaction. Besides, the character of Austrian despotism is stable, permanent, petrified, hopeless of change. French despotism is intermittent and proverbially subject to fluctuation, and if the people of Italy prefer it, and can get nothing better, let them have it.

We have already spoken of the new horrors which war would put on if it should break out between any two of the greater powers of Central Europe. We might add that not only would the bloodshed be terrible beyond anything hitherto known, but the commercial ruin which it would involve would be beyond any example. At no period of the world have the commercial interests of nations been so interwoven and dependent on each other as now; war would rend them apart, uproot, scatter and destroy them; it would break up gainful occupations, throw thousands out of work, condemn thousands to starvation. We may expect also that a war waged at the present day will be diversified by strange accidents, new to military history. It is an important part of the science of war to cut off the communications of the different portions of an army with each other, and to obstruct their progress. We may hear of hosts on their rapid journey by railway towards the seat of war, suddenly stopped by finding the iron rails taken up and carried off, or we may hear of railway bridges treacherously rendered insecure and whole squadrons dashed to pieces by their giving way. The clandestine cutting of the wires of a telegraph may interrupt the best-laid plan of operations, and bring it to a disastrous conclusion. Spies in the enemy's camp, and in the enemy's country, have been a part of the machinery of war in all ages, and there never was an opportunity for so much mischief to be accomplished by this class of men as now, when so many of the facilities which modern science has lent to the art of war, are placed at their mercy.

The Effect of the Sardinian War on American Travel
May 7, 1859

Bryant's reassurance of prospective travelers to western Europe is a reminder that he had, less than a year earlier, returned from extended travel through much of the territory to which he refers. The Thirty Years' War, 1618–1648, involving most of western Europe, had caused great devastation in Germany and the breakup of the Holy Roman Empire.

We suppose there were never as many American travellers in Europe as at the present moment. Last winter there was a mob of them in Rome—three hundred at one time—and the number of those who have already sailed for Europe this season, or who have made preparations to go abroad, is very large. The return of prosperity has brought back with it the inclination for foreign travel. The question is naturally raised, whether this migration will be checked by the threatened war in Europe, and whether, in case war should arise, it will much obstruct the movements of American travellers, or otherwise put them to very considerable inconvenience.

It is very likely many persons of a timid nature will be induced, by the probability of a coming war, to pause in their arrangements for going abroad; but, after the first shiver of apprehension has passed away, the greater part of them will proceed as if nothing had occurred, except that they may vary somewhat the plan of their tour. They will see some countries more thoroughly than they otherwise would have done, and of some countries which they would have been glad to visit they may see little or nothing; but this will be nearly all the difference the war will make. The British isles will be open to them from the Land's End to the Shetlands, with their great variety of climates, the cool summers of their northern parts and the soft winters of Torquay and the Isle of Wight, their antiquities, their arts and repositories of art, and their monstrous London—largest city of Christendom. There is no probability that the war will come nigh France, the capital of which, with its spectacles and amusements, is the great attraction for idle people who have no higher aim than to pass life pleasantly; so that all the empire, from Valenciennes southward to the calm and windless sky of Pau, and the breezy coast of Montpelier, and the majestic mountain ranges and green valleys of the Pyrennees, will be spread before the sojourner in search of health or pleasure, to allow him ample choice of places of residence; or if he be a little enterprising, a speedy voyage will take him from Marseilles to Algeria and give him a sight of Oriental life. Or he may enter Spain, now open to the traveller by a railway connecting the capital with the sea coast, and find himself in Madrid, gazing at the pictures in its magnificent gallery, before his acquaintances at Paris are aware of his absence. There will reign internal quiet in all the countries north of France to Spitzbergen. There is no motive to draw Belgium, or Holland, or Denmark, or Sweden into the strife, and every reason why they should resolutely insist on remaining neutral. Switzerland will, of course, follow her ancient policy of neutrality; the valleys of the Alps are no battle ground; and the tourist on the mountain sides in that region will only learn the progress of the conflict by what he reads of it in the journals of the day.

In the meantime France will be mistress of the Mediterranean. Not a corvette will venture out from the ports of Venice or Trieste while the French fleet, now rivalling the British in the size and number of its ships, rides those waters. In the Mediterranean, therefore, there will be peace, and unless a civil war should break out at Rome, there will be nothing to prevent the usual winter concourse of strangers in that city, coming thither in steamers by way of France. The probability of any internal disturbance at Rome, it seems to us, will be much lessened by the war between France and Austria. The theatre of that war will be on the plains of Lombardy and the banks of the Po, and already the more restless spirits of Rome and other parts of Italy are flocking northward to the Sardinian standard, that they may take part in the conflict. In the fierce but brief warfare which will follow—for as it will be terribly destructive of life and rapid beyond all previous example in its operations, it will necessarily be brief—the dissatisfied among the subjects of the Italian principalities will naturally be content to await the result of the strife in which their friends are engaged. Wars like these give employment to that unquiet and enterprising class by whom revolutions and insurrections are fomented, and turn their impatience for adventure into another channel.

On a review of the whole matter, therefore, we see little cause why those who contemplate going abroad should take alarm at the apparent certainty of a European war. The commerce between the United States and Western Europe will be carried on as before, without the slightest interruption, since Austria has no marine, and there can nothing occur, in consequence of the war, to disturb or render uncertain the pecuniary relations of the two continents. The greater number of places worth visiting as objects of a rational curiosity will be as accessible as ever; the most genial climates of Europe; the south of France, Sicily and Malaga, will still invite and welcome the invalid, and beyond them the way to Egypt and Western Asia, now so often visited, will be as little obstructed as ever.

The very destructiveness of the war, as warfare is now carried on, must operate to deter from engaging in it all those governments which are able to maintain their neutrality. There can be no Thirty Years' War in these days. A war of that duration would literally unpeople the countries engaged in it and leave them a desolate wilderness. We may rely upon it that, with the spectacle before them of nations dashed against each other with such immense bloodshed, the strong motives of self-interest and self-preservation will withhold all but the immediate parties to the dispute from mingling in the strife.

The European War
May 10, 1859

Henry Wellesley, Earl Cowley, was the British ambassador to France, 1852–1867. With the help of French Troops, the Piedmontese, who had rejected the Austrian ultimatum, repelled the invaders at Palestro on May 30.

The attitude and movements of the Great Powers of Europe furnish the absorbing topic of the day. Our only sources of intelligence in regard to them, the telegraphic reports, are unfortunately meagre and fragmentary, and do not enable us to form a decisive judgment as to the actual position of things. By the arrival of the *Anglo-Saxon* yesterday at Quebec, we learned, on the one hand, that the English government, on the 25th of April, had despatched "to Vienna and to Paris a joint representation offering to take up the mediation of England at the point at which it was left off by Lord Cowley, and to endeavor to arrange the difficulties, subject to one of these two conditions, either the immediate, absolute, and simultaneous disarmament of the three Powers, or the consent on the part of all, pending the result of the mediation, to retain their armies precisely in their present condition, and to maintain a position, if not of peace, at all events of inaction," and that an official intimation of the acceptance of the offer, by Austria, had been received in London on the 27th. But, on the other hand, we learned by the same arrival that French troops were rapidly pouring into Sardinia by the passes of the Alps and the seaports of the Mediterranean, that the Emperor of France and Prince Napoleon would quit Paris on the evening of the 27th, to place themselves in communication with the army, and that the King of Sardinia, the same day, attended a ceremony at the Cathedral of Turin, preparatory to his departure to Alessandria, where he would probably assume the command of his troops.

A subsequent arrival at St. Johns, however, of the steamer *Adelaide*, from Galway the 30th of April, bringing three days' later news, reconciles this apparent contradiction, or rather, it says nothing of the acceptance of the English propositions by Austria, while it does say that the Austrian soldiers have passed the Ticino, and that eighty thousand French troops were expected to be in Italy by the day the *Adelaide* sailed. The war then is actually begun; the armies of the empires are marching towards each other; and before this a decisive collision, either between the Austrians and the Italians, or the Austrians and the French, may have occurred.

The most interesting report brought by the *Adelaide* is of the alliance offensive and defensive, said to have been concluded between France and Russia, which seems to have fallen upon the English money market like a clap of thunder. Several journals, both in Paris and London, and some we perceive in this country, are disposed to question the accuracy of the report, although we cannot, for our part, see much reason for doubt. As early as the 5th of April last, the St. Petersburg *Vaidomostee* foreshadowed such an alliance by the terms in which it spoke of the *Moniteur*'s article on the Peace Congress proposed by Russia. "The Emperor," it said, "through the instrumentality of his official paper, entrusts his honor to the Emperor of all the Russias. And that great and generous nation, so proud and so touchy in matters of honor, France, whose self-esteem is so intimately connected with that of her Emperor, both shares and confirms the confidence placed in us. No better pledge of alliance can be imagined between two nations and sovereigns than this, and Russia's conduct in this affair is deserving of the highest praise, and has gained it." Again, in the same article, it was said: "Apart from all other considerations this event shows the solidity of the Russo-French alliance, and the amicable character of this intimate relation between the two Powers." It is true, the St. Petersburg journal added that this league had nothing to do with any purposes of conquest or war, but the disclaimer was a mere matter of form, which did not change the nature of the fact.

Thus, for the second time within the present century, we behold an alliance, offensive and defensive, between the great empires at the eastern and western extremities of Europe. The former was entered into in 1809—just fifty years ago—and at the prospective expense of Austria, as the present one seems likely to be. Owing to the overweening ambition of Napoleon I., and to an unexpected train of events, the first alliance did not long continue; but the second one, formed under different auspices, and under European conditions which have greatly changed since the Napoleonic wars, may attain a greater longevity. There is no essential opposition between the interests of France and those of Russia, and since the latter power appears to be inclined to push her gigantic developments towards the East, rather than the West or South, the probabilities of a future break or collision are lessened.

The combination, however, is one that England and Germany will not stomach so readily; England, on the pretence, doubtless, that it may furnish Russia a better opportunity for threatening her preponderance in India, and also because of her speculative apprehensions as to the dangers of uniting two great despotisms; and Germany, because she lies between the parties, and may be crushed, or at least wounded, by the embrace of two such ponderous bodies. The London *Times*, from the start, denounces the alliance as a menace to England, and we may expect to hear similar objurgations from the German press, as soon as its voices shall reach us. But they are the immediate consequences of the alliance, we suspect, rather than its possible remote effects, which these nations dread. It may interrupt the cordial understanding that England and France have cultivated since the outbreak of the Crimean war, and gain to the side of France the liberal sympathies of the continental populations, which England has repulsed by the dilatory policy of her Tory statesmen, to say nothing of their open approval of the conduct of Austria in Italy. Again, in respect to Germany, it will operate as a severe rebuke to the proclivities of the Germans towards the Austrian cause. Russia has no occasion or motive, that we see, to weaken Prussia, or any other German state, and the practical meaning of her alliance with France is simply a protest against the schemes of Austria. Russia proclaims to the Germans that in the war about to open they must keep their hands off. France has made no demonstrations against them; France does not mean to make any demonstrations against them; her quarrel is with Austria in the interests of Italy; and Russia sends her armies to the German frontier, in order to see and to maintain fair play. Should the result of this announcement be to circumscribe the war to Austria, France and Sardinia, as the parties to it, and to Italy as the theatre of it, the cause of humanity will be the gainer.

Austria is, by the late turn of events, completely isolated from the other powers of Europe. The feeble and cautious approbation of a few English statesmen will avail her nothing, and of course the English nation will not support her by force of arms; France and Sardinia are her enemies; Denmark is reported to have taken the same unfriendly course as Russia; Prussia, the most powerful of the German states, has expressed a surprise at the precipitancy of her action; and a chief vassal in Italy, the Grand Duke of Tuscany, has run away from his indignant people, leaving their example of revolt to be followed soon in the other principalities of the Peninsula. Not a solitary weapon is raised in her behalf, outside of the limits of her own empire, save in the Estates of the Church, and in some of the smaller German kingdoms. Neither of them are of much import in contrast to the overwhelming force, moral and physical, arrayed against her; and, when we add to these sources of difficulty, the hopeless embarrassment of her finances, and the hazard she runs with her Hungarian dependents, it would seem doubtful whether, with all her military strength, she will be long able to continue the war.

The Flight of the Duke of Tuscany
May 10, 1859

The first government overthrown by the present European convulsion is, singularly enough, one of the most liberal. Leopold II., Grand Duke of Tuscany, has, we learn by the latest European intelligence, brought by the *Adelaide,* fled from Florence. No further particulars are given, and though it was to be naturally supposed that the expatriation of the Grand Duke would be one of the necessary results of an Italian revolution, the event has taken place sooner than we had reason to expect. As yet, until we have additional news, it is almost impossible to speculate with propriety upon the causes which led to this premature flight, but it certainly shows the imminence of the great crisis in Italian affairs.

Leopold II., Grand Duke of Tuscany, is the second son of the Grand Duke Ferdinand III., and was born at Florence, on the third of October, 1797. During his infancy his family suffered political reverses, being driven out of their dominions by the French. Retiring to Germany his father caused the young Leopold to be educated, first at Salzburg and afterwards at Würzburg. In 1814, on the fall of Napoleon, Florence was restored to the Grand Duke, and Leopold returned with the family to his native city. In 1817 he married a Saxon princess, and in 1824, on the death of his father, succeeded to the ducal chair. During the troubles of 1848 he was again expelled, but soon returned to his capital, and on the 22d of June 1850, a Convention was signed by which ten thousand Austrian troops should occupy Tuscany and support the authority of the sovereign.

Frequent vicissitudes proved to Leopold that direct tyranny would endanger his government, but as a scion of the house of Hapsburgh, and the grandson of the German Emperor, his feelings naturally inclined towards imperial rather than republican traditions. Indeed, whatever might have been his inclinations, the influence of Austria was so decided that he dared not be too liberal. Yet, he has certainly done a great deal for the moral and material improvement of Tuscany, than which no Italian country now exhibits greater evidence of prosperity. It is chiefly to Leopold II. that the Tuscan people owe their splendid roads, their substantial stone bridges, their new railways, and many of their institutions of education. The traveller is at once struck with the contrast between Tuscany and the Papal States, in regard to these internal improvements. In the former he rides by easy paths, crosses magnificent stone bridges, such as are never met in this country, passes by cultivated fields and through towns where modern improvements are constantly taking place, and where the monumental buildings of mediæval ages are preserved with pious care. Crossing the boundary into the domains of Pius IX., he finds the roads neglected, the fields untilled, old cathedrals falling to decay, and the streams often impassable from want of proper bridging. In Florence, also, Leopold has been projecting and carrying on improvements that reflect the highest credit on his liberal taste. The great cathedral, perhaps next to St. Peter's, the most magnificent of Italy, and which has been for centuries unfinished, he had undertaken to complete. The Church of Santa Croce—that Pantheon of Florence, wherein repose the remains of Michael Angelo, and other great men whose genius has shed such lustre on the name of Italy—had long offended the eye by its imperfect front, and Leopold II. had commenced erecting a façade that was worthy of the edifice. The "Lung' Arno" the picturesque, promenade of Florence, a noble street bordering the east bank of the Arno, has been extended and adorned with new palaces. Indeed, had he been allowed to perfect his plans, Leopold II. would have done for Florence what Napoleon III. has already done for Paris.

As a patron of the Fine Arts, the Grand Duke of Tuscany also deserves mention. By his direction the invaluable art treasures of Florence were freely thrown open to public inspection, including the galleries of his own palace. In religion he has exhibited considerable tolerance, as the Protestant communities of Pisa, Leghorn and the capital city, will confess; although the persecution, in his dominion, of the Madiai has prejudiced against him many Protestant countries.

In person the Grand Duke is rather prepossessing. He is now sixty-two years of age, but looks much older. His hair is of a light gray color, and he stoops slightly while walking. His countenance betrays certain marks of care and suffering, which are attributed by many of his people to domestic trials, a cherished relative being afflicted with insanity. In manners he is affable and pleasant, and was accustomed to ride out daily in the Cascine, sometimes in a carriage, with the members of his family, and sometimes on horseback, his equipage being only distinguished by the respect with which the bystanders gaze upon it, from the more dashing turn-out of my Lord Noodle of England, the wealthy Mr. Smith of the United States, or the lesser lights of the Florentine nobility. In the more retired parts of the Cascine—the beautiful wooded park that lies upon the banks of the Arno, but a short distance from the city—he was often fond of strolling alone, and many strangers at Florence have passed him carelessly by without a thought. Those who recognised him would raise their hats, to which the Grand Duke would respond by a similar salute, there being no further formality or etiquette in this than what would mutually pass between the President and a citizen of the United States.

But with all these excellent qualities, Leopold is not popular in Tuscany. The presence of the Austrian troops constantly irritates the people, who do not think the music they gratuitously afford to the public, on the open space in front of the Ducal Palace and in the Cascine, a sufficient reward for the unwelcome presence of the "Tedeschi." Indeed, the presence of these troops can never be forgotten by the people, for a daily parade takes place in the principal streets. To a stranger it is very interesting to listen to the music of the band, and to see the well-trained file of soldiery passing along in their picturesque costumes—some with helmets adorned with waving plumes, others with the jaunty cap and feather of the Savoyard mountaineers, while their well-burnished bayonets cast lightning-like flashes of light upon the frowning walls of the palaces of the Strozzi and Medici. To a stranger this is all delightful—but then strangers do not have to pay for all this glitter and parade.

This, with other causes, has combined to make Leopold II. unpopular. He knew it, and was prepared for any coming political event. He had just returned from a visit to the dying king of Naples, when he heard the rumble of the political earthquake, and timid and nervous as he is, notwithstanding his refined tastes and his benevolence, he fled from Tuscany at the moment when she is in danger.

In this flight Leopold leaves the most beautiful city of Continental Europe, and the most luxurious home that any living monarch has occupied. Windsor Castle is graced with its battlements and towers—the Palace of the Tuileries is rich in treasure, and gorgeous with everything wealth can command—the Czar resides in halls where barbaric splendor is toned by modern art—Pius IX looks from the windows of the Quirinal or the Vatican upon the most classic ground the earth knows—but none of these regal homes can equal in luxurious delight the Pitti Palace of Tuscany. Its massive walls, its peculiar architecture, its domestic conveniences, its refined accessories, its superb position, are all unsurpassed. It contains some of the richest art treasures in the world. In its marble galleries are the peerless Madonna della Segiola of Raphael, the Madonna of Murillo, the richest sunlights of Salvator Rosa and Claude Lorraine, the Venus of Canova, and the cherished souvenirs of many of the greatest artists of Italy. Behind the palace stretch the Boboli gardens, with their quaintly-trimmed foliage, their refreshing fountains and their rare statuary, while from the higher terraces the now exiled Duke could enjoy the noblest view the vicinity of Florence affords. In the distance, bounding the horizon, are the white peaks of the Appenines, while near by lies the "fairest city of the earth," Florence, with the Arno winding through it, spanned by bridges that are themselves a feast to the eye. Rising from the clustered houses are the mighty dome of Brunelleschi, and the fairy campanile of Giotto, while beyond is the rich front of Santa Maria Novella, where is enshrined the famed Madonna of old Cimabue. Palaces and churches are scattered at intervals, and as a beautiful back ground there are the wide steps that lead up to the heights of San Miniato, where the dark cypresses stand like sentinels guarding the city below. In front, beyond the mediæval tower of the Palazzo Vecchio, beyond the Cathedral, and beyond the city walls, is the first billow of the rolling Appenines, and on its summit stands Fiesole, and the little tower where Galileo worked out his mighty problems. All this Leopold II. leaves, in his hurried flight, and who can tell whether the complications of European politics will ever allow his family again to occupy that palace and enjoy those scenes?

Nuisances on Railways
September 3, 1859

There are several nuisances to which travellers on our railways are exposed, concerning which we have long thought of saying a word or two.

One of them is the clouds of dust in which trains travel, and which, in warm weather, are continually drifting in at the open windows. The greater the speed of the train the more dense the whirlwind of sand which it raises from the ground below, so that the few who are in no haste to reach the end of their journey prefer the slower trains. Those who travel on the New York and New Haven railway, or on that which follows the track of the Hudson to Albany, experience this inconvenience to its fullest extent. Except immediately after a shower, they breathe an atmosphere of pulverized flint, fearfully unwholesome to certain constitutions, and come out of the cars with their hair and clothes the color of the soil. In no part of the world—at least in neither England, France, Germany or Italy—does this nuisance exist to so intolerable a degree as here. In some countries the railway track is covered with grass, in others it is paved with stone, and the wind of the train is in both cases prevented from drawing the dust into the air; but in our country a long time will pass before our railways will be so constructed that there will be no dust for the trains to raise. That there is a method by which this inconvenience may be got rid of is shown by the experience of the Housatonic Railroad. There the process of ventilation is effected in this manner: a current of air is made to enter at the top of the baggage-car, beyond the reach of the dust, and passes through all the cars that compose the train, the doors at both ends being open and all the windows closed, while the spaces between the cars are protected against the intrusion of dust by curtains on each side, meeting at the top. In that way the air in the cars is constantly renewed without bringing in either dust or smoke, and the travellers journey in comparative comfort, unless some of them are so indiscreet as to open the windows, which renders the air within no cooler and much less pure. We have hitherto seen no method of excluding dust so effectual as this of the Housatonic Railroad.

Another inconvenience experienced by travellers is the confusion and hurry which prevails in receiving and checking baggage at the New York stations. None of them is worse managed in this respect than the station of the New York and New Haven Railroad in Twenty-seventh street. A great deal of the baggage is collected and brought to the station in large loads by the express wagons. They do not generally arrive till very shortly before the moment for the trains to set out, and as soon as they are on the ground a sense of indescribable bustle and jostling begins. All those enormous piles of trunks at the door have to be tumbled in a few minutes into a little office, through which they must pass to the train, and where they must be fitted out with checks, which are to be handed to the owners. It is almost at the peril of your life that you adventure into this place, which is crowded with travellers dodging the heavy trunks which the porters are bringing in upon their shoulders, in dangerous neighborhood of your head, and hurling upon the counter. None of this confusion is seen upon the European railways. At their stations is space enough to enable you to keep out of harm's way, and though there is more consumption of time, every thing proceeds in an orderly and quiet manner. The confusion and jostling here might be avoided by proper regulations, since it is not the same at all our railway stations.

We have a third nuisance to mention, which is an abomination of the most disgusting sort. The habit of spitting is almost as freely indulged in by our countrymen in the cars as in the bar-rooms of our taverns. If a seat happens to be occupied by a tobacco chewer he soon makes it unfit to be occupied by anybody else. If you observe one of this class, you will see that the very first thing he does, on taking his seat in a car or an omnibus, is to drop his saliva. It is true that when the trains reach their destination the floors undergo a deal of cleansing, or, at least, are suffered to become dry, before they set out again, but it frequently happens that they are vacated and filled again by way passengers before they finally stop. A passenger goes out, a lady comes in and takes his seat, because there is no other; she finds the floor in such a pickle that she cannot sit down without allowing her skirts to absorb the pollution with which her predecessor has covered the floor. Some persons of this class are still more liberal of their salivary ejections, and bestow them upon the passage between the seats. It has been thought that a sense of decency would by degrees put an end to this uncleanly practice, but the progress of reformation is exceedingly slow. A beginning has been made, with some success, under the attentive management of the Housatonic Railroad. By a printed notice put up over every seat, passengers are requested not to spit on the floor, but, for the most part, those who must relieve themselves in this way open the window. There is an evident disposition to observe the regulation, and this is a good sign; the reform may, in good time, be extended to other railways. If no other method will answer, certain cars may be set apart for the tobacco chewers, as, on the French railways, a certain number of the cars are specially assigned to smokers.

John Brown and a Slave Insurrection
October 18, 1859

On October 16, 1859, the Abolitionist John Brown, with a handful of followers including two of his remaining sons, had raided a federal arsenal at Harper's Ferry, Virginia, with the aim of inciting a slave rebellion. But, as Bryant was writing this editorial, a body of local militia and a company of United States marines under Colonel—later General—Robert E. Lee captured the insurgents after killing several, including Brown's sons. Brown's nickname, "Osawatomie," came from a free-soil settlement he had established at that Kansas town, and from which he was driven in 1856 in reprisal by pro-slavery men for his murderous raid on their headquarters on the Pottawatomie Creek.

The stories connecting the name of "old Brown of Osawatomie," as he is called, with the leadership of this fanatical enterprise are, we are induced to think, well-founded; and in that event the whole affair might be regarded as a late fruit of the violence which the slaveholders introduced into Kansas. Brown was one of the early settlers in that territory; he was a conspicuous object of persecution all through the troubles; his property was destroyed; he and his family were cruelly treated on several occasions; three or four of his sons were killed by Southern desperadoes; and these many exasperations drove him to madness. He has not been regarded since, we are told, as a perfectly sane man. He has been known to vow vengeance against the whole class of slaveholders for the outrages perpetrated by their representatives in Kansas, and this insurrection, if he is at the head of it, is the manner in which he gluts his resentments. Frenzied by the remembrance of his wrongs, his whole nature turned into gall by the bitter hatreds stirred up in Kansas, and reckless of consequences, he has plunged into the work of blood.

Passion does not reason; but if Brown reasoned and desired to give a public motive to his personal rancors, he probably said to himself that "the slave drivers had tried to put down freedom in Kansas by force of arms, and he would try to put down slavery in the same means." Thus the bloody instructions which they taught return to plague the inventors. They gave, for the first time in the history of the United States, an example of the resort to arms to carry out their political schemes, and dreadful as the retaliation is which Brown has initiated, must take their share of the responsibility. They must remember that they accustomed men, in their Kansas forays, to the idea of using arms against their political opponents, that by their crimes and outrages they drove hundreds to madness, and that the feelings of bitterness and revenge thus generated have since rankled in the heart. Brown has made himself an organ of these in a fearfully significant way.

No one can think of the possible results of an outbreak of this kind, should it become general, without shuddering; without calling up to his imagination the most terrible scenes of incendiarism, carnage, and rape. In nearly all the Southern States the negroes greatly preponderate in number. Many of them, it is true, are too ignorant and stupid to take any effective part in an insurrection; others, too, are profoundly attached to their masters or their families; but these excepted, there are yet thousands able and willing to strike for their emancipation. It has been impossible to keep them in entire ignorance of the blessings of freedom, and of the possibility of attaining it by force of arms; the fugitive slaves of the North have found means of communicating with their old comrades; the Abolitionists have spoken to them by pictures, if not by language; Democratic orators have told them falsely that the entire North was engaged in a crusade against the South for the sake of the slaves; and as servants in the cities they have heard the talk of the parlor and barrooms, and in innumerable other ways have been made to think and to desire. When the hour comes, therefore, they will not be found either so incapable or so docile as the slaveholders seem to suppose.

But what a condition of society is that in which half the population constantly menaces the other half with civil war and murder; in which the leading classes go to sleep every night, carelessly, it may be, over the crater of a volcano; and in which the dangers do not lessen, as in other societies, with time, but grow with its growth until an explosion becomes as inevitable as the eruptions of Etna or Vesuvius! What a condition of society, to be extended over the virgin territories of the West, the seat of our future empire, and for which politicians should clamor and sear their consciences, and desperadoes should fight!

How insane the policy which would recruit and extend this form of social existence, even while it is becoming unmanageable as it is! Open the gates to the slave trade, cry the Southerners, who are as great fanatics as Brown; tap the copious resources of Africa, let new millions of blacks be added to the enormous number that now cultivate our fields, let the alarming disproportion between them and the whites be increased; it is a blessed institution, and we cannot have too much of it! But while they speak the tocsin sounds, the blacks are in arms, their houses are in flames, their wives and children driven into exile or killed, and a furious servile war stretches its horrors over years. That is the blessed institution you ask us to foster and spread and worship, and for the sake of which you even spout your impotent threats against the grand edifice of the Union!

The Execution and Its Effects
December 5, 1859

Following his capture at Harper's Ferry, John Brown was hanged on December 2, at Charlestown, Virginia. The Kentucky lawyer Thomas Corwin had been a United States Senator, 1845–1850, and Secretary of the Treasury, 1850–1853. Wendell Phillips was a Boston reformer and prominent Abolitionist. The Hungarian patriot

Louis Kossuth had led an insurrection against Austrian Emperor Franz Josef in 1848.
Between his conviction of insurrection and murder on November 2 and his execution a month later, as his stature as a martyr grew in the Northern states and across the seas, Brown was permitted freely by the Virginia authorities to write anyone he pleased. It is therefore a tantalizing, if unanswerable, question whether one of his communications was addressed to Bryant, for among the editor's surviving papers is the message, scrawled on a scrap of brown wrapping paper, "Tell W-C Bryant in my dying hour I freed the slaves of America." Unfortunately, the subjoined signature is undecipherable.

The manner in which popular feeling has manifested itself at the North with regard to Brown's execution proves the wisdom of his own remark when he said he could in no way so well serve the cause he had at heart as by hanging for it. We do not so much allude to the outward manifestations of respect for his name and memory,— the devotion of the hour of his death to prayer in a great number of churches, the tolling of bells in many towns, the firing of minute-guns in others,—though these have in themselves a marked significance—as to the pity which every one whose pity is worth having has openly expressed for the old man's fate, the sympathy which almost every one seemed glad to avow for his simple and manly virtues, and the silence with which, for the sake of those virtues, the faults and follies of a wild and wayward life have been covered almost by the whole community.

The death of a criminal on the gallows of whom half the nation speaks tenderly, and whose last hours the prayers and fastings of many thousands of sincere religious men have sought to hallow, is certainly not an incident to be dismissed with newspaper paragraphs. It is an event in our national history which warrants every thoughtful man amongst us in pondering over it deeply. Except those whose property he sought to damage—of whose power and privilege he avowed himself the mortal enemy—there is, we venture to assert, hardly a man outside the circle of professional politicians and southern traders who accuses Brown of more than legal guilt, or claims for Virginia in her dealings with him more than legal vantage ground. Her warmest apologists do not venture to invoke on her behalf against her enemy any higher law than the law of self-preservation, any stronger right than the right of self-defence. Thomas Corwin, even, in defending her the other night against the "misguided" Wendell Phillips, did not go behind the "necessity of the case" in order to justify her and condemn Brown. All the conservative and pro-slavery newspapers which have defended the rigor of her justice, and heaped reproaches on the head of the fanatic who assailed her, have invariably relied on her legality and his illegality for the support of their whole argument.

But neither Brown nor his friends have ever taken issue upon one of these points. That Brown's attempt was illegal, and that Virginia, if she meant to preserve her existance as a body politic, was not only justified in inflicting violence, but bound to inflict it, his warmest friends have not ventured to deny. Upon this side of his case any lawyer's clerk could overwhelm him and his sympathizers. There was no deception about the matter. Brown knew upon what terms half a dozen malcontents may challenge a state to the field. He knew that if, as Corwin says, society did not meet rebellious minorities, rope in hand, society would soon cease to be possible. He ran the risk, and we know from his conduct that he was prepared to pay the forfeiture. But as he prophesied before his death, rebel, traitor, convict, though he be in the eye of the Virginia law, there is a court of last resort, a higher one than the Virginian Court of Appeals, to which he managed to carry his case before he died, and in that he has triumphed. It is mere sophistry to assert that when a criminal court has pronounced its sentence, and its justice has been done on the culprit, that the atonement is complete and that society has vindicated itself.

It is an axiom in jurisprudence that the action of a court of law and of the executioner is but half the process by which crime is repressed and order maintained. The other half is to be found in the sympathies and feelings of the public. If these be on the side of the law, the criminal is indeed condemned; if they be against the law, his blood has been spilt not only in vain, but to the detriment of society. Take away popular approbation from the hangman, and he becomes a hired assassin. In this court of last resort the worst thing that has been said of Brown is, that he was foolhardy. He has been dismissed from the bar, with his judgment indeed impeached, but with no weightier condemnation of his acts than that they were marked by folly. In war all is folly which does not succeed: the rule is harsh, perhaps, but necessary. Napoleon said Leonidas was no doubt a very fine fellow, but "he let himself be turned at Thermopylae." Virginia, to be sure, thinks Brown more of a knave than fool, but in this matter the Virginians bear much the same relation to him, in the eyes of the world at large, that Francis Joseph bears to Kossuth. A large part of the civilized public will, as a large part of the world does already, lay on his tomb the honors of martyrdom, and while those honors remain there, his memory will be more terrible to slaveholders than his living presence could ever have been, because it will bring recruits to his cause, who would never have served under his banner while he was wielding carnal weapons.

If all these be facts, they are no doubt unpleasant facts for every one who has the future welfare of this country at heart to contemplate. But that is certainly not a reason for trying to hide them; the fact that a thing which in Virginia is deemed worthy of a shameful death, is in New England deemed worthy of Christian benison is not a fact to be avoided, but to be met and provided for. Two people whose standards of morality are so widely different need to look well to the bonds which unite them, and look well, too, to the feuds which threaten to sever them. But we should have already fallen upon worse days than God, we would fain believe, has in store for us, if loyalty to our common country called upon us to repress our sympathy for courage, for truth, for adherence to honest convictions, for faithfulness unto death in the cause of those whose gratitude or applause can bring neither fame nor honor. We have been long training ourselves to stand in the slaveowners' place, contemplate his dangers, and sympathise with his difficulties. But we should despair of the country if we thought a regard for its welfare required us to heap execrations on the first man's head who has put himself in the place of the slave, and sought to realize *his* trials and privations, the sorrows he has to undergo, and the obstacles he has to encounter. It is, therefore, we think, a sign, not of national decline, but of growth in all the real elements of national greatness, that sorrowing hundreds of thousands should have been found to overlook this man's errors in admiration for his heroism, for his fortitude, and for his hatred of oppression. It is to such qualities as these, and not to a holy horror of mere disorder, that we owe our existence as a nation, and when the day comes in which no man will be found in America to cry bravo! when he sees them, our final extinction will not be very far distant.

A Calm Word Respecting the Union—A Union Party at the South
December 23, 1859

At a Union meeting in New York—one of a number held throughout the North both to reassure the South after Brown's raid and to suggest Republican complicity in it—Postmaster John Adams Dix called Brown's invasion a "vast conspiracy," and his fellow Democrat, the lawyer Charles O'Conor, said that if the North "continued to elect fanatics to Congress" he would not blame the South for seceding. George Washington Bethune was a prominent Dutch Reformed clergyman; Benjamin Harvey Hill, a moderate Georgia legislator who opposed secession.

The Union meeting having been held, the speeches all made and published in the newspapers, the resolutions passed, the guns fired and the smoke of the powder dispersed by the winds, perhaps those who are anxious for the safety of the confederacy, having slept two or three nights upon the matter, will be prepared to listen to a few calm words.

We are not of that class who have any objection to Union meetings. It causes us neither surprise nor regret that people here, perceiving that there is a great excitement at the South, and conscious that neither they nor the great majority of the northern people have done anything to provoke it, should desire to make such representations as will appease it. It is very proper, in fact, that this should be done. We feel that the prejudices which have been fomented against us at the South are unfounded; we know that the resentment of our brethren in that quarter is without a just occasion; and we owe it to the cause of good neighborhood to set them right.

But, in attempting to do this, we should take such steps as to do it effectually. We should interest the largest possible number of our citizens in the movement, and particularly those against whom the charge of hostility to the South is most freely made. Unless this is done, nothing is done.

The excitement which prevails at the South has been got up by representations which are false. The mad project of Brown was falsely charged upon the Republican party; the leaders of that party were accused of being privy to Brown's proceedings, and of having favored, encouraged and even counseled them, though they were as innocent of the charge as Mr. Everett or Dr. Bethune, who have spoken at the Union meetings. The charge was made and urged for party purposes—made to influence the election of speaker at Washington—to influence the next election of President. Those who first gave it currency knew that it was not true, but a great many persons of the South have been persuaded to believe it, and are both indignant and alarmed. To satisfy those who are sincere in their belief, the Republican party should have been allowed in all the Union meetings the fullest opportunity of acquitting themselves of any responsibility of the acts of Brown, any approval of his undertaking and any design to interfere with slavery where it exists. The Republican party, in a general sense, constitute the people of the North. Here they govern, public opinion is on their side, and they hold the power of legislation. Let those at the South who are really alarmed but once see that they are guiltless of the charge brought against them, and the cause of alarm is done away.

But those who raise the cry of disunion at Washington, and those who were the leaders in getting up the Union meeting here, do not mean the people of the South shall see this. It is for their interest, so they certainly seem to think, that the people of the South should be kept in a state of excitement, for the present at least. It was therefore that the call for the Union meeting the other day was so drawn up that thousands of Republicans could not sign it. The *Journal of Commerce* commended the call because it had the effect to exclude the Republicans. It was for this reason that the Republican speakers were not allowed the opportunity to address the meeting. It was for this reason that a pro-slavery partisan, Charles O'Conor, the principal speaker of the evening, was put forward to affront northern feeling by speaking of slavery as a good, as a benign and beneficent institution, worthy of all favor; and to encourage the animosity of the South against the North, by declaring that, if the North continued to send such men to Congress as now represented it, the slave states were justified in dissolving the Union.

If a different course had been taken, if the call had been made general, so that the Republicans could sign it; if they had been allowed a place on the platform and an opportunity to vindicate their loyalty to the Union and their respect for the rights of the states, how different might have been the effect! If the well-meaning part of the southern people could have been satisfied by anything, this would have satisfied them, provided their party leaders and those who conduct their journals had but permitted them to see our proceedings. But the preparations for the meeting were in party hands, and such was the management that the effect on the South will, most assuredly, be worse than nothing.

Let it be considered that the meeting was the work of a party who are greatly in the minority in the free states, and that it was managed in such a way as not only to prevent any expression of the views of the party which forms the large majority, but to keep alive those misrepresentations of the designs of the Republican party by which the anger of the South is inflamed, and the necessary conclusion from this is, that more mischief than good has been done. If any slave-owner of the South really fears that we are about to instigate his slaves to cut his throat, what assurance does he get from Mr. O'Conor's speech that the danger does not exist? What syllable did John A. Dix or James S. Thayer utter, among all their many words to tranquilize him on this point? Did either of these men make himself responsible for the pacific intentions of the party which forms the mass of the people here, and which will remain faithful to its organization and to its purpose in spite of ten thousand Union meetings? On the contrary, the whole tendency of the proceedings was to let it be understood that the great and powerful Republican party is for exterminating slavery at the South by direct political interference, or by the dreadful expedient of servile insurrection.

We are sure that many who signed the call were innocent of any intention to encourage this kind of misrepresentation. We are ready to extend the same exemption to some who spoke at the meeting, and to others whose letters were read from the platform. But that the whole effect of the call and meeting was to give new currency to a shameless calumny, and to pour oil on the flame which blazes in the slave states, is undeniable.

Meantime, let it not be supposed that the sudden gust of ill-feeling at the South, caused by the calumnies uttered for party effect against the people of the North, is the same thing with a determination to break away from the Union. The formation of a Union party is begun in the slave states, and it will grow stronger and more numerous every day until the election of a President. The moment the Republican candidate for the Presidency is nominated, he will receive assurances of loyalty to the Union from tens of thousands at the South. That was the case when we were contending for the election of Frémont with far greater odds against us than we now have. Frémont was almost buried under showers of letters from the South, assuring him that the writers shared his opinions and prayed for his success. Republicanism at present is the rising sun, and it has already its worshippers at the South, the fervency of whose adorations will increase as its orb rises higher towards the meridian.

Already Southern members of Congress begin to declare that they will have no part or lot with those who talk of dissolving the Union, in case a President shall be elected whose political opinions do not agree with their own. Mr. Hill, of Georgia, avowed this determination in the most solemn manner, and we pledge ourselves that the avowal will do him no harm with his constituents. Mr. Anderson, of Kentucky, made himself responsible, in the same debate, for the firm attachment of Kentucky to the Union. Kentucky is not for going out of the confederacy, whatever the Virginia politicians may think of doing.

The other day, when the medical students in the southern states assembled in Philadelphia, and, in spite of the Union meetings held in that city, resolved to return to the South, their fathers sent messages by the telegraphic wire, desiring them to stay where they were. The old people, it seems, saw no particular cause to expect a dissolution of the Union.

In another part of this paper we place several extracts from journals at the South, which have been provoked by this clamor for the destruction of the Union, to speak of the mad project in terms of decided condemnation. The Baltimore journals are among the foremost to denounce this vile outcry—for Maryland has no idea of going out of the Union—but other journals published in more southern latitudes are scarcely less fearless and firm in their language. We ask our readers to look to the passages we have quoted, and judge for themselves, whether the cause espoused by the journals in question is not likely to prevail at the South.

SOUTHERN LITERATURE
December 28, 1859

British-born James Iredell of North Carolina, an ardent supporter of the American Revolution, was an Associate Justice of the United States Supreme Court, 1790– 1799. In 1857 Bryant had hailed publication of The Impending Crisis of the South, *a forthright attack on slavery as an obstacle to Southern growth by the North Carolinian Hinton Rowan Helper, which was furiously attacked by Southern Congressmen. Martin Jenkins Crawford was a Democratic representative from Georgia, 1855–1861. John Sherman, a brother of Civil War Union General William Tecumseh Sherman, was a leading Ohio Congressman from 1854 until 1861, when he was elected to the Senate. The cowardly braggart Captain Bobadil appears in Ben Johnson's play* Every Man in His Humour *(1598); "Put money in thy purse" is the repeated advice of Iago in Shakespeare's* Othello, *I, iii [345]. The* National Era *(1847–1859), an anti-slavery journal, had published* Uncle Tom's Cabin *serially in 1851–1852.*

The encouragers of southern literature in the northern states have lately been visited with gross abuse on the floor of Congress and in several of the journals of the southern cities. We must say few words in their favor.

A citizen of North Carolina two or three years since was compelled to leave the state, because he thought slavery was evil and said so— because he entertained and expressed the same views respecting slavery that were entertained by Washington and Jefferson of Virginia, and by Judge Iredell of North Carolina. He came to the North and published a book called "The Impending Crisis of the South," addressed to the white citizens of the southern states, with a view of convincing them that slavery is both morally and economically wrong, and that they ought to get rid of it. He afterwards made an abridgement of the work, to which he gave the title of "Compendium of the Impending Crisis," &c. This man was Hinton Rowan Helper. It is this "Compendium" which makes all the noise we hear about "Helper's book"—it is this which stirs the rage of the Crawfords, and the Foukes, and the Extra Billys in Congress.

Mr. Helper is a North Carolinian, addressing his countrymen of the slave states on a most important subject. We ourselves united with others to ask for him a candid hearing from the people of the South. The request was a very proper one. If Mr. Sherman, the Republican candidate for Speaker, was one of those who joined in this request, we hope he is not ashamed of it, and is ready to do the same friendly act for the next exile for opinions' sake from the same quarter of the country. We certainly are, for our own part.

Mr. Helper, however, did not seem likely to obtain the hearing he desired. The book found little sale and made no noise, and we dare say, produced no effect, good or bad, until the Bobadils of the South began to bluster about it in Congress, and to shower their filthy abuse on those who reccommended it. From that moment it began to sell. There was an immediate demand for it at Washington; every southern man at the seat of government must have a look at it. Then followed a demand for it in every quarter of the Union; a universal curiosity was awakened concerning a book which was to act like a torpedo affixed to the ship of state, and to blow it into fragments. Every speech made in Congress denouncing it produced an order to Mr. Burdick, the bookseller, for several thousand copies. Mr. Burdick is making his fortune, and Mr. Helper, we hope, is agreeably occupied in obeying the Shakespearean injunction, "Put money in thy purse." He now finds the audience at the South which he asked for; we only hope it will be a candid one.

The main defect of Helper's book is, that it deals too much in epithets; but its assemblage of facts to prove that the South can never be prosperous while the institution of slavery exists is most valuable, and if the people of the South will but give it their attention they must be convinced by it. One of the best parts of the book is that which has given, perhaps, the greatest offence. He urges the whites of the South who do not own slaves not to send any more slaveholders to Congress. He belongs, himself, to this class, and exhorts his brethren to make their voice heard in the halls of legislation. The advice is very natural for such a man to give, and very sound advice it is. The slaveholders and their tools in Congress are the pest of the republic. There are quite too many of them—men who can think of nothing but the propagation of slavery, and talk of nothing but northern aggression, while they are getting up a new scheme for their own aggrandisement every year. It is quite time that the South should have a representation of a more popular character, and if any recommendation of ours can have the effect of directing the attention of the southern nonslaveholding class to this subject, we are ready to give it.

Meantime there is nothing in the book which has the least incendiary tendency. There is nothing addressed to the slaves, nothing which could have the effect of making them discontented or uneasy; but there is much that should make the whites so. It is not circulated among their negroes any more than the *National Era* is, and if it were, a sensible planter said the other day, it could do no mischief, since it would be impossible for them to understand it. The book is called by some of the southern declaimers infamous; their denunciations have at least made it famous. If it be infamous to speak of slavery as the greatest and noblest and largest-minded men of the South have spoken of it, then Helper's book is infamous; but if they were right, he deserves to be honored for adopting their opinions and repeating their counsels in despite of the present fanatical attachment of the slave states to the institution which is at once their calamity and their reproach.

We close, therefore, with a sincere and earnest recommendation to every southern man who may see this article, to look at the statements in Mr. Helper's book, without regard to the rhetoric with which they may be accompanied, and to ask himself seriously whether he does not think that slavery is an evil to which an early remedy ought to be applied by the slave states themselves.

A Change of Tune
December 30, 1859

In Southampton County, Virginia, in 1831, a Negro preacher, Nat Turner, led a slave rebellion in which fifty-seven white men, women, and children were killed; in reprisal, about one hundred Negroes were tracked down and slain, and twenty more executed after trial. In 1835 Northern resentment of Abolition led a Boston mob to attack and nearly kill William Lloyd Garrison. During race riots in Cincinnati in 1841 the press of Dr. Gamaliel Bailey, then conductor of the anti-slavery Philanthropist, *was destroyed by a mob. In 1834 Lewis Tappan, a founder of the New York City Abolition Society, was stoned and his home attacked by a mob which burned his furniture in the street. "An appeal from Philip drunk to Philip sober" is a saying attributed to the Roman historian Valerius Maximus, ca. A.D. 14. James McDowell, a planter who strongly opposed slavery as fomenting disunion, governed Virginia from 1843 to 1846. Charles James Faulkner was a Democratic Congressman from Virginia, 1851–1859, and minister to France, 1857–1861.*

It is a constant subject of complaint on the part of the southern members of Congress that we of the North not only entertain opinions strongly adverse to the justice and wisdom of slavery, but are continually urging those opinions in an offensive manner. Most of the speakers on the southern side, during the pending discussions in the House of Representatives, have assigned this as one of the principal reasons why they regard the existence of the Union no longer either desirable or possible.

We copy on our first page to-day an article from the *National Era*, in which extracts are given from the speeches of the leading men of Virginia, after the suppression of the Southhampton insurrection in 1832.

It would not be easy to match the emphatic condemnation of the institution conveyed in those speeches from the severest attacks that have proceeded from any northern men. It is held up to view in every aspect, moral, political, and economical, and on all these grounds it is pronounced unworthy of defense. There are no more unmeasured denunciations of slavery in Helper's book; no fuller denials of its rightfulness, and acknowledgements of its calamitous effects on society, than are uttered by these Virginian statesmen and legislators.

Let it be remembered that these things were said in the Virginia legislature before Lovejoy was shot at Alton, before Garrison was led up State street with a halter around his neck, before Dr. Bailey's press was thrown into the Ohio at Cincinnati, and before a proslavery mob sacked Lewis Tappan's house in this city. The North was then "sound on the goose," and abolitionists were few and destitute of influence.

What a change has been wrought in twenty-seven years! Now Virginia ignores the sober utterances of her best men in those days, and is represented by men who not only defend slavery as right and profitable, but demand of the North to unlearn the lessons she taught it at a time when it gave no quarter to those who questioned the divinity of the institution.

What right has she to require of us that we shall adopt just that one of her recorded opinions which it suits her present purpose to patronize? It is a sufficient answer to all her modern gasconade that we hold precisely the doctrines of her best men in her better days. We appeal from Philip drunk to Philip sober. Virginia has no statesman above ground who is distinguished for a more enlarged and generous spirit, or for greater dignity of character, than Governor McDowell, whose speech is one of the strongest condemnations of slavery on record.

A striking proof of the great change brought about in twenty-seven years appears in the contrast between the views then held by Mr. Charles J. Faulkner and his present position in the ranks of the pro-slavery disunionists in Congress.

A still more noticeable fact is the vast difference between the temper in which slavery is dealt with immediately after an insurrection panic in 1832 and in 1859. Can it be that Virginia will calmly and deliberately prefer the vaporing and bluster of Wise and his partisans to the dignified and candid discussions of McDowell, Rives, and Randolph?

It is to be remembered that slavery has undergone no change since 1832, and that the census has, twice since that time, demonstrated with silent but unerring logic the truth of every word then uttered against the economy of its maintainance.

Benignity and Beneficence
December 31, 1859

Our readers have not, perhaps, forgotten Mr. Charles O'Conor's eulogy, pronounced at the late Union meeting, on that "just, benign and beneficent institution," slavery. A remarkable example of the kindly and humanizing effect of this benign and beneficent institution has just been given, the history of which we copy in another part of this sheet, under the title of "An Irishman's Sufferings in South Carolina." Mr. O'Conor will see that the person to whom the adventure happened was one of his own kindred, and will not fail, we hope, when he next repeats his oration, to adduce it as a convincing example of the effect of slavery in softening the manners and heightening the civilization of those regions which are blessed with its influences.

An Irish mechanic named James Power, who had always been a good democrat and voted with the pro-slavery party, went to South Carolina, and was employed as a stone-cutter on the State House, a magnificent building, the pride of the state, now going up in Columbia, where there is a college and professors, and a population not more barbarized, we suppose, than is to be found in other towns of its size at the South. This man made the discovery that a white laborer at the South, in consequence of slavery, which makes labor disgraceful, is looked upon as belonging to a degraded class. He said so. For this offence his apprehension was ordered by a Vigilance Committee; he attempted to make his escape, was pursued and seized two miles from town, was imprisoned for three days, without liberty to communicate with any of his friends, was then brought before the Mayor, where the remark he had made was proved, on which he was remanded to jail, kept there six days longer and half-starved.

At the end of this period two marshals took the Irishman out of his cell and made two negroes drag the poor man through all the muddy puddles on the way to the State House yard, where a crowd of several persons were assembled, headed by a troop of horse. They marched him in a procession to a place three miles out of the city, where, amidst brutal cries of vengeance from the crowd he received thirty-nine lashes from a cowhide, drawing blood at every stroke; his lacerated body was then daubed with tar from the head to the waist, and next covered with feathers. In this half naked state he was taken to the railway, and put on board the negroes' car. Here the crowd detained the train, made a fresh application of tar, and stuck it over with cotton. The train took him to Charleston, but at every stopping-place on the way a mob gathered to inflict fresh insults. At

Charleston he was kept in jail for a week, and visited by a physician, who comforted him by informing him that his case was a mild one, since there was another man then lying in the City Hospital, who had received five hundred lashes instead of thirty-nine, and was nearly killed by the infliction.

Last Saturday the poor Irishman was taken out of jail, being supposed now able to travel, and put on board a steamer for New York, where he arrived on Monday, and is here trying to get well and looking for work. The particulars we have given, it will be seen, are parts of Power's own story, but the Charleston *Mercury* had already informed the public that this man had been publicly whipped and then tarred and feathered, and that his crime was that he entertained "anti-slavery opinions," as a white mechanic at the South naturally would. The principal facts are admitted, and the minor circumstances are probably true. The remarkable feature of the case is the revolting brutality of the southern population it discloses. It seems to be one of the effects of the "benign and beneficent institution," that it nourishes a wolfish ferocity in the mass, and makes men indifferent to human suffering. The narrative of James Power is made probable by the examples which we have of the atrocities committed on other persons—such as the tarring and feathering and riding on a rail of two poor Italian organ-grinders in Alabama, on suspicion of being abolitionists—the tarring and feathering of a man in Clayton, in the same state, for the same reason—the tarring and feathering and ducking of Sandy Tate, a Scotchman, at Salisbury in North Carolina; and we might add to these the indignity to which two gentlemen who arrived in the steamer *Huntsville* from Savannah on the 19th instant had been subjected: a mob having seized them, shaved their heads on one side, and sent them out of South Carolina.

The institution which has these blessed effects is the one which Mr. Buchanan tells us is established and legalized by the Dred Scott decision in all the territories of the United States, until they become states and are allowed to legislate for themselves. We are sure that the single case of James Power is enough to make every right-minded man pray that an institution which encourages such horrid brutalities may never be extended a single rood beyond the space it now occupies, and exert himself to exclude it at any sacrifice from the territories. Wherever it goes, neither the personal liberty nor the personal safety of the whites can coexist with it; not only the black but the white population are the slaves of the oligarchy.

Who Is For a Coat of Tar and Feathers?
January 9, 1860

Probably there are few of our readers who would like to be smeared with tar and then equipped with a covering of feathers. Nor would many of them, we fancy, be much delighted with receiving thirty-nine lashes with a cow-skin, well laid on. A ride on a rail might be less unpleasant, but we doubt whether many of them would think it an agreeable diversion. To come down to matters of less moment, we do not suppose that they would take pleasure in being summarily expelled from the country for the offence of speaking their minds respecting a political institution which they desired to reform, or that they would be even satisfied to have the newspapers for which they subscribed, withheld from them by the creatures of the government. A reasonable man, let him live in what part of the country he might, would, we are sure, pardon any of our readers for not taking a fancy to be treated in either of the ways we have enumerated.

In saying this we but state some of the objections to the extension of slavery which have not hitherto received the attention they deserve. We of the free states object to legalizing the relation of master and slave in the territories, because, if slavery goes thither, we are not allowed to go. It is true that those who favor the enlargement of the area of slavery tell us that, although they claim the right of carrying it into the territories, yet the moment the inhabitants of any territory in which it is established frame their constitution, they have the liberty to abolish it.

That is not true; every mail that we receive from the slave states brings evidence that it is false. Wherever slavery goes, whether into a territory or a state, there is no longer any liberty of speech or even of thought in regard to that question. If any man denies its benefits, the practice of the day is to mob him, to shave his head on one side, to push him off a railway train to the danger of his life, to tar and feather him, to give him a public flogging. If he simply comes from the North, and endeavors to escape this rough treatment by observing a prudent silence in regard to slavery, his trunks are opened, his baggage searched for incendiary publications; if a northern newspaper is found, he is a subject for Lynch law; if the search be fruitless, he is warned to leave the state immediately. A bare suspicion of abolitionism is enough to cause the unfortunate traveler to be ejected from the community without further ceremony. A man selling maps, who never troubled himself to know whether he was an abolitionist or not, is admonished that he is regarded as a dangerous personage, and obliged to decamp with the next train. Commercial travelers who attend Union meetings at home, and do their best to keep on good terms with the slaveholders, are met by committees, who tell them that they will save their friends at the North a good deal of anxiety by making the best of their way back again.

Is not the theatre in which these enormities are acted large enough already, but must we open to them all that mighty area of territory which lies between the states on the Atlantic and those on the Pacific coast? Are we, are citizens of the free states, comprising two-thirds of the whole population of the Union, ready to introduce into the territories a system which will bar the whole of that vast region against us and against our children? Are we willing that the territories should become a part of the country into which we cannot enter without the certainty of being mobbed and the danger of losing our lives; in which we cannot express our opinions on public questions with that freedom which has hitherto been the boast of our institutions; in which we cannot read what books we please, and into which the newspapers of the free states, for the very reason they discuss public questions freely, are not allowed to circulate? Are we ready to establish over those extensive regions a censorship of opinions and a censorship of the press which shall make a residence in them impossible to a northern man deserving of the name of freeman?

Yet this is precisely what we are asked to do. The institution of slavery, when it reaches its full and consummate growth, which it now seems to have done in the southern states, demands all these sacrifices, all these abnegations of personal liberty. Wherever it goes it establishes a cruel, relentless, remorseless despotism, which exacts a conformity as rigid as is required in the absolute governments of the Old World, and punishes men on mere suspicion with the same ferocious severity.

No, we must keep the territories open for freedom—open for freedom of speech, open for freedom of the press; hospitably open for emigrants who carry with them only their own strong arms and their love of liberty; freely open to the commerce of the free states, and to all the civilizing influences of the older settlements. If we allow, upon any pretext, the institution of slavery to be established in them, we sign away our own birthright and the birthright of millions of freemen besides; we give them up to be the patrimony of an oligarchy which will remorselessly exclude us the moment they have it in their possession.

Mr. Carey's Challenge
January 14, 1860

Henry Charles Carey, a son of the Philadelphia publisher and economist Matthew Carey, an ardent protectionist, was himself an exponent of free trade until about

1844, when he was converted to protectionism. His Principles of Political Economy *was published in 1837–1840.*

Mr. Henry C. Carey of Philadelphia, known by various works on political economy, has challenged Mr. Bryant, one of the editors of this paper, to a discussion, in the newspapers, of the question of Custom-house taxation. In behalf of Mr. Bryant we would state that challenges of this kind he neither gives nor accepts. It would almost seem like affectation on his part to say that he has not read the letters—two in number, he is told—in which this defiance is given on the part of Mr. Carey, having, unfortunately, too little curiosity to see in what terms it is expressed; but as such is the fact, it is well perhaps to mention it. His duties as a journalist and a commentator on the events of the day and the various interesting questions which they suggest, leave him no time for a sparring-match with Mr. Carey, to which the public, after a little while, would pay no attention; and if he had ever so much time, and the public were ever so much interested in what he had to say, he has no ambition to distinguish himself as a public disputant. His business is to enforce what he considers important political truths, and refute what seem to him errors, just as the occasions arise, and to such extent as he imagines himself able to secure the attention of those who read this journal, and he will not turn aside from this course to tie himself down to a tedious dispute concerning the tariff question at any man's invitation.

The question of the tariff is not the principal controversy of the day. It may seem so to Mr. Carey, who is suffering under a sort of monomania, but the public mind is occupied just now with matters of grave import. To them it is proper that a journalist should principally address himself until they are disposed of. He may make occasional skirmishes in other fields of controversy, but here is the main battle. When the tariff question comes up again, it will be early enough to meet it, and even then, a journalist who understands his vocation would keep himself free to meet it in his own way.

If Mr. Carey is anxious to call out some antagonist with whom to measure weapons in a formal combat, and can find nobody who has an equal desire with himself to shine in controversy, we can recommend to him a person with whom he can tilt to his heart's content. One Henry C. Carey, of Philadelphia, published, some twenty years since, a work in three volumes, entitled "Principles of Political Economy," in which he showed, from the experience of all the world, that the welfare of a country is dependent on its freedom of trade, and that in proportion as its commerce is emancipated from the shackles of protection and approaches absolute freedom, its people are active, thriving and prosperous. We will put forward Henry C. Carey as the champion to do battle with Henry C. Carey. This gentleman, who is now so full of fight, will have ample work on his hands in demolishing the positions of his adversary, with which he has the great advantage of being already perfectly familiar. When that is done, which will take three or four years at the least, inasmuch as both the disputants are voluminous writers, we would suggest that he give immediate notice to his associates, the owners of the Pennsylvania iron mills, who will doubtless lose no time in erecting a cast-iron statue in honor of the victor.

THE DANGER TO THE UNION—THE CAUSE AND REMEDY
January 17, 1860

Alfred Iverson was a Georgia Democratic Senator from 1855 to 1861. A few weeks earlier he had called the enmity between North and South "deeper than hell," and said nothing could now prevent secession. Virginia Senator James M. Mason had long seen the relation between the two sections as an intolerable conflict between two social and economic systems.

We extract elsewhere a few paragraphs from the speech of Mr. Iverson of Georgia, delivered in the Senate on the 9th instant, showing the past and future requirements of the southern oligarchy upon what he calls the northern democracy. It will be seen that, whilst he commends them for the humiliations to which they have heretofore submitted, all this goes for nothing unless, like Mr. Charles O'Conor, they abjure and renounce the doctrines heretofore taught both at the North and at the South, that slavery is a moral, social, and political evil. There can be, he says, no party association with men holding such doctrines, and no union with states governed on such principles. This aspect of public affairs demands serious considerations by all patriots. The solution of this question, consistently with justice and safety to the Union, is indeed the object of all patriots. How it is to be accomplished is the only inquiry.

To us it seems that the further submissions demanded are impossible, and if possible would be most unwise. It must be apparent to all, indeed, that the submission which Mr. Iverson recounts and commends, and which have encouraged Mr. Mason to characterize the northern states as the "servile states," have drawn the government into its present danger. What but the unwise concessions which Mr. Iverson recounts has brought about that revolution in the South itself, touching the nature of slavery? If the northern democrats had resisted manfully the adoption of Mr. Calhoun's subtle dogmas in the party creed, and refused to be its apologists, or to defend the double-faced platforms on which nullification raised itself to power, the South would not have abandoned its own teachings, adopted the monstrous doctrine that slavery was a blessing to be perpetuated and extended, and now demanded, as a condition of the continuance of the Union, the acquiescence in this principle by the North.

If, instead of resorting to the gambling device of squatter sovereignty which Mr. Iverson now reprobates, though he confesses that he condescended to play the southern game with it in 1848, the northern democrats had adhered to the accepted doctrine of all parties and sections previously, we should not now be called upon to recognise slavery as a national institution and a blessing to be perpetuated and extended as the condition of the continuance of the government. While the North remained faithful to the true and time-honored constitutional doctrine the South also adhered, and not a murmur was uttered against the adminstration of the government upon that principle. It was only when the northern democracy had abandoned it, and by a delusive pretence the principle of "squatter sovereignty" was substituted, that the nullifiers were enabled to maintain possession of the government and consolidate the South. Now we are presented with the alternative of conforming our opinions to the new doctrines of the South, and recognising slavery as a national institution to be perpetuated as a blessing, or submitting to a dissolution of the government.

What is the instruction to be derived from these facts, as to the safest course to extricate the government from the dangers with which it is threatened? Is it not that in this, as in all other cases, it is by a firm adhesion to the truth we are to find the rock of safety? Are not those who would frustrate the efforts of the true lovers of the Union to consolidate the North on the principles upon which the government was administered from the beginning, with the unmeaning cry of sectionalism, playing precisely the game of the northern democracy, by whose treachery the dangers were originated? No man who acts on his judgment, and not on his fears, can fail to see that it is only by a manly assertion of the true principles of the government against the false and odious doctrines announced by the President and his party, that this government can be preserved or be worth preserving. Many well-meaning men, sick of this slave question, who will not give themselves thought enough in reference to it to comprehend its moment, are deluded by the cry of sectionalism, and surrender their own convictions out of a vague fear that the persistence in the assertions of them will aggravate difficulties. The very reverse is, however, the result. All that is needed at this moment to put down at once and forever the abominable doctrines set forth by the President and his adherents, and the mischiefs which flow from them, is that the people of the North should express with emphasis and with unanimity their real opinions on the subject. The absolutisms of Europe even bow before public opinion. The division of the North, through the contrivance of party organization, has for the moment, effected at the South what the armies of Napoleon enable him to do in France—to muzzle the press.

This has withdrawn all moral support from the true champions of the constitution at the South. They live there under a reign of terror, which now seems at its worst, but which, if the voice of the North is again palsied in the contest of the present year, will deepen into horrors which will sicken the heart. The maltreating and expelling from the southern states not only northern men, but native-born sons of the South, is the fruit of northern treachery. Let the northern people continue to take counsel of unworthy fears, and suppress their convictions, and another year will not pass till they will have witnessed barbarisms perpetrated on the noblest of their own race at the South, which ought to sear their eye-balls. Will the men of the North suffer the base traffickers for place to dull and deaden their sense of right by appeals to their fears and mercantile interests, and deprive them of an effective word for freedom, and the safety of their own race, at the approaching election, when it is manifest that a failure to give effect to these two sentiments involves the lives of multitudes of their own race at the South, continues their own exclusion from any share or influence in the government, (for no northern man of either party has now any power over the policy of the government,) re-opens the African slave trade, and dooms Mexico and all the Gulf region to slavery?

The disciples of Jefferson in the South ask no interference from the North. Such interference is mischievous to the cause, and even more dangerous to them than a refusal of northern men to act on the side of freedom within their constitutional powers. All that is asked, and all that is required, is, that the North shall be outspoken for its convictions, to put the government on the side of freedom, and return again to the policy under which so many of the states have abolished slavery.

Proof of Our Progress in Civilization
January 19, 1860

During a two-month conflict between December 1859 and February 1860 over organization of the House of Representatives and the election of Speaker John Sherman of Ohio, it was said that nearly all members of both chambers of the Congress were armed; Senator Hammond of South Carolina is reported to have remarked that *"the only persons who do not have a revolver and a knife are those who have two revolvers." Galusha A. Grow, a Pennsylvania Congressman, was the author in 1862 of a Homestead Act which gave any family head over twenty-one years of age 160 acres of public land. Roger A. Pryor was a fiery Virginia pro-slavery Congressman who was quick to challenge his Northern opponents to duels. Thomas Lanier Clingman of North Carolina was a Democratic Senator from 1858 to 1861.*

It is pleasant to observe the advances in civilization which our beloved country is making.

It is agreed that those who, in eating, convey their food to their mouths with their fingers, are in a savage state. The chopsticks of the Chinese are an improvement upon this method, but knives and forks are the climax of progress in this direction. The like is the case with weapons. In a mere state of nature, man employs only those which nature gave him; he pummels his adversary with his fists, tears out his hair, gouges out his eyes, scratches, bites and kicks him. The club, the bow and arrow, and the tomahawk indicate the first stage in civilization; the sword is the weapon of a people still more refined; the common pistol is a greater and higher triumph of human ingenuity; but the revolver is the consummation of all the resources of art and science in this line.

We may with perfect justice style ourselves not only the "freest and most enlightened," but the most civilized nation on earth; and the proof that we are so is to be found in the practices of our representatives at Washington. A stranger coming into our country, while our Congress is in session, naturally posts off to the seat of government, to observe us at that central point of intelligence, morality and refinement, to which every part of our country sends the men who are chosen as proper personifications of their character and their practices. He cannot but be astonished at the evidences of a high state of civilization that meet his eyes.

In the English Parliament, and in all the deliberative assemblies of the old world, the members attend furnished solely with the means of offence and defence which bare nature has provided. They bring only their hands and the nails at the ends of them, their feet and their teeth. They put themselves back into the savage state for the occasion. If they should get into a fray they could only kick, strike, scratch and bite, and it is very doubtful whether anybody would be killed. Here at Washington, on the contrary, we find more than half the members bearing, not clubs or tomahawks, or even the sword, which every gentleman wore in Queen Anne's time, but that blossom of modern civilization, the revolver. The members of Congress are little walking armories; miniature magazines of powder and ball. They debate as bandits debate when the question is a division of booty—armed to the teeth; they can hardly gesticulate but out drops a revolver.

The traveller from the old world, who sees all this, must be profoundly impressed with the rapid progress our country has made within a few years past. The clash of a pistol dropping on the floor would furnish him with ample matter for painful reflection upon the distance at which the people of his own hemisphere are lagging behind us. It might amuse him a little to see how the other members, particularly those from the South, leered at each other when this happened, and turned up the whites of their eyes, and exclaimed "shocking"; but even this would prove but a slight alleviation of his chagrin.

It must be confessed, however, that it is not in every part of our country that the great improvement of which we speak is to be observed. Here, in our state legislatures of the North, we go on in the old-fashioned way, debating and voting as if revolvers had never been invented, and behaving all the while as if a row was out of place in a legislative chamber, or anywhere else. It is only till, in proceeding south, we come to the Potomac, that we find evidences of that greater refinement of which we have spoken. This is the case at present, but southern ideas are diffusing themselves all over the rest of the Union, as is evident from the applause bestowed on Mr. O'Conor's speech at the late Union meeting, and we have every encouragement to expect that the legislative use of revolvers will go with them.

It has been objected to the practice of carrying pistols into a legislative chamber, that it must tend to make the debates dull by repressing those keen personalities which render them lively and interesting. No such effect is observed at Washington, on the contrary, the more pistols the more personalities. No member seems to be withheld from abusing another member by the knowledge that he carries a pistol; and the pistol-bearers seem to hold themselves bound to speak bullets as well as to carry them. The behavior of Mr. Branch of North Carolina, towards Mr. Grow of Pennsylvania, is an example of this kind: he first insulted Mr. Grow, and then challenged him because he naturally said that the insult was "unparliamentary and ungentlemanly." Last evening, Mr. Pryor [of Virginia], one of the "chivalry," gave Mr. Hickman of Pennsylvania the lie on the floor of the House of Representatives, because he said he believed the democratic members were determined to prevent the organization of the House. It would be naturally inferred from this that Mr. Pryor is a blackguard, but he redeemed his character on the instant, and proved himself a gentleman by offering to fight. It matters not it seems, in what vulgar and brutal foulness of abuse a member of Congress indulges, if he be only willing to wind up with a duel.

Not only do pistols thus encourage personal abuse, but their wearers seem to take it for granted that, by way of keeping up their warlike character, they must bluster on all occasions. Night before last Mr. Clingman, in the Senate after repeating the old rant that if a Republican should be elected President of the United States the slaveholders would dissolve the Union, went on to threaten the Republican members with driving them out of the Capitol at the cannon's mouth.

Bravo! Mr. Clingman, and three cheers for the progress of civilization in this free and enlightened country!

The Real Danger to the Union
January 20, 1860

In the summer of 1859 a New York doctor, Meigs Case, had gone to Salem, Alabama, to reorganize a female college; in the fury aroused by Brown's raid that fall on Harper's Ferry, Case was run out of town. Two years earlier the Irish journalist Edwin Lawrence Godkin, traveling in the South, was told by an otherwise mild-mannered former Mississippi governor that he could "see no harm in lynch law when directed against abolitionists or Frémonters." John Letcher, a lawyer and editor, and governor of Virginia 1859–1865?, opposed secession until Lincoln's call for troops at the start of the Civil War.

Yesterday we placed on record another example of the regard which the people of the slave states have for the rights of their northern brethren. A citizen of New York, who had made himself a resident of Alabama, and was entitled by the constitution to protection in that state, was expelled on twenty-four hours notice, for the simple reason that he was a northern man.

There are not wanting here in the northern states, among the firmest and most resolute men we know, some who have their serious fears for the integrity of the Union. "It is not that we suppose the southern states inclined to set up for themselves," they say. "Of that we have no fear; the slaveholders understand their own business better than to do that. They may threaten and bluster, but they have an object to serve by it, and when that is gained, or when they perceive that it cannot be gained, they will once more be quiet. What we fear is, that the people of the North will be roused to uncontrollable indignation by the outrages heaped upon their brethren who visit the southern states, and will rise as one man to say that such atrocities are not to be repeated. The feeling which has already been kindled here by whipping, imprisoning and banishing citizens of our common country from the southern states, unoffending men, guiltless of any crime save that of being suspected to entertain the very opinions which, at the North, are universal, is already strong and deep; it may smolder for a while, but a few more instances of such insolent cruelty will make it burst forth into a flame. Let these proceedings go on until at length a person of sufficient consequence to interest the community, shall be seized and imprisoned, on the charge of not being friendly to slavery, and the blood of every man in the free states will be on fire. The North and the West will start at once to their feet, and the men of that class who poured into Kansas and conquered it for freedom, in despite of the efforts of the federal government to hold it for slavery, will collect in a body against which resistance will be hopeless and will set the prisoner free. This will be the beginning of events on which may hang the whole future existence of the Union. If the popular feeling be not appeased by immediate concessions and guaranties of future good conduct given by the slave states, the decree of a dissolution of the Union may be passed. The free states may decline to live any longer under a government administered, in part, by the representatives of a semi-barbarous population, and may insist upon a division of the region which now forms our Republic. If this is done, most assuredly, the lion will take the lion's share. All the territories, every inch of them, will be ours. Ours will be the Potomac, with both its banks, from its springs to where the Chesapeake widens into the sea. Ours will be the entire Mississippi, with a broad belt on each of its borders, and the islands at its mouth. Ours will be northern and western Texas and the entire Pacific coast. Two regions in which slavery will continue to exist will be left, one to the east, and the other to the west of the Mississippi, and there it will be allowed to remain until the negroes run away or the white population become tired of it."

This is the way in which men at the North are beginning to talk. The constitution of the United States directs, in one section, that "the citizens of each state shall be entitled to all the privileges and immunities of citizens in the several states";—in another section that "no person shall be deprived of liberty without due process of law." Two provisions of the constitution are violated at once when a man is banished from one state because he had previously lived in another. It is difficult to imagine that such outrages upon personal liberty as these can be committed with any other design than that of showing in what utter contempt the South holds all who inhabit our half of the republic, and how confident it is that we shall never resent the most wanton insults and the grossest indignities. There is a class of journals, the *Constitution*, Mr. Buchanan's organ at Washington is among the number, which expatiate [on] what they call the *ferocious hate* borne by the people of the free states to those of the South. The evidences of hatred are all on the other side. Here, in the free states, the southern citizen travels unmolested, comes and goes with pleasure and without danger, expresses his opinions with freedom, declaims in favor of slavery, and is quiety allowed to convert as many as he can to the doctrine that it is a benign and beneficent institution. He is not mobbed for this; nobody proposes to lynch him; nobody suggests a coat of tar and feathers or an airing on a rail as a remedy for his case; no vigilance committee waits upon him to bid him leave the state within twenty-four hours. Everywhere he meets toleration, good nature and hospitality. Let a man go from the free states to the South, and he is treated as Powers and Crangale and Dr. Case were treated—he meets the cat-o'-nine tails; he encounters men ready for him with buckets of tar and bags of feathers; or he is suddenly ejected from the state, with the hint that if he remains beyond twenty-four hours he remains at the peril of his life—a threat of murder.

Of course there is a limit to the patience of communities as well as to that of individuals. We cannot say how far these outrages may be carried, nor exactly at which repetition of them the forbearance of the North will be exhausted and the moment will arrive for that reaction which, when it once begins, will sweep everything before it—even the counsels of the peaceful, moderate and philanthropic. If matters should be pressed to that extremity of which some persons speak, the free states will consent to no partition of the Union which does not correspond to their own overshadowing predominance in present population and activity, and their prospects of future growth. Theirs must be the vacant lands, theirs the great rivers, theirs the broad estuaries of the continent; they will be faithless to liberty if they do not claim these as her birthright. The North, the hardy, populous North, fertile in men, mighty in resources, with no internal cause of weakness, will make her own terms. Somebody, we believe it was Governor Letcher of Virginia, made a silly proposal the other day to call a convention for the peaceable division of the Union. If the controversy ever comes to a division of the Union, the North will wait for no convention; the people of the free states will occupy first and negotiate afterwards with the advantage of possession on their side. The communities which tolerate slavery will find themselves confined to the narrowest limits. Slavery will be surrounded, to use the eloquent words of General John A. Dix, with a wall of fire, within which, like the fabled scorpion, it will sting itself to death.

Mr. Sumner on the Barbarism of Slavery
June 7, 1860

On June 4, 1860, Senator Sumner, having just returned from convalescence in Europe after having been attacked four years earlier by Representative Brooks, broke a long silence on the subject in an impassioned four-hour speech on "The Barbarism of Slavery." Kansas was finally admitted to statehood on January 29, 1861.

Although we could not admit that Mr. Sumner, in his late speech in the debate on the admission of Kansas as a state, took the most certain course to persuade the majority of the Senate to vote for its admission, we think he is entitled to the benefit of a full statement of the provocation which called forth his eloquent denunciations. Whatever may be pretended, the real objection to the immediate reception of Kansas as one of the members of our confederacy is that she offers to come in with a free constitution. The friends of slavery had exhausted themselves in florid eulogies of the benign effects of the institution, and had lavished a vast deal of rhetoric on the calamitous and degraded condition of those communities in which it does not exist. With these views on the matter, acquired by that species of self-deception which men who are in the wrong are always so apt to practice, they seem to imagine themselves justified in laying every possible obstacle in the way of enlarging the Union by the admission of free states. Any pretext which comes to hand, on which their ingenuity can put a plausible face, is seized upon and made to serve as a reason for keeping the new state out of the Union.

Mr. Sumner intended his speech as an exposure of the fallacy on which this policy of excluding free states is founded. He designed to meet those who, in the same breath, pronounced eulogies of the institution of slavery and voted no on the admission of Kansas, by showing, as he has done with extraordinary ability, the inconsistency of slavery with a high and virtuous civilization. When they went yet further, and reviled the system of voluntary industry under which it is our happiness to live in this part of the Union, he thought it important to repel their calumnies with proofs that under that system alone can the highest welfare of society, both as respects its moral and natural condition, both as regards the practice of morality and the prosperity of the arts of life, be attained.

Without intending to abate anything from the essential force of the remarks made on this speech in our Tuesday's number, we have thought it but justice to Mr. Sumner that the attention of our readers should be directed to this view of the matter. In another part of this sheet our readers will find that portion of the speech to which we have referred.

The Old-Line Whigs
June 7, 1860

On May 18 at the Republican national convention in Chicago Abraham Lincoln had been chosen as its candidate for the Presidency, with Hannibal Hamlin, a Maine Senator, as his running mate. After the defeat of Frémont in 1856, efforts had been made in several states to bring together anti–Democratic Party factions in a Union party.

The support given to the nomination of Lincoln and Hamlin by the Buffalo *Commercial Advertiser,* an organ of the old-line whig party, seems to make the *Journal of Commerce* uncomfortable. In noticing the fact it remarks:

> "It is melancholy to see so many secessions and desertions from that respectable and once powerful old whig party in this state. These desertions: appear, however, to be confined, so far as the leaders are concerned, to ambitious gentlemen whose chances for distinction seemed too closely confined, so long as they remained attached to the old-line whigs. They go for freedom—at least, for a free choice for promotion, and failing to realize *that* among their friends, go to their enemies."

If the whig party has been respectable and powerful in this state, and if it is going over so largely as the *Journal* pathetically declares to the support of the Republican candidates, the chance of their success must be very greatly increased. For the party which calls itself democratic the prospect is, no doubt, what the print from which we have quoted calls it, exceedingly "melancholy." Let it be considered, however, that if this circumstance is painful to the pro-slavery party, it is a pleasant one to the friends of freedom. The desertion of the whigs from their ancient standard, and their adhesion to the Republican party, for the present election at least, is not one of those events which dissatisfies everybody; a fact which we mention for the comfort of our pensive neighbors of the *Journal.*

Meantime, however, we do not see the justice of imputing bad motives to such of the old-line whigs as, upon a careful review of the political field, prefer giving their votes for Mr. Lincoln, to the alternative of supporting a candidate of their own who has not the slightest chance of succeeding, or else absenting themselves from the polls altogether. The whig party, already lessoned by defections, to the Republican party on the one side and to the democratic party on the other, has been of late still further diminished by the formation of the Union party in which a few of them have taken refuge from the political inaction to which an adherence to their ancient party, now in superannuation, would have condemned them. That others should prefer to take their station in the ranks of the Republican party, and that these should be, in the language of the *Journal of Commerce*, many, may be easily imagined, without ascribing to them motives of personal ambition and the desire of distinction.

Certainly nothing could be imagined of a nature more proper to discourage the imputation of selfish motives than the circumstances under which so many of the old-line whigs have now come to the support of Mr. Lincoln's nomination. Our political platform was agreed upon by the members of the Chicago Convention, and our nomination was made without consulting them. With our declaration of principles and our selection of a candidate they had nothing whatever to do. No bargain was made with them for their assistance in electing the candidates, no offer of advantage held out to tempt them. All that can be said is, that they have considered the resolutions adopted at Chicago, and find nothing in them to condemn; they have considered the qualifications and character of our candidates, and approve them. We believe there was never a case in which the imputation of a desire to obtain office was less deserved. We cannot, indeed, answer for every old-line whig who comes at this hour of the contest to the support of our party, but this we affirm, that, as a class, they enter our ranks in a manner which makes the reproach of interested motives wanton injury, unsustained by a particle of proof.

We can only recommend to the party which finds the prospect before it so discouraging not to forget its charity in its melancholy. Adversity is said to be wholesome, but if we allow ourselves under its chastisements, to calumniate our neighbors, we pervert it from its proper uses.

Popular Sovereignty
ca. June 7, 1860

The territorial governor of Nebraska who vetoed the bill abolishing slavery was Samuel W. Black.

We have a practical proof of the manner in which the sovereignty of the people in the territories is regarded by the existing administration in Nebraska. Not long since a bill was passed by the Council and House of Representatives of that territory, to abolish slavery. It was a short bill, whose phrases were borrowed from the Jeffersonian ordinance of 1789, as follows:

> "Sec. 1. Be it enacted by the Council and House of Representatives of the territory of Nebraska, That slavery or involuntary servitude,

except for the punishment of crime, be and the same is forever prohibited in this territory.

"Sec. 2. This act shall take effect and be in force from and after the first day of July, A.D., 1860."

This measure was maturely considered, and once rejected by the Council, which put it in its present shape, when it received the concurrent vote of the House. But the Governor of the territory, properly named Black, and representing the federal government, has placed his veto upon the bill. In the legislature, the opponents of it took the ground that the prohibition was unnecessary; but Governor Black flies higher in his objections, and applies the decision of the Supreme Court in the Dred Scott case to the matter.

It is true, the organic act constituting the territory allows "the people" to regulate their own domestic matters, and this the Governor meets by asserting that the legislature are not "the people." They were elected by the people and represent the people, but nevertheless are not the people, and consequently have no right to prohibit slavery. Mr. Douglas and the other democratic friends of popular sovereignty will have to teach Black his duty. He is playing into the hands of the fire-eaters, and will damage the western branch of the democratic party. Congress, having conceded the power to legislate on slavery to the territory, the legislature was perfectly justified in the exercise of it, and nothing shows the necessity of positive prohibition more than this attempt to defeat it by a federal officer.

The Slave Interest Is a Spoiled Child
ca. October 1860

For the last fifteen years, the slaveholders have had their own way in the councils of the nation. The affairs of the Government have been managed in their interest; their wishes have been gratified so far as the Executive and the majority of Congress could gratify them; the laws have been made and administered as they would have them made and administered; their partisans have been placed on the federal bench; every ministerial office has been bestowed upon their creatures; their schemes of policy have been directly adopted by the Federal Government, or, when not directly adopted, connived at, favored, and promoted in every possible manner by the Government. The journals which speak as the organs of the ruling party are all in the slave interest.

If this were the proper method of putting the North and South at amity with each other, the work would have been accomplished long ago. If, by giving the country a government devoted to the slave interest, the jealousies and animosities between the different quarters of the country could have been laid asleep and forgotten, the four last administrations should have done it so effectually that slavery, as a topic of dispute between the people who inhabit different parts of the United States, would be no more thought of.

So far is this from being the case, that the longer the Government follows this policy, the more unreasonable these jealousies and the fiercer these animosities become. In the whole series of our federal administrations, no one has been so absolutely devoted to the slave interest as that of Mr. Buchanan; and certainly under no administration has the ill-humor of the South been exasperated to such a pitch. There has never been a time when the people of the North, adventuring to show themselves in the Southern States, have been so shamefully treated. There is neither liberty of speech nor of press at the South for a citizen of the Northern States, nor even for citizens of the slave States who do not avow themselves to be the partisans of slavery. From a state of things which permitted free discussion on this subject, the slave States have lapsed into an oligarchical tyranny, as absolute as the monarchical despotism in Austria. Men have been shot, hanged, tarred and feathered, exiled, expelled by force, on the bare suspicion of not being friendly to slavery.

The slave interest is a spoiled child; the Federal Government is its foolishly indulgent nurse. Every thing it has asked for has been eagerly given it; more eagerly still if it cries after it; more eagerly still if it threatens to cut off its nurse's ears. The more we give it the louder it cries, and the more furious its threats; and now we have Northern men writing long letters to persuade their readers that it will actually cut off its nurse's ears if we exercise the right of suffrage, and elect a President of our own choice, instead of giving it one of its own favorites.

The Election of Lincoln
November 7, 1860

Bryant was one of several prominent New York Republicans who had invited Lincoln to make his first appearance before an Eastern audience, at Cooper Union in New York on February 28, 1860. Elected president of the meeting, Bryant introduced the speaker as one of those "children of the West [who] form a living bulwark against the advances of Slavery, and from [whom] is recruited the vanguard of the armies of Liberty." In the November election Lincoln defeated three opponents for the Presidency: Senator John Bell of Tennessee, Vice President John Cabell Breckinridge of Kentucky, and Stephen A. Douglas. Edward Everett of Massachusetts was Bell's running mate. By polling a clear majority in the Electoral College, Lincoln avoided what must surely have been a stormy and perhaps losing struggle in a hostile House of Representatives. The Wilmot Proviso was explained in the headnote to March 8, 1850.

What the more sagacious calculators of chances in the different political parties were prepared for has now become a fact; the Republican party has triumphed, and Abraham Lincoln, if he lives to the Fourth of March next, will be President of the United States. An immense majority in the free states are now rejoicing in the result; a large minority of the citizens of southern states, hitherto trampled under the iron heel of an oligarchy which has shown itself as impatient of the freedom of thought as any of the despotisms of the Old World, are rejoicing with still more intense delight. Even in the slave states the elections have taken a turn which shows how strongly a large proportion of their people sympathize with their brethren of the North. Virginia, the most powerful of them all, has emphatically rebuked the disunionists and their treasonable schemes by giving her voice for Bell and Everett. In Kentucky, one of the most flourishing of the offshoots from Virginia, the disunionists are beaten by a large majority; Breckinridge, one of her sons, who should have had her vote, if he had not held opinions and cherished views offensive to her people, is set aside, and electors who are to vote for Bell are chosen by a large majority. In Maryland the struggle between Bell and Breckinridge is close, but the state would have gone for Bell by a considerable majority had not the friends of Lincoln nominated and supported a ticket of their own. Wilmington, one of the most busy, enterprising and prosperous towns in any slave state, gives a majority of two hundred for the Lincoln ticket. Missouri turns her back on Breckinridge, and gives her vote to Douglas. It is impossible to regard these results of the election in that great belt of slave states which immediately adjoin the free, otherwise than as the strongest expression they could give of their inflexible determination to abide by our federal Union.

There are various causes of congratulation in this survey of our successes. It is most gratifying to see what we believe to be a righteous cause—the cause of justice and humanity—after a long and weary struggle, closed by a decisive triumph. It is consoling to those who cherish high hopes of the destinies of our race, to see a great people, after a long discussion, in which the subtlest skill has been employed to varnish over wrong and give it a semblance of fairness, and, after allowing itself for a time to be misled by these sophistries, at length breaking through them all, and deciding boldly and firmly for the right.

We congratulate the country, moreover, on having escaped the confusion, the agitations and the corruption which must almost necessarily attend the choice of a President by the House of Representatives. These dangers have of late been so strongly pressed upon the public attention that we need not dwell upon them here. This consideration had no doubt its effect in enabling us to foil the scheme of those who hoped, by a combination of all the factions opposed to the Republican party in the free states, to carry the choice of a President into Congress, and to convulse the Union with another series of manœuvres and intrigues, such as were put in motion last winter to prevent the election of a Republican Speaker.

We congratulate the country also in the termination of the almost frantic struggle of the slaveholders for the introduction of their baleful institution into the territories. How violent that struggle has been; how reckless those who were engaged in it have been of the plainest rules of justice, and how indifferent to the peace of the country, we need not stop to describe. The contest is now necessarily at an end; it can go no further. The controversy is closed. There can be no hope of influencing the Executive to favor their designs; the expectation of re-opening the slave trade to people these territories with African bondmen is at an end, never, probably, to be revived.

We might enlarge this list of reasons for congratulation to an indefinite extent; but we rather pass on to remark that our rejoicing at the success we have obtained should be sobered by the reflection that we have taken upon ourselves immense responsibilities which we must consider how we shall faithfully discharge. For two years to come we must expect to find a majority in both Houses of Congress influenced by a spirit of distrust, if not of hostility, to the Republican administration. We must have patience to wait till, by a wise and impartial course of conduct, by a strict regard to the rights of the states, by a careful abstinence from every doubtful exercise of authority, by a frugal administration of the finances, and by the selection of wise, able and upright men as the agents of the government in every post, distrust shall be changed to confidence, and hostility disarmed of its weapons. We have pronounced in favor of a most conscientious as well as most able man to fill the Executive chair. The administration of the federal government must be conformed in all respects to the character of our Chief Magistrate, or the hold which we have obtained on the people is lost. Our success in the election, by deciding one question, the extension of slavery to the territories, has deprived our party of one important bond of union, one of the most powerful causes which have attracted to it the interest and favor of the people. Its place can only be supplied by an earnest endeavor to distinguish the Republican administration by an enlightened zeal for the public welfare.

In closing our remarks we take this occasion to congratulate the old friends of the EVENING POST, who have read it for the last score of years or thereabouts, on this new triumph of the principles which it maintains. The Wilmot Proviso is now consecrated as a part of the national public policy by this election; but earlier than the Wilmot Proviso was the opposition of our journal to the enlargement of slavery. It began with the first whisper of the scheme to annex Texas to the American Union, and it has been steadily maintained from that moment till now, when the right and justice of our cause is proclaimed, in a general election, by the mighty voice of a large majority of thirty millions of people.

A MODERATE VIEW OF THE SOUTH CAROLINA QUESTION
November 15, 1860

At an annual Southern Commercial Convention in Montgomery, Alabama, in May 1858, a Charlestonian named L. W. Spratt, a persistent advocate of reopening the African slave trade, which had been banned since 1808 by the United States Constitution, had made a passionate speech urging its revival. Despite Bryant's optimism expressed here, on December 20, 1860, a state convention convened by the legislature passed without dissent an ordinance declaring that "the union . . . between South Carolina and the other states . . . is hereby dissolved."

There is one point of view in which the people of South Carolina may be said to have behaved quite as well since the election as we had any right to expect; and we say this with a sincere desire to do them justice.

It should be recollected that the southern, especially South Carolina, politicians, in the hope of preventing the election of Mr. Lincoln, had again and again threatened that the whole South, the entire body of the slave states, would leave the Union the moment his election should be certain. It should be borne in mind also, that the election of a Republican President puts an end to the dominion of the slaveholding interest over our republic probably forever. It should be remembered, moreover, that there is in South Carolina a party, comprising a good many men of considerable distinction and of a restless temper, who have long cherished the hope of establishing, on the ruins of the Union, a southern confederacy of slave states, and who have stood for many years ready to take instant advantage of any convenient pretext which should offer itself, to revolt against the federal government. It should furthermore, be taken into the account that there is a class of men, some of them probably citizens of the northern states, who hope, under the protection of a southern confederacy, to drive an immensely lucrative trade in bringing slaves from Africa, and who wish for nothing so much as the breaking up of the Union, and the removal of all restraints on that cruel and infamous traffic.

When we put these considerations together; when we reflect that those who threatened disunion so loudly and so perseveringly felt that they must make a show of keeping their promise or become ridiculous; that those who strove so hard to keep the power in their own hands must be cut to the heart at seeing it wrested from them; that the nullifiers, who have so long wanted a pretext for pulling down the Union upon their own heads, would naturally seize upon so promising an opportunity for making the attempt, and that the champions of a revival of the slave trade should second their purpose with all their might, and endeavor to inflame the vexation of the defeated party to absolute madness, we confess we do not see anything more violent or hasty or ill-considered in the conduct of the people of South Carolina hitherto than we might naturally have expected from so excitable a population.

When we consider, moreover, that no northern journals of any credit circulate in that state, that all Republican newspapers are rigidly excluded, that the people are consequently in utter ignorance of the real character and purposes of the Republican party, and are made to believe by their orators and journalists that those who have won the day in the late election have conspired to use the power of the federal government to set the negroes free and divide the plantations among them, or still worse, to encourage the blacks to fly at the throats of the whites and fill the land with bloodshed, we can hardly help admiring the moderation which has been shown, not by the leaders, for they know better, but by the mass of the people whom they are seeking to stir up to treason and insurrection. We even wondered if the multitude believed what they were told, that they did not demand to be immediately led against the enemy. We are not surprised that they should be willing to be drilled as militia-men all day in rainy weather, and march to the sound of the drum through muddy streets on dark nights, or that they should regard with approbation the forecast of the state legislature in putting them into decent equipments [f]or the defence of their household hearths.

We confess that when we heard the leaders in this movement of secession counselling the system prevalent in Mexico and the other semi-barbarous republics of Spanish America, of resorting to the bayonet after having been fairly beaten at the ballot-box, we almost looked for an immediate *pronunciamiento* after the Mexican and South American fashion, thinking that the arms and the ammunition in Castle Pinckney and Fort Sumter would be distributed among the raw recruits drummed together in haste, and that since Mr. Buchanan makes no objection, South Carolina would be independent the next morning. Instead of that, calmer and wiser counsels have prevailed; the independence of South Carolina is postponed; a convention is to be called, and the convention will see what is to be done.

It is true that some extravagant and violent speeches have been made, and that Mr. Spratt, the champion of the slave trade, and other speakers of the disunion school, have made every use in their power of the general vexation felt at the defeat of the democratic party. But words break no bones. We ought not to make the least objection when a defeated party relieves itself in that manner. It is one of the most admirable features of our political system, that it allows vehement discontent to dilate itself into wordy and harmless complaint. The liberty of railing is with us the substitute for revolution. Political discontent, when pent up in silence, is like confined steam that rends its boiler and flings it about in fragments; give it air and it hisses, shrieks, snorts and sputters for a while, and at last is quiet. This flux of words is a favorable omen. Grim and calm determination would portend a different issue.

A friend who lived many years in a slave state south of Virginia, who once owned a plantation and negroes there, and whose children were all born there, said to us as we were writing this article: "I know the South well. I have been a citizen of the South and a slaveholder, and am sure that if nothing is done to increase their irritation while they are chafing under defeat, this excitement will soon subside. I have just written to a distinguished friend of mine in that part of the country, whose name I must not give, to inquire what, in his opinion, will be the end of all this. His answer was, 'It will end as all such things at the South have ended; but you must let us down easy.' Patience and good nature on the part of the northern states are all that is required to make the conclusion speedy and sure."

We may well be good-natured, for we are the victorious party. We may well have patience, for we feel that we are victorious in a good cause, and having nothing to reproach ourselves with, we can wait a little while for those whose vexation is the greater because they know they are in the wrong, to come gradually round to the right.

There is nothing which the Republican party can do at present to disabuse their southern brethren of their groundless prejudices and apprehensions. They have no way of speaking to the South; a general interdict closes against them all communication by means of the only practicable medium, the press. When the Republicans enter upon the administration of the government, the work of dispelling the delusions of which we speak, by a wise, just and moderate policy, will be easy. Until then, if the South is to be soothed, it must be by those who have labored to embitter and envenom its feelings towards the North. It is the presses and orators who have slandered the Republican party that must retract their calumnies with what speed they may, and teach those who listen to them that whatever views the people of the North may hold in regard to the questions that divide political parties at the present time, they have no intention of violating the least of the constitutional rights of the slave states.

The Fifty-Ninth Anniversary of the *Evening Post*
January 1, 1861(?)

In his advice to the players, Prince Hamlet admonishes them to "hold, as 'twere, the mirror up to Nature; . . . and the very age and body of the time his form and presence." Hamlet, III, ii, 25–28.

The year which has just drawn to a close has been an eventful one to the civilized world; it has been a specially eventful one to our country. The world has witnessed during this period the comparative emancipation of Europe from a political and ecclesiastical thraldom against which truth and justice have struggled in vain for centuries, and in this country the overthrow of an oligarchy which has conducted our government for many years in open defiance of the popular will and of the vital principles of popular sovereignty upon which our government is founded. The readers of the Evening Post have also witnessed, after a desperate struggle of near fifteen years duration, the complete triumph of a public policy to which the columns of this journal have been specially devoted, oftentimes against most discouraging adverse influences, and which has finally received its most suitable national vindication in the choice of Abraham Lincoln, the candidate of the Republican party, for President of the United States.

It has been the misfortune of the Evening Post, since its establishment, now nearly three-quarters of a century distant, to advocate measures which at first met the approval of but a small minority of the public, and the active opposition of the multitude; but it has been its good fortune in every instance, when questions of national policy were concerned, to have its course ultimately vindicated by the people. Thus it was the first and for many years the only journal north of the Potomac which pleaded for an amelioration of the restrictions upon our foreign commerce, and in behalf of those fundamental principles of legislation which are at war with all monopolies of legislative origin. It was one of the earliest champions of the rights of the states under the federal compact, so flagrantly abused by some of the provisions of the Fugitive Slave law, and so seriously menaced by the early policy of the present Administration in Kansas. It resisted successfully the elaborate system of internal improvement, which at one time threatened the budding enterprise of our country with the unequal and fatal opposition of the general government. It early discerned and denounced the abuses to which the system of using the public funds for banking purposes was exposed, and it labored with no ordinary devotion to establish the Sub-Treasury system, which is justly regarded as one of the most durable and conspicuous monuments of American Statesmanship.

It was one of the earliest as it was one of the most earnest advocates of the cheaper postage rates, of which the nation is now in the partial enjoyment. It defended the right of Petition when statesmen of distinction were expelled from Congress for following its example. It resisted the assumption of State Debts by the general government. It has resisted—thus far successfully—the extension of human slavery under the protection of the national flag, whether by the conversion of our free into slave territory, by the purchase of new slave territory, or by re-opening the slave trade with Africa, and it has been permitted at least to see if not yet to enter the promised land toward which it has been pursuing its wearisome journey so many years. Upon the course of the EVENING POST in reference to all these great questions of public polity, the American people have placed the seal of their approbation. If we refer to the fact with some degree of pride, and even exultation, we are sure those who have been regular readers of our columns, through good report and through evil report, will excuse us.

The EVENING POST and our common country are now commencing a new era; a new class of questions are to agitate the public mind; the great republic is passing into its adult stage of existence, when its strength is to be tested and its virtue to be sorely tried. Upon no class will a greater weight of responsibility rest than upon the journalist, who is called upon daily to anticipate the deliberate judgment of the nation, often without time himself to deliberate, and whose utterances shape the views of thousands for good or for evil.

That we shall endeavor to conduct the EVENING POST for the future with a full sense of the growing responsibilities of our profession, we hope may be inferred from its past history. It has never failed to plead the cause of truth and justice because they chanced for the time to be unpopular, nor has it shrunk from the discharge of any public duty because it involved the rapture of party associations; when it ceases to be either of these respects what it has been heretofore, it will cease to be the EVENING POST.

To all who think that what we have stated are merits in a public journal, we beg to commend the EVENING POST, with the assurance that its editors do not mean to permit its political shadow ever to be less. They mean, also, to make the other departments of the paper more and more interesting. Convinced that political questions will soon cease in this country to possess the same relative importance as heretofore, the editors contemplate the introduction of a class of topics to its readers which have hitherto been too much excluded from the public journals, for the want, mainly, of the necessary ability to treat them in a popular way, but which must sooner or later usurp the prominence hitherto given to political topics by the American press.

We believe we have kept the pledges, made a few years ago, to make the EVENING POST a satisfactory repository of the latest news from all parts of the world. That the public appreciates our efforts in this respect is shown by the demand which exists for our paper. Our daily issue is four times what it was five years ago, and our circulation has not been so large in any former year as it is now, by two thousand and upwards. We have much yet to do, however, to make the news department of the EVENING POST realize all our wishes and expectations, and it is our ambition to have each succeeding edition an improvement in some particular upon the preceeding one, so that no one shall feel that they know "the very age and body of the time" till they have read the last EVENING POST.

Such of our readers as approve of the course of the EVENING POST, and desire to see its doctrines on public questions more generally adopted, may contribute effectively towards such a result, and greatly oblige us, by commending it to such of their neighbors as stand in need of such a guide or family companion.

INDEX

Abolitionists, 22, 47–50, 78–80, 127–28
Adams, Charles Francis, xviii
Adams, John, 281–82
Adams, John Quincy, 1, 23, 110, 147, 183
Aethelbert, King of Kent, 291–92
African Americans, 4–5, 62–64; see also slavery
Albany Argus, 50–52
Albany Evening Journal, 214
Allen, Charles, 273–74
Alley, Saul, 249–50
Alton Observer, 78–80
Alton Telegraph, 79
American Anti-Slavery Standard, xvii–xviii
Amistad (ship), 109–111
Andrews, Garnett, 286
Anne, Queen, 169–70
Appleton, Nathan, 194–99, 202–213, 216–20
Appleton, Thomas, 26–27
architecture, 114
Ariosto, Ludovico, 80
Ashburton, Alexander Baring, Baron, 175
Asia, 329–331
Astor, John Jacob, 45–46
Atchison, David R., 283–84
Aubrey, John, 14–16
Austin, Elbridge G., 80

Bacon, Leonard, 133–34
Badger, George E., 275–76
Bailey, Gamaliel, 361
Bancroft, George, xxi, 102, 174
Bank of the United States, xxi, 6, 8–10, 18–19, 21, 108, 111–12, 161–62, 167–69, 191–92
banking, 103–105, 107–109, 121–22, 126, 128–31, 143, 164–65; see also Bank of the United States
Banks, Nathaniel P., 295–96
Barnes, John, 4–6
"Battlefield, The" (Bryant), xxii

Beecher, Henry Ward, 304–305
Bell, John, 380–81
Bellamy, Edward, xviii
Belser, James E., 286
Benton, Thomas Hart, xviii, 157
Bethune, George Washington, 355–56
Bible-reading in public schools, 326–28
Biddle, James, 277, 279
Biddle, Nicholas, xxi, 8, 18, 108, 165, 167, 191–92
Bigelow, John, xvii, xix
Birney, James G., 243
Black, Samuel W., 378–79
Blackstone, 34
Blair, Francis Preston, xviii, 8
blue laws, 228–29
Boccaccio, Giovanni, 80
Boston Courier, 209
Boston Morning Post, 198, 203
Boston Quarterly Review, 155–56
Boston *Sentinel*, 80–82
Botts, John Minor, 294, 296
Brandon (Miss.) *Platform*, 286
Breckinridge, John Cabell, 380–81
Briggs, Charles A., xviii
Bright, John, 186
Brooks, Preston S., 289–90, 293–94
Brown, Aaron Venable, 335–36
Brown, Albert Gallatin, 318
Brown, John, xxiii, 350–56
Brownson, Orestes, 229–30
Bryant, John, 67
Buchanan, James, 153, 190, 294–300, 302–308, 316–17, 319–20, 323–26, 334, 364, 374, 380, 385
Buffalo *Commercial Advertiser*, 377
Bürger, Gottfried August, 99–101
Burke, Edmund (New Hampshire Representative), 270
Burke, William, 47
Burlingame, Anson, 293–94
Burr, Aaron, 25, 53–54
Butler, Andrew P., 289
Butler, Samuel, 27
Byron, George Gordon, Lord, 14, 19

Cade, John ("Jack"), 84–85
Caesar, Julius, 11
Calhoun, John C., 12–13, 19–21, 23, 74, 223, 231, 235, 262–64, 311, 368
campaign practices, 76–78
Campbell, Alexander, 184
Campbell, John, 310
canals, 96–98
Canute, King of England, 54
Carey, Henry Charles, 366–68
Carey, Matthew, 366
Case, Meigs, 373, 375
Cass, Lewis, 259–61, 308
Casti, Giambattista, 80
Catherwood, Frederick, 58–59
Catron, John, 310
Central Park, idea of, 226–28, 268–69
Century Club, xviii
Chandler, Joseph Ripley, 318, 321
Charles II, 237
Charleston *Courier*, 13
Charleston *Mercury*, 307
Chase, Salmon P., xii, 265, 273
Chaucer, Geoffrey, 133
Cheves, Langdon, 191
Chicago *Tribune*, xviii
Choate, Rufus, 318, 321
cholera epidemic, 7
Churchman, The, 184
Cincinnati *Enquirer*, 307
Cincinnati *Whig*, 49
Cincinnatus, 165–66
Civil War, xvii–xviii
Clark, George Rogers, 140
Clay, Henry, 9, 12, 19, 20, 60–61, 65, 80, 90, 92, 112–13, 158–60, 165–67, 176, 193, 202, 238, 245, 264
Clemens, Jeremiah, 273–74
Clingman, Thomas Lanier, 371, 373
Cobb, Howell, 321
Cobden, Richard, xviii, 186
Cole, Thomas, xviii, 58, 60
Coleman, William, xvii
Collins, Edward Knight, 270
Commercial Advertiser, 146, 157, 229–30, 270
Congreve, Sir William, 72, 131
conservatism, political, 125–26
consuls, 26–27
Cooper, James Fenimore, xviii, 93–94, 174
Cooper Union, xxiii

copyright and patents, xxi–xxii, 57–58, 65–67, 171–75
Corn Law, 186–88
Corwin, Thomas, 352–54
Courier, Paul Louis, 80
Courier and Enquirer, The, 153
Cowley, Henry Wellesley, Earl, 342
Cowper, William, 163
Crabbe, George, 1, 2
Crawford, Martin Jenkins, 359
Crayon, The, xviii
credit, financial, 44–47
Croghan, George, 140–41
Curtis, Benjamin R., 312
Curtis, George William, xix
Cushing, Caleb, 286–87

Daily Advertiser, 208
Dana, Richard, xxi–xxii
Daniel, Peter, 310
Dante, 73
Davis, John, 153–54
Decatur, Stephen, 312
Defoe, Daniel, 169–71
Demosthenes, 60–61
Dewey, Orville, xiv, 107, 304, 306
Dexter, Andrew, 168
Dickens, Charles, xxi, 65, 173
Dix, John Adams, 273, 275, 355, 357, 375
Dixon, Archibald, 275
Dorr, Thomas W., 237
Douglas, Stephen A., 273, 275, 289, 319, 324, 379–81
Downing, Andrew Jackson, 226
Dwight, Timothy, 25

Edwards, Jonathan, 25, 53
Edwards, Ogden, 25–26, 31, 36, 38–40
Eggleston, George Cary, xviii
Emancipator, The, 52–53
Esterházy, Prince Pál Antal, 87–88
European affairs, 337–48; *see also* Italy, liberation of
Evening Star, 138
Everett, Edward, 273–75, 380–81

Faulkner, Charles James, 361–62
Federalists, 90–92
Felton, Cornelius, xx
Fenno, John Ward, 80
Fielding, Henry, 83

Fillmore, Millard, 272, 276, 295–96, 300, 302–304
Fish, Hamilton, xviii, xx
Florida *Sentinel*, 286
Floyd, John Buchanan, 9, 294
Follen, Charles, 123
foreigners and immigrants (rights of; hostility toward), 44–45, 75–76, 148–50, 200–202, 214–15, 223–24, 241–43, 246–48, 252–53, 281–86
Forney, John Wien, 303, 304–25
Forrest, Edwin, 84–85
Forsyth, John, 295–96
Fountain and Other Poems, The (Bryant), xx
Fowler, Orson Squire, 107–108
Fox, George, 184–85
Franklin, Benjamin, 70–72, 87–88
Franklin, Morris, 200–202
Free Soil Party, xvii, xxii, 260
freedom of speech, press, and assembly, 1, 22–25, 47–50, 78–80, 169–71, 223–26, 289–91, 324, 363–64
Freeman, J. D., 286
Freeman's Journal, 327–28
Frémont, John C., 294–97, 301–303, 305, 377
Fugitive Slave Act, 265–67, 387

Gales, Joseph, 8–9
Gallenga, Antonio, 102
Gardener, Henry J., 285
Garrison, William Lloyd, 293–94, 361
Gay, Sydney Howard, xvii
Gazette of the United States, 80
Geary, John White, 299–300, 304, 306, 309
George IV, 2, 3
Gifford, William, 14–15
Gisborne, Thomas, 222
Godkin, Edwin L., xviii, 373
Godwin, Parke, xvii–xviii, 82
Goldoni, Carlo, 136–37
Gorchakov, Prince Aleksander Mikhailovich, 297, 299
Grant, Ulysses, xxiii
Gray, Thomas, 277
Greeley, Horace, xviii, xxiii, 200–201
Greenville *Patriot*, 283
Gresset, Jean Baptiste Louis, 99, 139
Grow, Galusha A., 371–72

Hale, Sir Matthew, 34
Hamilton, Alexander, xvii, xx, 13, 53
Hamlin, Hannibal, 377
Harper, James, 200, 249–52
Harrison, William Henry, 83, 122–23, 131–33, 135–36, 138–41, 145, 159, 161
Harte, Bret, xviii
Harvard College, xx
Harvey, George, xviii–xix
Haskell, Job, 248
Havemeyer, William F., 249, 252
Hawkins, William, 34
Hawley, Curtiss, 285
Heckwelder, John Gottlieb Ernestur, 184–85
Hedrick, Benjamin S., 297
Helper, Hinton Rowan, 359–61
Henry VIII, 23
Hill, Benjamin Harvey, 355, 358
Hill, Rowland, 243, 245
Hilson, Thomas, 4, 6
Hobbes, Thomas, 14–15
Holt, Joseph, 335–36
Homer, 163
Hone, Philip, xxi, 16
Hone, William, 84
Hood, Thomas, 173
Horace, 165

Independent, The, xvii
Indians, American, 9–10
Iredell, James, 359
Irving, Washington, 75
Italy, liberation of, 253–55
Iverson, Alfred, 368

Jackson, Andrew, xvii, 1, 5–6, 9–13, 16–18, 20, 22, 60, 64–65, 80, 92–93, 102, 135, 146, 155, 165–66, 192, 283–84, 296, 304
James II, 169–70
Japan, relations with, 276–81
Jefferson, Thomas, 2, 53, 109, 269–70, 286
Jeffreys, George, 169–70
Johnson, Richard M., 51
Johnson, Samuel, 107
Jones, George Wallace, 275
Jonson, Ben, 14–15, 112, 359
Journal of Commerce, 28, 42, 44, 85, 153, 196–99, 237–38, 240, 261, 290, 357, 377–78

journalism, 135–36, 153–54; *see also* political theory; political writing
Kansas-Nebraska Act, 273, 300
Keitt, Lawrence M., 289–90
Kent, William, xviii
Keppel, Blanche, 4, 6
King, Charles, 90
King, John Alsop, 259–60
King, Preston, 273–74, 287–88
King, Samuel W., 237
King, Captain, 279
Kitchener, William, 1, 2
Know-Nothing Party (American Party), 281–83, 296, 302
Kossuth, Louis, 353–54

Landor, Walter Savage, 102
Law, John, 168
law and jurisprudence, 150–52
Lawson, James, xx
Lee, Robert E., 350
Leggett, William, xvii, xxi–xxii, 95, 231
Leonard, William Ellery, xix
Leopold II, Grand Duke of Tuscany, 345–48
Lepidus, Marcus Aemilius, 11–12
Letcher, John, 373, 375
Levitt, Joshua, xvii
Lewis, Charles T., xvii
Lexington (ship), 123–25
Lincoln, Abraham, xxiii, 377–78, 380–83, 386
Loco-Focos, 50–51
London Courier, 2
Longfellow, Henry Wadsworth, 194
Longstreet, Augustus Baldwin, 285–86
Lopez, Narciso, 277
Louis XI, 17
Louis XVI, 88
Louis XVIII, 2, 3
Lovejoy, Elijah, 78–80, 362
Lowell, Francis, 194
Lowell, James Russell, xviii, 194

Macgregor, Robert, 222
Macready, William Charles, xxi
Madisonian, The, 90–92
Mann, Abijah, 286–88
Marcy, William L., 92
Marshall, John, 9
Martineau, Harriet, xxii
Mason, James M., 263, 368
Mason, John Y., 304

McDowell, James, 361–62
McDuffie, George, 216
McElrath, Thomas, 200–201
McLean, John, 312–13
Mexican War, 255–57, 259
Milton, John, 245–46
Mississippi *Free Trader*, 286
Missouri *Argus*, 78–79
Mobile *Register*, 295
Monmouth, Duke of, 169–70
Monroe, James, 191
Morris, Robert, 268
Mott, Frank Luther, xix
Mozart, Wolfgang Amadeus, 133
municipal finance, 250–52

Nashville *Union*, 286
National Academy of Design, xvii
National American, 285, 296
National Era, 359–60
National Gazette, 17–18
National Intelligencer, 295
National Road, 98–99
Native American Party, 241–43
Nativists. *See* foreigners and immigrants
Necker, Olivier, 17
Nevins, Allan, xiii
New Haven *Register*, 283
New Orleans *Courier*, 286
New Orleans *Crescent*, 286
New York *American*, 1, 90–91, 96, 138
New York *Athenaeum*, xvii
New York *Courier*, 101
New York *Evening Post*, xvii, xix–xxiv, 49, 52, 62, 92, 95–96, 100, 116, 135–36, 196, 200, 202, 204, 231–35, 243, 269–70, 293, 383, 386–88
New-York Express, 214
New York *Gazette and General Advertiser*, 99–101
New York *Herald*, xvii
New York *Republic*, 238–39
New York Review, xvii
New York Society Library, 114
New York *Tribune*, xviii–xix, 200, 277
Newman, John Henry, 184
Noah, Mordecai, 153
Nordhoff, Charles, xvii
North, Sir Dudley, 216
North American Review, xxii
nullification, 12–13

O'Conor, Charles, 355, 357, 363, 372
Octavius, 11

Index

Ogle, Charles, 153–54
Ostend Manifesto, 304–305

Parrington, Vernon Lewis, xxiv
Paulding, James K., xviii
Perry, Matthew Galbraith, 277, 279, 281
Philadelphia *Gazette*, 191
Philadelphia *Press*, 303, 324
Philanthropist, The, 49
Phillips, Wendell, 352–53
Pierce, Franklin, 270, 287, 299, 304–305, 310
pilot guild, 61–62
Pinckney, Henry, 23–24
Pius IX, 253, 256
Placide, Henry, 4, 6
Plaindealer, The, 65
political theory, 106–107, 129–31, 257
political writing, 99–103, 238–39, 270–72; *see also* journalism
Polk, James K., 190, 220, 231, 233, 244, 333
Pope, Alexander, 82, 138, 165
Porter, David Rittenhouse, 125
postage, 188–90
postal service, 335–37
Povey, John, 4, 6
Power, James, 363–64, 375
Preble, George Henry, 277, 279
Preston, William, 319, 321
Providence *Journal*, 315
Pryor, Roger A., 371–72
public debt, 117–20
public works, 96–99
Pusey, Edward, 184–85

Rabelais, François, 80
railroads, 96–98
Randolph, John, xviii, 312–13
Raynor, Kenneth, 299, 301
Reconstruction, xviii
Reed, William Bradford, 318, 321
religious denominations, 184–86
religious freedom, 168–71
Ricardo, David, 202
Richmond Enquirer, 269–70, 283, 285, 287
Rolfe, John, 75
Rousseau, Jean-Jacques, 87
Ruxton, George Frederick Augustus, 257–58

Sainte-Beuve, Charles, xviii
Savannah *Georgian*, 286
Savannah *Republican*, 285
Say, Jean Baptiste, 202
Scarron, Paul, 80
Scott, Dred, 309–310, 312, 315, 364
Scott, Sir Walter, 14, 17, 222
Scott, Winfield, 12, 157
Seaton, W. W., 8–9
Sedgwick, Theodore, III, xviii, 92, 110, 231
Selden, Dudley, 249–50
Seward, William H., 92, 148–49, 273–75
Shakespeare, William, 14–16, 76, 82, 131, 176, 202, 233
Shannon, William, 304, 306
Shays, Daniel, 50–52
Sherman, John, 359, 370
slavery, xxii–xxiv, 1, 4, 23–25, 52–53, 109–111, 127–28, 263–67, 289–91, 305–317, 324–25, 332–33, 351–52, 363–64, 374–76, 378–80, 382–86
Slidell, John, 333–34
Smith, Adam, 216
Socinius, Faustus, 184
Soulé, Pierre, 304
Soult, Jean de Dieu, 87–88
Southern Literary Messenger, xviii
Spratt, L. W., 383, 385
Squatter Sovereignty, 308–309
Stevens, Thaddeus, 321
Stevenson, Andrew, 87–88
Stiles, William H., 286
Stillman, William J., xviii
street cleaning, 317–18
strike (labor), 25–44
Stringfellow, Benjamin F., 283–84, 308–309
Sumner, Charles, 273–74, 289–91, 293, 376
Swedenborg, Emmanuel, 163–64

Talisman, The, xvii
Tallmadge, Nathaniel P., 22
Taney, Roger B., 309–310, 312–15
Tappan, Lewis, 78, 361–62
tariffs, xviii, 12, 20–21, 176–78, 180–83, 192–200, 204–214, 216–20, 222–23, 239–41, 320–23, 366–68
Tate, Sandy, 364
taxation, 117–19

Taylor, Bayard, 277, 280
Taylor, William, 35
Taylor, Zachary, 259–60
Tazewell, Littleton, 140–41
temperance, 89–90, 133–35
Tennyson, Alfred, Lord, 131, 173
Texas, annexation of, 68–70, 223, 231–33, 235–37
Thayer, James, 357
Thayer, William Sydney, xvii
theater riots, 58–60
Thompson, Benjamin, 226
Thompson, Jacob, 308
Thompson, John R., xviii
Tilden, Samuel J., xviii
Trollope, Frances, 4
Troy *Morning Mail*, 148
Turner, Nat, 361
Tyler, John, 161–62, 165, 178, 235–37

Underwood, John Curtiss, xxii, 304
United States Military Academy (West Point), 1
United States Review, xvii
unjust laws, resistance to, 265–67
Urban II, 136
usury laws, 54–57

Van Polanen, Roger Gerard, 1
Van Buren, John, xviii, 273–74
Van Buren, Martin, xviii, xxi, 9–12, 60, 73, 80–84, 126, 131, 133, 141, 146, 148, 153–56, 165–67, 220–21, 259, 324
Vattenmare, Nicolas Marie Alexandre, 220
Verplanck, Gulian, 11, 90, 154
Victoria, Queen, 87–88
Virginia *Enquirer*, 294
Volta, Count Alessandro, 136–37
vote fraud, 243–44
voting rights, 62–64, 75–76, 237–38

Waller, William, 304
Walsh, Mike, 223

Walsh, Robert, 17
Ward, Artemus, xviii
Washington, George, 16, 335
Washington *American Organ*, 300
Washington *Constitution*, 374
Washington *Globe*, 8
Washington *Intelligencer*, 320–24
Washington *Star*, 290
Washington (Ark.) *Telegraph*, 286
Washington Union, 287, 295–96, 323–24
Wayne, James, 310
Webster, Daniel, 9, 19, 21, 80–82, 90, 92, 141–46, 157–60, 193, 241–45, 257–59, 261–65, 272–73
Webster, David, 142
Webster, John Fletcher, 261
Webster-Ashburton Treaty, 159
Weir, Robert, 1
Welles, Gideon, xviii
West, settlement of, 67–68, 258
Whig Party, 76–78, 82, 90, 156, 178–80, 200–202, 214–15, 241–43
White, Gilbert, 90, 92
White, Peregrine, 75
Whitman, Walt, xviii, 16
Whittier, John Greenleaf, 261
Wilberforce, William, 4
William III and Mary II, 169
Williams, Chief Justice, 35
Williams College, xx
Wilmot, David, 261–63
Wilmot Proviso, 260–61, 383
Wirt, William, 9
Wise, Henry Alexander, 99–100, 294, 296
Wolcot, John ("Peter Pindar"), 122
Woodbury, Levi, 80–81
Wright, Frances ("Fannie"), 84–85
Wright, Silas, xii, 143

youth, idealism of, 86–86

Zeno, 92–93